Futures f

Futures for the Public Sector

Edited by
Geert Bouckaert, Annie Hondeghem,
Trui Steen, and Steven Van de Walle

LEUVEN UNIVERSITY PRESS

The publication of this book was supported by KU Leuven Fund for Fair Open Access, and the DemoTrans project. DemoTrans is funded by the European Commission in its Horizon Europe framework (grant 101059288).

Views and opinions expressed are however those of the author(s) only and do not necessarily reflect those of the European Union or the European Commission. Neither the European Union nor the granting authority can be held responsible for them.

Published in 2025 by Leuven University Press / Presses Universitaires de Louvain / Universitaire Pers Leuven. Minderbroedersstraat 4, B-3000 Leuven (Belgium).
Selection and editorial matter © 2025, Geert Bouckaert, Annie Hondeghem, Trui Steen, and Steven Van de Walle
Individual chapters © 2025, the respective authors
This book is published under a Creative Commons Attribution Non-Commercial Non-Derivative 4.0 License. For more information, please visit https://creativecommons.org/share-your-work/cclicenses/

Attribution should include the following information:
Geert Bouckaert, Annie Hondeghem, Trui Steen, and Steven Van de Walle (eds.), *Futures for the Public Sector*. Leuven: Leuven University Press, 2025. (CC BY-NC-ND 4.0)

ISBN 978 94 6270 450 3 (Paperback)
ISBN 978 94 6166 624 6 (ePDF)
ISBN 978 94 6166 627 7 (ePub)
https://doi.org/10.11116/9789461666246
D/2025/1869/3
NUR: 805
Layout: Crius Group
Cover design: Daniel Benneworth-Gray
Cover illustration: *Babel*, Oil on panel, 100 x 120 cm, © Sven Van Dorst

Table of Contents

Preface   9
by Annie Hondeghem and Trui Steen

INTRODUCTION

Looking at futures for the public sector   15
by Geert Bouckaert

PART 1: FUTURES OF THE POLITICO-ADMINISTRATIVE SYSTEM

Strategies for democratic public administration in an era of populism   25
by Michael W. Bauer

The trend towards fragility in the 21st century   45
by Alasdair Roberts

Undermining the administrative state: The case of the United States   59
by Donald Moynihan

Shifting power structures in the US: The rolling back of Diversity, Equity, and Inclusion policies   75
by Norma M. Riccucci

PART 2: FUTURES OF CONTAINING CRISES AND DISRUPTION

Are poly-crises the new normal? Challenges for public administration in liberal-democratic states   89
by Brian W. Head

The rise of hybridity in the new 'normalcy' of crises   101
by Tiina Randma-Liiv and Steven Nõmmik

The future role of government in cybersecurity   123
by Greta Nasi

The dawn of disruptive technology-driven future government   141
by M. Jae Moon, Seulgi Lee, Seungkyu Park, and Ire Park

The digital transformation as a double governance challenge   157
by Albert Meijer

PART 3: FUTURES OF CITIZEN-STATE INTERACTIONS

The rise of sceptical citizens about public administration communication   175
by María José Canel

Politicisation and populism: The future of the frontline of public services   193
by Gabriela Lotta

PART 4: FUTURES OF ADMINISTRATING THE STATE

The transformation of the regulatory state?   211
by Martin Lodge

Why we need more public value   227
by Sandra Van Thiel

Ecosystems: the word that would be king?   241
by Adina Dudau

PART 5: FUTURES OF MANAGING THE CIVIL SERVICE

Shifting dynamics of advice: Non-state experts and private sector consultancies in public policy   257
by Rosie Collington

Flexibilisation of work and the future of public sector employment   273
by Adrian Ritz, Guillem Ripoll, and Lorenza Micacchi

The future of bureaucratic merit   289
by Marina Nistotskaya

The functional politicisation of the merit civil service: From responsive to subservient bureaucracy?   309
by Tobias Bach

The disappearance of lower-grade bureaucrats   323
by Steven Van de Walle

PART 6: FUTURES OF STUDYING PUBLIC ADMINISTRATION

Using Public Administration research to strengthen 'futures thinking' in the public sector — 335
by Jeroen Maesschalck

The future of a scattered field: Challenges and opportunities — 351
by Asmus Leth Olsen

The rise of open science and public access: Implications for Public Administration research — 363
by Mary K. Feeney

CONCLUSION

Which futures for the public sector? — 381
by Geert Bouckaert

List of contributors — 397

Preface

by Annie Hondeghem and Trui Steen

Point n'est besoin d'espérer pour entreprendre, ni de réussir pour persévérer
Attributed to William, Prince of Orange (1533–1584)

This book is written in honour of Prof. dr. Geert Bouckaert, on the occasion of his retirement. Geert started his career at KU Leuven in 1984, and ended it officially at KU Leuven in 2023. For 40 years he has been at the service of the academic community, of the discipline of Public Administration, and of society. As the quote at the beginning of this preface states, despite personal setbacks, he has shown an entrepreneurship that none can emulate.

During those 40 years, Geert has taken up various leadership positions. For the purposes of this book, we limit ourselves to five of these: Director of the KU Leuven Public Governance Institute (1997–2012), President of the Vlaamse Vereniging voor Bestuur en Beleid (VVBB) (2000–2010), President of the European Group for Public Administration (EGPA) (2004–2010), President of the International Institute of Administrative Sciences (IIAS) (2013–2019), and Vice-President of the UN/ECOSOC Committee of Experts on Public Administration (2018–2021). In all these roles, Geert has shown himself to be a visionary and strategic leader. He has set organisations in motion, empowering them to address new challenges.

As director of the KU Leuven Public Governance Institute, he initiated the research institute's movement for internationalisation. Looking beyond the local or regional context has always been important to Geert. He has put international comparative research on the agenda and has taken the initiative to invite international fellows for a research stay in Leuven, which has resulted in influential publications. Initially, his focus was mainly on OECD countries, but soon this was extended to all continents.

As chairman of the VVBB (the Flemish Association for Public Administration), he has taken a leading role in the community of Public Administration experts, both scholars and practitioners, in Flanders/Belgium. This has resulted in long-term research programmes funded by the Flemish government (from 2001 to the present), which enhanced Public Administration in Belgium as a discipline, but also prompted academics to step out of their ivory tower.

As chairman of the EGPA (European Group for Public Administration), Geert has transformed the organisation into a research community by setting up study groups in various domains, which are now the forums par excellence for researchers to present their work. He has set up dialogues with other Public Administration communities which have made it possible to transcend Eurocentrism: the Trans-Atlantic Dialogue (TAD) with the American Society for Public Administration (ASPA), the Trans-European Dialogue (TED) with the Network of Institutes and Schools of Public Administration in Central and Eastern Europe (NISPAcee), and EURO MENA with the Middle East and North Africa Public Administration Research network (MENAPAR).

As chairman of the IIAS (International Institute of Administrative Sciences), Geert was strongly focused on broadening the membership of countries worldwide, with the goal of realising mutual, bi-directional learning. This broadening was also aimed at building stronger governance systems, based on the conviction that good governance is a necessary basis for performance and sustainability.

Finally, as vice-chairman of UN/ECOSOC (CEPA), Geert introduced the Sustainable Development Goals (SDGs) to the discipline of Public Administration. Building effective, accountable, and inclusive governance institutions not only is one of the SDGs, but also forms the basis for achieving the other SDGs. This is not only relevant for the Global South, but also for Western democratic systems, which are increasingly under pressure.

The core areas of Geert's research during his academic career were public management reform, performance management and financial management, and trust. The most visible output for the first theme is the book with Christopher Pollitt, his friend and *companion de route*. The book *Public Management Reform: A Comparative Analysis*, four editions of which have been published by Oxford University Press, has been translated into eight languages (including Spanish, Chinese, Japanese, and Italian) and is one of the classics in the field of Public Administration worldwide.

Geert has always linked performance management, as one of the major innovations of New Public Management, to innovations in the financial systems of government. After all, performance information should feed the financial cycle of budget, accounting, and audit. However, such systems do not achieve their purpose if there is no trust. Geert's merit has been to expand the concept of trust in government. In addition to citizens' trust in government, which is essential for legitimacy, there is also the trust of government in the citizen, and trust within government, both in and between organisations. The issue of trust has been acknowledged more and more in recent years as a critical success factor for public organisations, as illustrated by the recent OECD publication *Government at a glance* (2023).

For these achievements (and many others that we do not mention in the scope of this preface, since otherwise this text would become a book in itself), Geert Bouckaert has been awarded eight honorary doctorates and numerous prizes. Honorary doctorates have been awarded by Aix-Marseille University, France (2008), Tallinn University of Technology, Estonia (2008), National School of Political Studies and Public Administration, Romania (2010), Corvinus University, Budapest, Hungary (2010), Université de Lausanne, Switzerland (2014), Babeș-Bolyai University, Cluj-Napoca, Romania (2014), Bucharest University of Economic Studies, Romania (2014), and Université du Québec (ENAP), Canada (2023). Of the numerous prizes, we mention only the two most recent ones: the Riggs Award for Lifetime Achievement in International and Comparative Public Administration (2023) and the Lifetime Achievement Award from the VVBB (2024).

In addition to his excellent performance as a researcher, we also mention Geert's role as a coach and mentor for young colleagues. As promotor, he has supervised 26 PhDs that were successfully completed. Many of his PhD students have dispersed and now hold important positions. Most of them still consult Geert regularly on important decisions in their careers. This also holds for many other researchers and colleagues.

Geert's efforts also apply in particular to researchers from the Global South. For example, Geert has set up a 10-year collaboration with Ethiopian universities, which resulted in the handbook *Public Administration in Ethiopia* (2020), strengthening the discipline in education, and starting the Ethiopian Public Administration Association.

The present book before us is in line with the intellectual path that Geert has walked in recent years. This path took him along a search for new concepts, analytical models, and normative systems to understand and guide governments in a changing context. This immediately raises the question of how the discipline of Public Administration can be strengthened in the future.

A previous result of this trajectory was the book *European Perspectives for Public Administration: The Way Forward* (2020), published by Leuven University Press and co-edited with Werner Jann. As the European version of the Minnowbrook conferences in the US that reflect on the discipline, the book outlined four major dimensions for our discipline: more attention to future thinking, diversity, interdisciplinarity, and the connection to practice.

Geert's current intellectual passion lies in further developing the model of the Neo-Weberian State. The idea is that the relationship between hierarchy, market, and networks needs to be re-examined to address the challenges of today's society. Global crises related to democracy, climate, migration, health, inequality, etc. call for a renewed role of the state: 'the return of the state'. To quote Geert himself: "We claim and hypothesise that NWS, much better and even contrary to NPM (market-driven) and NPG (network-driven), will ensure the three core functions of a whole of government strategy within a whole of society context: performing, inclusive and equitable service delivery, resilient crises governance, and effective innovation for government and society" (Bouckaert, 2023, p. 45).

The current book continues by discussing future trends for the public sector and will hopefully inspire many scholars and public servants.

Finally, Geert's approach to Public Administration scholarship is also influenced by his broader interest in art, culture, politics, and society in general. Not only does his strength as an academic scholar builds on his in-depth knowledge of Public Administration as a subject area and his experience in conducting robust social-scientific research, he also understands the functioning of Public Administration in its broader social context.

We hope (and assume) that the Public Administration community, both scholarly and professionally, will be able to build on Geert Bouckaert's scholarship for many years to come. This is what we wish him and the community.

Prof. dr. Annie Hondeghem, Director of the KU Leuven Public Governance Institute, 2013–2024

Prof. dr. Trui Steen, Director of the KU Leuven Public Governance Institute, 2024–present

Reference

Bouckaert, G. (2023). The Neo-Weberian state: From ideal type model to reality? *Max Weber Studies*, 23(1), 13–59.

INTRODUCTION

Looking at futures for the public sector

by Geert Bouckaert

In line with the German philosopher Kant (1724–1804), we all need to ask ourselves three questions: What can we know? What should we do? What may we hope for? These are also three key questions for social scientists. When we transfer these three questions to our academic field of public policy and its governance, we need to take uncertainties and disruptions into account which encompass not only the known unknown, but even more so the unknown unknown. The question of what we should do is complicated in environments of populism and illiberalism, which also triggers the question of who should do what? Since social sciences are likewise value-driven, it is important to make explicit what we may hope for. Realising the Sustainable Development Goals while keeping a rule-of-law-framed democracy is under pressure from crises and system quakes.

As academic social scientists, we need to know how we should organise ourselves to answer or at least discuss these possible futures. It is a common saying that we often neglect strategic and systemic topics since we are absorbed by urgent and operational issues. In the 20th century the number of dystopias was much larger than the number of utopias. Just like Malthus (1766–1834) or the Club of Rome, which was founded in 1968, there is a kind of evidence-based pessimism which is fuelled by chronic crises, political polarisation, and unreachable sustainable objectives linked to people, planet, prosperity, peace, and partnerships.

Another dimension in this academic debate is about a grounded belief in our capacity and agency to effectively change realities in fields of hunger, poverty, climate, peace, inclusion, and all the related policies. This is about voluntarism versus fatalism. Voluntarism and optimism are a moral academic duty, I believe, and therefore we need to push the relevance of our social sciences in general, and the field of Public Administration in particular, since the public sector should be part of the solution and of possible futures.

In this book, it is our ambition to map and discuss important topics on 'futures for the public sector', and how this affects social sciences in general, and our academic field of Public Administration in particular. It always was my conviction that the academic field of Public Administration needs to be ahead of problems and should anticipate possible futures, rather than just studying what happened. When, not if, we want to be relevant, we need to be prospective with our questions, and push to be self-fulfilling with our answers.

Obviously, we are not the first to discuss such a strategic topic. The most significant effort in the second half of the 20th century has been the Minnowbrook conferences, which have taken place every 20 years, starting in 1968, and then in 1988, and 2008, with a celebratory event on the 50th anniversary of Minnowbrook, in 2018 (Nabatchi and Carboni, 2019). The fourth Minnowbrook will be in 2028.

On the European side, and as former president of the European Group for Public Administration (EGPA), I also wanted such a future-oriented fundamental European debate (see also Bouckaert and Van de Donk, 2010). In 2018, Werner Jann and myself launched, embedded in the EGPA, the European Perspectives for Public Administration (EPPA) initiative (Bouckaert and Jann, 2018), also intended to happen every 20 years, we hope, and alternating with the US-based Minnowbrook. The next EPPAs should be in 2038 and 2058.

Reflecting on the future is risky business when it becomes speculation. It certainly requires critical observations and reflections on the past and the present. There is always the risk of a blind spot in observing and reflecting when the 'known unknown' is bypassed by the 'unknown unknown'.

Mapping the 'known known' was done by the American Society for Public Administration's (ASPA) stock-taking on its 75th anniversary (Guy and Rubin, 2015). The Minnowbrook events involve all frontline US researchers in Public Administration. Perhaps that selection was already a source for a structural blind spot on the future (see Bouckaert and Jann, 2018).

From the Minnowbrook I perspective (1968), according to Marini (1971, p. 353), there was a major shift in Public Administration to post-positivism, relevance, adaptation to turbulence (including the Vietnam War), and the emerging new organisational formats with a client focus. However, what Minnowbrook I totally missed, probably because new schools of economists were not part of the debate, was the emerging economics revival focusing on public choice, and in its wake the new competition in public policy analysis.

From the Minnowbrook II perspective (1988), interdependence and interconnectedness of policy issues, private–public organisations, and nation-states, combined with a cultural diversity in a variety of forms (workforce, public, and the world in general), became a central concern. This resulted in a focus on a central actor taking on several new roles such as facilitator, negotiator, and ameliorator, resulting in a renewed paradigm, which also emphasised a feminist view on and in Public Administration (Bailey and Mayer, 1992). However, what Minnowbrook II missed was the emerging New Public Management. This was probably because the debates were too US-centred, suffering from a lack of international comparative research, and therefore ignoring key developments within the OECD, and also because political philosophers which could have observed the emerging neoliberal movements were absent.

From the Minnowbrook III perspective (2008), the main topics that emerged were the impact of globalisation, collaborative governance, and information technology. A major observation was made by O'Leary "that while governance has become more global, diverse, and represented by complex governing arrangements and value, it also has departed from the long dominant norms embedded in Western notions of democratic governance" (O'Leary et al., 2010, pp. 284-285). However, what Minnowbrook III missed was the 2008 global economic and financial crisis and its impact on the public sector. The question here is whether this was 'known but unnoticed', or a genuine 'unknown unknown'. Consequences of massive structural and institutional deregulations, including in the banking sector, obviously enhanced major risks, especially since these practices were subject to organised blind spots.

From these three Minnowbrook meetings, it seems that combinations of disciplinary blindness, ignored or unnoticed consequences of ideological dominance, and unexpected chance events resulted in a lack of fundamental visions and their impacts. A derived question for academic visions for the future in all disciplines should therefore be how to create a burning platform and a sense of emergency which feeds an academic FOMO (Fear of Missing Out), by conducting relevant research. How can we anticipate these futures, or how can we be ahead of crises and trends, or even better, how can we as an academic field of Public Administration set trends ourselves?

In authoritarian systems, the official future is always certain and bright; however, the official past is always difficult to predict. Democratic countries' pasts, presents, and futures are different due to their checks and balances, their constitutional protection of the rule of law, their conception of responsibility and accountability, and their interactions with their administration (Koliba, 2024; Bertelli and Schartz, 2022; Bertelli, 2021). One consequence is that futures are permanent and dynamic, and therefore our critical reflections on futures within Public Administration should also be permanent, dynamic, and forward rolling.

By 2030 17 SDGs should have been realised, or at least we should have made significant progress on most of them (2015–2030). There are thus five more years to go. Will we have the strength and the willingness, after the

Millennium Objectives (2000–2015) and the Sustainable Development Goals, to mobilise and launch a subsequent global Programme for People, Planet, Prosperity, Peace, and Partnerships? The recent COVID-19 pandemic demonstrated that we have shifted from solving a crisis to handling crises (plural), to coping with system quakes. It proves that risk calculations are blended with uncertainty, and that environments, knowledge quality, degrees of dependence, and degrees of sustainability of 'solutions' make not just a VUCA world (Volatile, Uncertain, Complex, and Ambiguous), but are also blended with a TODO world (Turbulent and disruptive environments, Oscillating/Unpredictable/Unknown knowledge quality, Dominos falling in an unknown sequences of interdependence, and Opposing/Disputed/Wicked 'solutions') (Bouckaert and Galego, 2024).

In January 2024, in Leuven, this academic ambition to reflect on futures for the public sector brought together a group of researchers to discuss our administrative systems, which are in political turmoil, if not a political vortex. It raises questions of how contingencies of politics, technology, and crises affect fragility. It demonstrates tensions between the branches of our states, and within our societies. It invites us to think critically about our research strategies in terms of topics, disciplines we need in our teams, or data and communication to gain trustworthiness and legitimacy, not only for the state and its administration, but also for our teaching, research, and service to communities.

This book collects the outcomes of these discussions in six different clusters. In the first cluster of contributions, the embeddedness of the administrative system in a changing political environment is discussed. There is emerging and dominant populism which, once in power, explicitly wants to deconstruct the administrative state. Moynihan's discussion of what this entails in the US is very well corroborated by Riccucci. She shows how imbalances between the branches of the state, and especially the politicised judicial branch (the US Supreme Court), impacts and even reverses policies, such as diversity, equity, and inclusion (DEI) policies. Bauer discusses strategies for democratic public administrations in this era of populism. Roberts demonstrates not only how 'stable' countries are not just a minority and therefore an exception in our global world, but that 'fragility' of states is, if not the norm, certainly very common. He also shows that most of our Public Administration research is on and organised within a limited and set of 'stable' countries, which blinds us as researchers to 'fragile' country models.

This political populist pressure on public administrations is multiplied with a range of crises, disruptions, and hybridity. In the second cluster, Head shows clearly how multiple crises are not the exception anymore but have become the new normal. In fact, in some illiberal countries these crises become a pretext for governments to even gain more control over administrations. As Randma-Liiv and Nõmmik state, it results in a rise of hybridity of hierarchies, markets, and networks, which affects mechanisms of responsibility and accountability. Special attention to cyberspace and digital environments and how this affects administrative systems is also needed. Nasi describes how cyber-attacks have become so disruptive for standard service delivery that a new approach is needed to ensure essential services. Moon, Lee, Park, and Park focus on how artificial intelligence also has a significant disruptive capacity, even when there is a potential benefit. In a political context of populism, cyberspace and artificial intelligence have a huge potential to be used against citizens, or certain groups of citizens, affecting their constitutional rights. Meijer discusses the digital transformation as a double governance challenge. There is the external challenge of societal transformation interacting with government, and there is the internal challenge for government itself.

This combined environmental context of populism and crises or digitally driven disruption impacts the interaction of the state and its citizens, and therefore of the public sector in its interaction with citizens. In the third cluster Canel discusses what the impact is of the rise of sceptical citizens for public administration communication. Along the same lines, Lotta unpacks how politicisation and populism affect frontline public services and street-level bureaucrats' behaviour.

In the fourth cluster some aspects are discussed of how the above affects the administration of the state. Lodge focuses on how the nature of the regulatory state is being transformed and possibly could be reshaped. Van Thiel connects the old specialisation/coordination debate with public value. Dudau looks at how a renewed vision through the lens of ecosystems could be beneficial.

The fifth cluster discusses the drastic impacts on the public sector itself. In line with weakening the public sector by reducing its capacity and numbers, contracting out has become a common practice for advice and design in strategic dimensions of many policies. Collington clearly shows how non-state experts and private consultants in public policy managed to trigger demand for their services, and also how they offer their own defined supply and capacity. This shift from internal to external capacity is significant and structural. For those who stay in the public sector, a shift to flexibility becomes obvious. Ritz, Ripoll, and Micacchi discuss in detail this shift towards flexibilisation of public sector work and the way it is managed. Once the flexibility is realised, another classical bureaucratic question is raised. Is 'merit' still the central focus in shaping a public sector, including beyond hiring people? Nistotskaya discusses this in all its dimensions, and to the extent of how and under what conditions merit is functional. Bach complements this discourse by showing a shift within merit to functional politicisation, which may result in a kind of responsiveness that ultimately turns into a subservient bureaucracy. A crucial trend is described by Van de Walle, who surfaces the disappearance of lower-grade bureaucrats, with some serious consequences.

The last cluster handles the debate of how this affects us as researchers of Public Administration. Maesschalck discusses how to upgrade research for the future and how this not only impacts Public Administration, but also how Public Administration can leverage critical thinking on possible futures. Olson emphasises that Public Administration should adjust and take interdisciplinary publication strategies into account to make sure it is a horizontal and consolidating academic field. Feeney demonstrates how open science and public access is the way forward to advance our field of study.

Finally, in a concluding chapter, I try to show how these six clusters are interconnected and suggest possible futures. The perspective is not just to take stock, or to extrapolate a bit, or to just react according to a normative framework. The perspective is to be ahead of problems and tensions, or even to curb dystopian futures into desirable futures. This is what all participants in the Leuven 2024 seminar share. Based on a voluntaristic attitude, we have a strong belief that our research makes a difference and contributes to possible futures for public sectors in society.

References

Bailey, M. T., & Mayer, R. T. (Eds.) (1992). *Public Management in an Interconnected World: Essays in the Minnowbrook Tradition*. Greenwood Press. https://archive.org/details/publicmanagement0000unse_l1m1/page/n7/mode/2up.

Bertelli, A. M., & Schwartz, L. J. (2022). *Public Administration and Democracy: The Complementarity Principle*. Cambridge University Press. https://doi.org/10.1017/9781009217613.

Bertelli, A. M. (2021). *Democracy Administered: How Public Administration Shapes Representative Government*. Cambridge University Press. https://doi.org/10.1017/9781316755167.

Bouckaert, G., & Galego, D. (2024). System-quake proof "Systemic Resilience Governance": Six measures for readiness. *Global Policy*, 15(S6), 97–105. https://doi.org/10.1111/1758-5899.13433.

Bouckaert, G., & Jann, W. (Eds.) (2020). *European Perspectives for Public Administration: The Way Forward*. Leuven University Press. https://doi.org/10.11116/9789461663078.

Bouckaert, G., & van de Donk, W. (eds.) (2010). *The European Group for Public Administration (1975–2010): Perspectives for the Future / Le Groupe Européen pour l'Administration Publique (1975–2010): Perspectives pour le Futur*. Bruylant.

Guy, M. E., & Rubin, M. M. (2015). *Public Administration Evolving. From Foundations to the Future*. Routledge. https://doi.org/10.4324/9781315718958.

Koliba, C. (2024). Liberal democratic accountability standards and public administration. *Public Administration Review*, 1–11. https://doi.org/10.1111/puar.13831.

Marini, F. (Ed.) (1971). *Toward a New Public Administration: The Minnowbrook Perspective*. Chandler Publishing.

Nabatchi, T. & Carboni, J. L. (2019). *Assessing the Past and Future of Public Administration: Reflections from the Minnowbrook at 50 Conference*. IBM Center for the Business Government. https://www.businessofgovernment.org/sites/default/files/Assessing%20the%20Past%20and%20Future%20of%20Public%20Administration%20-%20Reflections%20from%20the%20Minnowbrook%20at%2050%20Conference_0.pdf.

O'Leary, R., Van Slyke, D. M., & Kim, S. (Eds.) (2010). *The Future of Public Administration around the World: The Minnowbrook Perspective*. Georgetown University Press. https://www.jstor.org/stable/j.ctt2tt4cr.

PART 1
FUTURES OF THE POLITICO-ADMINISTRATIVE SYSTEM

Strategies for democratic public administration in an era of populism

by Michael W. Bauer

1. Introduction

The surge of political illiberalism is a manifest trend haunting democracies in general and administrative systems more specifically. This chapter examines the challenges deriving from this trend, delving into its nature, and exploring the repercussions it holds for Public Administration (PA) as a discipline, and for public management as a practical enterprise. It demands increased intellectual efforts to innovate administrative legitimacy and foster a more democratic and responsive public administration aligned with its pluralistic mission.

The illiberal challenge is a trend that will not end any time soon; it is fuelled by the structural shortcomings of existing liberal democracies. The positive effects of the trend are hard to discern and might emerge only if ongoing transformations were to lead to innovative and greater democratisation of executive policymaking. PA as a discipline is called upon to improve the participatory and interactive basis of how "democracy administered" (Bertelli, 2021) works in the 21st century and, by teaming up with political philosophers and pioneers of new forms of legitimacy in complex governance configurations, to provide realistic models to experiment with (even) more collaborative and inclusive forms of public administration in practice. Because the only realistic solution for strengthening democratic administration under illiberal pressure lies in further democratising it (Zeitlin et al., 2023; Trondal, 2023; Torfing et al., 2024).

With a view to contributing to this necessary debate, this chapter proceeds as follows. Section 3 sketches the reasons behind the rise of authoritarian populism which, once in government, constitutes the illiberal challenge referred to in the chapter's title. Following cleavage theory in its structural argumentation, there appears to be little hope that populist success is ephemeral and will end soon. What authoritarian governments do once they have executive power to transform liberal institutions (Peters and Pierre, 2020;

Peters, 2023), policy substance, and the administrative system is briefly outlined in section 4. Two ensuing dilemmas such state transformation poses for PA and democratic bureaucracy are then discussed in section 5. Section 6 examines the ethical and normative implications of the illiberal challenge for PA as a discipline. The conclusions summarise the main argument and discuss implications for our research agenda. It is, however, the concept of illiberalism that needs to be addressed first.

2. Political illiberalism on the rise

Conceptual and theoretical discussions about 'illiberalism' – aiming to establish and explain the concept on its own terms – usually distance it from being merely the opposite of liberalism (Waller, 2023; Sajó et al., 2019; Plattner, 2000; Wagrandl, 2021). The definitional complexities are compounded by the fact that some controversial leaders – first and foremost Victor Orbán in Hungary – have embraced the labels 'illiberal' or 'illiberal democracy' to characterise their own political visions of regime transformation (Hajnal, 2021; Hajnal and Boda, 2021; Zakaria, 1997, 2002; Bustikova and Guasti, 2017). However, in most instances, 'illiberal' and 'illiberalism' serve as descriptors for populist movements or regimes, particularly those of a right-wing, authoritarian nature (Holmes, 2021; Inglehart and Norris, 2016; Schäfer, 2022). This chapter adopts the same stance, conceiving illiberalism as a pivotal element within the political ideology of authoritarian populists.[1]

Authoritarian populists' illiberalism runs on what can be called 'political negativism' (see Urbinati, 2019a, p. 22; Zürn, 2022). It is anti-elitist (the 'old' elites are corrupted); it is anti-internationalist (membership in international organisations and treaties bind the nation unfairly); it is anti-pluralist (procedures are deemed unimportant and an imagined homogenous notion of the 'majority' is advocated); and it is also anti-liberal. The latter concerns the lack of respect for individual and minority rights and for the rule of law (Plattner, 2020; Sajó, 2019). The 'illiberal challenge' embodied by authoritarian populists in government comprises all those features (Schäfer and Zürn, 2023).[2]

In summary, the chapter shares concerns about the increasing fragility of our Western liberal-democratic regimes (see also the contributions by Roberts, Moynihan, and Lotta in this volume). This being so, it argues that the illiberal challenge makes it necessary for PA to engage (yet again and more eagerly, see Waldo, 1952) in a dialogue with political philosophy and other (normative) political and social sciences about the potentials and limits of democratic administration in the democracies of the 21st century (Bertelli,

2021), and about how public administration can contribute to safeguarding popular trust in the liberal-democratic project (Bouckaert, 2012; Yesilkagit et al., 2024).

Against this background, democratic bureaucracy under populist rule faces tough choices. If 'democracy' is conceived primarily as popular sovereignty and as a chain of command deriving from elected government down to implementation (Finer, 1940; Bertelli and Schwartz, 2022; Jackson, 2009), then, under authoritarian populist rule, bureaucracy is in danger of becoming an accomplice of illiberal regime transformation (Bauer, 2024a). This means that the natural tension between the 'liberal' parts of our democratic regimes (in the form of counter-majoritarian components) and its features of 'electoral sovereignty' – which have so successfully been balanced in the second half of the 20th century – are dramatically reappearing in the current age of the rise of populism (Krastev, 2011; Heath, 2020; Bertelli, 2021).[3]

In straightforward terms, PA must therefore re-examine fundamental value questions, which have been neglected while the discipline's main focus was, rather, on more pragmatic aspects of optimising bureaucratic management (as discussed by Roberts in this volume; see also Stoker, 2021). Thus, there is a need for PA to contemplate its ethical and deontological ideals to a much greater extent than has been done in recent decades (du Gay, 2020; Cooper, 2012; Spicer, 2015; Bertelli, 2021; O'Leary, 2013, 2017).

The question might be whether public administration theorising ought to conceive 'democratic' in a *popular-electoral* or in a *liberal-pluralist* sense (Bertelli and Schwartz, 2022; Heath, 2020; Manow, 2021; Schäfer and Zürn, 2023; Koliba, 2024), i.e. whether bureaucracy's main role is (limited) to be an instrument of the elected leadership or whether it needs (to be extended) to become (and be understood accordingly as) an institution of pluralist government in its own right; and how to balance unavoidable tensions between these two legitimating principles (majoritarian will versus deliberating expertise) in bureaucratic practice (Dean, 2023).[4]

3. Evidence of authoritarian populism in action: more than a political strategy

Without being able to review the whole debate about the new populism here (but see Moffitt, 2020; 2016; Norris and Inglehart, 2019; Mudde and Kaltwasser, 2012; Müller, 2016), it is important to note that populism is typically debated with regard to its definition, its substance, its ability to mobilise citizens and antagonise societal groups, its impact on party systems, and political radicalisation (Kriesi,

2014). The nexus and impact of populist governments on public administration has only recently received more attention (Rockman, 2019; Spicer, 2018; Bauer et al., 2021; Peters and Pierre, 2020; Bauer, 2024a). The point is that the public administration system in general, and the state bureaucracy in particular, are the first institutions of the democratic state to 'suffer' populist rule while also, attributable to their mission, having to 'serve' their new masters (Bauer and Becker, 2020). It is argued that populist governments – in particular under what is called charismatic, one-person leadership – can become dangerous for democracy when the connection between leader and people remains unmediated for a longer period of time, thus bypassing and surpassing mediating institutions, among which one can also count, implicitly at least, the bureaucracy (Urbinati, 2019a, b; Mansbridge and Macedo, 2019). In other words, the populist leader draws on the core antagonism of 'the good people versus the corrupt elite', thus justifying impatience with the necessary compromises and frustrations of procedural democracy and its constraining checks and balances. The top ranks of the bureaucracy, if not the whole public administration system, are seen by populists as being part of this 'corrupt' elite, fighting against which constitutes the core mandate of populists elected to power.

For some observers, populism, particularly when emanating from the opposition, is viewed as a necessary political force that provides neglected segments of the electorate with a renewed representation (Mouffe, 2018; Moffit, 2020). Yet there is a broad consensus that populists *in government* pose a threat for the proper functioning and even for the future of democracy (Galston, 2017; Peters and Pierre, 2020; Bauer et al., 2021; Askim et al., 2022; Bellodi et al., 2022).[5] The pivotal questions then become: why are populists so successful, and is populism, especially authoritarian populism, merely a mobilising strategy to seize political power, or are there functional or structural features aiding its ascent (Manow, 2021)?

Why such a presumably political science question is also of interest for PA is obvious. If populism is merely a transient political trend, the situation may potentially revert once the electorate's attention shifts elsewhere. However, if there are structural reasons behind the success of populists – and I agree that there are – then public administration must also undergo a more profound re-evaluation of its role under populist governments and determine the stance it legitimately can and wishes to adopt amid ongoing transformations of the politics–administration relationship (Stoker, 2021).

Regrettably, the latter scenario appears to be the reality, as indicated by a majority of the literature on the current wave of populism, particularly within cleavage theory (Marks et al., 2021). In essence, the argument revolves around the growing incapacity of our representative democracies to present disadvantaged segments of the electorate with a genuinely political choice, because of the liberal embeddedness of the nation-state in inter- and supranational regimes and the delegation of decisions to non-majoritarian national institutions (Schäfer and Zürn, 2023). This increasing incapacity, coupled with the entrenched effects of prior policy and institutional decisions (which are difficult to change subsequently because of lock-in effects and the need for super-majorities, like, for example, establishing a transnational currency), tends to favour a specific 'liberal' spectrum of policy options in Western democracies, promoting neoliberal economic policies, libertarian societal models, and a general cosmopolitanism (Urbinati, 2019a, b). Consequently, those on the periphery or in opposition to these choices feel progressively less represented, and – aggravated by economic crises – feel existentially threatened and thus withdraw their support from the established institutions and policies of the system. This, at least, is the crux of the argument (Zürn, 2022).

What is more, the rise of the new cleavage is said to have been propelled by the increasing similarity among political parties, transforming them into 'catch-all parties'. Simultaneously, policymaking has faced escalating constraints from non-majoritarian institutions at both the national level (constitutional courts, central banks, regulatory agencies) and the international level (ECB, IMF, etc.) (Strijbis et al., 2020).[6] "Unfavorable policies alone" do not "cause dissatisfaction, but the feeling that these policies cannot be changed within the 'old system'" (Zürn, 2022, p. 790). Or, as Nadia Urbinati puts it, the confidence that "no majority is the last one" (2019, p. 91) has been lost.[7] Consequently, this cleavage has become manifest, with authoritarian populism on one side (majoritarian, nationalist, anti-liberal) and liberal cosmopolitanism on the other (emphasising individual rights, open borders, and international integration) (Strijbis et al., 2020; Koopmans and Zürn, 2019; de Vries, 2018).

The debates surrounding this development are more complex than can be addressed here. However, for the purpose of our discussion, a crucial point emerges: authoritarian populism should not be regarded as a transient or external phenomenon but as a novel political ideology inherent to the evolution that Western liberal democracies have undergone in the last decades (see Zürn and De Wilde, 2016; Schäfer and Zürn, 2023). The emerging cleavage appears to be a lasting condition, shaping new political realities, and consequently, it also introduces a new context for politics–administration relations, particularly where populists successfully conquer executive power (Yesilkagit et al., 2024; Bauer, 2024a; Peters and Pierre, 2020). Before delving into what that development means for public administration, the question is: what do we know about the authoritarian populist agenda once these forces have seized control of executive government?

4. The authoritarian populist agenda: system transformation, illiberal policy change, and administrative deformation

To state the obvious: governments, including authoritarian populist governments, can only execute – in the sense of performing and implementing – decisions through their administrative apparatus. Consequently, any envisioned governmental action, beyond mere party political communication or grassroots mobilisation by a party that constitutes that government, must be meticulously outlined, and set in motion by segments of the bureaucracy. This underscores the critical role played by the bureaucracy in what is commonly referred to as democratic backsliding.

To provide a brief reminder, democratic backsliding signifies the gradual deterioration of democratic institutions and norms, leading to the erosion of the democratic quality of a system and the concentration of power in the executive (referred to as 'executive aggrandizement') (Bermeo, 2016, 2022; Coppedge, 2017). Authoritarian populists contribute to this backsliding by undermining democratic checks and balances, restricting political pluralism, compromising electoral integrity, diminishing minority rights, and weakening the rule of law. There is also evidence suggesting that authoritarian populist governments promote nationalism and xenophobia, exacerbate corruption and cronyism, and, additionally, exhibit economic under-performance (Albertazzi and McDonnell, 2015; Levitsky and Ziblatt, 2018; Biard, 2019; Peters and Pierre, 2022; Bellodi et al., 2024; Zhang, 2023). Beyond systemic-level change in the form of democratic backsliding, authoritarian populists in government also attempt to implement their preferred illiberal policies as well as to reform the state bureaucracy into a submissive instrument centrally steerable by their personal command (Peters and Pierre, 2019).

Analysis of illiberal *policy* change has focused so far on how populist leaders engage in backsliding by manipulating bureaucratic capacities to bring about changes in public policies (see for an overview Morais de Sá e Silva and Gomide, 2024). These changes often involve covert and subversive methods to avoid public and institutional scrutiny. Examples include President Trump's efforts to sideline the Environmental Protection Agency and weaken the capabilities of the US foreign policy bureaucracy (Dillon et al., 2018). The short-term tactics involve strategies to impede accurate bureaucratic management, such as publicly criticising administrators, dismissing experts, reducing budgets, and appointing loyalists. Over time, these administrative changes can significantly influence policy design, demonstrating how backsliders use bureaucratic politics and reorganisation strategies as shortcuts to achieve their policy objectives through subterfuge.

Propelled by distrust of what they perceive as a 'runaway' and 'establishment-elitist' civil service, populist administrative reformers also follow their anti-pluralist script when transforming democratic public administration itself. Such reforms usually have the ambition to transform bureaucracy into a mere instrument at the disposal of their leadership, and their leadership alone. Backsliders employ a variety of strategies to mould bureaucracies into instruments with which to execute their illiberal policy agendas. These tactics encompass centralising administrative structures, bolstering top-down control, implementing budget cuts, purging staff based on ideology, subverting democratic norms in civil service management, and diminishing external accountability and interaction with society (Bauer et al., 2021; Bauer and Becker, 2020).

In recent years a rich body of PA literature has emerged covering illiberal policy change and administrative deformations as attempted by populists in government (see for an overview Yesilkagit et al., 2024; Bauer, 2024a). While the intensity and patterns of the achieved transformation vary, the intention and direction of authoritarian change, as well as the centrality of the bureaucracy as a means *as well as* an object of that change, can be taken for granted. This chapter can therefore explore the dilemmas that arise for democratic administration due to such developments.

5. The limits of the instrumental role

One could argue that public administration as the instrument of the government of the day has to do what that government wants, provided that said government enjoys legitimacy based on fair elections (Finer, 1940). Even if one embraces such a purely instrumental role, there are at least two dilemmas for democratic administration under populist rule: an epistemological and a backsliding dilemma.

The epistemological dilemma derives from the policy expertise vested in the bureaucracy and in individual bureaucrats. Expertise is almost by definition the basis of non- or even counter-majoritarian influence, and that makes the administrative elites (as part of the old elite against which populism campaigns) suspicious of populists in government. The bureaucracy is trained to be the guard of the kind of professional standards of policymaking populists detest because they understand them, most of the time, as constraints to their claim of an intuitive understanding of what is "the right thing to do" to "make things great again" (Urbinati, 2019a; Christensen, 2022). In view of the unprincipled demands of populists in power, civil servants will have to weigh to what extent they can implement populist policy choices that are in conflict with professional standards and scientific knowledge (Schuster et al., 2022; Kucinskas and Zylan, 2023; Story et al., 2023). The dilemma is: should bureaucrats acquiesce when asked to design and implement policies that are to the best of their knowledge ineffective or counter-productive in view of the problem to be solved, or potentially not in harmony with national laws or international commitments (Bertelli, 2021; Mosler and Potrafke, 2020; Dijkstra et al., 2022)? To what, in the first place, ought bureaucrats ideally be loyal – the elected government or professional standards?

The backsliding dilemma has been debated more extensively and consists, as detailed in the previous section, in the risk of populists in government using their bureaucracies to dismantle liberal-democratic standards, procedures, and democratic political cultures (Bermeo, 2016, 2022). Not opposing such government action may make civil servants the accomplices of democratic backsliding. But again, the question is whether and to what extent bureaucrats can shed responsibility and do what they are told to do by their populist superiors when the latter go against liberal or pluralist values and established democratic culture. PA research has started to consider these aspects (Bertelli, 2021; Yesilkagit et al., 2024; Bauer, 2024a; Koliba, 2024). The dilemma is that in a traditional instrumental view on public administration, it is very difficult to justify bureaucratic counter-action, save, perhaps, when populist governments clearly and ostensibly breach the constitution. It appears that without a robust and fundamental debate about the ethical principles underlying a good civil service and the nature of appropriate administrative behaviour in times of crisis, this dilemma remains intractable, or at least risks being shifted to the conscience of individual civil servants. Instead of leaving individual bureaucrats in a particular situation to figure out what to do, this problematic requires examining whether our current conception of a democratic public administration system is adequate to address such challenges and, if the conclusion is that it is not, how, potentially, to adapt it. The implied question is whether the liberal state is too liberal in the face of those who attempt to undermine the democratic constitutional order and thus whether the civil service needs to be enabled to act as a guardian (Raadschelders, 2022; Yesilkagit et al., 2024). At any rate, both the epistemological and backsliding dilemma point to the fundamental question of whether civil servants can uphold their neutrality when professional standards, or even the bedrock principles of their liberal-democratic order, are threatened by the very government they serve.

6. How to respond to the illiberal trend? Populism as an ethical challenge for PA

If the previous argumentation has some validity, the illiberal challenge poses tricky ethical and normative questions for PA as a discipline (Stivers, 2008; Stivers and DeHart-Davis, 2022; Bertelli, 2021). How can the civil service be prepared to 'stand up to' the populist challenge, and what can be expected from individual democratic bureaucrats under pressure to advance illiberal agendas (Bauer, 2024a; Yesilkagit et al., 2024)? The orthodox image of bureaucracy as, first and foremost, an instrument of government seems too narrow (see Jackson, 2009), and so does the conception of the bureaucratic ethos as deriving exclusively from values like efficiency, neutrality, loyalty, expertise, hierarchy, and a chain of command from elected leaders to implementation (Cooper, 1990). Rather, what is needed is a renewal of the debate about administrative responsibility and the adequate kind of democratic ethos for modern public bureaucracies (Rohr, 1986, 1998; Bertelli, 2021; Meier et al., 2019; Brugué and Gallego, 2003; Železnik and Fink-Hafner, 2023; Bauer, 2024b). Such a debate needs to explore the fine balance between professional neutrality and the need for practical integrity if the democratic system itself is at stake. To what extent individual bureaucrats need to ground their behaviour on higher-order moral principles such as constitutionalism, citizenship, public interest, social equity, and justice in order to preserve the liberal-democratic order will have to be discussed (Nabatchi et al., 2011; Heath, 2020). Yesilkagit et al. (2024) have provided a manifesto for just such an active guardianship of democratic administration in the face of democratic backsliding by incumbent governments (see also Terry, 2003; du Gay and Lopdrup-Hjorth, 2022). Similarly, balancing the formal competences of civil servants, their necessary independence to do their job, and their duty to advance pluralist democratic values, Bertelli (2021, Ch 6) develops a 'complementary principle' as a normative orientation for individual 'policy workers' to remain truthful to democratic values in their governance work. According to such considerations, bureaucracy is not just an instrument, but a democratic institution with its own normative and organisational intrinsic values (which are usually shared with the society in which it is operating). The necessary legitimacy for the bureaucracy to act in such a way needs to be further discussed and probably spelled out more clearly than is currently the case in constitutional principles, rule of law, due process, and impartial expertise (Heath, 2020). In addition, if clashes with backsliding governments are to be expected, deontological ethical standards on which to base democratic administrative performance need to be developed and their practicability explored and assured (Stivers, 2008; Nabatchi et al., 2011).

Beyond defending pluralist values against illiberal backsliders in government, a further point for consideration is that our 'models' of a bureaucracy in liberal representative democracies need to come to grips with the intensifying centrality of the executive in modern governance, and the challenge ever-greater executive powers pose for conceiving of adequate forms and ways to keep 21st-century government legitimate and democratic. This is probably via a mixture of increasing deliberative, participative, representative, and other forms and mechanisms of popular engagement and control. If there is any potentially positive impact of the current trend of rising authoritative populism, then perhaps it is to raise questions of how to further democratise public administration in practice.

Only in the tradition of democratic administration thinking can one expect to find a solid theoretical basis for conceiving of active administrative responsibilities against the potential exaggerations of illiberal governments (Etzioni-Halevy, 2013; Brugué and Gallego, 2003; Wood et al., 2022; Železnik and Fink-Hafner, 2023). In particular, a shift of focus away from external controls towards internal responsibility would be necessary; and this would mean a shift away from concerns of hierarchical control and towards those of how to make civil services democratically resilient. Potential solutions might be to make it harder for incumbent governments to abolish the institutional accountability of the bureaucracy to parliament and organised society, to intensify the participation of citizens in the management of the res publica, and to ensure that recruitment and career progression cannot be monopolised by the political leadership of the day. Staff at all levels need to be trained in how to actively stand for democratic values. Grasping the democratic mission of public administration and upholding trust in professional standards can empower staff to recognize when it is appropriate to resist the demands of political superiors—a complex challenge for public sector leadership. Taking actions along these lines could potentially 'toughen up' the bureaucracy and thus make it harder for anti-liberalists to succeed (Yesilkagit et al., 2024).

At any rate, in times when populists take over government with the aim of using the executive to implement an illiberal transformation in order to accomplish democratic backsliding, the responsibility of the bureaucracy for the liberal order as such appears to point in the direction of overcoming a purely instrumental conception of bureaucratic loyalty. Perhaps only a stern change of perspective can help, one that conceives of democratic bureaucrats in the first place as "the servant and guardian of legal and professional rules and a constitutional order, not of the rulers" (Olsen, 2008, p. 17; Yesilkagit et al., 2024).

7. Conclusion

The illiberal challenge has tangible consequences for public administration by elevating authoritarian populists to positions of power in liberal democracies, exposing our political systems to the perils of deliberate democratic regression, policy dismantling, and administrative deformation (Box, 2017). From the perspective of Western democracies, the unprecedented situation is that danger to the liberal order comes 'from within', from its elected government itself; that public administration, as part of the executive government, may potentially suffer an illiberal transformation itself while being in danger of becoming a tool to execute authoritarian ambitions (Bauer, 2024c). What one expects from PA in such dire times depends, first and foremost, upon whether one adheres to a popular-electoral or counter-majoritarian conceptualisation of the role of bureaucracy in politics–administration relations. While democratic bureaucracy alone is unlikely to save bureaucracy (Yesilkagit, 2021), it is necessary – normatively speaking – for PA to reconsider the role and commitment of existing public administration systems to constitutional values and to work out prospectively how best our bureaucracies can become part of what can be conceived as a "Guardian State", if need be (Yesilkagit et al., 2024; Bertelli, 2024). If there is a call for the PA research agenda, then it comes from this direction.

Unfortunately, the evidence from empirical studies on the reactions of civil servants in authoritarian regimes so far provides little hope for substantial administrative guardianship but rather suggests that even in the best-case scenario, the bureaucracy may only be able to moderate the anti-liberal effects of authoritarian rule, perhaps delaying its transformation. However, in a direct confrontation with an elected government, democratic public administration seems unlikely to prevail, especially if that government has gained popular legitimacy through successive electoral cycles (Schuster et al., 2022; Story et al., 2023; Lotta et al., 2023; Kucinskas and Zylan, 2023; Guedes-Neto and Peters, 2021).

Therefore, placing the fate of representative democracy solely on the shoulders of civil servants would be not only unfair but also short-sighted. This is not to imply that democratic civil servants should not be held accountable for upholding the political integrity of the system to which they have pledged their allegiance (Terry, 2003, 2015). Quite the contrary, PA should, of course, debate how democratic administration can be encouraged and reformed to stand by the liberal-democratic order. However, if it is correct that authoritarian populism is a structural phenomenon, occasional individual administrative resistance will not be enough.

From that point of view, the rise of authoritarian populism must be put into the context of an intensifying crisis of representative democracy, which seems correlated – and this is important from a PA perspective – with the increasing dominance of the executive branch vis-à-vis other Montesquieuean powers. While citizen engagement and participatory mechanisms have expanded over the years (Ansell et al., 2023), no consensual model has yet emerged for how representative democracy under 21st-century executive dominance should be redesigned. In such a model the executive – and the bureaucracy as its core component – would continue to play a crucial role. Major questions would however be how public management can be further 'democratised', while PA is to contribute to the strengthening of the liberal-democratic quality of the political system that it is itself part of. PA must therefore engage in a dialogue with political philosophy, other social sciences, and practice to explore frameworks for producing a liberal theory of public administration able to help revitalise the representative liberal-democratic model (Heath, 2020). That might be by transforming the bureaucracy from a mere instrument of representative government into a platform for intensified and novel forms of citizen participation with which we can forge new avenues for legitimacy in republican governance (Rosanvallon, 2011; Heath, 2020; Bertelli, 2021; Ansell et al., 2024).

Notes

1. This means left-wing populism and left-wing or liberal populist governments are put aside most of the time for the argumentation. That seems justified as – perhaps with the exception of Macron in France – the success of these movements has not so far been able to match authoritarian right-wing populists' successes. It also does not contradict the general definition of populism, i.e. that populism can be seen as an ideology with a 'thin core', i.e. it can combine with many specific political programmes, denouncing the political elite as corrupt and claiming to re-empower the true people by vesting leadership in an untainted leader who promises swift solutions to the unfairly neglected 'true' majority (see Mudde and Kaltwasser, 2012; Müller, 2016; Norris and Inglehart, 2019; Mansbridge and Macedo, 2019; Lotta, 2024).
2. It would probably be more precise to speak of a comprehensive 'anti-liberalism' instead of 'illiberalism' to catch the negativism behind this ideology (Holmes, 2021; Waller, 2023; Urbinati, 2019b; Zürn, 2022). But for the sake of comprehensibility and following established custom, this chapter sticks to the 'illiberalism' terminology.
3. Let me just remind the reader that classical democratic theory used to be full of distrust of popular sovereignty – for example in the form of universal suffrage – specially to avoid the excesses of the French Revolution.

4. To oversimplify polemically, PA may need to choose between Caesarism and constitutionalism as the ultimate frame for defining its future institutional design and mission (Arato and Cohen, 2021; Zürn, 2023). See Max Weber's endorsement of 'Caesarism' as the ultimate political power against runaway bureaucracy (Caspar, 2007); and for an advocate of administrative constitutionalism, Spicer, 2015.
5. See also Laclau, 2025; Kriesi, 2014; Müller, 2016; Mansbridge and Macedo 2019; Norris and Inglehart, 2019 for the broader debate.
6. See Zürn and de Wilde, 2016, p. 282: "Peter Mair identifies three separate components that need to be present in order for a conflict to be a cleavage: a structural component, an organizational component and a normative component: 'In other words, the shift from society to politics occurs when a particular social divide [structural component] becomes associated with a particular set of values or identities [normative component], and when this is then brought into the political world, and made politically relevant by means of an organized party or group [organizational component]'". See also Schäfer and Zürn, 2023 for further references to the cleavage argumentation.
7. To simplify: a new cleavage arose because policymaking realities are constrained by an international (often neo)liberal consensus from which nationally, at least unilaterally, it is difficult to escape. The existing party system proves insufficient in providing an adequate 'voice' for the growing dissatisfaction, especially amidst the challenges posed by globalisation pressures, economic downturns, and ongoing crises in the distribution of resources. It is this cleavage between economic disadvantaged, identity-wise estranged parts of the electorate on the one side, and cosmopolitan liberals on the other which populists exploit.

References

Albertazzi, D., & McDonnell, D. (2016). *Populists in Power* (1st ed.). Routledge. https://doi.org/10.4324/9781315725789.

Ansell, C., Sørensen, E., Torfing, J., & Trondal, J. (2024). *Robust Governance in Turbulent Times*. Cambridge University Press. https://doi.org/10.1017/9781009433006.

Ansell, C., Sørensen, E., & Torfing, J. (2023). The democratic quality of co-creation: A theoretical exploration. *Public Policy and Administration*, 39(2), 149–170. https://doi.org/10.1177/09520767231170715.

Arato, A., & Cohen, J. L. (2021). *Populism and Civil Society: The Challenge to Constitutional Democracy*. Oxford University Press. https://doi.org/10.1093/oso/9780197526583.001.0001.

Askim, J., Karlsen, R., & Kolltveit, K. (2021). Populists in government: Normal or exceptional? *Government and Opposition*, 57(4), 728–748. https://doi.org/10.1017/gov.2021.30.

Bauer, M. W. (2024a). Public administration under populist rule: Standing up against democratic backsliding. *International Journal of Public Administration*, 47(15), 1019–1031. https://doi.org/10.1080/01900692.2023.2243400.

Bauer, M. W. (2024b). Administrative backsliding. In A. Croissant, L. Tomini (Eds.), *The Routledge Handbook of Autocratization* (362-376, 1st ed.). Routledge.

Bauer, M. W. (2024c). Democratic backsliding and administrative responsibility: Seeking guidance for bureaucratic behavior in dark times. In M. Morais de Sá e Silva, A. de Ávila Gomide (Eds.),

Public Policy in Democratic Backsliding: How Illiberal Populists Engage with the Policy Process (pp. 315–355). Palgrave Macmillan.

Bauer, M. W., & Becker, S. (2020). Democratic backsliding, populism, and public administration. *Perspectives on Public Management and Governance*, 3(1), 19–31. https://doi.org/10.1093/ppmgov/gvz026.

Bauer, M. W., Becker, S., Peters, B. G., Pierre, J., & Yesilkagit, K. (Eds.) (2021). *Democratic Backsliding and Public Administration: How Populists in Government Transform State Bureaucracies*. Cambridge University Press. https://doi.org/10.1017/9781009023504.

Bauer, M. W., Peters, B. G., & Pierre, J. (2021). Pathways to administrative resilience: Public bureaucracies ruled by democratic backsliders as a transnational challenge. *STG Policy Analysis, 2021/03*, 1–13. https://doi.org/10.2870/752884.

Bellodi, L., Morelli, M., & Vannoni, M. (2024). A costly commitment: Populism, economic performance, and the quality of bureaucracy. *American Journal of Political Science*, 68(1), 193–209. https://doi.org/10.1111/ajps.12782.

Bermeo, N. (2016). On democratic backsliding. *Journal of Democracy*, 27(1), 5–19. https://doi.org/10.1353/jod.2016.0012.

Bermeo, N. (2022). Questioning backsliding. *Journal of Democracy*, 33(4), 155–159. https://doi.org/10.1353/jod.2022.0054.

Bertelli, A. M. (2021). *Democracy Administered: How Public Administration Shapes Representative government*. Cambridge University Press. https://doi.org/10.1017/9781316755167.

Bertelli, A. M., & Instituut voor de Overheid, KU Leuven (n.d.). *Values rather than control: Rethinking the democratic deficits of administrative agencies*. [Paper]. International Seminar on Future Trends for the Public Sector, Leuven, Belgium.

Bertelli, A. M., & Schwartz, L. J. (2022). *Public Administration and Democracy* (1st ed.). Cambridge University Press. https://doi.org/10.1017/9781009217613.

Biard, B. (2019). The influence of radical right populist parties on law and order policy-making. *Policy Studies*, 40(1), 40–57. https://doi.org/10.1080/01442872.2018.1533110.

Bouckaert, G. (2009). Trust and public administration. *Administration*, 60(1), 91–115. https://lirias.kuleuven.be/retrieve/216467.

Box, R. C. (2014). Into a new regressive era: Implications for public administration. *Public Integrity*, 19(6), 576–592. https://doi.org/10.1080/10999922.2017.1344515.

Brugué, Q., & Gallego, R. (2003). A democratic public administration? Developments in public participation and innovations in community governance. *Public Management Review*, 5(3), 425–447. https://doi.org/10.1080/1471903032000146973.

Bustikova, L., & Guasti, P. (2017). The illiberal turn or swerve in Central Europe? *Politics & Governance*, 5(4), 166–176. https://doi.org/10.17645/pag.v5i4.1156.

Christensen, J. (2022). When bureaucratic expertise comes under attack. *Public Administration*, 102(1), 79–94. https://doi.org/10.1111/padm.12905.

Cooper, T. L. (1990). *The Responsible Administrator: An Approach to Ethics for the Administrative role* (3rd ed.). Jossey-Bass.

Coppedge, M. (2017). *Eroding Regimes: What, Where, and When?* V-Dem Working Paper 2017:57, 1–32. https://doi.org/10.2139/ssrn.3066677.

De Vries, C. E. (2018). The cosmopolitan-parochial divide: Changing patterns of party and electoral competition in the Netherlands and beyond. *Journal of European Public Policy*, 25(11), 1541–1565. https://doi.org/10.1080/13501763.2017.1339730.

Dean, R. (2023). Deliberating like a state: Locating public administration within the deliberative system. *Political Studies*, 72(3), 924–943. https://doi.org/10.1177/00323217231166285.

Dijkstra, H., Von Allwörden, L., Schuette, L. A., & Zaccaria, G. (2022). Donald Trump and the survival strategies of international organisations: When can institutional actors counter existential challenges? *Cambridge Review of International Affairs*, 37(2), 182–205. https://doi.org/10.1080/09557571.2022.2136566.

Dillon, L., Sellers, C., Underhill, V., Shapiro, N., Ohayon, J. L., Sullivan, M., Brown, P., Harrison J., Wylie, J., & "EPA Under Siege" Writing Group (2015). The environmental protection agency in the early Trump administration: Prelude to regulatory capture. *American Journal of Public Health*, 108(S2), S89–S94. https://doi.org/10.2105/AJPH.2018.304360.

Du Gay, P. (2020). The bureaucratic vocation: State/Office/Ethics. *New Formations: A Journal of Culture/Theory/Politics*, 100, 77–96. https://doi.org/10.3898/NEWF:100-101.06.2020.

Du Gay, P., & Lopdrup-Hjorth, T. (2022). *For Public Service: State, Office, and Ethics* (1st ed.). Routledge. https://doi.org/10.4324/9780203093603.

Etzioni-Halevy, E. (2013 [1985]). *Bureaucracy and Democracy. A Political Dilemma*. Routledge.

Finer, H. (1941). Administrative responsibility in democratic government. *Public Administration Review*, 1(4), 335–350. https://doi.org/10.2307/972907.

Galston, W. A. (2017). *Anti-pluralism: The Populist Threat To Liberal Democracy*. Yale University Press. https://doi.org/10.2307/j.ctt21668rd.

Goodsell, C. T. (2022). Strengthening American democracy through public administration. *The American Review of Public Administration*, 52(6), 403–408. https://doi.org/10.1177/02750740221098348.

Guedes-Neto, J. V., & Peters, B. G. (2021). Working, shirking, and sabotage in times of democratic backsliding: An experimental study in Brazil. In M. W. Bauer, B. G. Peters, J. Pierre, K. Yesilkagit, & S. Becker (Eds.), *Democratic Backsliding and Public Administration: How Populists in Government Transform State Bureaucracies* (pp. 221–244). Cambridge University Press. https://doi.org/10.1017/9781009023504.011.

Hajnal, G. (2015). Illiberalism in the making: Orbán-era governance reforms in the view of the administrative elite. In P. Kovač & G. Gajduschek (Eds.), *Contemporary Governance Models and Practices in Central and Eastern Europe* (pp. 133–156). NISPAcee Press.

Hajnal, G. (2021). Illiberal challenges to mainstream public management research: Hungary as an exemplary case. *Public Management Review*, 23(3), 317–325. https://doi.org/10.1080/14719037.2020.1752038.

Hajnal, G., & Boda, Z. (2021). Illiberal transformation of government bureaucracy in a fragile democracy: The case of Hungary. In M. W. Bauer, B. Peters, J. Pierre, K. Yesilkagit, & S. Becker (Eds.), *Democratic Backsliding and Public Administration: How populists in Government Transform State Bureaucracies* (pp. 76–98). Cambridge University Press. https://doi.org/10.1017/9781009023504.005.

Heath, J. (2020). *The Machinery of Government: Public Administration and the Liberal State*. Oxford University Press. https://doi.org/10.1093/oso/9780197509616.001.0001.

Holmes, S. (2021). The Antiliberal Idea. In A. Sajó, R. Uitz, & S. Holmes (Eds.), *Routledge Handbook of Illiberalism* (1st ed., pp. 3–15). Routledge. https://doi.org/10.4324/9780367260569-2.

Inglehart, R. F., & Norris, P. (2016). *Trump, Brexit, and the Rise of Populism: Economic Have-Nots and Cultural Backlash.* HKS Working Paper No. RWP16-026. https://doi.org/10.2139/ssrn.2818659.

Jackson, M. (2009). Responsibility versus accountability in the Friedrich-Finer debate. *Journal of Management History*, 15(1), 66–77. https://doi.org/10.1108/17511340910921790.

Kessler, J. (2022). Illiberalism and administrative government. In A. Sarat, L. Douglas, & M. M. Umphrey (Eds.), *Law and illiberalism* (pp. 62–77). University of Massachusettes Press. https://doi.org/10.2307/j.ctv2x8v62m.7.

Koliba, C. (2024). Liberal democratic accountability standards and public administration. *Public Administration Review*, 1–11. https://doi.org/10.1111/puar.13831.

Koopmans, R., & Zürn, M. (2019). Cosmopolitanism and communitarianism: How globalization is reshaping politics in the twenty-first century. In P. de Wilde, R. Koopmans, W. Merkel, O. Strijbis, & M. Zürn (Eds.), *The struggle over borders* (pp. 1–34). Cambridge University Press. https://doi.org/10.1017/9781108652698.001.

Krastev, I. (2011). The age of populism: Reflections on the self-enmity of democracy. *European View*, 10(1), 11–16. https://doi.org/10.1007/s12290-011-0152-8.

Kriesi, H. (2014). The populist challenge. *West European Politics*, 37(2), 361–378. https://doi.org/10.1080/01402382.2014.887879.

Kucinskas, J., & Zylan, Y. (2023). Walking the moral tightrope: Federal civil servants' loyalties, caution, and resistance under the trump administration. *American Journal of Sociology*, 128(6), 1761-1808. https://doi.org/10.1086/725313.

Laclau, E. (2005). *On Populist Reason.* Verso.

Levitsky, S., & Ziblatt, D. (2018). *How Democracies Die.* Crown.

Lotta, G., Gustavo, G. M., & Story, J. (2023). Political attacks and the undermining of the bureaucracy: The impact on civil servants' well-being. *Governance*, 37(2), 619–641. https://doi.org/10.1111/gove.12792.

Manow, P. (2021). The political economy of populism in Europe: Hyperglobalization, migration, capital and diverse political protest. *Rechtstheorie*, 52(2–3), 209–223. https://doi.org/10.3790/rth.52.2-3.209.

Mansbridge, J., & Macedo, S. (2019). Populism and democratic theory. *Annual Review of Law and Social Science*, 15, 59–77. https://doi.org/10.1146/annurev-lawsocsci-101518-042843.

Marks, G., Attewell, D., Rovny, J., & Hooghe, L. (2021). Cleavage Theory. *The Palgrave Handbook of EU Crises* (pp. 173–193). https://doi.org/10.1007/978-3-030-51791-5_9.

Meier, K.J., Compton, M., Polga-Hecimovich, J., Song, M., & Wimpy, C. (2019). Bureaucracy and the failure of politics: Challenges to democratic governance. *Administration & Society*, 51(10), 1576-1605. https://doi.org/10.1177/0095399719874759.

Moffitt, B. (2014). *The Global Rise of Populism: Performance, Political Style, and Representation* (1st ed.). Stanford University Press. https://doi.org/10.2307/j.ctvqsdsd8.

Moffitt, B. (2020). *Populism.* John Wiley & Sons.

Morais de Sá e Silva, M. (2021). Beyond ordinary policy change: Authoritarian policy dismantling. *SciELO Preprints*, 1–21. https://doi.org/10.1590/SciELOPreprints.2692.

Morais de Sá e Silva, M., & Gomide, A. (Eds.). (2024). *Public Policy in Democratic Backsliding: How Illiberal Populists Engage with the Policy Process*. Palgrave Macmillan.

Mosler, M., & Potrafke, N. (2020). International political alignment during the Trump presidency: Voting at the UN General Assembly. *International Interactions*, 46(3), 481–497. https://doi.org/10.1080/03050629.2020.1719405.

Mouffe, C. (2018). *For a left populism*. Verso.

Moynihan, D., & Roberts, A. (2021). Dysfunction by design: Trumpism as administrative doctrine. *Public Administration Review*, 81(1), 152–156. https://doi.org/10.1111/puar.13342.

Mudde, C., & Kaltwasser, C. R. (2012). *Populism in Europe and the Americas: Threat or Corrective for Democracy?* Cambridge University Press. https://doi.org/10.1017/CBO9781139152365.

Mudde, C., & Kaltwasser, C. R. (2017). *Populism: A Very Short Introduction*. Oxford University Press. https://doi.org/10.1093/actrade/9780190234874.001.0001.

Müller, J.-W. (2016). *What is Populism?* University of Pennsylvania Press. https://doi.org/10.9783/9780812293784.

Nabatchi, T. (2006). Addressing the citizenship and democratic deficits: The potential of deliberative democracy for public administration. *The American Review of Public Administration*, 40(4), 376–399. https://doi.org/10.1177/0275074009356467.

Nabatchi, T., Goerdel, H. T., & Peffer, S. (2011). Public administration in dark times: Some questions for the future of the field. *Journal of Public Administration Research and Theory*, 21(suppl_1), i29–i43. https://doi.org/10.1093/jopart/muq068.

Norris, P., & Inglehart, R. (2019). *Cultural Backlash: Trump, Brexit, and Authoritarian Populism*. Cambridge University Press. https://doi.org/10.1017/9781108595841.

O'Leary, R. (2013). *The Ethics of Dissent: Managing Guerrilla Government* (2nd ed.). CQ Press. https://doi.org/10.4135/9781506335681.

O'Leary, R. (2017). The ethics of dissent: Can President Trump survive guerrilla government? *Administrative Theory & Praxis*, 39(2), 63–79. https://doi.org/10.1080/10841806.2017.1309803.

Olsen, J. P. (2008). The ups and downs of bureaucratic organization. *Annual Review of Political Science*, 11(1), 13–37. https://doi.org/10.1146/annurev.polisci.11.060106.101806.

Peters, B. G. (2019). Public administration in authoritarian regimes. *Asia Pacific Journal of Public*, 45(1), 7–15. https://doi.org/10.1080/23276665.2023.2169820.

Peters, B. G., & Pierre, J. (2019). Populism and public administration: Confronting the administrative state. *Administration & Society*, 51(10), 1521–1545. https://doi.org/10.1177/0095399719874749.

Peters, B. G., & Pierre, J. (2020). A typology of populism: Understanding the different forms of populism and their implications. *Democratization*, 27(6), 928–946. https://doi.org/10.1080/13510347.2020.1751615.

Peters, B. G., & Pierre, J. (2022). Politicisation of the public service during democratic backsliding: Alternative perspectives. *Australian Journal of Public Administration*, 81(4), 629-639.

Plattner, M. F. (2020). Illiberal democracy and the struggle on the right. In B. Vormann & M. D. Weinman (Eds.), *The Emergence of Illiberalism* (1st ed., pp. 43–57). Routledge. https://doi.org/10.4324/9780429347368-4.

Raadschelders, J. C. N. (2025). The evolution of bureaucracy as a political actor: From instrument for power, via iron cage, to container and guardian of democracy. In A. Ladner & F. Sager

(Eds.), *Handbook on the Politics of Public Administration* (pp. 13–23). Edward Elgar Publishing. https://doi.org/10.4337/9781839109447.00008.

Rohr, J. A. (1982). *To Run a Constitution: The Legitimacy of the Administrative State*. University Press of Kansas.

Rohr, J. A. (1998). *Public Service, Ethics, and Constitutional Practice*. University Press of Kansas.

Rosanvallon, P. (2011). *Democratic Legitimacy: Impartiality, Reflexivity, Proximity*. Princeton University Press. https://doi.org/10.1515/9781400838745.

Sajó, A. (2019). The constitution of illiberal democracy as a theory about society. *Polish Sociological Review, 208*(4), 396–412. https://doi.org/10.26412/psr208.01.

Sajó, A., Uitz, R., & Holmes, S. (Eds.) (2019). *Routledge Handbook of Illiberalism* (1st ed.). Routledge. https://doi.org/10.4324/9780367260569.

Sasso, G., & Morelli, M. (2021). Bureaucrats under populism. *Journal of Public Economics, 202*. https://doi.org/10.1016/j.jpubeco.2021.104497.

Schäfer, A. (2020). Cultural backlash? How (not) to explain the rise of authoritarian populism. *British Journal of Political Science, 52*(4), 1977–1993. https://doi.org/10.1017/S0007123421000363.

Schäfer, A., & Zürn, M. (2023). *The Democratic Regression: The Political Causes of Authoritarian Populism*. John Wiley & Sons.

Schuster, C., Mikkelsen, K. S., Correa, I., & Meyer-Sahling, J.-H. (2022). Exit, voice, and sabotage: Public service motivation and guerrilla bureaucracy in times of unprincipled political principals. *Journal of Public Administration Research and Theory, 32*(2), 416–435. https://doi.org/10.1093/jopart/muab028.

Spicer, M. W. (2015). Neutrality, adversary argument, and constitutionalism in public administration. *Administrative Theory & Praxis, 37*(3), 188–202. https://doi.org/10.1080/10841806.2015.1053363.

Stivers, C. (2005). *Governance in Dark Times. Practical Philosophy for Public Service*. Georgetown University Press.

Stivers, C., & DeHart-Davis, L. (2022). Introduction to the Symposium Issue on Reappraising Bureaucracy in the 21st Century. *Perspectives on Public Management and Governance, 5*(2), 77–83. https://doi.org/10.1093/ppmgov/gvac014.

Stoker, G. (2018). Public administration: How to respond to populism and democratic backsliding. In M. W. Bauer, B. G. Peters, J. Pierre, K. Yesilkagit, & S. Becker (Eds.), *Democratic Backsliding and Public Administration: How Populists in Government Transform State Bureaucracies*. Cambridge University Press. https://doi.org/10.1017/9781009023504.012.

Story, J., Lotta, G., & Tavares, G. M. (2023). (Mis)led by an outsider: Abusive supervision, disengagement, and silence in politicized bureaucracies. *Journal of Public Administration Research and Theory, 33*(4), 549–562. https://doi.org/10.1093/jopart/muad004.

Strijbis, O., Helmer, J., & De Wilde, P., (2020). A cosmopolitan–communitarian cleavage around the world? Evidence from ideological polarization and party–voter linkages. *Acta Politica, 55*(4), 408–431. https://doi.org/10.1057/s41269-018-0122-0.

Terry, L. D. (2001). *Leadership of Public Bureaucracies: The Administrator as Conservator* (2nd ed.). Routledge. https://doi.org/10.4324/9781315669236.

Trondal, J. (2023). *Governing the Contemporary Administrative State: Studies on the Organizational Dimension of Politics*. Springer Nature Switzerland AG. https://doi.org/10.1007/978-3-031-28008-5.

Urbinati, N. (2014). *Democracy Disfigured: Opinion, Truth, and the People*. Harvard University Press. https://doi.org/10.4159/harvard.9780674726383.

Urbinati, N. (2019a). *Me the People. How Populism Transforms Democracy*. Harvard University Press.

Urbinati, N. (2019b). Political theory of populism. *Annual Review of Political Science, 22*, 111–127. https://doi.org/10.1146/annurev-polisci-050317-070753.

Wagrandl, U. (2021). A theory of illiberal democracy. In A. Sajó, R. Uitz, & S. Holmes (Eds.), *Routledge Handbook of Illiberalism* (1st ed., pp. 94–117). Routledge.

Waldo, D. (1950). Development of theory of democratic administration. *American Political Science Review, 46*(1), 81–103. https://doi.org/10.2307/1950764.

Waller, J. G. (2018). Elites and institutions in the Russian thermidor: Regime instrumentalism, entrepreneurial signaling, and inherent illiberalism. *Journal of Illiberalism Studies, 1*(1), 1–23. https://doi.org/10.53483/VCHS2523.

Waller, J. G. (2023). Distinctions with a difference: Illiberalism and authoritarianism in scholarly study. *Political Studies Review, 22*(2), 365–386. https://doi.org/10.1177/14789299231159253.

Wood, M., Matthews, F., Overman, S., & Schillemans, T. (2022). Enacting accountability under populist pressures: Theorizing the relationship between anti-elite rhetoric and public accountability. *Administration & Society, 54*(2), 311–334. https://doi.org/10.1177/00953997211019387.

Yesilkagit, K. (2023). Can Bureaucracy Save Liberal Democracy? How Public Administration Can React to Populism. *Turkish Policy Quarterly, 20*(3), 1–10.

Yesilkagit, K., Bauer, M. W., Peters, B., & Pierre, J. (2024). The Guardian State: Strengthening the public service against democratic backsliding. *Public Administration Review, 84*(3), 414–425. https://doi.org/10.1111/puar.13808.

Zakaria, F. (1994). The rise of illiberal democracy. *Foreign Affairs, 76*(6), 22–43. https://doi.org/10.2307/20048274.

Zakaria, F. (2000). Illiberal democracy five years later: Democracy's fate in the 21st century. *Harvard International Review, 24*(2), 44–48. https://www.jstor.org/stable/i40104444.

Zeitlin, J., Van Der Duin, D., Kuhn, T., Weimer, M., & Jensen, M. D. (2021). Governance reforms and public acceptance of regulatory decisions: Cross-national evidence from linked survey experiments on pesticides authorization in the European Union. *Regulation & Governance, 17*(4), 980–999. https://doi.org/10.1111/rego.12483.

Železnik, A., & Fink-Hafner, D. (2023). Theoretical perspectives on bureaucrats: A quest for democratic agents. *Administration & Society, 55*(7), 1432–1456. https://doi.org/10.1177/00953997231165998.

Zhang, D. (2023). Draining the swamp? Populist leadership and corruption. *Governance, 37*(4), 1141–1161. https://doi.org/10.1111/gove.12829.

Zürn, M. (2020). How non-majoritarian institutions make silent majorities vocal: A political explanation of authoritarian populism. *Perspectives on Politics, 20*(3), 788–807. https://doi.org/10.1017/S1537592721001043.

Zürn, M., & De Wilde, P. (2016). Debating globalization: Cosmopolitanism and communitarianism as political ideologies. *Journal of Political Ideologies, 20*(3), 280–301. https://doi.org/10.1080/13569317.2016.1207741.

The trend towards fragility in the 21st century

by Alasdair Roberts

1. The trend: an increasingly fragile world

Since World War II, the foundation of world political order has been the state. Each modern state consists of a governmental apparatus that asserts control over a defined territory and claims the loyalty of people living in that territory, as well as recognition of its authority by other states. There are roughly 194 states in existence today. The number varies slightly because countries disagree about whether a small number of aspiring states ought to be admitted to the global community of states.

The world of states can be divided into three groups. According to research by the Fund for Peace, about 30 states are very stable, while 80 are very fragile. Another 70 exist in a liminal condition between stability and fragility (Table 1). Less than 10% of the world's population lives in very stable states, located mainly in the Global North. 55% live in very fragile states located mainly in the Global South. As we shall see later, though, the experience of fragile states is largely overlooked in top-ranked Public Administration journals. The scholarly field of Public Administration, as it is usually defined, is concerned mainly with the governance of very stable states.

The bubble of stability that has enveloped countries in the Global North over the last 70 years is historically unusual. Moreover, it is unlikely to persist. A critical trend in the coming decades will be the decline of political and social order around the world, including in the Global North. Fragility will become a universal concern. Leaders and citizens in the Global North, like those in the Global South, will worry more about fundamental problems of state integrity, societal cohesion, and public order.

Even today, the field of Public Administration ought to show more concern for problems of governance in fragile states. This is a matter of simple justice, because most people live in such countries. The case for taking fragility seriously within the field will become stronger as stability in the Global North declines. It is relatively easy to identify the ways in which scholarship ought to change if fragility is to be taken seriously. We can enumerate the topics that require more attention. The harder question is whether scholars and institutions within the field of Public Administration are willing to make the adjustments necessary to preserve its relevance in the coming decades.

Table 1. Fragility of states

Fragile States Index category	Number of states	Share of world population
Very stable or better	28	6%
Stable or more stable	37	11%
Warning	31	28%
Elevated warning or worse	81	55%

The Fragile States Index categorises 178 countries that account for more than 99% of the global population. The 11 FSI categories have been reduced to four in this chart. Source: Fund for Peace, 2023a.

2. Explaining the trend toward fragility

A fragile state is one in which governments struggle to perform the basic functions associated with statehood. A government may find that its capacity to exercise physical control over territory is compromised, perhaps because the governed population no longer acknowledges that government as the rightful authority. Or a government may become paralysed, in the sense that it is incapable of making decisions or translating those decisions into action. A national government may also lose the capacity to engage constructively with governments of other countries and retain their respect (Brinkerhoff, 2007, Ch 1; Brock, 2012, Ch 1; Fund for Peace, 2023b).

It is tempting to ask: what makes a state fragile? But this may be putting the question the wrong way around. As I have already noted, fragility is the natural condition for states. Stability, rather than fragility, is the anomaly that must be explained. Of the 20 most populous countries, accounting for 70% of the global population, only three – Germany, Japan, and the United States – could be counted as very stable in 2023, according to the Fund for Peace. Twelve of those 20 countries – including behemoths like India, Nigeria, and Brazil – were so fragile in 2023 that the Fund for Peace put them on its warning list. Many of these states are not merely fragile, but also relatively young. They were created when European empires collapsed after World War II. Indeed, most countries that exist today are less than 65 years old.

Even in the Global North, stability is a relatively new phenomenon. Consider, for example, the set of powerful countries that make up the G7. Since 1900, all these countries have been convulsed by wars, economic crises such as the Great Depression of the 1930s, and waves of internal unrest and domestic terrorism. The Federal Republic of Germany is less than 80 years old. In 1991 it absorbed the remnants of a failed state, the German Democratic Republic, which had survived for only 40 years. The current French Republic, established in 1958, is the fifth in that country's history. The Italian and Japanese states are also post-World War II constructions. The United Kingdom has spent the last century dismantling its empire, a painful and often violent process. The territory of the United Kingdom itself has shrunk by almost 25% since 1900. Canada escaped disaster when a referendum on the secession of Québec was narrowly defeated in 1995.

Scholars who study Public Administration in the Global North tend to underestimate the tenuous condition of the states within which they work. A scholarly career lasts 30 or 40 years, and the current generation of scholars may take stability for granted because they have not personally experienced disruption. But this is not the whole explanation for our neglect of fragility. If scholars of Public Administration were trained to think historically, and to recognise the state as a unit of analysis, evidence of fragility would be easy to see. However, academics in the Global North are generally not trained to think this way. Instead, they are encouraged to focus on lower-level problems of policy design and management, with an emphasis on the recent past (Roberts, 2019, Introduction and Ch 12).

Even so, it has been hard for scholars in the Global North to avoid evidence that the brief epoch of stability in that region is coming to an end. Since 2000, countries in the Global North have faced a series of major crises: a resurgence of terrorism between 2001 and 2005, an international financial and economic crisis between 2007 and 2012, the COVID-19 pandemic between 2020 and 2022, and wars in Iraq, Afghanistan, Ukraine, and the Middle East.

Other disruptive forces are also at work. Faith in the neoliberal economic formula has given way to anger about inequality and precarity. Governments have struggled to manage a surge in unauthorised immigration, which has often triggered a populist backlash. The quality of public discourse has been corroded by the rise of social media and the collapse of traditional journalism. Jürgen Habermas has recently warned that technological shocks are shredding the "delicate fabric" of political culture in the Global North. He warns that

Western democracies have already entered "a phase of increasing internal destabilization" (Habermas, 2023, pp. 22 and 28).

Habermas is not alone in his warning. The 2023 report of the Fund for Peace rejects the "facile notion" that fragility is a problem only in poor countries. Western democracies, it says, may also be "more fragile than we think" (Fund for Peace, 2023a, p. 10). After conducting its 2023 global survey, the Edelman Trust Institute found a worldwide decline of faith in societal institutions, "triggered by economic anxiety, disinformation, [and] mass-class divide." The Global North was not exempt from this global trend. Every G7 country except Canada was found to be severely polarised, or in danger of severe polarisation (Edelman Trust Institute, 2023, p. 16).

Decay in political stability is especially marked in the United States. The ideological gap between major political parties has widened substantially over the last 30 years (Moskowitz et al., 2019). Ideological polarisation has a clear regional basis: conservative and liberal states are demarcated more sharply than they have been in many decades. Among conservatives, antipathy toward Washington – expressed as hostility toward the 'deep state' or 'administrative state' – has deepened. One result of polarisation is political gridlock in Washington.

Gridlock is one of the main indicators of fragility. Another is political violence. In a 2023 survey, one-quarter of Americans agreed that "because things have gotten so far off track, true American patriots may have to resort to violence to save our country" (Public Religion Research Institute, 2023, p. 6). One-third of Republicans felt that way. One expert observed in 2022 that the United States was "closer to civil war than any of us would like to believe" (Walter, 2022, p. 159). A former chair of the US National Intelligence Council agreed: "It seems plain that a civil war is coming, and the only question is whether it will be fought with lawsuits and secessions or with AK-15s" (Treverton and Treverton, 2021). The United States, Stephen Marche observed in 2022, "is a textbook case of a country on the brink of civil conflict" (Marche, 2022). Instability in the United States can be expected to increase following Donald Trump's second inauguration as president in January 2025.

Instability and governmental dysfunctionality can be seen in Europe as well. Politics in the United Kingdom has roiled since the country opted to leave the European Union in 2016. The capacity of government to deliver public services and respond effectively to crises appears to have declined markedly, while political tensions have mounted (Richards et al., 2022). One analyst wrote in 2022: "No other major power on Earth stands quite as close to its own dissolution" (McTague, 2022). Elsewhere in Europe, the political stability of many states has been undermined by the rise of right-wing extremism (Judis, 2016, Ch 4). In Hungary, the government of Viktor Orbán has pursued a self-declared project of "regime change", aimed at establishing a form of "illiberal democracy", for more than a decade (Orbán, 2014). The recent success of the far-right politician Geert Wilders in Dutch elections has been described as "a warning to the rest of Europe" (The Guardian, 2023).

The European Union, a confederal structure that plays an increasingly large role in governance across Europe, is not counted as a state by the Fund for Peace and therefore not included in its Fragile States Index. If it were included, though, the European Union would undoubtedly be classified as fragile. Since 2007, EU leaders have reeled from crisis to crisis, improvising responses and struggling to hold the European project together. During the early months of the COVID-19 pandemic, some observers predicted the EU's imminent demise. George Soros warned Europeans about "the tragic reality" that the EU "may not be able to survive the challenges it currently confronts" (Soros, 2020). In a 2019 survey, most Europeans saw the EU as a good thing, but also expected that it would collapse within 20 years (Boffey, 2019). Concern about the durability of the European integration project is longstanding and unlikely to dissipate in the coming decades.

3. Two powerful drivers of fragility

Of all the factors that will contribute fragility in the Global North in the coming decades, climate change may be the most important. Throughout history, climate change has been one of the main drivers of political and social instability, contributing to the collapse of many political systems (Harper, 2017). Geoffrey Parker has suggested that a global wave of political upheaval in the 17th century, an epoch known among historians as "the general crisis", was caused by a decades-long phase of atmospheric cooling (Parker, 2017, pp. 49–51). Thomas Hobbes' *Leviathan*, with its dark view of the struggle to preserve political order, was a product of this era.

Of course, modern-day governments are more capable of responding to climate shocks than were governments of the 17th century. On the other hand, climatic changes over the next 30 years will be much more substantial than those of four centuries ago. Modern-day polities are also more complex and vulnerable to disruption. The population that needs protection in 2050 will be 20 times larger than it was in 1650.

Countries in the Global North will experience direct and indirect effects of climate change. The direct effects include an increase in weather emergencies, setbacks in economic productivity, and an increase in internal migration.

Developed countries will compete more aggressively for access to resources such as water, habitable and arable land, and minerals that are critical to low-carbon technologies. The indirect effects of climate change are those caused by disruptions in other countries. Large countries in the Global South that are already fragile, such as those in South Asia, will be severely affected by climate change. This may lead to mass migrations, civil and interstate wars, and a breakdown of public health systems. All these developments will have repercussions in the Global North.

Climate change will not be the only destabilising force in the coming decades. At the same time, technological changes are likely to disrupt many industries (Ford, 2015). Professions that have been largely protected from technological shocks over the last half-century may be jeopardised by advances in artificial intelligence. The whole history of economic development in the West over the last two centuries reminds us that economic disruption is usually a prelude to social and political disruption as well, often inflaming ethnic, racial, and religious conflicts (Schumpeter, 1976).

4. Implications for governance: adaptability

We can enumerate the topics that are likely to preoccupy governments, and which ought to preoccupy scholars of public administration as well, as fragility spreads around the world. Governments will likely give more emphasis to security functions – national defence, border control, and domestic policing – as global and internal order is shaken. These topics have generally been neglected within the scholarly literature on public administration (Raadschelders and Lee, 2011, p. 27). There may also be more emphasis on crisis management as natural disasters and international conflicts increase. At the same time, governments may be pressed to expand the "protective state", by insuring citizens and businesses against major hazards (Ansell, 2019). Leaders may put more emphasis on measures to promote social cohesion, and bolster democratic processes, as domestic political conflicts intensify.

In 2017, the National Intelligence Council, an analytic body within the United States government, published an assessment of pressures that were likely to confront the United States and other countries in the future. The Council predicted "more intense and cascading global challenges" that would produce "widespread strains on states and societies as well as shocks that could be catastrophic." The Council concluded that *adaptability*, the capacity to adjust to rapidly shifting circumstances, would be "an imperative" for states to survive and thrive in this new world (National Intelligence Council, 2021, pp. 1–3, 70). In a series of reports, the OECD has reached the same conclusion. "Nimbleness", it says, will be essential for countries to thrive in a turbulent and crisis-prone environment (OECD, 2013, p. 58).

Adaptability will be an essential quality of states in coming years (Roberts, 2024). Adaptability is not the same as resilience, which is often defined as the capacity of a system to preserve its core purpose and functionalities in the face of new conditions. An adaptable system must do something more than preserving itself. It must be capable of reimagining goals and reconstructing functionalities to meet new conditions. An adaptable state is adept at shapeshifting.

The idea that adaptability is an essential quality for political systems has a long intellectual pedigree. More than two thousand years ago, the Indian statesman Kautilya warned that rulers should be attentive to dangers and ready to adjust quickly to new threats (Kautilya, 1992). In the 15th century, Niccolo Machiavelli gave the same advice, warning Florentine rulers that inflexible regimes would soon die. Four hundred years later, the American theorist John Dewey said that the design of government ought to be regarded as a never-ending "experimental process" (Dewey, 1927, p. 83). In Dewey's view, a constant stream of new challenges requires the unrelenting reconstruction of public institutions.

The notion that states must be capable of continual reinvention may seem self-evident. In fact, it is not. There is a substantial body of thought which denies the importance of shapeshifting. For example, many American legal scholars regard the United States Constitution, a document drafted a quarter of a millennium ago, as inviolable. In the 1990s, reformers associated with international institutions such as the World Bank also promoted a package of government reforms designed to work in all circumstances and at all times. Some of these reformers believed that we had reached the "end of history", and that, as a result, it was possible to establish "the final form of human government" (Gray, 2007, p. 29). Of course, the experience of the last quarter of a century has demonstrated that history is definitely not over. Countries have encountered a series of powerful shocks, each one requiring a dramatic reconstruction of governmental capabilities.

At a high level of abstraction, we can define four functions that must be performed if a governmental system is to remain adaptable (Roberts, 2024, Ch 1):

- The system must be capable of *anticipating dangers*. That is, people within the system must be capable of thinking about the future and foreseeing dangers that might arise. Whether a system is adept at anticipating dangers is determined by culture and institutional design. Decision-makers and

the public at large must have a mindset that orients them toward the long term and sensitises them to risks. Decision-makers must also be supported by experts with the skills and resources necessary to identify and appraise risks successfully.
- The system must also be capable of not only apprehending dangers but also *inventing strategies to manage them*. Moreover, dangers cannot be addressed in isolation because their effects are usually intertwined. A master strategy for managing multiple dangers is required, and crafting one requires skill and creativity.
- The system must be effective at *legitimating strategies*. That is, the system must be capable of building support for different strategies among politically influential constituencies. There must be some degree of agreement within the leadership group of a state, and within the public at large, that a plan for overhauling institutions to fit the requirements of a new strategy ought to be adopted.
- And finally, the system must be skilled at *execution*, or translating strategy into action. The implementation of any strategy requires a substantial overhaul of important institutions. Even the best-designed strategy might be mangled by incompetent or corrupt public servants, or by public agencies that refuse to coordinate their work.

A critical question that will have to be answered in the remainder of this century is whether Western systems of government are capable of performing these four functions well. Western systems are those that fill key positions through free elections, separate the three branches of government, provide guarantees of individual rights, and sometimes divide authority between central and sub-national governments.

Conventional wisdom about the adaptability of Western systems is built on several premises. Because power is widely shared, and people enjoy free speech, it seems more likely that warning flags will be raised about looming dangers. Political freedom might also allow more creativity in crafting strategies for addressing those dangers. Open political competition allows for reform ideas to be examined closely and helps build broad support for action. Federalism also allows sub-national governments to act as laboratories for potential reforms.

All of these arguments have some merit. However, the case for the adaptability of Western systems is not open and shut. For example, academics have worried for decades about the short-term bias of Western politics. Politicians have an incentive to worry more about the next election rather than the long term. The intensification of political competition in several countries may aggravate this short-term bias. A related danger is the decay of public institutions that have a long-term focus. Long-term planning went out of fashion in the West after the 1980s. In some countries, agencies that were responsible for thinking about the future were shut down. Policy offices within government departments were downsized as governments tried to control spending.

The capacity of Western systems to build broad agreement about long-term strategies may also have been damaged by recent developments. In the United States, for example, political polarisation appears to be intensifying. There is increasing evidence that technological change is undermining the quality of public discourse. The decline of old media and the rise of social media have had several adverse effects. This transformation has destabilised the public agenda, encouraged a fixation on passing controversies, and coarsened public debate.

Added to this are worries about the capacity of Western governments to execute major reforms effectively (Fukuyama, 2014). Systems such as that of the United States, with strict divisions of power between branches and levels of government, have always been prone to gridlock and miscoordination. Some observers believe that the performance of Western bureaucracies has also decayed due to mounting red tape within government, underinvestment in people and systems, and declining public respect for expertise.

Of course, we should avoid sweeping statements about the adaptability of Western systems. They are not all the same. Some are federal, while others are not. Some are strict about the separation of powers between branches, while others are not. Some have a long tradition of public service, while others do not. Still, the broad point is that the adaptability of Western systems cannot be taken for granted. Some observers think that the COVID-19 pandemic has provided evidence of the vulnerabilities of the Western model (Roberts, 2022, Ch 8). In some Western countries, the pandemic response was marred by a lack of preparedness, confusion among agencies and governments, and widespread public resistance to government directives. In the initial phases, China's authoritarian government seemed to do a better job than several Western states of protecting public health and the economy.

Authoritarian regimes such as China's offer a different approach to adaptability. The functions of anticipation and strategy-making can be performed by technocrats working under party control. The task of building political support is simplified because leaders can resort to propaganda and repression. Centralised control over all levels of government simplifies execution, allowing the rapid mobilisation of resources in the face of new threats. In practice, of course, China's model has its own pitfalls. Still, there are observers who worry that the world will lurch toward the authoritarian model as crises multiply in the coming decades. If Western systems prove incapable of responding competently to new challenges, the appeal of authoritarian or 'strongman' rule may grow.

5. Are academics ready for fragility?

The remaining decades of the 21st century will be tumultuous for all states. Fragility, a condition once associated exclusively with governance in the Global South, will become a reality in the Global North as well. The challenge for political leaders will be to devise regimes that are capable of adapting to new circumstances without compromising their commitment to democracy, the rule of law, and human rights. The role of scholars in Public Administration should be to provide advice on how this can be done.

Presently the scholarly field of Public Administration, as it is conventionally defined, is not well equipped to provide this sort of advice. As many scholars have noted, the system of knowledge production in Public Administration – which is composed of faculties, degree programmes, journals, associations, and research conferences – is essentially neocolonial in structure (Moloney et al., 2023). The field purports to generate universal propositions but it draws predominantly from the experience of a small number of Global North countries, almost all of them former imperial powers. Scholars working in the Global North, and writing about problems of governance in the Global North, dominate the pages of scholarly journals (Hattke and Vogel, 2023, Figure 3).

As I noted earlier, all these countries have spent the last 80 years in an unusual bubble of stability. The 18 countries that contributed 90% of articles to top-ranked Public Administration journals in 2020 had an average FSI fragility score that would put them in the "very stable" category (see Table 2). The only exception to the rule of stability is China, which contributed less than 3% of articles. And China is an authoritarian regime; it cannot tell us much about handling fragility while respecting democratic norms. Large fragile countries with democratic aspirations – such as India, Indonesia, Nigeria, Brazil, or the Philippines – do not make significant contributions to top-ranked journals in Public Administration.

In short, the Public Administration literature takes stability for granted. It assumes that all the fundamental problems of governance – maintaining order, achieving a basic level of political and social cohesion, establishing a workable system of executive decision-making, operating a competent and corruption-free public service – have been resolved. Working from this assumption, the literature then focuses on second-order problems of governance: that is, making an essentially sound machine work more smoothly. Colloquially, these are known as First World problems.

Table 2. Contributions to top 10 Public Administration journals, by location of author's institution

Country	Percentage of articles	Cumulative percentage	FSI category
USA	32.9%	32.9%	Stable or more stable
United Kingdom	11.8%	44.7%	Stable or more stable
Netherlands	7.6%	52.3%	Very stable or better
Germany	6.8%	59.1%	Very stable or better
Italy	4.1%	63.2%	Stable or more stable
Denmark	4.0%	67.2%	Very stable or better
Switzerland	3.1%	70.3%	Very stable or better
Australia	3.0%	73.3%	Very stable or better
China	2.8%	76.1%	Warning
Canada	2.8%	78.9%	Very stable or better
Belgium	2.6%	81.5%	Very stable or better
Sweden	2.1%	83.6%	Very stable or better
South Korea	1.8%	85.4%	Very stable or better
Spain	1.5%	86.9%	Stable or more stable
Norway	1.4%	88.3%	Very stable or better
Israel	1.3%	89.6%	Stable or more stable
Austria	1.3%	90.9%	Very stable or better

Data obtained from Journal Citation Reports. Contributions to the 10 journals in the public administration category with the highest impact factor in 2020. For FSI categories, see Table 1.

A scholarly literature that takes fragility and adaptability seriously will have four features. It would be adept in thinking about large questions relating to regime design, and also normative questions about democracy and human rights. The literature would also suggest a strong historical awareness: that is, a sense of how regimes have changed in the face of shocks and strains in the past. And it would have the capacity to speculate intelligently about the future: about the pressures that are likely to arise, and how states ought to be constructed to manage those pressures.

Presently the field is deficient in all four dimensions. In some respects, it is not merely indifferent to the kind of scholarship that will be necessary but strongly opposed to it. There are some scholars who see Public Administration research as a form of hard science that is entirely divorced from normative questions, and others who question the reliability of historical methods. Hardly anyone accepts the legitimacy of scholarship that speculates about the future. So a profound change in mentalities will be necessary, as well as a change in practices. Doctoral students will need to be trained differently, and institutions within the field will have to develop new standards of relevance and rigour in research.

It is not clear that the field of Public Administration will make these changes quickly. The writer and activist Upton Sinclair once observed that "it is difficult to get a man to understand something, when his salary depends on his not understanding it" (Sinclair, 1935, p. 109). The reality is that many scholars in the Global North make a good living by playing the academic game as presently constructed. Changing the rules of the game may help new players, including those from the Global South, but it will also disadvantage incumbent players who are invested in the status quo. In this respect, the academic industry is not unique. It is just as vulnerable to sclerosis as other industries (Olson, 1982). Indeed, academia may be more sclerotic since it is less exposed to market forces. The scholarly factory of the Global North keeps running even when consumers no longer value its outputs.

In sum, we face a double problem of adaptability. States themselves must be adaptable if they are to thrive in the turbulent conditions of the 21st century. Public administration scholars ought to provide advice on how states can improve their adaptability. But this can only be done if the scholarly field of Public Administration itself can perform the four functions that are essential to adaptation. That is, the field must think carefully about how the needs of its clients are likely to change in the coming decades; consider how research ought to be reoriented; reach some level of agreement about the adjustments to institutions and practices that will be required for a change in orientation; and make those adjustments in a timely way. Scholarly fields that cannot adapt will wither and die, just as unresponsive states do.

References

Ansell, C. (2019). *The Protective State*. Cambridge University Press. https://doi.org/10.1017/9781108667081.

Boffey, D. (2019, May 15). Majority of Europeans Expect End of EU within 20 Years. *The Guardian*. https://www.theguardian.com/world/2019/may/15/majority-of-europeans-expect-end-of-eu-within-20-years.

Brinkerhoff, D. W. (2007). *Governance in Post-Conflict Societies: Rebuilding Fragile States* (1st ed.). Routledge.

Brock, L., Holm, H.-H., Sørensen, G., & Stohl, M. (2012). *Fragile States: Violence and the failure of intervention*. Polity Press.

Carr, J. (2020). George Soros Says Coronavirus May Spell the End of the EU. *Daily Mail*. https://www.dailymail.co.uk/news/article-8348669/George-Soros-says-coronavirus-spell-end-EU.html.

Dewey, J. (1927). *The Public and Its Problems*. H. Holt & Company.

Edelman Trust Institute (2023). *Edelman Trust Barometer Report 2023*. https://www.edelman.com/trust/2023/trust-barometer.

Ford, M. (2015). *Rise of the Robots: Technology and the Threat of a Jobless Future*. Basic Books.

Fukuyama, F. (2014). America in Decay. *Foreign Affairs*, 93(5), 3–26.

Fund for Peace (2023a). *Fragile States Index Annual Report 2023* (E. Bassey, Ed.). https://fragilestatesindex.org/wp-content/uploads/2023/06/FSI-2023-Report_final.pdf.

Fund for Peace (2023b). *Fragile States Index: What Does State Fragility Mean?* https://fragilestatesindex.org/frequently-asked-questions/what-does-state-fragility-mean/.

Gray, J. (2007). *Black Mass: Apocalyptic Religion and the Death of Utopia*. Allen Lane.

Habermas, J. (2021). *A New Structural Transformation of the Public Sphere and Deliberative Politics* (C. Cronin, Trans.). Polity Press.

Harper, K. (2017). *The Fate of Rome: Climate, Disease, and the End of an Empire*. Princeton University Press.

Hattke, F., & Vogel, R. (2023). Theories and theorizing in public administration: A systematic review. *Public Administration Review*, 83(6), 1452–1563. https://doi.org/10.1111/puar.13730.

Judis, J. B. (2016). *The Populist Explosion: How the Great Recession Transformed American and European Politics*. Columbia Global Reports.

Kautilya (1992). *The Arthashastra*. India Penguin Classics.

Marche, S. (2022). *The Next Civil War: Dispatches from the American Future*. Simon and Schuster.

McTague, T. (2022). How Britain Falls Apart. *The Atlantic*. https://www.theatlantic.com/international/archive/2022/01/will-britain-survive/621095/?utm_source=copy-link&utm_medium=social&utm_campaign=share.

Moloney, K., Sanabria-Pulido, P. & Demircioglu, M. A. (2022). Interrogating hegemonic embraces: Representative bureaucracy, methodological whiteness, and non-west exclusions. *Public Administration Review*, 83(1), 195–202. https://doi.org/10.1111/puar.13512.

Moskowitz, D., Rogowski, J., & Snyder Jr, J. (2019). *Parsing Party Polarization in Congress*. National Bureau of Economic Research. https://bpb-us-w2.wpmucdn.com/voices.uchicago.edu/dist/2/3167/files/2022/02/polarization_agenda.pdf

National Intelligence Council (2021). *Global Trends 2040: A More Contested World.* https://www.dni.gov/files/ODNI/documents/assessments/GlobalTrends_2040.pdf.

OECD (2013). *Poland: Implementing Strategic-State Capability.* OECD Public Governance Reviews. OECD Publishing. https://doi.org/10.1787/9789264201811-en.

Olson, M. (1980). *The Rise and Decline of Nations.* Yale University Press.

Orbán, V. (2014). *Speech at the Bálványos Free Summer University and Youth Camp 26th July, 2014.* Bálványos Free Summer University and Youth Camp. https://2015-2019.kormany.hu/en/the-prime-minister/the-prime-minister-s-speeches/prime-minister-viktor-orban-s-speech-at-the-25th-balvanyos-summer-free-university-and-student-camp.

Parker, G. (2017). *Global Crisis: War, Climate Change and Catastrophe in the Seventeenth Century.* Yale University Press. https://doi.org/10.2307/j.ctt32bksk.

Public Religion Research Institute (2023). *Threats to American Democracy Ahead of an Unprecedented Presidential Election: Findings from the 2023 American Values Survey.* https://www.prri.org/wp-content/uploads/2023/10/2023-AVS-Presentation.pdf.

Raadschelders, J. C. N., & Lee, K.-H. (2011). Trends in the study of public administration: Empirical and qualitative observations from public administration review, 2000–2009. *Public Administration Review, 71*(1), 19–33. https://doi.org/10.1111/j.1540-6210.2010.02303.x.

Richards, D., Warner, S., Smith, M. J., & Coyle, D., (2018). Crisis and state transformation: Covid-19, levelling up and the UK's incoherent state. *Cambridge Journal of Regions, Economy and Society, 16*(1), 31–48. https://doi.org/10.1093/cjres/rsac038.

Roberts, A. (2019). *Strategies for Governing: Reinventing Public Administration for a Dangerous Century.* Cornell University Press. https://doi.org/10.7591/cornell/9781501714405.001.0001.

Roberts, A. (2022). *Superstates: Empires of the Twenty-First Century.* Polity Press.

Roberts, A. (2024). *The Adaptable Country: How Canada Can Thrive in the Twenty-First Century.* McGill-Queen's University Press.

Schumpeter, J. A. (1976). *Capitalism, Socialism, and Democracy* (5th ed.). George Allen & Unwin.

Sinclair, U. (1935). *I, Candidate for Governor: And How I Got Licked.* Farrar & Rinehart.

The Guardian (2023, November 26). Editorial: The Observer View on Geert Wilders' Win: Far-Right Victory is a Warning to the Rest of Europe. *The Guardian.* https://www.theguardian.com/commentisfree/2023/nov/26/observer-view-geert-wilders-far-right-victory-warning-to-europe-editorial.

Treverton, K., & Treverton, G. (2021). Civil War Is Coming. *The Article.* https://www.thearticle.com/civil-war-is-coming.

Walter, B. F. (2022). *How Civil Wars Start.* Crown.

Undermining the administrative state: The case of the United States

by Donald Moynihan

1. Trend: undermining the administrative state

This chapter considers the legitimacy of the administrative state, by which I mean the delegation of government powers to unelected state officials, incorporating civil service systems. The administrative state is under attack in many quarters (Bauer et al., 2021). This trend aligns with the increase of populism as a mode of political campaigning. It includes attacks from left-wing parties in Mexico and parts of Latin America, but more frequently is seen from right-wing populists, who marry anti-immigrant and anti-elitist rhetoric.

Rather than offer a broad comparative account, I focus on understanding the attacks in one setting, the United States. The core claim is straightforward: we are witnessing an attack on the administrative state, primarily driven by right-wing political movements, which will undermine state capacity and grant power to authoritarian actors, undermining democratic values. While the particular patterns, tactics and tools will vary by country, we see common trends between the US and countries such as Hungary and Turkey: politicians delegitimate the administrative state through threatening rhetoric like 'the deep state', deconstruct safeguards intended to protect the broader public interest from narrow partisan capture, and seek to establish control of the administrative apparatus (Moynihan, 2022a). While the ultimate goal of political parties is to more closely control the state, their attacks on state capacity may do significant and lasting damage to both the public's beliefs about the state and its internal functioning.

I offer evidence for this claim by describing contemporary American politics. The attacks come most prominently from Donald Trump, the Republican Party that he leads, and a broader right-wing political-judicial movement that has developed novel judicial philosophies that call for reducing administrative power. The details of the case illustrate how the attacks on the administrative state risk undermining the quality of public services, but also undermine democratic values. The fragility of the administrative state in the most powerful country in the world represents something of a failure for the field of Public Administration, which has been sidelined by the actors most intent on its demise.

The return of Trump to office engenders the most dramatic change to the administrative state since the creation of the civil service in 1883. In the midst of the election, Supreme Court decisions curbed administrative state powers to significant degrees. Aspects of the attack on the administrative state presaged Trump and have become deeply embedded in one of the two main political parties in America.

My account here is primarily descriptive. Rather than offer a grand underlying theory of state legitimacy, I provide an account of specific mechanisms seeking to undermine and control administrative power in one setting. Such work is made necessary by the severity and immediacy of the threats to the administrative state. While left-wing progressives may undermine administrative capacity in other ways, such as excessive proceduralism, the scale of their threat is smaller, and not addressed here (Lindsey, 2021).

2. Evidence for the trend: Trumpism and the attack on the administrative state

Trump represents a myriad of characteristics that do not offer a coherent ideological or policy agenda, but centre on Trump himself. When his term ended, Alasdair Roberts and I (Moynihan and Roberts, 2020) catalogued the defining qualities of Trumpism as an administrative doctrine. This included a divisive populism that presented state actors as part of a corrupt elite, a delegitimisation of public service values and public employees, a preference for political and personal loyalty over competence, a blurring of personal, political and presidential powers and interest, and a deep aversion to traditional modes of presidential accountability. This combination was not an effective strategy for governing. And the administrative state survived largely intact, though not without damage.

Trumpism as an administrative doctrine has not changed fundamentally. But some things have changed. The first is the intensity of his focus on the administrative state. The 'swamp' and 'deep state' has gone from being a rhetorical punchline to a genuine target. Second, Trump has developed specific plans and the machinery of the Republican Party stands behind him. Political parties – or military coups – remain the central mechanism by which administrative states are captured. The Republican Party not only failed to jettison Trump despite his efforts to stay in power despite losing the 2020 election, they in fact amplified his messages and embraced many of the tactics. With his party behind him, Trump is better positioned to wrangle the administrative state in a way he failed to previously do. Third, the purpose of the attack on the administrative state is much less the traditional conservative goal of a smaller government, and much more converting it into a tool of control. The end result would be both a weaker administrative state, and one more amenable to anti-democratic leadership. The next sections update prior accounts of Trumpism as an administrative doctrine, more directly tying it to effects on the administrative state.

3. Conspiracist messaging delegitimating state actors

Trump moved the paranoid style that Richard Hofstadter described in the 1960s from the fringes to the heart of the Republican Party. This worldview has been given a contemporary spin with conspiracy theories such as QAnon (the claim that Satan-worshipping paedophiles control the government and other major institutions) (Scott et al., 2020), the Big Lie (denying the 2020 election outcome), and Great Replacement Theory (the idea that elites are deliberately replacing native whites with immigrants of colour). Trump has offered support for these theories, with varying but increasing degrees of explicitness. His greatest enthusiasm is for the Big Lie, reflecting how closely it matters to his political survival, and his denial that he lost an election.

The direction of Trump's conspiracy messaging is not random. It reflects a key theme of populist thought, which is that powerful state actors are secretly working against the interests of the true people, although in Trump's case there is a stronger-than-usual conflation between his specific legal and political challenges and those of his supporters, with claims such as "I am being indicted for you."

Trump appealed to a deep tradition of anti-statism in Republican politics, but has taken it in a different direction. It is less philosophical, and more personal than the libertarianism of Goldwater or Reagan. This is in no small part because of Trump's frustrations with the 'deep state' that was not sufficiently obedient to him, and his various legal and political troubles – related to tax avoidance and business fraud in his private life, as well as legal violations as President, including withholding aid to Ukraine, refusing to return classified documents, instigating an attack on the Capitol in order to overturn the election, and engaging in election interference in the state of Georgia. The effigy of the 'deep state' burned in his speeches simultaneously explains both the failures of his administration and why he is a victim of unfair prosecution for behaviour that would have been disqualifying for any previous generation of American political leaders.

With Trump's help, conspiracy theories have become dangerously popular. About half of Republicans believe in the tenets of Great Replacement Theory (Bump, 2022) and QAnon (Bote, 2020). About 69% of Republicans believe that Biden's win in 2020 was illegitimate, and 39% believe that there is clear evidence of election fraud (Agiesta and Edwards-Levy, 2023).

The Republican response to Trump's embrace of deep state conspiratorial language revealed a conservative movement that had evolved from a scepticism of government to embrace a peculiar brand of anti-statism. Trump-era anti-statists are not libertarians. They portray the 'deep state' as something to be controlled rather than minimised. Previously, ambitious Republican politicians would have distanced themselves from being associated with such theories. Indeed, Trump built his political base within the Republican Party by aggressively embracing birtherism – the claim that Obama was not the legitimate President because he was born outside of the United States – in a way that other Republicans did not. Now, members of the party see a commitment to conspiracist messaging as a path to maintaining credibility with Trump.

Effect: justifying real abuse of state power

Anti-statist rhetoric is encoded with a promise: that once we return to power, we will use this power to punish the wicked. *Our victimhood necessitates our extremes.* As the next section discusses, Republicans under Trump have devised new means of controlling the administrative state, especially the national security and justice systems needed to protect Trump from legal risk.

A political philosophy that is both anti-statist and promises to use state power will inevitably struggle with contradictions and hypocrisies. It holds others to account while denying such accountability applies to those wielding state power. This is less discomfort with state power, and rather with the idea that state power used without favour will be power that is sometimes used against them, and is therefore illegitimate. By denying the possibility that the state can play any legitimate role, it justifies obvious abuses of power by their side. This approach abandons the idea of the state as an even-handed actor designed to serve a pluralistic public and multiple factions, one that can be controlled by formal democratic processes. Legitimate processes of democratic accountability become the justification for anti-democratic abuses of state power.

Effect: undermining trust in government

Governments need trust to function. It is difficult to maintain broad faith in democracy if one party believes they have been unfairly denied an electoral win. Criticism and scrutiny are warranted, but conspiracist messaging makes impersonal administrative action impossible since it assumes that power is only legitimate when it is held by your tribe. As long as this anti-statist philosophy holds, it makes it more difficult to gain support for investments in state institutions.

Effect: targeting state actors

There are other ways that the conspiracist messaging hurts state capacity. Far-right attacks are the main source of domestic terrorism in the US, and have dramatically increased since Trump became a candidate (Doxsee et al., 2022). These are cultivated by a rhetoric that identifies political opponents as existential threats, and encourages extremist action (Feuer, 2022). Actual violence is the most extreme outcome of threats against public officials. Threatening political rhetoric, personal threats, and intimidation have become more common. Violent threats to Congress increased tenfold since Trump was elected (Edmondson, 2022). Trump's worsening legal problems after the 2020 election saw a massive increase in serious threats to federal judges, threats which increased when Trump was in court (Tanfani et al., 2024).

In such a context, the ability to impose fear for personal safety is a form of power. Educators, tax collectors, election administrators, librarians, and public health officials must now worry that they will be subject to harassment or worse (Brennan Center for Justice, 2021; Wines, 2023; Bryant-Genevier et al., 2021; Will, 2022; Harris and Alter, 2023). These include employees at the state and local level, and, when Trump was not in power, not just national government employees working under Trump. State and local employees vulnerability reflect how rhetorical messaging that feeds threats and intimidation can coerce officials that may not be under the formal control of the political principal in question.

The negative construal of public employment and harassment will make it harder to recruit good people to public work. The anti-statist moment comes at an especially bad time for the US public sector. The US has an aging federal workforce – almost one in five is eligible to retire (Partnership for Public Service, 2019). Just 7% of the federal workforce is under 30, compared to almost 20% of the broader US labour force (Partnership for Public Service, 2022).

4. Personalism and loyalty in governing

While Trump is often described as a populist (Bauer and Becker, 2020), another useful construct from political science is personalism. Personalism is driven "mainly by loyalty to that leader rather than, for example, organizational rules, ideological affinities, or programmatic commitments" (Kostadinova and Levitt, 2014, p. 492). Personalist political leaders are also more likely to oppose accountability and democratic constraints, and to use state power for personal benefit. Personalism is therefore largely the enemy of administrative structures that value impersonal processes and sharp divisions between public offices and private interest.

We could find many measures of personalism in the Republican Party, but the clearest is that party officials are reluctant to accurately characterise Trump's actions or criticise him, and those that do are likely to not remain in the party. Of the 10 Republicans who voted to impeach Trump after the January 6th attack on the Capitol, only two remain in office; the rest either retired or lost to a primary challenger. While there is no shortage of charismatic figures contesting the American presidency, none have drawn the accusations of a cult of personality that Trump does.

The holding of office did not temper Trump's tendencies towards personalism. Indeed, the lesson he drew from his first term is that he needed to better institutionalise mechanisms of personal loyalty to deal with perceived betrayals by both political appointees and career officials. Presidents typically draw on a constellation of experts, associates, campaign officials, and hangers-on to populate their office (Lewis, 2008). Much of this is built up via political associates over time, or from the broader constellation of party associates and supporters. Trump did not have this, and has acknowledged as much: "When I went there, I didn't know a lot of people; I had to rely on, in some cases, RINOs [Republicans in name only] and others to give me some recommendations, but I know them all now. I know the good ones, I know the bad ones, I know the weak ones, I know the strong ones."

Trump did face resistance that limited his ability to govern. But it is important to understand the nature of this resistance. Much of it came from his own political appointees (Pfiffner, 2022). And much of it centred on stopping Trump from breaking the law, such as Bill Barr refusing to use the Department of Justice to go along with false claims or election fraud, or Chief of Staff John Kelly pushing back against using the government to investigate Trump's political enemies (Schmidt, 2022).

Though the first Trump administration might be seen as a marriage of convenience between Trump and traditional Republicans, this coalition largely no longer exists. A second Trump administration is populated by supporters personally loyal to Trump and his vision. Moreover, it is one with a clearer blueprint for how to govern. This change was driven by three processes. First, Trump became hostile to anyone who did not pass his criteria for loyalty, and loyalty became a more important quality as he violated more and more governing norms. Second, Trump has a real constituency that were willing to serve him, though it took time to find them. Third, Trump and his loyalists learned from the failings of his administration, which centred on not going far enough in imposing Trump's control.

The emerging elites surrounding Trump fit very much with Li and Wright's (2023) description of the category of loyalists who undermine state capacity: their power and influence is closely tied to the leader, and they do not value an impersonal bureaucracy. Indeed, in this case, Trump loyalists have made opposition to an impersonal bureaucracy a central theme of their goals for power. Plans for a second administration include a three-fold strategy that involves hiring loyalists as political appointees, removing job protections from career civil servants, and building a legal infrastructure that allows for extreme action.

Hiring loyalists as political appointees

The US civil service system emerged in the aftermath of, and in response to, a spoils system where political leaders provided government jobs to party loyalists. Elements of the spoils system remain, with about 4,000 political appointees remaining in place, with the normative goals of providing a different type of political responsiveness that a Weberian civil service system is judged unable to do. While the number of civil servants has stayed relatively constant since the early 1960s, the number of appointees has steadily increased. So too has the number of contractors and consultants who deliver both policy advice and public services. The turn to such actors represents not just a rejection of Weberian norms of hierarchical control, it also creates levers of using government power for those who do not wish to be subject to such controls. In the US setting, government contractors are also potential campaign donors, creating the risk of corruption if accountability controls are relaxed.

Trump has founding existing tools of political control such as appointees to be insufficient. In the aftermath of his first impeachment, Trump went from a President who complained about the deep state to one who seemed to firmly believe it. He recalled a young aide, Johnny McEntee, who had been fired for not revealing his gambling debts. McEntee was made Director of the Presidential Personnel Office. McEntee had no real qualifications for the job, except for the one that he sought in those hired: absolute loyalty to Trump. The office controlled political appointment positions. McEntee started to interview appointees to verify their loyalty, including checking their social media (Diamond et al., 2020).

In 2023, the Heritage Foundation and about 80 other conservative organisations expanded this model of loyalty-first recruitment, seeking 20,000 screened appointees-in-waiting who will serve Trump. The President of Heritage summed up the strategy: "In 2016, the conservative movement was not prepared to flood the zone with conservative personnel. On Jan. 20, 2025, things will be very different. This database will prepare an army of vetted, trained staff to begin dismantling the administrative state from Day 1" (Swan and Haberman, 2023). John Kelly, Trump's former Chief of Staff said: "The lesson the former president learned from his first term is don't put guys like me […] in those jobs. The lesson he learned was to find sycophants" (Arnsdorf et al., 2023). The screening of appointees is part of a broader project to prepare for the next Republican administration, called "Mandate for Leadership" (The Heritage Foundation, 2023). Heritage has performed this role for GOP (Grand Old Party) candidates since the Reagan administration. Its adoption of Trump's standard for greater politicisation and the prioritisation of loyalty symbolised how the power structure of the Republican Party adopted Trump's more radical standards for governing.

Removing job protections from career civil servants

In October 2020, Trump signed an executive order that would allow Trump to convert any official in a policymaking or policy advisory role into a political appointee (a 'Schedule F' appointee), thereby removing the civil service protections intended to stop the politicisation of the public service, and allowing them to be fired by Trump's appointees without cause (Moynihan, 2022b). The order was rescinded by the Biden administration and reinstated under Trump.

In speeches, Trump has left little doubt about the purpose of Schedule F: "We will pass critical reforms making every executive branch employee fireable by the president of the United States. The deep state must and will be brought to heel" (Katz, 2022). Former Trump appointees reportedly have lists of career civil servants they plan to fire if they return to office (Arnsdorf et al., 2023). James Sherk, the Trump official who authored the order, has said he expects Schedule F will be reinstalled on day one of a second Trump administration, and about 50,000 career officials will be involuntarily converted to political appointees. Schedule F represents an extraordinary increase in politicisation of government expertise, in an administration where expertise matters less than loyalty. It makes it dramatically less likely that public officials would offer evidence contrary to partisan preferences, or report on wrongdoing by partisan actors.

Building a legal infrastructure that will allow extreme action

The actions of radical political appointees can be checked by government lawyers who raise objections. Trump supporters have focused on finding loyalist lawyers that would allow them to build a legal infrastructure to allow Trump to pursue goals that previous lawyers would have categorised as illegal (Swan et al., 2023; Arnsdorf et al., 2023). For example, Trump fired his Attorney General Jeff Sessions for allowing an investigation into Trump's ties with Russia to move forward (Baker et al., 2020), and installed a loyalist to oversee the investigation. When the Mueller report was released, Bill Barr, Sessions' replacement, then withheld information in crafting a misleading announcement that the investigation had cleared Trump (The Associated Press, 2022).

A model for the type of lawyer Trump is seeking is Mark Paoletta, the former General Counsel at the Office of Management and Budget. When Trump ordered the withholding of military aid to Ukraine that Congress had appropriated, Paoletta rejected the career staff objections about the illegality of such actions (Werner et al., 2020). Paoletta was also accused of misleading investigations about what actually happened (Brannen, 2020). The non-partisan Government Accountability Office concluded that withholding funds was, contrary to Paoletta's legal advice, clearly illegal (Government Accountability Office, 2020), and triggered Trump's first impeachment. All of this was done to enable Trump to blackmail Ukraine for damaging information on his political opponents. Some career officials who raised concerns resigned and were denied promotions in the aftermath. With Schedule F, Trump could simply have fired them.

Other lawyers in the Trump orbit argue that the Department of Justice should not be independent of the President, thereby allowing the President to more aggressively curtail investigations into his own conduct while using the justice system to target his political enemies. Gaining control of other parts of the national justice system, and the military, is a preoccupation of the second Trump administration.

5. The political-judicial attack on the administrative state

Historically, courts have recognised and deferred to agency expertise on issues where the law was unclear, and especially where judgments were based on technical knowledge. This system that has allowed politicians to delegate power to the administrative state, though within the context of democratic values and guardrails (Rosenbloom, 2002). The logic of such deference was relatively uncontroversial a generation ago. In 1984, John Paul Stevens wrote in a unanimous ruling establishing 'Chevron deference' that "[j]udges are not experts in the field and are not part of either political branch of the government."

Recent decades have seen the right-wing organise around a judicial ethos that opposes the administrative state, and targeted Chevron deference. This is not an organic outcome of judicial reasoning, but of political organisation of the judiciary, who are political appointees at the federal government level. This is best reflected in the role of the Federalist Society, a private organisation formed in 1982, which quickly became a pipeline of conservative political appointees in Republican administrations and judicial nominees. The Society developed an elaborate operation to recruit and train law school students and sitting judges, direct them toward right-wing policy positions, and reinforce that influence through ongoing retreats, training and events for judges. The majority of the Supreme Court are now affiliated with the Society, who screened Trump's judicial candidates for adherence to their values. Since its beginning, the Federalist Society has been supported by corporations and right-wing donors opposed to the rise of the administrative state. It should, therefore be understood as part of a broader political network.

In a 2024 court decision, *Loper Bright Enterprises v. Raimondo*, the Supreme Court's 6–3 conservative majority overruled its own precedent on Chevron. In doing so, it overturned decades of case law and practice. The ability of regulatory agencies to function had been premised on the use of administrative power and expertise, which the Supreme Court unceremoniously upended, without providing a roadmap to an alternative vision of governing. Agencies lost their ability to interpret vaguely worded statute, giving them less ability to exercise power against well-funded adversaries who could take their cases to court. As Chevron deference fell, two other novel legal doctrines arose:
- 'Unitary executive' theory proposes that the President is the embodiment of the executive branch. The court has shown openness to this idea, giving the president increased authority in the dismissal power of some positions (Moynihan, 2022b). An extreme version of this doctrine provides for little constraints on the President.

- 'Major questions' doctrine proposes that some administrative actions are simply too important to be undertaken without clear Congressional permission. Major questions doctrine offers a means to constrain regulatory authority. What is, or is not, a major question is not well defined, leaving the limits of administrative power unspecified, but giving judges extraordinary power to make such determinations.

Unitary executive theory would sharply strengthen the hand of a President like Trump to take control of the administrative state. If one leg of Trump's legal strategy is to intimidate judges, and another is to recruit government lawyers that will agree to violating legal norms, the third component is to rely on judges, appointed by Republican presidents, who will sign off on expansions of Trump's power using theories such as unitary executive. By contrast, major questions, and the removal of Chevron deference, disempowers both the President and the administrative state, and empowers the judiciary. The one common theme across approaches is a desire to weaken the administrative state, reducing its power and ability to rely on expertise as a core basis for public decisions.

The judges who impose their novel interpretations of the Constitution claim as their primary goal to understand an 18th-century document as faithfully as possible, not to align it with the needs of modern governance. A scenario where, for example, judges with strong ideological views decide on the technical details of drug regulation for abortion medication, or climate regulation, offers a preview of how state power will be used in partisan ways at the expense of consistency and expertise. The administrative state will be able to make fewer decisions, and those decisions are more likely to be second-guessed by the courts. This significantly restricts the capacity of the state to act on major challenges like climate change.

The different aspects of right-wing actions, legal and political, precipitate a broader realignment of power among the three branches of government. The executive branch and judicial branch actively seek to expand power using novel legal theories and tools, at the expense of administrative actors, and fuelled by ideological goals rather than broader consideration of government capacity. Meanwhile, Congress could reassert power, but has proven unable to do so. The body that created the civil service system has made itself increasingly irrelevant. It has delegated more and more authority to the President on personnel issues, while failing to update the civil service system since 1978, or to respond to threats like Schedule F. It has proven unable to write the type of detailed and specific laws that judges demand as they erode administrative authority. This weakness by the legislative branch reflects a combination of factors: polarisation that prioritises party loyalty over protecting institutional prerogatives, and a lack of attention to protecting the capacity of the administrative state as a core political task. It also reflects the limits of governing. Congress cannot, for example, anticipate all of the legal specifics necessary for laws protecting the environment, or responding to AI. For complex and changing policies, some degree of delegation is necessary.

6. Conclusion: how should Public Administration respond?

Neither Trumpism nor the political-judicial attack on the administrative state is concerned with cultivating government capacity. Both have an ideology that draws on anti-statism, and primarily benefits monied interests: the business community that has lobbied against regulation, and a donor class reluctant to pay taxes. As citizens see a government engage in real abuses of power, and unable to perform core tasks, anti-statism becomes a self-fulfilling prophecy; a weakened and politicised state gives the public little reason to trust it. In seeking a loyalist administrative state, one willing to use state power to ignore wrongdoing by Trump, including overturning elections, Trump also sought an administrative state that is shorn of basic democratic qualities: transparency, loyalty to the Constitution and rule of law, and based on rationality.

The academic field of Public Administration has largely slept through the growing alarm until recently (e.g. Bauer and Becker, 2020). Such indifference reflects two characteristics (Moynihan, 2009; Roberts, 2013). The first is a bias towards normalcy – the idea that functioning administrative democracies are inevitable, and therefore the foundations of such can be taken for granted. Such a bias reflects the privilege of academics accustomed to such conditions, even if never reflected the lived reality of most citizens around the world. The second is an abandonment of modes of analysis where administrative scholars considered the role of the administrative state in the context of contemporary challenges. Descriptive accounts of real time challenges are often judged atheoretical and unscholarly, contributing to an inability for scholars to competently and confidently speak publicly about the most relevant events reshaping the field of practice. Exceptions, such as Pollitt and Bouckaert (2017), are too few.

One obvious opportunity for Public Administration is to engage more directly on questions of administrative capacity, and the political forces shaping that capacity (e.g. Oliveira et al., 2023). This engagement has been fitful within our field, representing a missed opportunity. We have been relatively inattentive to the issues of politicisation. Much of the empirical evidence on the effects of politicisation in the United States comes from political science (Lewis, 2008; Richardson, 2019; Wood and Lewis, 2017). Attention to the role of the courts largely comes from the field of administrative law. Useful concepts such as populism, democratic backsliding, and personalism draw from comparative politics.

A narrowing of specialisation within the field of Public Administration, for example to behavioural issues, and a failure to build statecraft as a muscle have left the field with few who can speak to the damage to state capacity. A preference for sophisticated modelling or causal design has overlooked the value of descriptive work. In the United States, at least, it is hard to make the case that the field of Public Administration has made a strong defence for the administrative state or offered much needed advice on how to modernise it. Instead, the political energy and institutional investment has been in the domain of those seeking to undermine the state.

One obvious response is to do more of what we have neglected: research on effects of merit and politicisation, reinvest in administrative capacity as a field-level focus, communicate to the public about threats. We must also consider what the practice and study of public administration will look like if the trends I identified come to pass. A weakened and more authoritarian state will offer rich opportunities to study, though perhaps a more restricted environment in which the results can be communicated.

References

Agiesta, J., & Edwards-Levy, A. (2023, August 3). *CNN Poll: Percentage of Republicans Who Think Biden's 2020 Win Was Illegitimate Ticks Back up near 70%*. CNN. https://www.cnn.com/2023/08/03/politics/cnn-poll-republicans-think-2020-election-illegitimate/index.html.

Arnsdorf, I., Dawsey, J., & Barrett, D., (2023, November 5). Trump and Allies Plot Revenge, Justice Department Control in a Second Term. *Washington Post*. https://www.washingtonpost.com/politics/2023/11/05/trump-revenge-second-term/.

Baker, P., Benner, K., & Shear, M. D. (2018, November 7). Jeff Sessions Is Forced out as Attorney General as Trump Installs Loyalist. *The New York Times*. https://www.nytimes.com/2018/11/07/us/politics/sessions-resigns.html.

Bauer, M. W., & Becker, S. (2020). Democratic backsliding, populism, and public administration. *Perspectives on Public Management and Governance*, 3(1), 19–31. https://doi.org/10.1093/ppmgov/gvz026.

Bauer, M. W., Peters, G., Pierre, J., Yesilkagit, K., & Becker, S. (Eds.) (2021). *Democratic Backsliding and Public Administration: How Populists in Government Transform State Bureaucracies*. Cambridge University Press. https://doi.org/10.1017/9781009023504.

Bote, J. (2020, October 22). Half of Trump Supporters Believe in QAnon Conspiracy Theory's Baseless Claims, Poll Finds. *USA TODAY*. https://eu.usatoday.com/story/news/politics/2020/10/22/qanon-poll-finds-half-trump-supporters-believe-baseless-claims/3725567001/.

Brannen, K. (2020, February 11). Exclusive: New Unredacted Emails Show How Deeply OMB Misled Congress on Ukraine. *Just Security*. https://www.justsecurity.org/68614/exclusive-new-unredacted-emails-show-how-deeply-omb-misled-congress-on-ukraine/.

Brennan Center for Justice (2021). Local Election Officials Survey. *Brennan Center for Justice*. https://www.brennancenter.org/our-work/research-reports/local-election-officials-survey-june-2021.

Bridging Divides Initiative (n.d.). *Understanding threats and harassment to local officials*. Princeton University. https://bridgingdivides.princeton.edu/UnderstandingThreats.

Bryant-Genevier, J., Rao, C. Y., Lopes-Cardozo, B., Kone, A., Rose, C., Thomas, I., Orquiolo, D., et al. (2021). Symptoms of depression, anxiety, post-traumatic stress disorder, and suicidal ideation among state, tribal, local, and territorial public health workers during the COVID-19 pandemic–United States, March–April 2021. *Morbidity and Mortality Weekly Report*, 70(26), 947–952. https://www.cdc.gov/mmwr/volumes/70/wr/mm7026e1.htm.

Bump, P. (2022, May 10). Nearly Half of Republicans Agree with "Great Replacement Theory". *Washington Post*. https://www.washingtonpost.com/politics/2022/05/09/nearly-half-republicans-agree-with-great-replacement-theory/.

Cortellessa, E. (2022, August 9). Trump Allies Are Attacking Biden For a Plan to Hire 87,000 New IRS Agents That Doesn't Exist. *Time*. https://time.com/6204928/irs-87000-agents-factcheck-biden/.

Diamond, D., Lippman, D., & Cook, N., (2020, July 15). Trump Team Launches a Sweeping Loyalty Test to Shore up Its Defenses. *POLITICO*. https://www.politico.com/news/2020/07/15/trump-appointees-loyalty-interviews-364616.

Doxsee, C., Jones S. G., Thompson, J., Halstead, K., Hwang, G. (2022, May 17). Pushed to Extremes: Domestic Terrorism amid Polarization and Protest. *Center for Strategic and International Studies*. https://www.csis.org/analysis/pushed-extremes-domestic-terrorism-amid-polarization-and-protest.

Edmondson, C. (2022, October 29). Pelosi Attack Highlights Rising Fears of Political Violence. *The New York Times*. https://www.nytimes.com/2022/10/29/us/politics/paul-pelosi-political-violence.html.

Feuer, A. (2022, August 15). As Right-Wing Rhetoric Escalates, So Do Threats and Violence. *The New York Times*. https://www.nytimes.com/2022/08/13/nyregion/right-wing-rhetoric-threats-violence.html.

Friedman, J., & Johnson, N. F. (2023, April 4). Banned in the USA: The Growing Movement to Censor Books in Schools. PEN America. https://pen.org/report/banned-usa-growing-movement-to-censor-books-in-schools/.

Government Accountability Office (2020, January 16). Office of Management and Budget – Withholding of Ukraine Security Assistance. https://www.gao.gov/products/b-331564.

Harris, E. A., & Alter, A. (2023, June 22). With Rising Book Bans, Librarians Have Come under Attack. *The New York Times*. https://www.nytimes.com/2022/07/06/books/book-ban-librarians.html.

Katz, E. (2022, July 25). If Trump Is Reelected, His Aides Are Planning to Purge the Civil Service. *Government Executive*. https://www.govexec.com/workforce/2022/07/trump-reelected-aides-plan-purge-civil-service/374842/.

Kostadinova, T., & Levitt, B. S. (2014). Toward a theory of personalist parties: Concept formation and theory building. *Politics & Policy, 42*(4), 490–512. https://doi.org/10.1111/polp.12081.

Lewis, D. E. (2008). *The Politics of Presidential Appointments: Political Control and Bureaucratic Performance*. Princeton University Press https://doi.org/10.2307/j.ctt7rnqz.

Li, J., & Wright, J. (2013). How personalist parties undermine state capacity in democracies. *Comparative Political Studies, 56*(13), 2030–2065. https://doi.org/10.1177/00104140231169014.

Lindsey, B. (2021). State Capacity: What Is It, How We Lost It, And How To Get It Back. In *Niskanen Center*. https://www.niskanencenter.org/wp-content/uploads/2021/11/brinkpaper.pdf.

Moynihan, D. P. (2009). "Our usable past": A historical contextual approach to administrative values. *Public Administration Review, 69*(5), 813–822. https://doi.org/10.1111/j.1540-6210.2009.02031.x.

Moynihan, D. P. (2022a). Delegitimization, deconstruction and control: Undermining the administrative state. *Public Administration Review, 699*(1), 36–49. https://doi.org/10.1177/00027162211069723.

Moynihan, D. P. (2022b). Public management for populists: Trump's Schedule F Executive Order and the future of the civil service. *Public Administration Review, 82*(1), 174–178. https://doi.org/10.1111/puar.13433.

Moynihan, D. P., & Roberts, A. (2020). Dysfunction by design: Trumpism as administrative doctrine. *Public Administration Review, 81*(1), 152–156. https://doi.org/10.1111/puar.13342.

Oliveira E., Abner, G., Lee, S., Suzuki, K., H. Hur, & Perry J. L. (2023). What does the evidence tell us about merit principles and government performance? *Public Administration, 102*(2), 668–690. https://doi.org/10.1111/padm.12945.

Partnership for Public Service (2019). Fed Figures 2019. *Partnership for Public Service*. https://ourpublicservice.org/wp-content/uploads/2019/08/FedFigures_FY18-Workforce.pdf.

Partnership for Public Service (2022). The federal workforce and the Trump administration. https://ourpublicservice.org/fed-figures/the-federal-workforce-and-the-trump-administration/.

Pfiffner, J. P. (2022). President Trump and the shallow state: Disloyalty at the highest levels. *Presidential Studies Quarterly, 52*(3), 573–595. https://doi.org/10.1111/psq.12792.

Pollitt, C., & Bouckaert, G. (2017). *Public Management Reform: A Comparative Analysis – Into the Age of Austerity* (4th ed.). Oxford University Press. http://ndl.ethernet.edu.et/bitstream/123456789/40090/1/102.Christopher%20Pollitt.pdf.

Richardson, M. D. (2019). Politicization and expertise: Exit, effort, and investment. *The Journal of Politics, 81*(3), 878–891. https://doi.org/10.1086/703072.

Roberts, Alasdair (2013). Large forces: What's missing in public administration. http://dx.doi.org/10.2139/ssrn.2424260.

Romano, A. (2020, November 18). Conspiracy theories, explained: Americans are embracing dangerous conspiratorial beliefs, from QAnon to coronavirus denial. *Vox*. https://www.vox.com/21558524/conspiracy-theories-2020-qanon-covid-conspiracies-why.

Rosenbloom, D. (2000). *Building a Legislative-Centered Public Administration: Congress and the Administrative State, 1946–1999*. University of Alabama Press.

Schmidt, M. S. (2022, November 13). Trump Wanted I.R.S. Investigations of Foes, Top Aide Says. *The New York Times.* https://www.nytimes.com/2022/11/13/us/politics/trump-irs-investigations.html.

Scott, D., Heilweil, R., Stewart, E., Ghaffary, S., Jennings, R., Estes, A. C., North, A., & et al. (2020, October 9). QAnon: The Conspiracy Theory Embraced by Trump, Several Politicians, and Some American Moms. *Vox.* https://www.vox.com/2020/10/9/21504910/qanon-conspiracy-theory-facebook-ban-trump

Swan, J. (2020, June 14). Scoop: Trump's Loyalty Cop Clashes with Agency Heads. *Axios.* https://www.axios.com/2020/06/14/john-mcentee-white-house-trump.

Swan, J., & Haberman, M. (2023, April 20). Heritage Foundation Makes Plans to Staff next G.O.P. Administration. *The New York Times.* https://www.nytimes.com/2023/04/20/us/politics/republican-president-2024-heritage-foundation.html.

Swan, J., Savage, C., & Haberman, M., (2023, November 1). If Trump Wins, His Allies Want Lawyers Who Will Bless a More Radical Agenda. *The New York Times.* https://www.nytimes.com/2023/11/01/us/politics/trump-2025-lawyers.html.

Tanfani, J., Parker, N., & Eisler, P. (2024, February 29). Judges in Trump-Related Cases Face an Unprecedented Wave of Threats. *Reuters.* https://www.reuters.com/investigates/special-report/usa-election-judges-threats/.

Tesler, M. (2021, December 7). Birtherism Was Why so Many Republicans Liked Trump in the First Place. *Washington Post.* https://www.washingtonpost.com/news/monkey-cage/wp/2016/09/19/birtherism-was-why-so-many-republicans-liked-trump-in-the-first-place/.

The Associated Press (2022, August 20). The DOJ Under Barr Wrongly Withheld Parts of a Russia Probe Memo, a Court Rules. *NPR.* https://www.npr.org/2022/08/20/1118625157/doj-barr-trump-russia-investigation-memo.

The Heritage Foundation (2023, April 21). Project 2025 Publishes Comprehensive Policy Guide, "Mandate for Leadership: The Conservative Promise". The Heritage Foundation. https://www.heritage.org/press/project-2025-publishes-comprehensive-policy-guide-mandate-leadership-the-conservative-promise.

Wagner, E. (2020, December 14). As White House Steps Up Schedule F Implementation, "Lawmakers Don't Get It". *Government Executive.* https://www.govexec.com/management/2020/12/white-house-steps-schedule-f-implementation-lawmakers-dont-get-it/170722/.

Werner, E. , J. Stein, & Dawsey (2020, January 28). Hard-Charging White House Budget Lawyer in Middle of Ukraine Decision Has Pushed Legal Limits for Trump. *Washington Post.* https://www.washingtonpost.com/us-policy/2020/01/28/hard-charging-white-house-budget-lawyer-middle-ukraine-decision-has-pushed-legal-limits-trump/.

Will, M. (2022, April 18). Teacher Job Satisfaction Hits an All-Time Low. *Education Week.* https://www.edweek.org/teaching-learning/teacher-job-satisfaction-hits-an-all-time-low/2022/04.

Wines, M. (2023, November 23). For Election Workers, Fentanyl-Laced Letters Signal a Challenging Year. *The New York Times.* https://www.nytimes.com/2023/11/22/us/fentanyl-letters-election-workers-threats.html.

Wood, A. K., & Lewis, D. E. (2017). Agency performance challenges and agency politicization. *Journal of Public Administration Research and Theory, 27*(4), 581–595. https://doi.org/10.1093/jopart/mux014.

Young, J. C., & Friedman, J. (2022, August 17). America's Censored Classrooms. PEN America. https://pen.org/report/americas-censored-classrooms/.

Shifting power structures in the US: The rolling back of Diversity, Equity, and Inclusion policies

by Norma M. Riccucci

1. Introduction

Every country across the globe has its own system of interconnected structures and processes of government, each organised in different ways to exert its powers (Bouckaert and Brans, 2019). The US is a federal republic with three branches of power – executive, legislative, and judicial – which compete among one another for control, along with the bureaucracy, interest groups, and other stakeholders. Currently in the US the judicial branch, via its own manoeuvring, is becoming the most powerful branch of government, and because of three conservative appointments to the US Supreme Court by Donald Trump, it has moved precipitously toward the right. The conservative ethos of this newly formed Supreme Court has set a trend for accepting the most politicised cases to upend its own longstanding precedents in a number of policy areas, including the evisceration of voting rights, abolishing the constitutional right to abortion, the expansion of gun rights, the ability of businesses on the basis of religious grounds to refuse services to same-sex couples, and most recently an assault on race-based affirmative action (AA) programmes. The Court's activism is threatening to roll back the trends on a number of other well-established rights and laws in the US, including the constitutionality of gay marriage, the legal rights of persons with HIV infections or with AIDS, and the ability of the federal Environmental Protection Agency to fulfil its goals and mission of developing and enforcing environmental regulations.

This chapter examines one area where the Supreme Court's regressive rulings will hinder the ability of institutions of higher education to diversify their student bodies: *Students for Fair Admissions (SFFA) v. Harvard & University of North Carolina* (2023), where the Court's unsound reasoning effectively justified its overturning decades of its own precedents. This is a significant ruling in that diminished diversity in academic programmes will limit the dissemination of diverse perspectives in the classroom, which is key for the educational experiences of everyone globally (Neamtu, 2020). Moreover, the lack of diversity in education will limit diversity in the labour pipelines in the US, a major setback for public sector employers which have worked assiduously over the past 50 years to diversify their workforces. The potential impact of the decision on public and private sector workforces will also be explored. This issue is important because AA promotes diversity, and diversity promotes social equity. And as H. George Frederickson (1990) has argued, social equity is one of the three pillars of public administration, along with efficiency and economy.

2. The *SFFA* rulings

In June 2023, the right-leaning US Supreme Court issued regressive rulings in two *SFFA* cases: a 6–2 ruling in *Students for Fair Admissions (SFFA), Inc. v. Harvard*[1] and a 6–3 ruling in *SFFA v. University of North Carolina*. The Court took great pains to justify its decision to eviscerate 45 years of its own precedent[2] and it did so by rounding up all *dissenting* opinions written by conservative members of the Court, who never intended for AA to survive. As such, the *SFFA* Court pivoted on the established analysis – strict scrutiny framework – for determining the constitutionality of race-based or AA programmes in higher education to create a new narrative.

The Court appears to have conflated the two prongs of the strict scrutiny test in an Orwellian 'newspeak' style. Based on Court precedent, strict scrutiny was defined as a two-pronged test which asks: (a) is there a compelling government interest in the programme or diversity, and (b) is the programme sufficiently narrowly tailored to meet its goal (where in previous rulings, the Court accepted race as a criterion for admissions decisions if it was but one factor in those decisions)?

According to Chief Justice Roberts, writing for the majority, "both programs lack sufficiently focused and measurable objectives warranting the use of race, unavoidably employ race in a negative manner, involve racial stereotyping, and lack meaningful endpoints" (*SFFA*, 2023, p. 2176). But then later, perhaps in an effort to depict the first prong, Roberts conceded that race can serve as a compelling government interest. However, ignoring years of its own precedent, where student-body diversity served as the justification for a compelling government interest, he bewilderingly argued that Harvard and the University of North Carolina (UNC) had not clearly stated their goals for the use of race-based admissions programmes. Next, further perverting the strict scrutiny framework, he pointed to the *dissenting* opinions in *Regents of Univ. of California v. Bakke* (1978), where four justices argued that the government may use race for the purpose of "remedying the effects of past societal discrimination", a much higher bar to be cleared. But what exact procedure would the *SFFA* Court accept in an effort to remedy the present *effects of past discrimination*? Here we could review another one of the Court's rulings – completely unrelated to AA – where Roberts wrote for the majority: in the 2007 decision in *Parents Involved in Community Schools v. Seattle School Dist. No. 1*, Roberts opined that the use of race was unconstitutional in a school's desegregation efforts as it could not demonstrate that the school was remedying the effects of past intentional discrimination. Despite bloviating on this issue, Roberts did not argue that Harvard or UNC must remediate specific, identified instances of past discrimination to satisfy the first prong of strict scrutiny.

To add to this ambiguity, Roberts then seems to equate compelling state interest in part with a requirement that universities specify *when* they will cease to rely on race-based admissions programmes. He completely misinterprets – or simply disregards – the majority opinion in *Grutter v. Bollinger* (2003), which stated that the Court expected the goal of diversity to become such a fixed and accepted norm in our society that race-based admissions programmes would no longer be necessary. Chief Justice Roberts wrote that in 25 years "the use of racial preferences will no longer be necessary to further the interest approved today" (*SFFA*, 2023, p. 2166, quoting *Grutter* at 343).

In an ostensible effort to apply the second prong, Roberts further places heavy emphasis on the dissenting opinions in *Grutter* as well as those in the 2016 *Fisher v. University of Texas at Austin* case. Scrubbing dissenting opinions from previous rulings, Roberts argued that there is no clarity in how to objectively measure the schools' diversity interests. Yet, as discussed earlier, Roberts stated that Harvard and UNC had not clearly stated the goals for their AA programmes. Why would he expect them to measure the goals, if there were no specified goals? Again, Orwellian newspeak or perhaps doublespeak.

The Court ultimately found that the schools' policies, "however well intentioned [sic] and implemented in good faith", were lacking in both respects (*SFFA*, 2023, p. 2166). Thus, the Court ruled that the programme was not sufficiently narrowly tailored to meet its goals. This ruling provides a clear illustration of this activist, regressive Supreme Court, and its efforts to insert itself as the most powerful branch of government in the US.

A final observation about Roberts' opinion in the *SFFA* cases: as a public university, UNC is bound by the Fourteenth Amendment's Equal Protection Clause and Title VI of the Civil Rights Act of 1964, which bars race discrimination by institutions that receive federal money. Harvard, a private institution, is subject only to the statute. Nonetheless, Roberts applied the Fourteenth Amendment, and hence the strict scrutiny test to Harvard's admission programme.

3. What is ahead for AA/DEI in higher education?

When we think about diversity, equity, and inclusion (DEI), the question arises as to how this compares with AA. In simple terms, as we have seen here, AA is mainly a legal tool, whose parameters have been drawn by the courts. Its ultimate aim is to create diversity, but the courts continue to focus on AA, a polemical issue to be sure. Diversity is more a managerial tool, as is the broader concept of DEI, which is aimed promoting equal opportunity, access, and sense of belonging to the organisation. It recognises and acknowledges the *value of* the perspectives of different groups of people, and seeks to integrate the worth and voice of all persons into an open, safe working environment. And DEI efforts, as with AA, have always been seen as important measure to create equity in the workplace.

The importance of DEI in higher education cannot be understated; it promotes diversity in the classroom, which enriches the learning experience for everyone. It is not only critical for the students seeking degrees to further their career aspirations, but diversity in university graduates also helps to build diverse labour pools. And an inordinate amount of research points to the benefits of organisational diversity in both the public and private sectors (Sabharwal et al., 2018; Ding and Riccucci, 2022). As the Chair of the US Equal Employment Opportunity Commission (EEOC), Charlotte A. Burrows, commented on the day the *SFFA* rulings were issued:

> Today's Supreme Court decision effectively turns away from decades of precedent and will undoubtedly hamper the efforts of some colleges and universities to ensure diverse student bodies. That's a problem for our economy because [... organizations] often rely on a diverse pipeline of talent for recruitment and hiring. Diversity helps companies attract top talent, sparks innovation, improves employee satisfaction, and enables companies to better serve their customers. (EEOC, 2023)

Organisations have made significant inroads into diversifying their workforces and, as such, are not willing abandon programmes such as AA, whose aims are to promote DEI. Indeed, hundreds of eminent American corporations (e.g. Apple, Google) and seven Ivy League schools submitted amicus briefs urging the *SFFA* Court to uphold AA. The Biden Administration along with

Democratic lawmakers, military officials, and civil rights leaders also filed briefs pressing the Court to support AA (Hamid and Orakwue, 2022). Thus, as discussed further below, it is unlikely that DEI initiatives will be abandoned, regardless of how the means to this end are specified.

Moreover, admissions staff at universities and colleges across the country have already begun to examine approaches to continue relying on race-based AA programmes, providing they fit the contours of the *SFFA* ruling. A key passage in Roberts' opinion in SFFA serves as providing guidance: "nothing in this opinion should be construed as prohibiting universities from considering an applicant's discussion of how race affected his or her life, be it through discrimination, inspiration or otherwise" (*SFFA*, 2023, p. 2176). Recognising the gratuitousness of Robert's inane statement here, Justice Sotomayor aptly wrote in her dissent that "[t]his supposed recognition that universities can, in some situations, consider race in application essays is nothing but an attempt to put lipstick on a pig" (*SFFA*, 2023, p. 2251).

Since the *SFFA* rulings, innumerable schools, including Ivy League schools, are introducing supplemental essay prompts to their applications so that students will write their essay about their identity in terms of 'lived experiences', and link this to their potential 'unique contributions' to the university's campus. As Cheung (2023) points out, all this language draws from Roberts's opinion in *SFFA*: "In essence, the colleges are asking students to respond indirectly to Roberts and provide the kind of answers that Roberts himself would deem permissible considerations of racial identity. These supplemental prompts represent a new kind of diversity essay question, replacing the old kind that relied on a previous Supreme Court ruling on affirmative action." She goes on to say that, "[t]hough barred from actively using race as a factor, [universities] will still 'see' race in signifiers such as name, ZIP code and, perhaps most notable, what students say about themselves in their essays" (Cheung, 2023).

Some colleges or universities may plan a strategy that emphasises economic or class-based diversity, which remains legal. Although some have claimed that relying on socio-economic status could increase racial diversity, it appears to mask a broader issue or problem. Many have argued that class-based AA does not accept or acknowledge the fact that race *matters* in America. As Bridges (2016, pp. 55–56) has pointed out:

> It denies that individuals – and groups – continue to be advantaged and disadvantaged on account of race. It denies that there is such a thing called race privilege that materially impacts people's worlds. Moreover, […] at least part of the reason why class-based affirmative action has been embraced by those who oppose race-based affirmative action is precisely because it

denies that race matters, has mattered, and probably will continue to matter unless we make conscious efforts to make race matter less.

4. The continued use of AA/DEI programmes in employment

In light of the US Supreme Court rulings in *SFFA*, a growing concern has been how the rulings will potentially affect AA programmes in employment. Although the decisions in the aforementioned cases are solely related to higher education admissions, employers and their legal staff have already begun to examine the rulings' implications for their AA programmes. But first, some clarification is in order around whether the AA programmes are race- or gender-based. This is strictly a constitutionality question.

Race-based versus gender-based AA

The US Supreme Court treats race as a suspect classification under the US Constitution because of the country's longstanding history of racial discrimination. As such, courts subject any race-based programme to close scrutiny when an Equal Protection Clause claim is made. Gender, however, *has not* been deemed a suspect classification, and therefore, gender-based programmes are not subject to same level of scrutiny. While strict scrutiny is applied to race-based programmes, intermediate scrutiny is applied to gender-based programmes, which only asks if there is a compelling government interest in a programme. In a landmark case here, the Supreme Court in *United States v. Virginia* (1996) opined that there was no compelling state interest in Virginia Military Institute's (VMIs) male-only admissions policy, thus ruling it violated the Fourteenth Amendment's Equal Protection Clause. In 1997, women were admitted for the first time to the VMI, which was established in 1839. Parenthetically, former US Supreme Court Justice Ruth Bader Ginsberg argued that gender classification should not lower the level of judicial scrutiny because this only perpetuates stereotypical assumptions about women (Ginsburg, 1985). In short, the *SFFA* rulings only pertain to race-based AA programmes.

Public versus private employer AA/DEI programmes

The *SFFA* rulings have no immediate impact on the continued use of race-based AA and DEI in private employment. The Fourteenth Amendment does not apply to private companies. Title VII of the Civil Rights Act of 1964, however, covers employment in both the public and private sectors. It prohibits employment discrimination on the basis of race, sex, colour, religion, sexual orientation, gender identity and national origin, but the constitutional-based strict scrutiny test is not applied. Rather, the courts are likely to ask if the private sector programme seeks to remedy past discrimination or is intended to promote racial or gender balance. As Kiely et al. (2023) point out, given the different legal frameworks and how they have been interpreted and applied by the courts, private sector employment is unlikely to be affected by the *SFFA* rulings. Moreover, given that private sector employers have been more progressive around diversity and AA, it is unlikely that private firms would cease to pursue their DEI goals (see e.g. Di Meglio, 2023; Riccucci, 2021, 2019). Indeed, private employers, as their customer bases have become more diversified, have long developed voluntary AA and DEI programmes and initiatives.

The Court's recent ruling does not directly affect precedent under Title VII with respect to *voluntary* AA programmes developed by government employers. But public sector employers are subject to the Equal Protection Clause of the Fourteenth Amendment. It is conceivable that plaintiffs may challenge public sector race-based AA programmes on the same grounds that the Students for Fair Admissions challenged colleges' and universities' race-conscious AA programmes.

However, it is unlikely that the *SFFA* rulings will affect AA in federal contracting in the US, as federal contractors and subcontractors are required by a number of AA legal measures to meet certain thresholds for contract amounts and employee counts. These measures, include, for example, Executive Order No. 11246 as amended, Section 503 of the Rehabilitation Act, and the Vietnam Era Veterans' Readjustment Assistance Act, which require covered employers to take AA to ensure applicants are employed, and that employees are treated without regard to race, colour, religion, sex, sexual orientation, gender identity, disability or national origin.

In addition, with respect to federal, state, and local government employment, Charlotte A. Burrows, Chair of the EEOC, made the following statement in a press release the day the *SFFA* decisions were issued:

> [T]he decision in *Students for Fair Admissions, Inc. v. President & Fellows of Harvard College* and *Students for Fair Admissions, Inc. v. University of North Carolina* does not address employer efforts to foster diverse and inclusive workforces or to engage the talents of all qualified workers, regardless of their background. It remains lawful for employers to implement diversity, equity, inclusion, and accessibility programs that seek to ensure workers of all backgrounds are afforded equal opportunity in the workplace. (EEOC, 2023)

This is certainly a harbinger of the endurance and stability of AA in government employment, especially to the extent government employers are pursuing DEI goals, and are not explicitly making race-based employment decisions.[3]

Moreover, as employment specialists, litigators and DEI advocates from Elarbee Thompson have argued that:

> [W]hen properly designed and lawfully applied, affirmative action programs and DEI initiatives [in state and local government employers] have never purported to authorize race-based employment decisions. Rather, they focus on increasing the diversity of applicant pools, removing unnecessary obstacles hampering the hiring and advancement of minority applicants and employees, educating the workforce on the benefits of diversity, and taking appropriate measures to ensure a welcoming work environment for all employees. Nothing in the Supreme Court's Harvard/UNC decision precludes state and local government employers from enacting, or from continuing to maintain and apply, such programs and initiatives. (Elarbee Thompson, 2023)

5. Conclusions

The US Supreme Court has positioned itself as the controlling branch of the federal government in the US in large part because of its willingness – indeed inclination – to address high-profile, controversial issues that the other branches of government are unwilling to tackle.[4] The two chambers of the legislative branch in the US – the Senate and House of Representatives – are too reliant on and subservient to the electoral system to risk their elected seats in Congress to even contemplate legislation addressing politicised issues such as abortion rights, AA, and gay marriage, among others. The President can request congressional members to introduce legislation on any of these issues, but even if the liberals in congress (i.e. the Democrats) controlled enough seats in Congress to pass such legislation, it is unlikely that the totality of Democrats would support a bill to address some of these politicised issues, as several Democratic members of Congress remain conservative. In effect, there currently exists an erosion of the system of government in the US which is intended to provide each branch of government with 'checks and balances', that is, the power to 'check' the other branches to ensure a balance of power among the three.

This chapter has provided an illustration of how the amassing of power in the judicial branch of government has had an extraordinarily negative impact on an important social policy in the US: affirmative action. To be sure, this portends a trend for this conservative Court to attack other longstanding rights and laws. In fact, some of the Court's justices are explicitly taking aim at landmark decisions. For example, Justice Samuel Alito has renewed his criticism of the Court's 2015 decision in *Obergefell v. Hodges*, which guaranteed the constitutional right of same-sex couples to marry. The High Court's activism in the abortion and AA cases has already violated the principle of *stare decisis*, which binds the Court to follow precedent. The quality of the Court's reasoning in some of the cases, especially AA, as seen above, has been inferior and its continual trend to weaken *stare decisis* will inevitably threaten the stability of law and order in the US (Gentithes, 2020).

Future research should continue to examine the trends around the extent to which the High Court is overturning its own precedents, creating new ones, and the implications of doing so in such highly politicised areas as gay marriage, gun rights, the regulation of social media companies, and the criminal prosecution of former President Donald Trump for his role in the January 6th riot on the Capitol of the US. Research might also monitor the extent to which universities have successfully circumvented the *SFFA* decisions without explicitly evading the common law established by the rulings, circuitous as they are. In addition to those mentioned earlier, a number of organisations are offering guidance on how to maintain their commitment to DEI in the wake of the *SFFA* decisions. For example, the non-profit Legal Defense Fund (2023) provides a number of important strategies universities and colleges can pursue to advance equal opportunity and diversity in higher education. Similarly, the American Council of Education has provided an inordinate amount of resources to guide universities in creating inclusive climates. These and other organisations are providing strategies for how universities could revise their admissions policies to comport with the Supreme Court's *SFFA* ruling, which allows "an applicant's discussion of how race affected his or her life, be it through discrimination, inspiration or otherwise." The irony here is that the byzantine *SFFA* ruling could potentially backfire because of this caveat in Roberts' opinion, thus ensuring that universities are legally considering race in their admissions decisions.

Notes

1. Justice Jackson recused herself from the *Harvard* case as she had served on the board of overseers at Harvard, where she earned her undergraduate and law degrees.
2. See *Regents of the University of California v. Bakke* (1978), which upheld for the first time the principle of AA; *Grutter v. Bollinger* (2003); *Fisher v. University of Texas* (2016).

3. It should further be noted that states have already banned the use of AA in higher education and/or public employment. They include: California (1996), Washington (1998), Florida (1999), Michigan (2006), Nebraska (2008), Arizona (2010), New Hampshire (2012), Oklahoma (2012), and Idaho (2020).
4. For a broader discussion of the potential impact of judicial control in and outside the US, see Bouckaert and Brans (2019).

References

American Council Education (2023). *Post-SFFA v. Harvard & UNC Decision Resources: Admissions and Beyond*. ACE: American Council Education. https://www.acenet.edu/Research-Insights/Pages/Post-SFFA-Decision-Resources.aspx.

Bouckaert, G., & Brans, M. (2019). The politics of bureaucracy in the face of different legal futures. *The British Journal of Politics and International Relations*, 21(3), 530–540. https://doi.org/10.1177/1369148119842026.

Bridges, K. M. (2016). Class-based affirmative action, or the lies that we tell about the insignificance of race. *Boston University Law Review*, 96(1), 55–108.

Cheung, J. (2023, September 4). Affirmative Action Is Over. Should Applicants Still Mention Their Race. *The New York Times*. https://www.nytimes.com/2023/09/04/magazine/affirmative-action-race-college-admissions.html.

Di Meglio, F. (2023, July 24). *How Does the End of Affirmative Action Impact Workplaces?* HR Exchange Network. https://www.hrexchangenetwork.com/dei/articles/how-does-the-end-of-affirmative-action-impact-workplaces.

Ding, F., & Riccucci, N. M. (2022). How does diversity affect public organizational performance? A meta-analysis. *Public Administration*, 101(4), 1367–1393. https://doi.org/10.1111/padm.12885.

EEOC (2023, June 29). *Statement from EEOC Chair Charlotte A. Burrows on Supreme Court Ruling on College Affirmative Action Programs* [Press release]. https://www.eeoc.gov/newsroom/statement-eeoc-chair-charlotte-burrows-supreme-court-ruling-college-affirmative-action.

Elarbee Thompson (2023, June 29). *Effect of the Supreme Court's Harvard/University of North Carolina Decision on State and Local Government Employers*. Elarbee Thompson: Labor, Employment and Complex Litigation Specialists. https://elarbeethompson.com/effect-of-the-supreme-courts-harvarduniversity-of-north-carolina-decision-on-state-and-local-government-employers.

Frederickson, H. G. (1990). Public administration and social equity. *Public Administration Review*, 50(2), 228–237. https://doi.org/10.2307/976870.

Gentithes, M. (2020). Janus-faced judging: How the Supreme Court is radically weakening stare decisis. *William & Mary Law Review*, 62(1), 83–142. https://scholarship.law.wm.edu/cgi/viewcontent.cgi?article=3871&context=wmlr.

Ginsburg, R. B. (1985). Some thoughts on autonomy and equality in relation to Roe v. Wade. *North Carolina Law Review*, 63(2), 375–386. https://scholarship.law.unc.edu/nclr/vol63/iss2/4.

Hamid, R. D., & Orakwue, N. L. (2022, August 4). Top Corporations, Universities Ask Supreme Court to Uphold Affirmative Action in Harvard Case. *The Harvard Crimson*. https://www.thecrimson.com/article/2022/8/4/affirmative-action-amicus-briefs/.

Kiely, C., Tyman, A., Gesinsky, L., & Olson, C. (2023, June 29). *Supreme Court Bans Affirmative Action in College Admissions: Exploring Potential Employment Implications*. Seyfarth. https://www.seyfarth.com/news-insights/supreme-court-bans-affirmative-action-in-college-admissions-exploring-potential-employment-implications.html#:~:text=Supreme%20Court%20Bans%20Affirmative%20Action%20in%20College%20Admissions%3A%20Exploring%20Potential%20Employment%20Implications&text=Seyfarth%20Synopsis%3A%20In%20two%20companion,of%20the%20college%20admissions%20process.

Legal Defense Fund (2023). Affirmative Action in Higher Education: The racial justice landscape after the SFFA cases. *Legal Defense Fund*. https://www.naacpldf.org/wp-content/uploads/2023_09_29-Report.pdf.

Neamtu, B. (2020). In Search of a Better Understanding of Cultural Diversity in European Public Administration Research and Practice, with a Focus on Religion and Language. In G. Bouckaert & W. Jann (Eds.), *European Perspectives for Public Administration: The Way Forward* (pp. 225–246). Leuven University Press. https://muse.jhu.edu/book/72918.

Riccucci, N. M. (2009). The pursuit of social equity in the federal government: A road less traveled? *Public Administration Review*, 69(3), 373–382. https://doi.org/10.1111/j.1540-6210.2009.01984.x.

Riccucci, N. M. (2021). *Managing Diversity in Public Sector Workforces* (2nd ed.). Routledge. https://doi.org/10.4324/9781003176534 .

Sabharwal, Meghna, Helene Levine, & Maria D'Agostino (2018). A conceptual content analysis of 75 years of diversity research in public administration. *Review of Public Personnel Administration*, 38(2), 248–267. https://doi.org/10.1177/0734371X16671368.

Case Law

Fisher v. University of Texas at Austin, 579 U.S. ___ (2016) (2016, June 23). https://supreme.justia.com/cases/federal/us/579/14-981/.

Grutter v. Bollinger, 539 U.S. 306 (2003). https://supreme.justia.com/cases/federal/us/539/306/

Obergefell v. Hodges, 576 U.S. 644. (2015). https://supreme.justia.com/cases/federal/us/576/644/.

Regents of Univ. of California v. Bakke, 438 U.S. 265. (1978). https://supreme.justia.com/cases/federal/us/438/265/.

Students for Fair Admissions (SFFA) v. Harvard College, Students for Fair Admissions v. University of North Carolina, 600 U.S. 181 (2023). https://www.supremecourt.gov/opinions/22pdf/20-1199_hgdj.pdf.

PART 2
FUTURES OF CONTAINING CRISES AND DISRUPTION

Are poly-crises the new normal? Challenges for public administration in liberal-democratic states

by Brian W. Head

1. Introduction: trends in crisis development on many fronts

There is a widespread view that modern liberal-democratic states, far from achieving their lofty visions of prosperity and social harmony, have become buffeted by crises and intractable problems. These challenges extend across many policy domains and are often interconnected in terms of causes and impacts. Governments and public institutions are generally held accountable for effectively managing these challenges. But the capacity of leaders and institutions to effectively manage such crises and problems has been seriously questioned.

Among researchers in public policy and Public Administration, these concerns are generating a reconsideration of the basic factors that facilitate or obstruct effective democratic governance. The fundamental issues include: the role of expert knowledge and stakeholder experience; the role of leaders in articulating the values that should guide the search for solutions; understanding the underlying causes of complex policy problems; the political framing of complex issues; the role of digital communications in stoking conflict; better processes for transparent decision-making; ensuring fair and effective policy responses; and the need for civic support and legitimation. In short, the research agenda for scholars in Public Administration and public policy is being transformed across all domains of organisational and institutional activities.

Since the 1960s, modern liberal-democratic states and their operational activities have become very complex, having moved well beyond their early 20th-century legal-bureaucratic focus on administration of core functional responsibilities. Governments have expanded their range of key social goals and priority issues. The boundaries between policy domains increasingly overlap, with multiple points of connection and coordination. Complex issues are recognised as multilayered, requiring higher levels of collaboration. And government agencies are increasingly partnering with private and community organisations for improved problem-solving.

Within this general evolutionary pattern, there are wide national and regional variations. The opportunities for greater convergence and mutual learning (as encouraged by the OECD and the European Commission) are reshaped and filtered by the unique institutional traditions and political histories of various countries (Kickert, 2008; Pollitt and Bouckaert, 2017, Ch 3). Moreover (and much to the chagrin of scholars), the quality of policy debates and associated political leadership has been highly variable, and often not conducive to achieving fair and effective policy solutions. Indeed, some policy areas have continually been marked by policy failures, policy inaction or gridlock, and poor political and managerial leadership.

Much of the global agenda is summarised in the UN Sustainable Development Goals (SDGs) for 2015–2030. These Goals are especially aimed at uplifting and supporting the Global South countries which have limited resources. Each of the 17 Goals is sufficiently challenging, but the collective interconnections among the Goals are incredibly complex. As noted in a study of these interdependencies (Le Blanc, 2015):

> The proposed goals and targets can be seen as a network, in which links among goals exist through targets that refer to multiple goals. Using network analysis techniques, we show that some thematic areas covered by the SDGs are well connected with one another. Other parts of the network have weaker connections with the rest of the system. The SDGs as a whole are a more integrated system than the MDGs were, which may facilitate policy integration across sectors.

These and other challenges, such as geopolitical competition and natural disasters, have also generated many concerns about the 'nexus' between core systems – food, energy, water, etc. – that are fundamental for human well-being. Some commentators therefore argue that we have entered a new age of 'poly-crises'. These are characterised by cascading crisis entanglements, which intensify the impacts of each particular challenge (Lawrence et al., 2024).

2. Evidence of the nature and extent of complex crises

The scope of major problems confronting public sector leaders has been extensive. There are many types of crisis. Some are generated by 'external' events, over which a particular government has minimal or no control. Examples include natural disasters such as storms, fires, floods, earthquakes, and tsunamis, which can cause immediate devastation and long-term disruption to food supplies, housing, and employment. For these natural disasters, public accountability issues have centred on the adequacy of emergency response services and the timely provision of accurate information to communities at risk. Other types of disasters arise directly from human agency, either by purposeful design (such as cyber-terrorism) or as a by-product of poor supervision and monitoring (such as toxic pollution from industrial facilities or nuclear power plants). Other types of major crises emerge within the financial system, such as credit bubbles or hyper-inflation, leading to economic recessions for which governments are ultimately held accountable.

Health crises are typically caused by the transmission of infectious diseases, such as the recent COVID-19 pandemic. Similar pandemics have recurred regularly, so that governments are now expected to have well-resourced response plans that can protect vulnerable populations, provide relevant medical services, and minimise overall disruptions to economic livelihoods. Other types of crises emerge from spill-over effects, such as the impact of events across national borders (e.g. civil wars or sectarian violence or regional famine) that lead to the displacement of populations. Refugee crises have become common, sparking serious political conflicts in countries receiving large waves of immigrants.

Finally, it is useful to distinguish between (a) crises that are sudden and acute, for which immediate responses are required; and (b) slow-burning (or 'creeping') crises that gradually build towards a critical juncture over many years (Boin et al., 2021). Governments will typically act quickly in response to a highly visible crisis event, but they have more discretion about when and how to deal with emergent longer-term risks such as the gradual destruction of biodiversity or the steady increase in greenhouse gas emissions. In addition to these acute and creeping crises, governments also face many ongoing socio-economic challenges in service provision that impact the well-being of citizens. Examples include the mitigation of severe social inequalities and the provision of effective services for healthcare, housing, education, and training. These ongoing challenges raise many questions about state capacity and political priorities.

To the extent that policy controversies and policy debates are generated both by intermittent crises and by ongoing socio-economic problems, the research literature has increasingly attempted to map the dynamics of crisis-induced policy conflicts and to examine the capacity of governmental systems to produce strategic policy responses (Wu et al., 2018). These responses need to be regarded as both fair and effective. The capacity of governmental systems to cope with multiple complex issues is one of the great challenges of the current era.

Some of these issues have been characterised as 'wicked' problems, which can be summarised as complex, contested, and intractable (Head and Alford, 2015; Head, 2022a). The relevant literature focuses on three main dimensions of a 'wicked' problem:

(a) complexity: the problem or issue itself has many dimensions and causal inter-connections, and it also involves several groups of key stakeholders and decision-makers;
(b) uncertainty: the knowledge base is insufficient for understanding the causes of the problems and for identifying the likely impacts of various potential policy responses, including their ripple effects and unintended consequences;
(c) divergence of values and perspectives: the stakeholders and decision-makers have a range of different interests, expectations and ideological preferences.

These features of 'wicked' problems complicate the politics of problem-solving. If the very nature of a problem is in dispute, the suggested solutions will similarly be incompatible. Some analysts have argued that the two key variables in understanding disputes about how to resolve a wicked problem are, firstly, the extent of agreement about the situation (factual and experiential knowledge about the problem), and secondly, the extent of agreement on values and norms that should guide the pathway towards agreed solutions (Heifetz, 1994; Hisschemöller and Hoppe, 1995: Head and Alford, 2015).

A key implication of this conceptual approach is that the construction of a satisfying solution (i.e. fair, effective, and legitimate) is unlikely to emerge either from seeking more reliable information (more science or 'more data'), or from delegating responsibility for the issue to a technocratic group ('leave it to the experts'). While it is always important to identify the key facts relevant to complex and contested problems, it is even more important to focus on how the values and norms that should frame the solutions can be articulated (Pal, 2023; Head, 2024).

3. Governmental responses to crises and wicked problems

With the benefit of hindsight, it is clear that since the 1980s the widespread adoption of neoliberal pro-growth policies, together with a deliberate weakening of regulatory oversight, not only contributed to the onset of the global financial crisis in 2008 but also undermined social cohesion and well-being in many countries (Fukuyama, 2022, Ch 2). The economic hardship produced by the lengthy recession was intensified by widespread implementation of fiscal austerity policies. This recession fostered the rapid growth of extreme disparities in income and wealth. In the face of social dissension and conflict, policy analysts increasingly highlighted the importance of ensuring that policymaking and administrative processes could rebuild trust and legitimacy (Bouckaert, 2012). Within international organisations, there was a discernible shift from promoting neoliberal pro-growth models towards advocating more 'balanced' approaches that took greater account of distributional outcomes. For example, the OECD developed a strategic framework that emphasised the need for social inclusion (OECD, 2014) and trust-building processes (OECD, 2017), which were seen as complementing its ongoing focus on best-practice delivery of effective services and best-practice principles for good governance and regulation (OECD, 2023).

Governmental capacity for effectively addressing problems depends on the capacities of both the political and administrative systems (Wu et al., 2018). This was evident recently in the highly variable policy responses to the COVID-19 pandemic (Capano et al., 2020). In general, policy failures are associated with serious deficiencies in state capacity (Howlett and Ramesh, 2016). The relevant capacities centre on core financial and organisational resources and a wide range of professional skills – political, managerial, and analytical. These resources and skills determine the strength of state capacities for steering, implementation, and coordination across the various sectors of the state, business, and community (Bouckaert et al., 2022; OECD, 2024). Leaders have to make wise choices about how to deploy these scarce skills and resources.

In the context of multiple problems that demand attention, and uncertainties about how these problems will evolve, prioritisation of issues becomes crucial. Research has shown that the policy-attention cycle fluctuates, with few matters retaining prominence over time. For example, in recent decades, international organisations and prominent management consultancy firms have compiled lists of serious risks, threats, or global shocks that could disrupt socio-economic stability. These lists have shown large changes in risk perceptions over time. For example, the OECD in 2011 drew attention to the need for states to anticipate the impacts of pandemics, financial crises, cyber-disruption, and catastrophic storms (OECD, 2011). Some years later, the World Economic Forum (a high-level multi-stakeholder group) nominated five 'likely' areas of major risk – extreme weather events, natural disasters, displaced populations, large-scale terrorism, and data fraud (WEF, 2017).

In 2020–2021 there was a global preoccupation with the COVID-19 pandemic, highlighting its massive health and economic impacts and the highly variable policy responses. But soon afterwards, the perceived salience and urgency of health-related crises again faded away, perhaps reflecting the short attention span of leaders. In early 2023 the WEF conducted a survey based on perceptions of both short-term and long-term global risks. While issues of social disharmony, refugees, and cyber-disruption remained prominent, a newly urgent concern focused on cost-of-living pressures, while the longer-range concerns focused on climate change and natural resource issues (WEF, 2023, p. 6). The WEF's 2024 update suggested that the global forward agenda would have to address significant regional conflicts (e.g. Ukraine and the Middle East) that were undermining the international cooperation necessary for tackling many of the other global threats. Moreover, this conflictual and competitive geopolitical context was seen as intensifying related risks such as involuntary population movements and the toxic spread of disinformation (WEF, 2024, p. 8).

A European Union research group has recently nominated 10 interconnected future trends that will shape the decision-making context for European countries (ESPAS, 2024). In brief, these include geopolitical competition and conflict, economic stability and energy transitions, managing environmental and climate crises, technological disruption and workplace changes, managing health challenges, concerns for social equality, and threats to democracy from political populism and misinformation.

Framing the forward agenda of governments is a crucial role for government leaders. They constantly engage in agenda-setting and problem-framing, not only in relation to ongoing complex social challenges (e.g. poverty alleviation) but also in relation to emergent crises (e.g. a sudden influx of refugees). In comparing the policy decisions of various governments, it is evident that they differ widely in terms of which problems should be prioritised, what level of policy change is tolerable, and what level of investment should be devoted respectively to preventative programmes and emergency responses. The policy literature has identified several types of responses to complex and contested problems, linked to varieties of leadership styles and the political and institutional contexts of each policy problem (McConnell and 't Hart, 2019). In other words, the policy steering activities of neo-Weberian liberal-democratic states may take many routes and directions.

Thus, in some instances, leaders adopt a wait-and-see stance, thus denying that the issue requires urgent governmental action. However, when governmental responses are demanded via media or stakeholder pressure, other strategies are necessary. In some cases, the challenge could be framed as a national security threat, allowing the executive government to undertake coercive responses with minimal public consultation. On other matters, such as intractable social problems, policy development might proceed through adaptive management and discussion informed by the diverse perspectives of managers, experts, and stakeholders. The array of responses options to complex and contested problems is outlined below (see also Head, 2022a, Ch3). These have different implications for the problem-solving and management capacities of states.

Firstly, a government may seek to deflect or avoid the issue, by denying its importance or relevance, or suggesting that responsibilities for resolving the problem lie elsewhere. When minimal action is seen to be necessary, symbolic reassurances or cosmetic adjustments may be undertaken. Secondly, in the face of complex interconnected issues, a government may decide to subdivide the concerns into a number of tightly defined elements which can be separately analysed and managed. This compartmentalisation of larger issues is typical of the project management approach found in most bureaucracies. Pragmatic and incremental adjustments of policy settings are likely outcomes, but deeper concerns about root causes and interconnected issues are likely to be discounted. Thirdly, a government may decide to invoke its executive decision-making authority to impose a regulatory solution to tame an unruly situation. For example, a government might issue emergency regulations regarding the use of coercive policing powers to address terrorist threats or various types of civil disorder.

Fourthly, a government might declare that the issue requires close analysis and deliberation by technical experts, and thus the government might delegate the issue to an expert advisory committee or an independent statutory advisory body. Technocratic problem-solving is well known as a preferred approach for managing many issues – such as credit supply and interest rates, quality of pharmaceuticals, bio-security challenges, and military weapons procurement. But the legitimacy of these elitist approaches for addressing issues such as social services, civil rights, or local environmental planning would be strongly contested. The 'output legitimacy' of top-down and exclusionary processes is widely questioned, and techno-elitist decision-making can feed populist distrust of public sector institutions.

Fifthly, many of the wicked issues impacting the everyday lives of citizens are socio-economic issues, in which the perspectives, values, and interests of affected stakeholders are paramount. Whether the issues are relatively novel, such as digital services and AI regulation, or long-term and familiar, such as education and family support payments, the case for continuous community engagement and stakeholder collaboration is overwhelming. For contentious social issues, collaborative approaches are important to ensure that the knowledge and experience of all stakeholders are gathered, and that differences are voiced, as part of a process for sharing information and negotiating compromises on agreed goals and cooperative actions.

While emphasising the core significance of *state capacities* for tackling crises and wicked problems, it is also important to appreciate the political context of debates and decisions. Crisis responses are heavily politicised, in terms of problem-framing, blame-shifting and different viewpoints about criteria for success (Boin et al., 2009). And the populist trend towards advocating simplistic solutions has shifted the political culture in many countries, including the deliberate undermining of liberal-democratic institutions (Bauer et al., 2021). Nevertheless, it remains very important to build the steering capacity of the state to undertake long-term policy development (Greve and Ysa, 2023). These capacity-building activities should be undertaken in ways that are more adaptive, flexible, and inclusive. A recent study of OECD countries identified several key functions and capacities needed for central governments to provide the necessary leadership and coordination for not only managing the core business of everyday administration but also for building skills and resources to address recurrent crises. Emphasis was placed on long-term strategy, foresight capacities, communication, and bridging between sectors (OECD, 2024).

4. Implications for the Public Administration research agenda

Scholarly research has continued to explore appropriate methods for addressing controversial areas of policy, planning, and administration. The majority of research projects are attempting to fill known gaps in knowledge, such as through case studies. This research strategy rewards the building of a deeper and wider stock of reliable knowledge. Policymaking can draw upon this increasing stock of evidence-based analysis. But gathering knowledge in the digital age is not a neutral scientific process. The advent of digital media information and AI computational analysis has generated deep debates about whether these new information capabilities will increase the scope, speed, and accuracy of policy-relevant knowledge, or whether they will more likely contribute to the dissemination of low-quality opinions and assist in the increased surveillance of citizens by corporations and governments (Vydra and Klievink, 2019).

It is arguable that, in the turbulent context of multiple crises, conflicts over wicked issues, and the politicised dissemination of disinformation, a primary reliance on better data and rational persuasion will be insufficient for good governance. This is because (a) the crisis situations are often ambiguous, volatile, or threatening, such that the knowledge base is unclear and rapidly changing; and (b) many organisations and community groups have conflicting perceptions about 'what is at stake'. In other words, stakeholders' own values and interests are divergent, and correspondingly they have varying views about the nature of the problem and how to respond. To the extent that these disputes are anchored in differing values and identities, and intensified by populist media channels, the issues will not be amenable to being resolved through appeals to empirical science and managerial efficiency.

Therefore, scholars have been developing research agendas to explore different kinds of policy processes that emphasise inclusion and transparency. Whereas the New Public Management agendas of the 1990s were focused on bureaucratic efficiency and performance, wider agendas soon emerged to promote more joined-up, integrated, and coherent public governance to tackle large and difficult issues. Recent research agendas have highlighted the value of active forms of multi-stakeholder deliberation, with special attention to inclusion of vulnerable groups (Torfing et al., 2012; Ansell 2023; Ansell et al., 2024). In particular, scholars and practitioners have been investigating a range of co-design processes (Blomkamp, 2018), and forums for hosting debate and conflict resolution among stakeholders, as alternatives to more expert-driven technocratic decision-making. These participatory options extend from small-scale 'design lab' workshops, to middle-level citizens juries, through to extensive online forums and crowd-sourcing experiments. These processes can inform good policy design and implementation and address some of the difficult trade-offs that need to be navigated. For example, in planning for sustainable development and renewable energy systems, governments could build on both scientific expertise and local stakeholder knowledge to identify localities for building wind farms where the likely damage to biodiversity and ecosystems would be minimal or zero. Good planning, informed by expert and stakeholder knowledge, is the hallmark of good public administration.

The policy learning literature suggests that several kinds of knowledge and experience – lay and expert, civic and professional – need to be brought together in order to develop transdisciplinary 'usable knowledge' for policy improvement. A core proposition, for further testing, is that enhanced civic engagement can facilitate 'hearing' a range of viewpoints, adjusting mutual understandings, reframing issues in dispute, and shifting the debate towards matters that can be broadly accepted and resolved. However, given the complexities involved in facilitating multi-stakeholder activities, these deeper forms of engagement are likely to be exceptional rather than mainstream. These processes require considerable time and effort, and iterative cycles of discussion. If designed carefully for achieving public-value outcomes, deep engagement can produce policy improvements, but it cannot be relied on for comprehensive solutions to complex issues. Indeed, the notion of a 'solution' for a complex and contested problem may often be rhetorical or utopian, because in many cases the best available outcome is to stabilise a problem through coping strategies and preventative programmes (Head, 2022b).

The other important theme for further research is how to promote the explicit integration of public-value norms with ongoing needs for efficient and impartial bureaucratic management. Many scholars have demonstrated that instrumental-managerial capabilities are necessary and desirable but one-sided. Over recent decades, the governance mechanisms that have evolved in OECD liberal-democracies for engaging citizens and experts, making informed decisions, and effectively implementing programmes have drawn upon three different forms of authority and cooperation – legal hierarchies, marketised contracts, and social networks (Bouckaert, 2023). Each of these can be fit-for-purpose and be more or less well managed, and the increasing proliferation of various hybrid forms can also be relatively successful in achieving stated goals. But the purposes and practices of the modern liberal-democratic state need to go beyond instrumental efficiency and effectiveness. States also need to demonstrate innovative capacity to manage crises and wicked problems; they need to highlight their normative commitment to equitable outcomes and inclusion of civic concerns; and they need to demonstrate commitment to stewardship of due process and probity.

References

Ansell, C. (2023). *Rethinking Theories of Governance*. Edward Elgar Publishing. https://doi.org/10.4337/9781789909197.
Ansell, C., Sørensen, E., Torfing, J., & Trondal, J. (2024). *Robust Governance in Turbulent Times*. Cambridge University Press. https://doi.org/10.1017/9781009433006.
Bauer, M. W., Peters, B. G., Pierre, J., Yesilkagit, K., & Becker, S. (Eds.) (2021). *Democratic backsliding and public administration: How populists in government transform state bureaucracies*. Cambridge University Press.

Blomkamp, E. (2018). The promise of co-design for public policy. *Australian Journal of Public Administration, 77*(4), 729–743. https://doi.org/10.1111/1467-8500.12310.

Boin, A., Ekengren, M., & Rhinard, M. (Eds.) (2021). *Understanding the Creeping Crisis*. Palgrave Macmillan. https://doi.org/10.1007/978-3-030-70692-0.

Boin, A., 't Hart, P., & McConnell, A. (2009). Crisis exploitation: Political and policy impacts of framing contests. *Journal of European Public Policy, 16*(1), 81–106. https://doi.org/10.1080/13501760802453221.

Bouckaert, G. (2012). Trust and public administration. *Administration, 60*(1), 91–115.

Bouckaert, G. (2023). The neo-Weberian state: From ideal type model to reality? *Max Weber Studies, 23*(1), 91–115. https://doi.org/10.1353/max.2023.0002.

Bouckaert, G., Peters, B. G., & Verhoest, K. (2022). Policy design for coordination. In B. G. Peters, & G. Fontaine (Eds.), *Research Handbook of Policy Design* (pp. 351–370). Edward Elgar Publishing. https://doi.org/10.4337/9781839106606.00032.

Capano, G., Howlett, M., Jarvis, D., Ramesh, M., & Goyal, N. (2020). Mobilizing policy (in) capacity to fight COVID-19: Understanding variations in state responses. *Policy & Society, 39*(3), 285–308. https://doi.org/10.1080/14494035.2020.1787628.

ESPAS (2024). *Global Trends to 2040: Choosing Europe's Future*. ESPAS: European Strategy and Policy Analysis System. https://espas.eu/files/espas_files/about/ESPAS-Global-Trends-to-2040-Choosing-Europes-Future.pdf.

Fukuyama, F. (2022). *Liberalism and its Discontents*. Profile Books.

Greve, C., & Ysa, T. (Eds.) (2020). *Handbook on Strategic Public Management*. Edward Elgar Publishing. https://doi.org/10.4337/9781789907193.

Head, B. W. (2022a). *Wicked problems in public policy: Understanding and Responding to Complex Challenges*. Palgrave Macmillan. https://doi.org/10.1007/978-3-030-94580-0.

Head, B. W. (2022b). Coping with wicked problems in policy design. In B. G. Peters, & G. Fontaine (Eds.), *Research Handbook on Policy Design* (pp. 155–175). Edward Elgar Publishing. https://doi.org/10.4337/9781839106606.00018.

Head, B. W. (2024). Reconsidering expertise for public policymaking: The challenges of contestability. *Australian Journal of Public Administration, 83*(2), 156–172. https://doi.org/10.1111/1467-8500.12613.

Head, B. W., & Alford, J. (2015). Wicked problems: Implications for public policy and management. *Administration & Society, 47*(6), 711–739. https://doi.org/10.1177/0095399713481601.

Heifetz, R. A. (1994). *Leadership without Easy Answers*. Harvard University Press. https://doi.org/10.2307/j.ctv1pncrt0.

Hisschemöller, M., & Hoppe, R. (1992). Coping with intractable controversies: The case for problem structuring in policy design and analysis. *Knowledge & Policy, 8*, 40–60. https://doi.org/10.1007/BF02832229.

Howlett, M., & Ramesh, M. (2015). Achilles' heels of governance: Critical capacity deficits and their role in governance failures. *Regulation & Governance, 10*(4), 301–313. https://doi.org/10.1111/rego.12091.

Kickert, W. J. M. (Ed.) (2008). *The Study of Public Management in Europe and the US: A Comparative Analysis of National Distinctiveness* (1st ed.). Routledge.

Lawrence, M., Homer-Dixon, T., Janzwood, S., Rockstöm, S., Renn, O., & Donges, J., (2024). Global polycrisis: The causal mechanisms of crisis entanglement. *Global Sustainability*, 7, 1–36. https://doi.org/10.1017/sus.2024.1.

Le Blanc, D. (2015). Towards integration at last? The sustainable development goals as a network of targets. *Sustainable Development*, 23(3), 176–187. https://doi.org/10.1002/sd.1582.

McConnell, A., & 't Hart, P. (2019). Inaction and public policy: Understanding why policymakers 'do nothing'. *Policy Sciences*, 52(4), 645–661. https://doi.org/10.1007/s11077-019-09362-2.

OECD (2011). *Future global shocks: Improving risk governance*. OECD Publishing. https://doi.org/10.1787/9789264114586-en.

OECD (2014). *Report on the OECD framework for inclusive growth*. OECD Publishing. https://www.oecd.org/mcm/IG_MCM_ENG.pdf.

OECD (2017). *Trust and public policy: How better governance can help rebuild public trust*. OECD Publishing. https://doi.org/10.1787/9789264268920-en.

OECD (2023). *The principles of public administration*. Sigma/OECD. https://www.sigmaweb.org/publications/Principles-of-Public-Administration-2023.pdf.

OECD (2024). *Steering from the centre of government in times of complexity*. OECD Publishing. https://doi.org/10.1787/69b1f129-en.

Pal, L. A. (2023). Speaking good to power: Repositioning global policy advice through normative framing. *Policy & Society*, 42(3), 347–358. https://doi.org/10.1093/polsoc/puad012.

Pollitt, C., & Bouckaert, G., (2017). *Public Management Reform: A Comparative Analysis – Into the Age of Austerity* (4th ed.). Oxford University Press. http://ndl.ethernet.edu.et/bitstream/123456789/40090/1/102.Christopher%20Pollitt.pdf.

Torfing, J., Peters, B. G., Pierre, J., Sørensen, E., & (2012). *Interactive Governance: Advancing the Paradigm*. Oxford University Press. https://doi.org/10.1093/acprof:oso/9780199596751.001.0001.

Vydra, S., & Klievink, B. (2019). Techno-optimism and policy-pessimism in the public sector big data debate. *Government Information Quarterly*, 36(4), 1–10. https://doi.org/10.1016/j.giq.2019.05.010.

World Economic Forum (2017). *Global Risk Outlook 2017*. http://www3.weforum.org/docs/GRR17_Report_web.pdf.

World Economic Forum (2023). *Global Risks Report 2023*. https://www3.weforum.org/docs/WEF_Global_Risks_Report_2023.pdf.

World Economic Forum (2024). *Global Risks Report 2024*. https://www3.weforum.org/docs/WEF_The_Global_Risks_Report_2024.pdf.

Wu, X., Howlett, M., & Ramesh (Eds.) (2018). *Policy Capacity and Governance*. Palgrave Macmillan. https://doi.org/10.1007/978-3-319-54675-9.

The rise of hybridity in the new 'normalcy' of crises

by Tiina Randma-Liiv and Steven Nõmmik

1. Background: crisis as the 'new normal' for public administration

This century has presented us with terrorist attacks, floods and wildfires, a global financial crisis, multiple refugee crises, the COVID-19 pandemic, and the war in Ukraine. These events have tested the crisis management capacities of most democratic states. The COVID-19 pandemic revealed extraordinary vulnerabilities arising from global uncertainty. There is a widespread perception that crises increase in number and frequency and accelerate in speed (Boin and 't Hart, 2010). Many of them are transboundary in scope and rapidly cross the borders of individual countries. The nature of the modern crises also tends to be more acute, with threats less contained and spilling over to different sectors and policy fields. In addition, emerging technologies such as artificial intelligence and DNA engineering are likely to create unforeseen and even unimaginable developments. Consequently, we can expect a future filled with fast-moving, cascading, and cross-national challenges and disturbances. Uncertainty and readiness for crises is no longer the context experienced by a handful of specialised public services, but it has become the 'new normal' for most public servants.

Any crisis is a serious threat to the basic structures and fundamental values and norms in public administration, which under time pressure and highly uncertain circumstances necessitates making decisions with potentially far-reaching consequences, while the continuation of business as usual is not an option (Ansell et al., 2021). This places public administrations in an environment of uncertainty, urgency, and pressure. Uncertainty in crisis context arises from two factors. First, the nature of crisis is uncertain. The course of a crisis is not perfectly predictable, and it is characterised by unexpected turns of events. Second, the expertise to inform decision-making is uncertain. Crises are often unprecedented, so the existing knowledge is limited, contested, and subject to change. Third, crises often require an urgent response. With the immediate consequences of the crisis, there is an amplified call for a timely response from the wider public as well as from within the public sector. As a result, the decision-making and policy implementation starts to follow the timeframe dictated by the crisis, which can diverge considerably from the pre-established approach for problem-solving. During the crisis response, governments face amplified pressure to the work they are conducting from external and internal stakeholders. The pressure arises within the organisation, with individuals perceiving there to be conflicting guidelines impeding their work; within the policy field, as stakeholders compete over resources and question the responses from different value perspectives; and in broader society, as decision-makers are subjected to a constant limelight of attention while the shifts in key values may be necessary.

The problem-solving environment is further complicated for public administrations, as the acute crises enter into an already existing state of turbulence. Turbulence is defined as "situations where events, demands, and support interact and change in highly variable, inconsistent, unexpected or unpredictable ways" (Ansell and Trondal, 2018, p. 43). Turbulence tends to amplify weaknesses and tensions from trade-offs present for public administrations due to constantly shifting conditions, interdependency, and shifts in time perspective (Ansell and Trondal, 2018). Turbulence leads to constant changes in the resources and instruments that are available for stakeholders to tackle problems. Turbulence also triggers shifts in the dynamics and relationships within a given policy process, with previously independent actors or arrangements becoming interdependent (Ansell and Trondal, 2018). Turbulent events can occur in forms we cannot yet imagine and they have no ready-made solutions, which results in a change of the amount of time available for addressing the challenges they pose. Through the interaction between crises and turbulence, public administrations face a normal state of long-term pressures interspersed with short-term shocks.

Addressing crises and turbulence is becoming a litmus test for administrative capacity. First, democratic systems must improve their adaptability instead of the temptation to centralise authority in the face of crisis. Second, public administrations are subjected to regular short-term shocks and long-term pressures, which require a shift towards flexibility. The stakeholders are likely to face constantly shifting challenges that are unpredictable and unknown. However, traditional public administrations have been designed to deal with routine and standardised processes in a stable environment. Governments have existing processes and structures designed towards carrying out tasks in the most cost-efficient manner, resulting in limited flexibility for crisis responses (O'Flynn, 2021). Situations of crisis combine dynamic and complex processes with a lot of new information – and therefore challenge routine bureaucratic life. Crisis management systems need to be able to cope with urgency and uncertainty, acquire political, societal and expert support for their policy responses, and ensure smooth implementation (Ansell et al., 2021). Decision-making in situations of deep uncertainty requires a different approach, as the established and routine responses based on rational models are not equipped and able to deal with complex and unstable problems.

Regardless of their nature, cause, scale, scope, and length, crises need to be managed. Hence, crisis management is a public policy (Rosenthal et al., 1991) that includes a set of preparatory and response activities aimed at the containment of the threat and its consequences. Crises are not phenomena that are managed by a single entity; rather, they are handled by complex cross-sectoral networks of organisations. Thus, an effective crisis response relies on "the breadth and depth of inter-organizational relations in its crisis management systems" (Boin and 't Hart, 2010, p. 365), requiring substantial coordination on political, strategic, and operational levels. This necessitates administrative structures and processes to adjust the existing sub-systems to handle the tasks and challenges relevant for crisis management. All in all, public sector organisations have to adapt to a more problem-oriented stance to seek pragmatic solutions. However, whilst the problem-oriented perspective provides a normative compass towards goals through the increased response capacity, the underlying transition regarding the structure and processes still remains vague (Carstensen et al., 2022).

The crisis-related Public Administration literature has been growing consistently in recent decades, providing more insight into the composition of actors, design of structures, decision-making processes and implementation. However, the existing literature has tended to remain fixed on monoparadigmatic perspective, with conflicting and contradictory strategies proposed for different stages of a crisis (Cristofoli et al., 2022; Wolbers et al., 2016). Ideal-type typologies provide a straightforward theoretical lens for comprehending the shifts, but they are less suited for understanding the endogenous and more subtle exogenous shifts that take place within governance systems as they shift over time from one configuration to another (Tenbensel, 2018). Whilst existing literature has highlighted some of the overlaps across the ideal types (e.g. Moynihan, 2009), hybridity, which focuses on the dynamics between the different configurations of ideal types, has so far received limited attention in crisis management literature.

2. Trend: hybridity as a crisis response

The use of a wide variety of concepts is present in the hybridity literature due to its broad appeal to different disciplines, including biology, linguistics, and cultural studies (Brandsen and Karré, 2011). Hybridity has also found considerable application within Public Administration literature, with a steady wave of publications since the 1980s and 1990s and a new wave since the new millennium (Koppenjan et al., 2019). Hybridity has been studied (a) from a variety of perspectives: actor perspectives, underlying norms, values, and logics (Skelcher and Smith, 2015; Hooge et al., 2022); and (b) from a variety of levels: from intra-organisational to cross-organisational to system level (Koppenjan et al., 2019). Whilst preeminent focus has gone towards the analysis of hybridity within single organisations and cross-organisational partnerships, there is also an increasing amount of literature on the system level looking at the dynamics between the different decision-making and implementation streams (Meuleman, 2008; Jessop, 2016). This became increasingly popular within academic literature from the 1990s through the works of Bob Jessop (2003, 2016) and Jan Kooiman (2003).

This chapter makes use of the definition of hybridity by Brandsen and Karré (2011) and combines it with approaches by Meuleman (2018) and Sørensen and Torfing (2019) – by analysing hybridity through the use of ideal types. Hybridity is an attempt to find common ground through specific mixtures (either in processes or products) that are combined through ideal types with seemingly contradicting or conflicting rationale (Brandsen and Karré, 2011). Hybridity in the field of governance reflects a configuration of coordinated decision-making and implementation through designing and managing sound combinations of ideal types to achieve the most suitable outcomes (Meuleman, 2018; Sørensen and Torfing, 2019). A configuration can be composed of single or multiple decision-making and implementation processes and structures that rely on a number of instruments based on the different ideal types (Tenbensel, 2018; Meuleman, 2018).

Adjusting and adapting governance to the needs of crisis response is possible through a variety of mechanisms and instruments. Over the years these mechanisms and instruments have been clustered together in different typologies. The hierarchy–market–network trichotomy (Bouckaert et al., 2010) is one of the most prominent toolsets used by scholars to differentiate between three ideal types of governance. The use of hierarchy–market–network in governance literature has been developed towards two connected goals: (a) to provide broad generalisations of specific public administration reform trends over the decades (e.g. Pollitt and Bouckaert, 2011); and (b) to provide a classification of governance modes (Bouckaert et al., 2010; Tenbensel, 2018). Whilst the former provides an overview of how public administration has evolved and developed over the years, the latter – which is also used in this chapter – has been used as a pragmatic tool to communicate the different ideal types of governance. Each ideal type possesses a distinct underlying logic and rationale enabling coordination between actors and encompasses distinct advantages and disadvantages for their usage.

According to the hierarchy–market–network trichotomy (Bouckaert et al., 2010), hierarchy relies on legitimate authority, which involves the use of management and structural instruments to establish a more direct and hierarchical control to achieve goals. The use of market utilises is based on instruments focused on incentivisation of specific outputs, and measurement of existing actions to foster spontaneous coordination through rationality. The use of networks focuses on solidarity and interdependency through process-related instruments that aim to provide the space for interactions, facilitating knowledge and values in order to improve learning and (joint) decision-making. In practice, most governance arrangements make use of the different ideal types in a variety of combinations that complement and conflict with each other (Jessop, 2016).

All of the above-mentioned ideal types of governance exhibit specific advantages and disadvantages in terms of governments' responses to crises:

- The instruments relying on *hierarchy* in crisis response have the advantage of providing clarity and transparency that can speed up decision-making (Meuleman, 2008). The use of authority by stakeholders can limit the amount of time spent on bargaining and negotiation, expediting decision-making and implementation and providing an urgent response to a crisis (Boin et al., 2021). However, the adherence to formalised measures can also result in considerable rigidity, as it may increase 'red tape', which can become problematic when facing crisis-induced uncertainty (Entwistle et al., 2007). Furthermore, the prioritising of the perspectives of a few actors may lead to the complexity and unpredictability of crisis situations being underestimated and may mean that sufficient societal support is not mobilised (Kersbergen and Van Waarden, 2004).
- *Market-based* instruments provide actors with flexibility and discretion to determine the best alternatives to achieve specific goals, which can bring about major change without feeling enforced (Braithwaite, 2020). Furthermore, the measures can incorporate new competencies that can provide invaluable insight in turbulent situations and provide competitiveness between different alternatives (Howlett and Ramesh, 2014). However, reliance on market-based mechanisms may cause market

failure. Actors may lose control over the process and incentives may become subject to manipulation (Entwistle et al., 2007). Furthermore, reliance on market mechanisms, outsourcing, and performance-related incentives may lead to a loss of control and transparency, which can be particularly detrimental in the context of a crisis.
- *Network-based* instruments expand available perspectives and provide more information for decision-making and implementation through broader inclusion. Furthermore, the inclusion of stakeholders and implementation of communicative tools can increase acceptance of the results, trust, and voluntary collaboration and compliance, which are particularly important during crises. However, the reliance on deliberations and dialogue can lead to high interaction costs and lead to indecisiveness in emergency contexts (Howlett and Ramesh, 2014). It might also lead to unclear roles and responsibilities, hence increasing risks for all parties and potentially blurring accountability (Hermannson, 2016). Lastly, the reliance on solidarity for government-to-citizen relations may result in public perceptions of inaction, resulting in loss of legitimacy (Pierre, 2020).

The advantages and disadvantages of the different ideal types, and the consequent limitations in choosing alternatives, have resulted in a balancing dilemma highlighted in crisis management literature – from the need for leadership, authoritative decision-making, and hierarchical command, to the need for collaboration and networks, as they are flexible and adaptive frameworks for responding to unique situational demands (e.g. Moynihan, 2009), to the need for markets to activate latent resources external to public actors and steer towards desired solutions (Braithwaite, 2020).

Whilst literature has highlighted the suitability of single ideal types for distinct contexts (see Meuleman, 2018; Howlett and Ramesh, 2014), this perspective has limitations due to the volatility of the crisis context and the shifts within the priorities of relevant stakeholders. Overreliance on single ideal types results in the amplification of the tensions, to the point where the configuration is required to look for alternative instruments. The endogenous and exogenous signals lead to constant shifts within the configurations from adapting, discarding, and adopting different instruments (Tenbensel, 2018). This is especially accentuated in a crisis context – as a result of the pressure to respond quickly and the uncertainty regarding the problem – meaning that the governance structure needs to have the flexibility to adjust and adapt to the different dimensions of the crisis (Ansell and Trondal, 2018). With the limitations of the individual ideal types and the volatility of the crisis environment, the need for hybridity becomes inevitable. When governance tools are unable to deal with a crisis, actors are directed to conduct a process of reconfiguration – often through a process of *ad hoc* improvisation – in order to handle the new pressures from the crisis (Boin et al., 2020). The need for adaptive and innovative solutions during crises drives the increase in the hybrid forms of governance through mixing the ideal types of governance. Hybridity serves as a tool to describe these situations that transcend the boundaries established through ideal types, with an emphasis on configurations lying between the ideal types (Skelcher and Smith, 2015). With the challenges from turbulence and crises, existing routines become ill-suited, meaning actors need to create new combinations with alternative routines to compensate for the vulnerability of existing configurations. Hybridity therefore provides a suitable theoretical lens for comprehending how different instruments, both complementing and conflicting, are able to coexist. While a few studies have attempted to expand the lens of hybridity towards specific crisis scenarios (e.g. Lee and Wong, 2021; Eckhard et al., 2021), these remain limited to single case studies rather than addressing hybridity in governments' crisis responses in a more systematic way.

3. Hybridity across the various phases of crisis: evidence and effects

The ability to respond to a crisis effectively is dependent on the different interconnected processes – from preparation for upcoming crises, to the ability to make sense of the initial chaos, to designing a working decision-making process and ensuring an implementation process (Boin and Lodge, 2016). Prior to the occurrence of a crisis, the existing administrative structures provide limitations as well as prescribe certain actions that can both impede and expedite the actual response to the crisis (Braithwaite, 2020). One of the more prevalent crisis response instruments during the pre-crisis period is contingency planning, with relevant stakeholders mapping resources and capacities for sense-making, decision-making, and coordination (Boin and Lodge, 2016). For instance, in relation to the COVID-19 pandemic, many countries had anticipated that a pandemic could spread and prepared contingency plans for pandemics based on previous experiences, with a variety of pharmaceutical and non-pharmaceutical tools to contain and combat the spread (Räisänen et al., 2023; Boin et al., 2020). The contingency plans vary in level of depth and prescriptiveness, encompassing very detailed scenarios as well as more generic events, which affect sense-making, decision-making, coordinating, and meaning-making (Ten Brinke et al., 2010; Alexander,

2005; McConnell and Drennan, 2006). Such variation leads to reliance on different coordination logics. The adherence to more detailed emergency plans tends to emphasise the use of hierarchy, whilst flexibility in relation to generic events enables a stronger market and/or network logic. The use of pre-crisis planning results in specific path dependencies, which limit the choice of alternatives that are compatible with the existing instruments, as well as affect the openness to deviating away from the existing configurations (Jessop, 2003; McConnell and Drennan, 2006). For example, during the COVID-19 pandemic, Sweden's approach was based on longstanding WHO guidelines, and reluctance to change strategy reflected the strength of existing configurations (Boin et al., 2020; Zahariadis et al., 2023). Although crisis planning has been one of the core tenets of crisis management, the ability to plan and have suitable plans for every contingency is impossible (Wolbers et al., 2021; Ten Brinke et al., 2010). As a result, actors may have to rely less on configurations with pre-crisis planning and more on an *ad hoc* combination of instruments (Capano and Toth, 2023).

Accompanying contingency plans is the design of emergency law(s) during the pre-crisis preparation. Through the formulation of emergency laws, the stakeholders agree upon the allocation of resources and tasks during the crisis response (McConnell and Drennan, 2006). On the one hand, these laws can serve as a tool of consolidation and centralisation, with prescriptive legislation providing specific agencies and taskforces with resources and power to steer the response (Räisänen et al., 2023). Alternatively, emergency laws can be oriented towards more inclusive strategies, with coordinating agencies' roles directed to facilitating the participation of other actors through framework legislation. This can be achieved through the establishment of participatory arenas for the crisis response, as well as by shaping the perspective of coordinating agencies to be more facilitative of including other actors during the pre-crisis planning (i.e. public forums for formulating contingency plans and emergency acts) (Therrien and Normandin, 2020; Larsson, 2017). With *ex ante* legislation, the public actors can also shape the relations with private partners. This can involve the framework for the inclusion of private partners through contractual relations (Alexander, 2005) or planning the allocation of emergency funds for recovery through incentives (Braithwaite, 2020). The various forms of using *ex ante* legislation, preparation and pre-determined role allocation can have an effect on the speed of implementation and also limit possible duplicate activities and accountability issues (Hermansson, 2016).

Once the crisis hits, instruments related to pre-crisis planning and legislation are used in combination with a number of *ad hoc* measures that adjust and adapt other existing instruments. The instruments for the initial phase of the crisis involve attempts to control the chaos resulting from the crisis, and to provide clarity and a timely response (Cristofoli et al., 2022). Whilst this can be achieved through a variety of rationales, there is a considerable reliance on hierarchy. This is shown by emphasising adherence to prescriptive emergency acts, as well as by adapting existing legislation to determine clear roles, procedures, and command lines for coordinating a response (Wolbers et al., 2016). Public agencies receive temporary emergency powers and resources to issue orders and coordinate a centralised response (Moorkamp et al., 2020). A prominent example during the COVID-19 pandemic was the use of positions of formal authority, with responsible politicians leaning on the use of scientific knowledge (often formalised through the position of 'chief scientist') for sense-making and decision-making or as the face (both practically and symbolically) of the crisis response (Boin and McConnell, 2007; Therrien and Normandin, 2020). In addition, hierarchical measures can involve prioritisation of one information stream over another through limiting those with less priority during sense-making (Wolbers et al., 2016; Christensen et al., 2022). From the government-to-citizen dimension, interactions can be shaped through prescriptive regulations, prohibiting certain behaviours and enforcing other behaviours, combined with a number of punitive measures, including the use of penalties and sanctions to enforce the desired meaning-making process (Christensen et al., 2022).

Whereas the initial response to a crisis tends to rely predominantly on hierarchy-based instruments, a variety of hybrid configurations are likely to emerge in the further course of the crisis. First, a market-based approach can be used alongside hierarchy in order to give actors flexibility and autonomy when adjusting to specific goals and including additional competencies in the crisis response. The market-based instruments enable coordination of the societal response through various incentive systems, including tax exemptions, emergency loans, subsidies, rewards, and other support measures to cover costs from adopting specific behaviour (Larsson, 2017; Wolbers et al., 2016; Christensen and Lægreid, 2020; Levi-Faur, 2014). Financial instruments can be both incentivising and constraining (Levi-Faur, 2014). For example, the promotion of vaccination certificates during the COVID-19 pandemic simultaneously attempted to incentivise desired behaviour through improved access to public spaces and to curtail undesired behaviour by restricting movement. This highlights how a single tool makes simultaneous use of different ideal types that can over time complement, contradict, and conflict with each other, which is reflected in the hybridity perspective. Market-based instruments can also be used to mobilise external expertise and competencies through contracting and outsourcing. Equally, they can play a supporting role during the crisis response, operating in parallel with the other decision-making and implementation arenas (e.g. providing critical services, like ensuring logistics for basic goods for citizens during critical infrastructure failure) (Boin and McConnell, 2007). This support can be seen through the key infrastructure that has been designed through contractual relations, e.g. ICT solutions, communication systems, and logistics (Larsson, 2017). In conjunction with pre-crisis preparedness, private stakeholders may become more important actors during the crisis response.

Second, network-based instruments may be utilised (especially in combination with hierarchy) to ensure broader comprehension within the cross-organisational networks and acceptance amongst the relevant actors. As a result, informal contacts, voluntary agreements, and calls for solidarity (as experienced during the COVID-19 pandemic) can become key in devising and complementing the crisis response. Crisis response can include volunteers, who provide critical resources as well as alternative decision-making and implementation arenas that are more flexible than public agencies. Such initiatives are often – but not always – initiated bottom-up (Boersma et al., 2019). Crisis management literature also highlights the role of frontline workers collaborating with volunteers to determine *ad hoc* responses in the event of limited resources (Boin and McConnell, 2007; Wolbers et al., 2016). During crisis response, societal actors can coordinate roles in service provision, decision-making, and exchange of resources and knowledge (Wolbers et al., 2016). These actors can opt to deviate from established power positions in contingency plans and provide *ad hoc* crisis response units (Moorkamp et al., 2020). Furthermore, the government can utilise the capital it has with the citizens to call for adherence to measures of varying levels, as seen during the rally-around-the-flag moments (O'Flynn, 2021). Network measures enable incorporating additional perspectives to be able to comprehend and gain familiarity with different viewpoints for sense-making, meaning-making, and decision-making.

Hybridity in crisis governance changes consistently, as the different ideal types and their measures interact, complement, and conflict with each other. For example, hierarchical measures in the form of commands and rules can complement network-based measures, network-based measures can replace hierarchical measures, and market-based measures can provide new competencies for existing hierarchical and network measures that fail to bring in all the relevant perspectives (Braithwaite, 2020; Meuleman, 2018). The existing governance literature on crisis response highlights prominently the combinations of hierarchy and network instruments (see Moynihan, 2009). The recent literature on the COVID-19 pandemic also emphasises the various combinations of hierarchical and network measures. For cross-organisational coordination, there was adherence to top-down policy guidelines and prescriptive regulation (Boin et al., 2021). With the legitimacy of top-down political support and emergency acts, taskforces and emergency committees reflected both hierarchical and network measures based on the inclusiveness of different actors, with both open and closed arenas highlighted (Christensen et al., 2022). The use of experts became an indication of the balancing act between hierarchy and network in terms of the role given to them – whether they were used to legitimise the top-down political-level decisions characteristic of hierarchy or whether they were used as participants within the decision-making process that is more characteristic of networks (Christensen et al., 2022). Although less reflected in studies regarding the COVID-19 pandemic, the European refugee crisis (2015) involved a considerable use of volunteers, who self-organised independently following the limited response by public agencies (Boersma et al., 2019). This reflects how parallel decision-making and implementation arenas can appear within configurations that adhere to different rationales. Whilst market-based measures were less reflected during the COVID-19 pandemic in cross-organisational dynamics, their role was present through relations between the public and private (Christensen and Lægreid, 2020).

4. How to make the best use of hybridity in responding to crises?

The factors impacting the choice of instruments reflect the ruggedness present in environments, with crises proving an especially challenging context (Tenbensel, 2018; Boin and Lodge, 2016). This is highlighted by the fact that organisations opt for different strategies despite often facing similar threats (Baekkeskov, 2016). As a result, rather than striving towards the most optimal solution, configurations are designed having in mind *what works* in a given context (Jessop, 2003; Tenbensel, 2018), so the choice between (a mix of) hierarchy, market, and networks is a matter of 'practicality' (Bouckaert, 2022a). Whilst the ideal types most similar to 'business as usual' operation may formulate the initial response to a crisis, over time they may become insufficient to handle the problems (Boin and Lodge, 2016; Boin et al., 2021). With the inability to provide an adequate response and the worsening conditions of a crisis, actors start to deviate away from existing instruments in order to find mixes that address the problems while meet the expectations of different stakeholders (Jessop, 2003). This iterative process, similar to patchworking, continues through the introduction of new instruments, discontinuing and combining existing instruments until the tensions and pressures have been resolved. Most often, the traditional hierarchy-based response will prove insufficient, and it will be complemented by market- and/or network-based mechanisms.

This brings us to simultaneous dynamics, which combine different intensities of hierarchy, market, and network into hybrid solutions (Bouckaert, 2022a). History shows that past crises, whether related to terrorism, banking, nature, health, or migration, have not been addressed by only market-based or only network-based systems. Moreover, only or predominantly market-based approaches, or only or predominantly networks, would not have been able to manage or handle crises like 9/11 (2001), the global financial and banking crisis (2008), the Japanese Fukushima disaster (2011), or the COVID-19 pandemic (2020–2022) (Bouckaert, 2022b). States and centres of government, as hierarchies, are necessary, and take the lead in handling crises and guiding markets and networks in a synergetic way (see e.g. Kuhlmann et al., 2021 for COVID-19; Kickert and Randma-Liiv, 2015 for the financial crisis). This implies that in crisis response, hierarchies are indispensable (Bouckaert, 2022a), not only by themselves but also in their role in building a strategic, legal, and operational foundation for hybrid solutions involving functional markets and functional networks.

The complementing effect between hierarchy and networks was reflected during the COVID-19 pandemic within Estonia through the Scientific Advisory Board. Prior to the COVID-19 crisis, scientific input in decision-making was quite limited, with a few consultative bodies and no pre-existing legal frameworks for including experts in decision-making. Over the first days of the COVID-19 crisis, there was a lot of uncertainty as well as mixed messages from opinion leaders and from public sector organisations due to uncertainty and considerable pressure to find solutions. In an effort to reduce uncertainty and limited knowledge and to moderate the overall discussion, the government mandated the creation of a consultative body of academic experts to provide the relevant scientific input. This created legitimacy for both the newly founded body as well as the Estonian government, due to perceptions of more informed decision-making together with coherent, clear narratives. Over the course of the crisis, hierarchical instruments were utilised to manage the organisation of collaborative networks and also to determine clear roles to reduce confusion for citizens and other stakeholders. Furthermore, the scientific input from the collaborative arenas in a cross-organisational dimension became hierarchical policy decisions in the government-to-citizen dimension, highlighting the shift of instrument depending on the interaction arena. Through the use of hierarchy, the Estonian government also created new market logic to steer citizen behaviour. For the uptake of vaccination passes, the government, working together with private companies, provided both incentivising (i.e. gift cards, ice cream) and constraining (i.e. access to public spaces, events) measures. The examples highlight both the framing role of hierarchy in establishing the space for markets and networks, and the complementing effect in shaping the overall goal of the configuration of instruments. Hierarchy has the capacity to ensure coordination and meta-governance of hierarchy, markets, and networks (Meuleman, 2008; Bouckaert, 2022a). As indicated by Bouckaert (2022b), the state and its public sector have not only the capacity but also *a duty* to organise public services, which will require involving partners with transparent, responsible, and accountable frames to facilitate hybrid solutions in crisis response.

Although hybrid solutions are often necessary and even indispensable during a crisis, they do not offer a panacea for effective crisis response. Creating configurations from different ideal types has inherent tensions, conflicts, and incoherence, requiring a constant matching process to create compatible combinations (Tenbensel, 2018). The configurations themselves reflect a compromise and are prone to failure, as the actors make decisions based on the advantages and trade-offs of specific ideal types in relation to the compatibility with solving the key problems and existing dominant rationales (Jessop, 2003). The reliance on the pre-crisis period for sense-making and decision-making through limited decision-making arenas, and through hierarchical implementation creates inflexibilities in being able to adjust to scenarios beyond the plan. The inability to deviate from a prescriptive plan creates notions of a false sense of control, limiting both timely and compatible responses (Ten Brinke et al., 2010). Fragmentation present within expanded decision-making arenas may result in confrontations between a variety of perspectives, with professionals from varying backgrounds, where compromise may be difficult to reach. Giving stakeholders more autonomy for individual *ad hoc* decisions and interpretation to adjust the tools to fit the context may result in problems of accountability. Furthermore, the increased reliance on contractual relations and outsourcing may result in the hollowing out of existing decision-making arenas, with the substantive role shifting towards the contractual partners, relegating existing arenas from co-creators to advisors and creating considerable legitimacy issues.

Stable and resilient organisations and policies are not sufficient to respond to continuous disruption, but overly agile configuration and reconfiguration of hybrid solutions may leave behind the core values and goals that are crucial for the maintenance of core elements of democratic legitimacy.

During crises, especially during long-term ones, democracies face particular challenges. Decisions have to be made quickly, which requires a strong degree of centralisation and less time for debate, negotiation and accountability. But precisely because difficult decisions are made and, frequently, fundamental rights are affected, the crisis management needs legitimacy and citizens' acceptance, to make sure that measures are successfully implemented. Hybrid solutions therefore are only able to create long-term viability once they have established a compatibility with the core values for democratic legitimacy, however, they [i.e. hypbrid solutions] also provide for the necessary urgency in crisis management.

The established legitimacy of institutions affects the behaviour of citizens and impacts adherence to the chosen measures, with low-legitimacy contexts reducing such adherence (O'Flynn, 2021). On the one hand, network-based measures can be a crucial instrument for providing necessary input and throughput legitimacy for hierarchies at crucial moments (Hendriks, 2022). This not only provides access to more options due to broader perspectives and resources, but also the opportunity to enact more options due to improved legitimacy (Eckhard et al., 2021). On the other hand, the urgency and efficiency of crisis management requires democratic trade-offs, which in turn raise legitimacy questions. For example, some policy measures to tackle crises may clash with fundamental rights, as in the case of austerity during the financial crisis (see e.g. Kickert and Randma-Liiv, 2015), movement restrictions during the COVID-19 pandemic (e.g. Schmidt, 2020), or the migrant crisis (e.g. Grigonis, 2016). Whoever decides on these issues must have the formal decision-making power to do so, as well as legitimacy and social capital in the eyes of citizens. Crises that disrupt society and have a considerable impact on the democratic regime and fundamental rights show how crucial the role of law and regulatory instruments are. Regulatory instruments are important for establishing the necessary learning ability in public administrations to critically analyse and evaluate the hybrids. Through law, public administrations are able to engage in configuration and reconfiguration processes during moments of tensions to establish the complementing effects from the different ideal types. Through positive supplementing dynamics, crisis management can look for efficiencies and effectiveness framed within the boundaries of the rule of law.

In order to maintain the legality of crisis management measures, countries usually adopt emergency laws, which frequently grant more powers to the executive branch, in order to increase efficiency and efficacy (Ansell and Trondal, 2018; Posner and Vermeule, 2009), thus also raising issues of democratic legitimacy (Kickert and Randma-Liiv, 2015; Schmidt, 2020). During a crisis, deviations from normal standards of policymaking are common in order to grant executives more efficient powers. During the COVID-19 pandemic, the involvement of parliaments in decision-making was narrowed in scope, since many urgent governmental measures (including hybrid solutions) were adopted by passing legislatures (Griglio, 2020). However, legislative control over the acts and actions of emergency authorities is of vital importance for safeguarding the rule of law and democracy; and emergency legislation adopted through fast-tracked procedures in response to urgent and compelling policy concerns is traditionally regarded as difficult to reconcile with requirements for good-quality legislation (Griglio, 2020). Crisis management performance depends not only on governance capacity but also on governance legitimacy, in its input, throughput, and output dimensions (Boin and 't Hart, 2010). This is likely to provide a challenge for the introduction of *ad hoc* measures and present barriers for the (re)configurations of hybrid solutions. The viability of hybrids is strongly dependent on the emergency laws, together with other pre-crisis instruments (e.g. plans and exercises) in establishing a clear responsibility and accountability structure throughout the crisis response. Through an active learning process and retroactive (de)legitimation of legislation from the acute phase, public administrations develop governance capacity for future crises. By limiting dysfunctionalities from inefficient crisis responses and violations of rule of law and democratic values, public administrations are able to establish more robust frames for hybrid solutions to operate in.

5. Future research agenda

The current discussion on hybrid crisis responses leads to (at least) four avenues in the future research agenda. First, despite the experience of a variety of crises over the past decades, Public Administration literature still tends to underestimate the increasing prevalence of turbulent environments. Traditional public administrations have been designed to deal with routine and standardised processes in a stable environment, and consequently a large part of Public Administration studies rely on rational decision-making processes, and focus upon planned changes and fine-tuning existing structures and processes. However, as governments are likely to face consistently shifting challenges that are unpredictable and unknown, and they are increasingly subjected to consistent short-term shocks and long-term pressures, scholarly literature should take turbulence and adaptability seriously. Public Administration literature should focus on developing governance systems that are able to cope with urgency and uncertainty, acquire political, societal and expert support for their policy responses, and ensure smooth implementation. Turbulent events can occur in forms we cannot yet imagine and they have no ready-made solutions. It is in the nature of crisis that pre-existing plans will not fit exactly the new or evolving nature of the crisis, which is why the capacity to learn from unexpected and unforeseen dynamics of the crisis is of critical importance. Crisis management literature should not be a niche topic within Public Administration but should be horizontally integrated into the analysis of various Public Administration sub-topics.

Second, in the crisis environment, governments need to shift to a problem-oriented approach to offer pragmatic solutions to 'what works' in terms of organisation, policies, or decision-making processes. Addressing real-life problems requires cooperation across academic disciplines and fields of study, because the complexities of a crisis do not correspond the boundaries of a single field. This calls for studying crisis management from the interrelated perspectives of public administration, democracy, and law, assuming a multi- or interdisciplinary approach to crisis response. For example, in Political Science, the aspects of democracy and power are at the core of scholarship, which is essential to cover when analysing governments' responses to crisis. Similarly, the input from Law is important, especially in the context of regulation of crisis response, emergency laws, and ensuring legitimate crisis response. Crisis management is not only about performance and efficiency, it is also about fairness and equality, as well as legality, the rule of law, and – ultimately – legitimacy (Hustedt et al., 2020). Democracy, legitimacy, and power serve as intersectional concepts, and the Public Administration, Political Science and Law communities should thus address crisis governance in collaboration. In terms of hybridity, the need for adaptive and innovative solutions during crises drives the emergence of hybrid forms not only in public administration (mixing the 'ideal types' of hierarchical, market-based and network approaches) but also in democracy (mixing representative, participatory/deliberative, and direct modes of democracy) and law (mixing substantive, framework, and reflexive forms of law). Hybridity in crisis response thus needs to address interactions both *within* specific ideal type typologies as well as *between* ideal type typologies (so-called 'mixing and matching'). This would enable a more holistic perspective towards understanding hybridity and better comprehending the shifts signalled from the surrounding governance system and crisis environment.

Third, instead of utilising a static logic of searching for optimal hybrid configurations for the crisis response, the dynamic nature of hybridity should be the focal point. The challenges within the ideal types, between the ideal types, and from the crisis-specific context result in consistent stress-tests for hybrid configurations. Whilst the choice of hybrid responses provides insights on the advantages of and trade-offs between ideal types, the optimal response in its static form remains inflexible to address the challenges brought about by crisis and turbulence. Rather than searching for a single optimal response to address the crisis situations, what matters is the government's capability to shift from one (hybrid) configuration to another. This includes the choice of alternative instruments adhering to different ideal types that fit the specific context and meet the expectations of stakeholders. The flexibility towards shifting from one configuration to another is dependent on the openness towards alternatives that is achieved through a learning process that necessitates overcoming the dominance of pure ideal-type solutions and pre-planned (hybrid) responses. Different types and phases of crisis are likely to require different responses and different hybrid configurations. the temporal dynamics of crisis response is what scholars should increasingly focus upon.

Finally, the Public Administration community should lend a hand to governments in the preparation of pragmatic solutions for crisis preparation and response. In terms of governance hybridity, this would entail addressing the following questions. How to prepare for the effective use of hybrid solutions during crises? What could 'hierarchy' do to facilitate and ensure the use of markets and networks during the crisis? What is the role and substance of contingency plans and emergency laws in order to provide dynamic hybrid response(s) to crisis? How could emergency laws and contingency plans shift towards more inclusive strategies, with coordinating agencies' roles oriented to facilitating the participation of other actors? How can participatory arenas for the crisis response be established? How can inter-organisational and interpersonal trust be built to ensure a place for flexibility, adaptability, collaboration, and innovation in crisis response? Is there any empirical evidence of specific hybrid solutions that prove effective in crisis response? What are the challenges in the use of hybrid solutions and how can they be overcome?

References

Alexander, D. (2005). Towards the development of a standard in emergency planning. *Disaster Prevention and Management*, 14(2), 158–175. https://doi.org/10.1108/09653560510595164.

Ansell, C., & Trondal, J. (2017). Governing turbulence: An organizational-institutional agenda. *Perspectives on Public Management and Governance*, 1(1), 43–57. https://doi.org/10.1093/ppmgov/gvx013.

Ansell, C., Sørensen, E., & Torfing, J. (2021). When governance theory meets democratic theory: The potential contribution of cocreation to democratic governance. *Perspectives on Public Management and Governance, 4*(4), 346–362. https://doi.org/10.1093/ppmgov/gvab024.

Baekkeskov, E. (2016). Same threat, different responses: Experts steering politicians and stakeholders in 2009 H1N1 vaccination policy-making. *Public Administration, 94*(2), 299–315. https://doi.org/10.1111/padm.12244.

Boersma, K., Krajukhina, A., Larruina, R., Lehota, Z., & Nury, E. O. (2019). A port in a storm: Spontaneous volunteering and grassroots movements in Amsterdam. A resilient approach to the (European) refugee crisis. *Social Policy & Administration, 53*(5), 728–742. https://doi.org/10.1111/spol.12407.

Boin, A., & Lodge, M. (2016). Designing resilient institutions for transboundary crisis management. *Public Administration, 94*(2), 289–298. https://doi.org/10.1111/padm.12264.

Boin, A., & Lodge, M. (2021). Responding to the COVID-19 crisis: A principled or pragmatist approach? *Journal of European Public Policy, 28*(8), 1131–1152. https://doi.org/10.1080/13501763.2021.1942155.

Boin, A., Lodge, M., & Luesink, M. (2020). Learning from the COVID-19 Crisis: An Initial Analysis of National Responses. *Policy Design and Practice, 3*(3), 189–204. https://doi.org/10.1080/25741292.2020.1823670.

Boin, A., & McConnell, A. (2007). Preparing for critical infrastructure breakdowns: The limits of crisis management and the need for resilience. *Journal of Contingencies and Crisis Management, 15*(1), 50–59. https://doi.org/10.1111/j.1468-5973.2007.00504.x.

Boin, A., McConnell, A., & 't Hart, P. (2021). *Governing the Pandemic: The Politics of Navigating a Mega-Crisis*. Palgrave Mcmillan. https://doi.org/10.1007/978-3-030-72680-5.

Boin, A., & 't Hart, P. (2010). Organising for Effective Emergency Management: Lessons from Research. *The Australian Journal of Public Administration, 69*(4), 357–371. https://doi.org/10.1111/j.1467-8500.2010.00694.x.

Bouckaert, G. (2022a). *The Neo-Weberian State: From ideal type model to reality?* UCL Institute for Innovation and Public Purpose, Working Paper Series (IIPP WP 2022-10). https://www.ucl.ac.uk/bartlett/public-purpose/sites/bartlett_public_purpose/files/bouckaert_g._2022_the_neo-weberian_state_from_ideal_type_model_to_reality_0.pdf.

Bouckaert, G. (2022b). From NPM to NWS in Europe. *Transylvanian Review of Administrative Sciences, 18*(SI), 22–31. https://doi.org/10.24193/tras.SI2022.2.

Bouckaert, G., Peters, G., & Verhoest, K. (2010). *The Coordination of Public Sector Organizations: Shifting Patterns of Public Management*. Palgrave Macmillan. https://doi.org/10.1057/9780230275256.

Braithwaite, J. (2020). Meta governance of path dependencies: Regulation, welfare, and markets. *The ANNALS of the American Academy of Political and Social Science, 691*(1), 30–49. https://doi.org/10.1177/0002716220949193.

Brandsen, T., & Karré, P. M. (2009). Hybrid organizations: No cause for concern? *International Journal of Public Administration, 34*(13), 827–836. https://doi.org/10.1080/01900692.2011.605090.

Capano, G., & Toth, F. (2022). Thinking outside the box, improvisation, and fast learning: Designing policy robustness to deal with what cannot be foreseen. *Public Administration, 101*(1), 90–105. https://doi.org/10.1111/padm.12861.

Carstensen, M. B., Sørensen, E., & Torfing, J. (2022). Why we need bricoleurs to foster robust governance solutions in turbulent times. *Public Administration, 101*(1), 36–52. https://doi.org/10.1111/padm.12857

Christensen, T., & Lægreid, P. (2020). Balancing governance capacity and legitimacy: How the Norwegian government handled the COVID-19 crisis as a high performer. *Public Administration Review, 80*(5), 774–779. https://doi.org/10.1111/puar.13241.

Christensen, T., Jensen, M. D., Kluth, M., Kristinsson, G. H., Lynggaard, K., Lægreid, P., Niemikari, R., Pierre, J., Raunio, T., & Skúlason, G. A. (2022). The Nordic Governments' Responses to the Covid-19 Pandemic: A Comparative Study of Variation in Governance Arrangements and Regulatory Instruments. *Regulation & Governance, 17*(3), 658–676. https://doi.org/10.1111/rego.12497.

Cristofoli, D., Cucciniello, M., Micacchi, M., Trivellato, B., Turrini, A., & Valotti, G. (2022). One, none, and a hundred thousand recipes for a robust response to turbulence. *Public Administration, 101*(1), 106–123. https://doi.org/10.1111/padm.12870.

Eckhard, S., Lenz, A., Seibel, W., Roth, F., & Fatke, M. (2021). Latent hybridity in administrative crisis management: The German refugee crisis of 2015/16. *Journal of Public Administration Research and Theory, 31*(2), 416–433. https://doi.org/10.1093/jopart/muaa039.

Entwistle, T., Bristow, G., Hines, F., Donaldson, S., & Martin, S. (2007). The dysfunctions of markets, hierarchies and networks in the meta-governance of partnership. *Urban Studies, 44*(1), 63–79. https://doi.org/10.1080/00420980601023836.

Griglio, E. (2020). Parliamentary oversight under the Covid-19 emergency: Striving against executive dominance. *The Theory and Practice of Legislation, 8*(1–2), 49–70. https://doi.org/10.1080/20508840.2020.1789935.

Grigonis, S. (2017). EU in the face of migrant crisis: Reasons for ineffective human rights protection. *International Comparative Jurisprudence, 2*(2), 93–98. https://doi.org/10.1016/j.icj.2017.01.003.

Hendriks, F. (2021). Key values for democratic governance innovation: Two traditions and a synthesis. *Public Administration, 100*(4), 803–820. https://doi.org/10.1111/padm.12738.

Hermansson, H. M. L. (2015). Disaster management and collaboration in Turkey: Assessing progress and challenges of hybrid network governance. *Public Administration, 94*(2), 333–349. https://doi.org/10.1111/padm.12203.

Hooge, E. H., Waslander, S., & Theisens, H. C. (2021). The many shapes and sizes of meta-governance: an empirical study of strategies applied by a well-advanced meta-governor: The case of Dutch central government in education. *Public Management Review, 24*(4), 1–19. https://doi.org/10.1080/14719037.2021.1916063.

Howlett, M., & Ramesh, M. (2014). The two orders of governance failure: Design mismatches and policy capacity issues in modern governance. *Policy and Society, 33*(4), 317–327. https://doi.org/10.1016/j.polsoc.2014.10.002.

Hustedt, T., Randma-Liiv, T., & Savi, R. (2019). Public administration and disciplines. In G. Bouckaert & W. Jann (Eds.), *European Perspectives for Public Administration: The Way Forward* (pp. 129–146). Leuven University Pres. https://doi.org/10.11116/9789461663078.

Jessop, B. (2002). Governance and metagovernance: On reflexivity, requisite variety and requisite irony. In H. P. Bang (Ed.), *Governance, as Social and Political Communication* (pp. 101–116). Manchester University Press. https://www.researchgate.net/profile/Bob-Jessop/publication/241024274_Governance_and_Metagovernance_On_Reflexivity_Requisite_Variety_and_Requisite_Irony1/links/5656279508aefe619b1d1a45/Governance-and-Metagovernance-On-Reflexivity-Requisite-Variety-and-Requisite-Irony1.pdf.

Jessop, B. (2016). Territory, politics, governance and multispatial metagovernance. *Territory, Politics, Governance*, 4(1), 8–32. https://doi.org/10.1080/21622671.2015.1123173.

Kersbergen, K. Van, & Waarden, F. Van (2004). "Governance" as a bridge between disciplines: Cross-disciplinary inspiration regarding shifts in governance and problems of governability, accountability and legitimacy. *European Journal of Political Research*, 43(2), 143–171. https://doi.org/10.1111/j.1475-6765.2004.00149.x.

Kickert, W., & Randma-Liiv, T. (2015). *Europe Managing the Crisis. The Politics of Fiscal Consolidation* (1st ed.). Routledge. https://doi.org/10.4324/9781315722689.

Kooiman, J. (2003). *Governing as Governance*. Sage Publications. https://doi.org/10.4135/9781446215012.

Koppenjan, J. F. M., Karré, P. M., & Termeer, C. J. A. M. (2019). *Smart Hybridity: Potentials and Challenges of New Governance Arrangements* (1st ed.). Eleven International Publishing. http://hdl.handle.net/1765/119689.

Kuhlmann, S., Bouckaert, G., Galli, D., Reiter, R., & Van Hecke, S. (2021). Opportunity management of the COVID-19 pandemic: Testing the crisis from a global perspective. *International Review of Administrative Sciences*, 87(3), 497–517. https://doi.org/10.1177/0020852321992102.

Larsson, O. L. (2017). Meta-governance and collaborative crisis management: Competing rationalities in the management of the Swedish Security Communications System. *Risk, Hazards & Crisis in Public Policy*, 8(4), 312–334. https://doi.org/10.1002/rhc3.12120.

Lee, S., & Wong, R. (2021). COVID-19 Responses of South Korea as hybrids of governance modes. *Frontiers in Public Health*, 9. https://doi.org/10.3389/fpubh.2021.654945.

Levi-Faur, D. (2014). The welfare state: A regulatory perspective. *Public Administration*, 92(3), 599–614. https://doi.org/10.1111/padm.12063.

McConnell, A., & Drennan, L. (2006). Mission Impossible? Planning and Preparing for Crisis. *Journal of Contingencies and Crisis Management*, 14(2), 59–70. https://doi.org/10.1111/j.1468-5973.2006.00482.x.

Meuleman, L. (2008). *Public Management and the Metagovernance of Hierarchies, Networks and Market: The Feasibility of Designing and Managing Governance Style Combinations*. Physica-Verlag. https://doi.org/10.1007/978-3-7908-2054-6.

Meuleman, L. (2018). *Metagovernance for Sustainability: A Framework for Implementing the Sustainable Development Goals* (1st ed.). Routledge. https://doi.org/10.4324/9781351250603.

Moorkamp, M., Torenvlied, R., & Kramer, E.-H. (2020). Organizational synthesis in transboundary crises: Three principles for managing centralization and coordination in the corona virus crisis response. *Journal of Contingencies and Crisis Management*, 28(2), 169–172. https://doi.org/10.1111/1468-5973.12294.

Moynihan, D. P. (2009). The network governance of crisis response: Case studies of incident command systems. *Journal of Public Administration Research and Theory*, 19(4), 895–915. https://doi.org/10.1093/jopart/mun033.

O'Flynn, J. (2021). Confronting the big challenges of our time: Making a difference during and after COVID-19. *Public Management Review, 23*(7), 961–980. https://doi.org/10.1080/14719037.2020.1820273.

Pierre, J. (2020). Nudges against pandemics: Sweden's COVID-19 containment strategy in perspective. *Policy and Society, 39*(3), 478–493. https://doi.org/10.1080/14494035.2020.1783787.

Pollitt, C., & Bouckaert, G., (2011). *Public Management Reform: A Comparative Analysis – New Public Management, Governance, and the Neo-Weberian State* (3rd ed.). Oxford University Press. https://www.academia.edu/11548460/Public_Management_Reform_A_Comparative_Analysis_New_Public_Management_Governance_and_the_Neo_Weberian_State?source=swp_share.

Poster, E. A., & Vermeule, A. (2009). Crisis governance in the administrative state: 9/11 and the financial meltdown of 2008. *University of Chicago Law Review, 76*(4), 1613–1682. https://doi.org/10.2139/ssrn.1301164.

Räisänen, H., Eronen, J. T., & Hukkinen, J. I. (2023). Imagining the next pandemic: Finnish preparedness for chronic transboundary crises before and during COVID-19. *Risks, Hazards and Crisis in Public Policy, 14*(3), 226–246. https://doi.org/10.1002/rhc3.12271.

Rosenthal, U, 't Hart, P., & Kouzmin, A. (1991). The bureau-politics of crisis management. *Public Administration, 69*(2), 211–233. https://doi.org/10.1111/j.1467-9299.1991.tb00791.x.

Schmidt, V. A. (2020). Conceptualizing legitimacy: Input, output, and throughput. In V. A. Schmidt (Ed.), *Europe's Crisis of Legitimacy: Governing by Rules and Ruling by Numbers in the Eurozone* (pp. 25–55). Oxford University Press. https://doi.org/10.1093/oso/9780198797050.003.0002.

Skelcher, C., & Smith, S. R. (2014). Theorizing hybridity: Institutional logics, complex organisations and actor identities. The case of nonprofits. *Public Administration, 93*(2), 433–448. https://doi.org/10.1111/padm.12105.

Sørensen, E., & Torfing, J. (2019). Towards robust hybrid democracy in Scandinavian municipalities? *Scandinavian Political Studies, 42*(1), 25–49. https://doi.org/10.1111/1467-9477.12134.

Tenbensel, T. (2017). Bridging complexity theory and hierarchies, markets, networks, communities: A "population genetics" framework for understanding institutional change from within. *Public Management Review, 20*(7), 1032–1051. https://doi.org/10.1080/14719037.2017.1364409.

Ten Brinke, W. B. M., Kolen, B., Dollee, A., Van Waveren, H., & Wouters, K. (2010). Contingency planning for large-scale floods in the Netherlands. *Journal of Contingencies and Crisis Management, 18*(1), 55–69. https://doi.org/10.1111/j.1468-5973.2009.00594.x.

Therrien, M.-C., & Normandin, J.-M. (2020). From policy challenge to implementation strategy: Enabling strategies for network governance of urban resilience. *Risks, Hazards & Crisis in Public Policy, 11*(3), 320–341. https://doi.org/10.1002/rhc3.12192.

Wolbers, J., Ferguson, J., Groenewegen, P., Mulder, F., & Boersma, K. (2016). Two faces of disaster response: Transcending the dichotomy of control and collaboration during the Nepal earthquake relief operation. *International Journal of Mass Emergencies & Disasters, 34*(3), 419–438. https://doi.org/10.1177/028072701603400304.

Wolbers, J., Kuipers, S., & Boin, A., (2021). A systematic review of 20 years of crisis and disaster research: Trends and progress. *Risk, Hazards & Crisis in Public Policy, 12*(4), 374–392. https://doi.org/10.1002/rhc3.12244.

Zahariadis, N., Petridou, E., Exadaktylos, T., & Sparf, J. (2023). Policy styles and political trust in Europe's national responses to the COVID-19 crisis. *Policy Studies, 44*(1), 46–67. https://doi.org/10.1080/01442872.2021.2019211.

The future role of government in cybersecurity

by Greta Nasi

1. Trends and challenges of governing the cybersecurity of essential services

The disruption of essential services, such as healthcare and electricity, presents a significant challenge due to its widespread and severe impact on society, the economy, and public safety, as they are necessary to ensure the inclusion of people, the competitive advantage of firms, and the national security of states. The role of governments is central because they are responsible for implementing robust regulatory frameworks, investing in infrastructure resilience, governing and orchestrating public and private capacities and operations, ensuring rapid response and recovery mechanisms, and maintaining continuous oversight – actions that are crucial to mitigate risks, address vulnerabilities proactively, and uphold the stability and well-being of the state and its stakeholders.

The safe and secure provision of essential services relies on core elements grounded in combined physical and digital infrastructures, which can be understood as assets, systems, networks, and facilities. They are often labelled as 'critical' as they contribute to the lives of people and a country's economy (Rinaldi et al., 2001). Natural disasters, internal failures, and cyber-attacks disrupt the functioning of critical infrastructures by impacting process operation, communication, and the prompts for service provision (Genge et al., 2015). In turn, the damage and the consequent loss of services may significantly impact citizens' well-being and national security beyond the specific value of the direct losses suffered (Zio and Sansavini, 2011).

Over the past decade, there has been a surge in cyber-attacks targeting essential services. This alarming trend has been particularly evident in the European Union. From 2012 to 2022, the European Union Agency for Cybersecurity (ENISA) reveals a staggering 92% increase in incident reporting. Notably, the escalation in reported incidents between 2021 and

2022 alone reached over 48%. These cyber-threats have most prominently targeted critical sectors such as health, energy, and telecommunications, underscoring the vulnerability of infrastructures on which the provision of these essential services heavily depends. Disruptions to critical infrastructures (e.g. power grids) interrupt essential services (electricity), with many serious consequences, like those resulting from physical hazards, which encompass health, societal, economic, and environmental effects (Yates, 2014).

Similar consequences may be hypothesised in the event of disruption of essential services due to cyber-attacks. To mitigate these possible serious cascading effects and societal harm, governments have increasingly focused on protecting these essential services, particularly from cyber-attacks (Apt et al., 2006). They have adopted several approaches, standards and regulations to secure critical digital and physical infrastructures, reduce interdependencies, and increase reliability. The focus has been on the resilience of computer and organisational security, despite the fact that the impact of disruption of essential services goes well beyond the boundaries of one organisation. We argue that what matters is the services those infrastructures provide and the value these services provide to their stakeholders and users. Indeed, in the specific case of cyber disruption to critical infrastructures, the significant impact of the disruption occurs when the service is used (Osborne et al., 2021).

The main limitation of the current government's approaches to the security of essential services is its narrow focus. Their policies and actions to foster risk mitigation concentrate on the organisations responsible for service provision and ensure they implement robust, usually technical, measures to reduce the risk of service disruption. Recovery recommendations often focus on key sub-organisations of critical infrastructures, like the dispatch unit of a gas infrastructure, which would create the greatest disruption to the critical infrastructure if attacked. However, this organisation-focused approach often neglects the context in which essential services are provided and misses the dynamic relationships among the other involved actors.

In this chapter, we argue that the current government's narrow perspectives on essential services must be broadened to consider the whole set of critical inter-organisational, network-based, and cross-sectoral relationships that deliver value. We argue the root of this limited view is the origin of much critical infrastructure and cybersecurity policy: the computer science and engineering view of computer security. Rather than considering multiple policy domains that the disruption of essential service provision may involve, policymakers have focused largely on the technical systems included in that ecosystem. These limits have generated a 'fatal flaw' in the governance, policies and actions themselves: protecting essential services has become about maintaining the continuous operations of particular systems rather than managing the wide and cascading effects of potential disruptions. Service disruption is, by and large, not about computer security and its interruption.

On the contrary, the value of essential services is in their use. System continuity represents a necessary, but not sufficient, condition to generate value in the context of essential services. What matters is the service these systems provide and their value for the people who rely on them. For essential services, the value at risk is enormous: the ongoing functionality of firms and institutions relies on this whole essential service ecosystem. Without these essential service ecosystems, we cannot include and care for people in society. Damages and disruption to the critical infrastructures providing such essential services may significantly impact the state's security and its citizens' well-being beyond the specific value of direct losses suffered because of the disruption event.

To make this argument, this chapter reviews the current trends and prevailing approaches of governments to essential services cybersecurity. Second, it explores the challenges that arise from them. Then, it proposes a value-informed cybersecurity theory that can generate new insights and models for cybersecurity framing that are more 'fit-for-purpose' for the contemporary, complex reality of essential services. It concludes by drawing a research agenda for Public Administration scholars.

2. Governing the disruption of essential services: a flawed approach?

Essential services, as defined in the Pillar of Social Rights of the European Union, are those necessary to ensure the full social inclusion of people in society and the labour market. They are interdependent; one essential service is often necessary for providing others. For example, electricity enables transportation and telecommunication, which in turn allow other firms to maintain their operations. We have witnessed how an increasing number of natural disasters, including ones starting in cyberspace, result in extended and costly power outages, which further cascade into the subsequent disruption of several other interconnected services, such as suspended hospital care, telecommunication service discontinuity, and other critical services and businesses not being able to operate (U.S. DOE, 2017; Zio and Duffey, 2021).

Much research on ensuring the continuity of essential services focuses on the critical infrastructure that underlies them, because "the damage to critical infrastructure, its destruction or disruption by natural disasters, terrorism, criminal activity or malicious behavior, may have a significant negative impact on the security [and] well-being of its citizens".[1] Science and technology research has focused on the safety and cybersecurity of particular assets – usually computers, networks, and other connected hardware – which, in the wrong event or scenario, could cause an undesirable outcome. In turn, the objective of standards and regulation is to help system operators and designers make decisions that minimise the risk of the system failing and improve the chances of resilient recovery in the event of damage. However, these approaches do not consider the impact on the interconnected networks of other actors and processes involved in the system.

Suppose a water supply management system is compromised, and water is contaminated due to an attack on the integrity of the water treatment equipment, as happened in Florida in 2021. The damage to the functioning of the infrastructure refers to its assets, the lost load, and the cost of recovering the status of the facilities before the damage. However, if the compromised water is serviced, drunk, or used for consumption, agriculture, and industry needs, it becomes a public health challenge, a social and economic problem with possible disruptions to the well-being of communities and the supply chain of the affected industries.

Disruptions generally lead to safety hazards, economic losses, social unrest, and human suffering, often stemming from cyber-threats and interdependencies among essential services (Chang, 2016; Herrera and Maennel, 2019). Despite the normative awareness of the impact that the disruption of essential services due to cyber-attacks may cause, more evidence is needed in the current body of knowledge to frame the problem and support adequate decision-making for prevention, mitigation, and recovery.

This concern is not hypothetical. The Colonial Pipeline attack showed how one company's seemingly rational decision to shut down its systems in response to an attack rippled across a regional economy and caused widespread emotional responses and social distress (Smith, 2022). This recent history shows how a focus on protecting assets may cause decision-makers to lose sight of broader societal consequences and fail to plan a broader response. The current approach is a narrow-sighted framing of the problem, and it may lead to non-optimal risk protection and mitigation decisions for the broader ecosystem if attacks like this example happen to be successful.

Our argument is about the impact of cyber disruption of essential service provision. If governments focus their governance, policies, and actions mainly on essential services as organisational systems, they may take decisions that miss out on important outcomes critical to the community and society. Indeed, the users of the services, the community, and the states may have different needs and priorities. The interdependencies between the critical infrastructure and societal systems may not become apparent until after the failure (Loggins et al., 2019). "Number of outages avoided" or "voltage variability prevented" may fail to capture how a particular system failure did (or did not) affect the needs of vulnerable people in society and firm competitiveness. What seems like a small change in systems performance may have a big impact on societal competitiveness. In other words, to build and manage essential services well, we must go beyond studying and analysing them as technical issues in siloed organisations. Instead, we must focus on the provision of essential services operating in cyberspace with a broad understanding of the interests and dynamic relationships among all the actors and stakeholders. Decision-making that considers all these interests and relationships implicates a broad set of domains from defence to foreign policy to internal affairs to individuals' interests. If we can build a better 'model' of all the actors and interests at hand in delivering essential services, we can create a policy that better considers all of the societal interests.

In the context of essential services, a new model starts with moving beyond solely considering the perspective of essential service operators and their resilience, taking into account the inter-organisational processes that lead to the essential service provision, the interconnectedness among essential services, and the possible impacts that multiple stakeholders may face in the event of disruption.

3. Responding to the challenges: a value-informed approach to cybersecurity

The safety and security of essential services cannot be understood and assessed only by identifying the technical vulnerabilities and the associated hazards and threats. The analysis must be supported by a comprehensive, dynamic modelling framework that reflects all elements of the essential service provision. Applying our value-informed approach, we argue that decision-making to mitigate risks or restore the disrupted infrastructure should be guided by the main stakeholders of the service, divided into three levels: the individuals involved, the organisations involved, and the state. Following this view, governments should focus on whatever elements, technical or not, contribute to the essential service provision. In the remainder of the chapter, we will consider this approach's potential contribution to cybersecurity policymaking for three core issues related to essential services: the loci and foci of the essential service, the value-based approach, and the dynamic relationships between elements.

Loci of essential services

Essential services have multiple loci or locations where they generate value. The first one is the individual citizen. Individuals are understood as the end-users of the essential service (Kessler and Bach, 2011). Thus, they may also benefit from the service when not using it as citizens or non-citizens (as asylum seekers). Finally, the individual can also be a 'collective individual' as a community that benefits from the provision of common goods (Shah, 2019). Individuals' interests in any essential service may differ, leading to a different definition of their priorities and what constitutes value for them. Building on existing literature from service management and public service logic (Osborne et al., 2021), we argue that the value of an essential service may be created through its use. Hence, critical infrastructures and essential services have no intrinsic value until used and created (Grönroos, 2019). A railway system has no value beyond its capital value until it becomes populated with trains, conductors, goods, and passengers. Second, the state and society have interests in the essential service provision as it ensures the well-being of the State's constituents, and they are expressions of societal values and address national priorities (Bryson et al., 2017). Thirdly, the critical infrastructure operator is interested in its functioning and the provision of its associated services, as it contributes to pursuing its mission and accumulating value. Often, essential services are provided by a plurality of actors that operate synergically, like how the fire department, ambulances, police, and other emergency services cooperate. These actors' roles, interests, and priorities may change in space and time. For example, in the context of energy, individuals are no longer mainly end-users as they are becoming prosumers if they install renewable energy infrastructure on their premises. Most cybersecurity approaches consider mainly dyadic relationships (e.g. critical infrastructure – state/policymakers; critical infrastructure – users). We contend that the current approaches to cybersecurity decision-making fail to grasp all of these loci.

Foci of cybersecurity approaches

Current approaches to policymaking in cybersecurity for essential services focus on the continuity and resilience of the internal processes of the critical infrastructure. This perspective must be rebalanced with a discussion of mitigating the risk of losing value for individuals and society, shifting away from focusing solely on the organisations that operate the service. The value of essential services is created out of the critical infrastructure and in the context of society, the service system, and the lives of service users and citizens.

The macro level concerns the impact on societal and national values and institutional norms. This level refers to the value at risk that is socially desirable, often enacted through political debate and public policy. This is typically the domain of safety and security studies in international relations, which looks at cybersecurity objectives through geopolitical and defence lenses. The objective is the broader protection of national security. National cybersecurity strategies focus on safeguarding critical infrastructure sectors such as energy, transportation, telecommunications, healthcare, finance, etc. These sectors are essential as they provide vital services for society and the economy. Protecting these infrastructures involves identifying and prioritising their vulnerabilities, establishing robust security measures, and implementing incident response and recovery plans. Thus, the characterisation of national security and the measurement of value in studies on the cybersecurity of critical infrastructures often remains normative, referring to "the need to protect national security and the well-being of individuals", without addressing the precise nature of this problem or its operationalisation (Cornish et al., 2009). Vakulyk et al. (2020) argue that cybersecurity is an essential element of national security as it should ensure the safety of individuals, institutions and firms in cyberspace.

The meso level draws upon the service system that consists of the organisational network of actors involved in providing the essential service, and their processes and technologies. This is the level within which the value at risk intersects with the interconnectedness among the actors and elements that contribute to providing the essential service. The value of cybersecurity at this level lies in the organisational learning and innovation that contributes to mitigating risks and building resilience. It is the value in the production of the service for use.

The micro level is the most investigated one. It builds on the safety and security of the network of computers, impacting the organisational or service performance. It may consider the service disruption costs for the provider and the cost of the power outage for society. In the context of electricity services, the most common way of valuing loss of electricity is the 'Value of Lost Load' (VoLL), a figure in £/MWh (Schmidthaler and Reichl, 2016).

The sub-micro level refers to the impact on the well-being of its citizens. It draws upon their utility and the individual's context for value disruption in the event of service discontinuity.

In sum, modern cybersecurity policy must balance all of these foci, the organisational, individual, and societal value. In the context of essential services, considering all the different foci shows the right range metrics and methodologies for comprehensively evaluating the value at risk. Unlike focusing on just organisations – where economic and monetary values are commonly used – determining the value at risk for essential services involves assessing factors such as public safety, societal impact, and potential loss of life. Defining and quantifying these non-monetary factors can be subjective and challenging.

The dynamic relationships of the essential service ecosystem logic

So far, cybersecurity has focused on the former and the physical, cyber, and geographical interdependencies among the critical infrastructure elements. But they must also consider the interdependencies between the critical infrastructure and the services themselves (Loggins et al., 2019). Policy must holistically consider the logical interconnections between the elements of essential services, systematically identify them, and jointly assess them to inform effective decision-making, considering the different political, economic, societal, technological, and behavioural perspectives involved. Addressing these questions advances the safety and cybersecurity disciplines and redefines the scope and methods of assessing risks to critical infrastructures. This approach is a value-informed and truly interdisciplinary perspective on risk management. Its aim is to support rational, informed decision-making to protect assets and systems of critical infrastructures essential for ensuring vital societal functions.

In this approach, the *value* of an essential service is a central, distinctive concept that evolves in space and time. Correspondingly, the safety and cybersecurity of essential services cannot be understood and assessed by statically identifying and considering the risks associated with the assets and infrastructures that provide them (Zio, 2018). Instead, the safety and cybersecurity of essential services must be considered within a dynamic framework that reflects all the elements of the essential service ecosystem (ESE), like contexts, processes, actors, rules, structures, and technologies, with their responses, behaviours, and dependence relationships. The framework for such comprehensive analysis enables the assessment of the value at risk for individuals, markets, and society. This requires the convergence of theories and cross-pollination of different, siloed perspectives that address the current deficiencies in the policymaking approaches (Falco et al., 2019).

An ESE is a "relatively self-contained, self-adjusting system of resource-integrating actors connected by shared institutional arrangements and mutual value creation through service exchange" governed by a network of actors, processes, and technologies, namely the critical elements of the ESE (Vargo and Lusch, 2016; Aarikka-Stenroos and Ritala, 2017). The ESE view draws attention to multiple loci that accrue value from the essential service, and to foci of value, including the context and social norms as drivers of value creation (Osborne et al., 2021; Akaka et al., 2013) as shown in Table 1, which represents the application of our theory and framework in the context of essential services.

The loci that influence by the disruption of essential services (Osborne et al., 2022) are: societal (macro level); elements of the ecosystem, such as actors, organisations, processes, networks, and institutions (meso level); organisational (micro level); and individual (sub-micro level). As discussed, most research focuses on the micro-organisational level for informing policymaking. But individuals may be affected individually and as groups of actors, and they can affect the dynamics of the ESE through their behaviours. From the macro perspective, society can gain value from safety and security strategies by maintaining societal values such as freedom and sovereignty (Haynes, 2018) or by addressing systemic societal issues such as the inclusive well-being of individuals and the competitiveness of firms and states (Bryson et al., 2017). In addition, public and non-public actors may accumulate public value by enacting an interconnected ESE that iteratively learns and integrates these elements to ensure the safety and security of essential service provision.

Table 1. The essential service ecosystem loci and value-added foci

Essential service ecosystem loci	Description of the impact in the context of essential services	Value-added foci
Macro level	Impact on the provision of public goods, societal norms, rules, inclusion, well-being, and competitiveness	**Value-in-society**
Meso level (elements of the ESE)	Impacts on the organisational actors, networks, communities, service processes, and technologies providing the essential service	**Value-in-production**
Micro level (organisational)	Impact on organisation performance, rules, and functioning	**Value-in-use**
Sub-micro level (individual)	Impact as a result of the use of the essential service and individuals' behaviours, beliefs, and actions	**Value-in-use** **Value-in-context**

In the ESE logic, the value-added foci of safety and cybersecurity decision-making and mitigation actions can be summarised as follows (adapted from Osborne et al., 2021):

- At a macro level of the ESE, it refers to value-in-society: the impact on societal values, institutional norms, the well-being and inclusion of individuals, and firms' competitiveness through safety and cybersecurity decision-making and actions. For example, the current policy debates in Europe focus on questions of 'digital sovereignty' as a key value for fostering individual well-being and maintaining economic advantage. If digital sovereignty is indeed a societal value, policymakers should clearly define and measure it, so they know whether related actions lead to their intended outcomes.
- The meso level concerns value-in-production: the impact of safety and cybersecurity decision-making and actions on all elements of the ESE, including individuals, networks of public and non-public organisations, and technologies, their network processes, rules, structures, and the norms as a milieu. As such, building a clear understanding of the ESE requires a multi-stakeholder, multidimensional, outcomes-focused model.
- The micro level concerns value-in-use, which draws upon the creation of value through safety and cybersecurity decisions and actions for the single actors, such as the organisation and its performance, rules, structure, and processes. This micro level is the one most often addressed in current approaches. Business continuity, resilience, organisational performance, and uptime are all outcomes that matter to single actors, largely organisations.
- The sub-micro level concerns value-in-use as a direct use of the service and value-in-context that influences individuals' behaviours and actions. The sub-micro level encompasses a particular person's well-being and satisfaction, and their use of a service that generates that kind of value.

This unified, structured and dynamic framework is fundamental for supporting effective policy decision-making for service protection. It takes a comprehensive view of the safety and cyber scenarios to assess and resolve the current tensions among different disciplines into a single, holistic, value-informed framework for enhancing the safety and cybersecurity of the ESE (Figure 1).

Figure 1. A simplified figure of the value-informed modelling for policy framing for safety and security of essential services

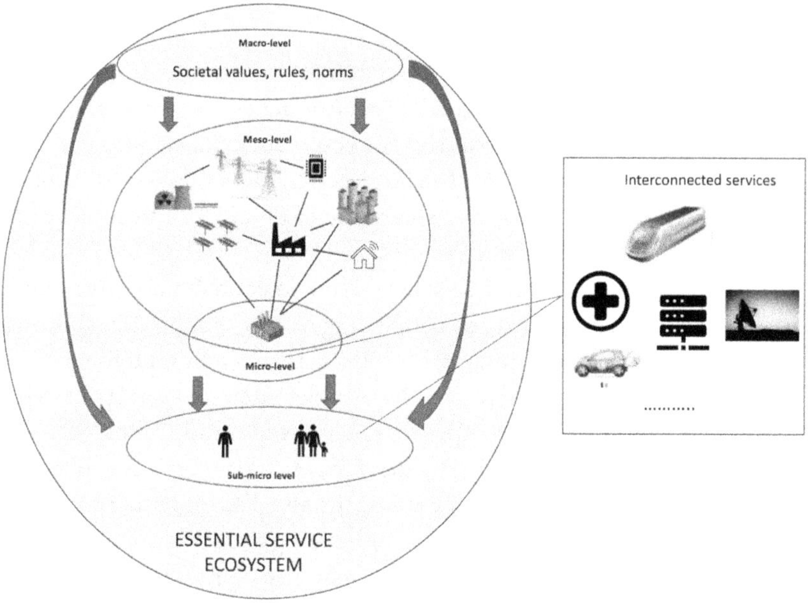

4. The future of cybersecurity of essential services: a Public Administration research agenda

This chapter argues that governments are taking a narrow perspective when it comes to the cybersecurity of essential services. So far, the approach has been dominated by a technical perspective grounded in computer security and risk management principles that inform policies, governance frameworks, and actions to ensure the business continuity and performance. This has led to overlooking the actual nature of essential service provision, which occurs at the inter-organisational level among networks of processes, technologies, and stakeholders; the interconnectedness among essential services that may be impacted in event of a cyber-attack on another service; and the actual value at risk in the event of cyber-disruption besides the effects on the performance of the attacked organisation.

Based on public administration and public service logic theories and value creation, we present a new approach to decision-making that aims at overcoming the existing flaws. This approach emphasises the distinctive characteristics of essential services and takes a holistic and systemic approach to assessing the value at risk in the event of disruption of the essential service provision, drawing upon performance measures that move beyond the efficient restoration of the service but taking into account the priority needs of all actors that may include other types of interests, including the reputational, economic, social, and societal ones.

Our inductive analysis shows the potential for major disruptions and crises even in a regular and normally functioning government. Therefore, we argue that the role of government in cybersecurity must be understood as a cross-cutting policy field at the intersection of technology and policy. This requires advancements in the literature of Public Administration and the call for more interdisciplinary work.

Firstly, Public Administration scholars should contribute to broadening perspectives on cybersecurity by conducting research in this domain about collaborative governance, in order to address the complex interdependencies among essential services and the broader societal impacts of cyber disruptions. A greater and comprehensive understanding of the effects of the current governance of cybersecurity for essential services can lead to more robust policies that protect not just the attacked entity but the entire ecosystem of essential services, thus preserving the social and economic fabric of society (Genge et al., 2015). This may also contribute to redefining the role of government in cybersecurity to reflect its cross-cutting nature and intersecting technology and policy domains. Current governance frameworks often isolate cybersecurity within specific sectors, failing to recognise the interconnectedness of essential services. A more integrated approach would see governments coordinating efforts across various sectors, ensuring that policies reflect the broader network of dependencies (Yates, 2014).

Secondly, to effectively safeguard essential services, it is crucial to adopt a holistic and systemic approach to value assessment in the event of service disruptions. Traditional performance measures often focus solely on the speed and efficiency of service restoration, neglecting broader impacts on stakeholders and the community. A more comprehensive assessment would consider the priority needs of all actors involved, including reputational, economic, social, and societal interests (Zio and Sansavini, 2011). For example, restoring power to a hospital must take precedence over other less critical services in order to protect human lives. By developing frameworks that account for these diverse impacts, policymakers can prioritise actions that maximise overall societal welfare, ensuring that essential services provide their intended value even under duress.

Thirdly, advancing cybersecurity for essential services requires interdisciplinary collaboration that bridges the gap between technology and policy in order to move beyond the current models aiming to solve policy problems at the expense of theory-building and methodological innovation (Eriksson and Giacomello, 2007).

Public Administration scholars can integrate insights from computer science, engineering, and social sciences to develop more holistic governance frameworks. This interdisciplinary approach acknowledges that cybersecurity is not just a technical issue but also a complex policy challenge that involves various stakeholders (Osborne et al., 2021). For instance, understanding the social implications of cyber disruptions can inform more effective communication strategies and public awareness campaigns. By fostering collaboration across disciplines, research can produce more comprehensive solutions that address the multifaceted nature of cybersecurity threats and enhance the resilience of essential services.

Finally, future research in Public Administration should explore the implications of political pressures on the resilience and functionality of governments, particularly in the context of cybersecurity for essential services. Our inductive analysis shows that even in normally functioning governments, significant disruptions can occur, highlighting inherent vulnerabilities. This issue becomes more complex under political pressure, where bureaucratic decision-making and stability are further compromised. Research should investigate how existing cybersecurity models and theories can adapt to the shifting political landscape, examining how political instability, policy changes, and varying governmental priorities impact the governance and protection of critical infrastructures. Additionally, studies should analyse the interplay between political actors and bureaucratic agencies in shaping cybersecurity strategies and assessing how political agendas influence resource allocation, regulatory frameworks, and inter-agency coordination. By understanding these dynamics, scholars can develop more robust models that account for the political dimensions of cybersecurity, ensuring that essential services remain resilient and secure even in politically volatile environments.

In advancing research, there may be some challenges that need to be addressed. The complex interdependencies among essential services make it difficult to isolate and quantify each essential service's specific value at risk. In addition, there is a lack of standardised metrics and methodologies for evaluating the value at risk in essential service cybersecurity. Moreover, historical data or publicly available information regarding cybersecurity incidents is often scarce in this context. This lack of data hampers the ability to accurately assess the value at risk and hinders the development of predictive models or risk quantification methodologies.

Stakeholders may have varying perceptions of risk and the value associated with essential services. Government entities, operators of critical infrastructures, and individuals may have different priorities and perspectives on what constitute valuable assets within essential services. Aligning these diverse viewpoints and developing a consensus on the value at risk can be complex and challenging.

Addressing the lack of measures to assess the value at risk in essential service cybersecurity requires not only the contribution of Public Administration scholars but also collaborative efforts among scholars of different disciplines, including computer engineering and security, international relations and securitisation studies, economics, and social sciences. Their contributions inform the value-based approach by supporting the development of standardised metrics for the different loci and foci, facilitating the definition of the data collection mechanisms and risk assessment frameworks specific to the context of essential services. Enhancing our understanding of the value at risk makes it possible to prioritise investments, allocate resources effectively, and implement targeted cybersecurity measures to protect critical infrastructure and ensure the continuous delivery of essential services.

Notes

1. European Pillars of Social Rights: https://ec.europa.eu/info/sites/default/files/access-essential-services_en.pdf.

References

Aarikka-Stenroos, L., & Ritala, P. (2017). Network management in the era of ecosystems: Systematic review and management framework. *Industrial Marketing Management*, 67(8), 23–36. https://doi.org/10.1016/j.indmarman.2017.08.010.

Akaka, M. A., Lusch, R. F., & Vargo, S. L. (2013). The complexity of context: A service ecosystems approach for international marketing. *Journal of International Marketing*, 21(4), 1–20. https://doi.org/10.1509/jim.13.0032.

Apt, J., Lave, L. B., & Morgan, M. G. (2006). Electricity: Protecting essential services. In P. E. Auerswald, L. M. Branscomb, T. M. La Porte, & E. O. Michel-Kerjan (Eds.), *Seeds of Disaster, Roots of Response: How Private Action Can Reduce Public Vulnerability* (pp. 211–238). Cambridge University Press. https://doi.org/10.1017/CBO9780511509735.016.

Bryson, J., Sancino, A., Benington, J., & Sørensen, E. (2016). Towards a multi-actor theory of public value co-creation. *Public Management Review*, 19(5), 640–654. https://doi.org/10.1080/14719037.2016.1192164.

Cavelty, M. D. (2018). Cybersecurity research meets science and technology studies. *Politics and Governance*, 6(2), 22–30. https://doi.org/10.17645/pag.v6i2.1385.

Cherdantseva, Y., Burnap, P., Blyth, A., Eden, P., Jones, K., Soulsby, H., & Stoddart, K. (2016). A review of cyber security risk assessment methods for SCADA systems. *Computers & Security*, 56, 1–27. https://doi.org/10.1016/j.cose.2015.09.009.

Christensen, K. K., & Petersen, K. L. (2017). Public-private partnerships on cyber security: A practice of loyalty. *International Affairs*, 93(6), 1435–1452. https://doi.org/10.1093/ia/iix189.

Corallo, A., Lazoi, M., & Lezzi, M. (2020). Cybersecurity in the context of industry 4.0: A structured classification of critical assets and business impacts. *Computers in Industry*, 114, 1–15. https://doi.org/10.1016/j.compind.2019.103165.

Cornish, P., Hughes, R., & Livingstone, D. (2009). *Cyberspace and the National Security of the United Kingdom: Threats and Responses*. Chatham House. https://www-chathamhouse-org.webpkgcache.com/doc/-/s/www.chathamhouse.org/sites/default/files/public/Research/International%20Security/r0309cyberspace.pdf.

Falco, G., Eling, M., Jablanski, D., Weber, M., Miller, V., Gordon, L. A., Wang, S. S., Schmit, J., Tomas, R., Elvedi, M., Maillart, T., Doavan, E., DeJung, S., Durand, E., Nutter, F., Scheffer, U., Arazi, G., Ohana, G., & Lin, H. (2019). Cyber riks research impeded by disciplinary barriers: Security progress requires cross-disciplinary collaboration. *Science*, 366(6469), 1066–1069. https://doi.org/10.1126/science.aaz4795.

Fang, Y. P., Pedroni, N., & Zio, Z. (2014). Comparing topological and physical approaches to network modeling for the optimization of failure-resilient electrical infrastructures. *Vulnerability, Uncertainty, and Risk: Quantification, Mitigation, and Management*, 725–735. https://doi.org/10.1061/9780784413609.074.

Genge, B., Kiss, I., & Haller, P. (2015). A system dynamics approach for assessing the impact of cyber attacks on critical infrastructures. *Journal of Critical Infrastructure Protection*, 10, 3–17. https://doi.org/10.1016/j.ijcip.2015.04.001.

Grönroos, C. (2017). On value and value creation in service: A management perspective. *Journal of Creating Value*, 3(2), 125–141. https://doi.org/10.1177/2394964317727196.

Haynes, P. (2018). Understanding the influence of values in complex systems-based approaches to public policy and management. *Public Management Review*, 20(7), 980–996. https://doi.org/10.1080/14719037.2017.1364411.

Kessler, I., & Bach, S. (2011). The citizen-consumer as industrial relations actor: New ways of working and the end-user in social care. *British Journal of Industrial Relations*, 49(1), 80–102. https://doi.org/10.1111/j.1467-8543.2009.00759.x.

Kröger, W., & Zio, E. (2011). *Vulnerable Systems*. Springer London. https://doi.org/10.1007/978-0-85729-655-9.

Leppänen, A., & Kankaanranta, T. (2017). Cybercrime investigation in Finland. *Journal of Scandinavian Studies in Criminology and Crime Prevention*, 18(2), 157–175. https://doi.org/10.1080/14043858.2017.1385231.

Loggins, R., Little, R. G., Mitchell, J., Sharkey, T., & Wallace, W. A. (2019). CRISIS: Modeling the restoration of interdependent civil and social infrastructure systems following an extreme event. *Natural Hazards Review*, 20(3). https://doi.org/10.1061/(ASCE)NH.1527-6996.0000326.

Liu, R., Vellaithurai, C., Biswas, S. S., Gamage, T. T., & Srivastava, A. K. (2015). Analyzing the cyber-physical impact of cyber events on the power grid. *IEEE Transactions on Smart Grid*, 6(5), 2444–2453. https://doi.org/10.1109/TSG.2015.2432013.

Moallem, A. (Ed.) (2017). *HCI for Cybersecurity, Privacy and Trust: First International Conference* (1st ed.). Springer International Publishing. https://doi.org/10.1007/978-3-030-22351-9.

Nazempour, R., Monfared, M. A. S., & Zio, E. (2016). A complex network theory approach for optimizing contamination warning sensor location in water distribution networks. *International Journal of Disaster Risk Reduction*, 30(1), 225–234. https://doi.org/10.1016/j.ijdrr.2018.04.029.

Osborne, S. P., Nasi, G., & Powell, M. (2021). Beyond co-production: Value creation and public services. *Public Administration*, 99(4), 641–657. https://doi.org/10.1111/padm.12718.

Osborne, S. P., Powell, M. G. H., Cui, T., & Strokosch, K. (2022). Value creation in the public service ecosystem: An integrative framework. *Public Administration Review*, 82(4), 634–645. https://doi.org/10.1111/puar.13474.

Palleti, V. R., Adepu, S., Mishra, V. K., & Mathur, A.(2021). Cascading effects of cyber-attacks on interconnected critical infrastructure. *Cybersecurity*, 4(1), 1–19. https://doi.org/10.1186/s42400-021-00071-z.

Ralston, P. A., Graham, J. H., Hieb, J.,L. & (2007). Cyber security risk assessment for SCADA and DCS networks. *ISA Transactions*, 46(4), 583–594. https://doi.org/10.1016/j.isatra.2007.04.003.

Rilla, N., Lima-Toivanen, M., & Myllyoja, J. (2018). *ASEAN Cybersecurity Innovation Ecosystem: A Co-creation Approach*. European Union. https://ec.europa.eu/research/participants/documents/downloadPublic?documentIds=080166e5c26b3ef7&appId=PPGMS.

Rinaldi, S. M., Peerenboom, J. P., & Kelly, T. K. (2002). Identifying, understanding, and analyzing critical infrastructure interdependencies. *IEEE Control Systems Magazine*, 21(6), 11–25. https://doi.org/10.1109/37.969131.

Schmidthaler, M., & Reichl, J. (2016). Assessing the socio-economic effects of power outages ad hoc. *Computer Science-Research and Development*, 31(3), 157–161. https://doi.org/10.1007/s00450-014-0281-9.

Shah, A., Sapatnekar, S., Kaur, H., & Roy, S. (2017). Financing common goods for health: A Public Administration Perspective from India. *Health Systems and Reform*, 5(4), 391–396. https://doi.org/10.1080/23288604.2019.1652461.

Smith, S. (2022). Out of gas: A deep dive into the colonial pipeline cyberattack. In *SAGE Business Cases*. SAGE Publications: SAGE Business Cases Originals. https://doi.org/10.4135/9781529605679.

Tweneboah-Kodua, S., Atsu, F., & Buchanan, W. J. (2018). Impact of cyberattacks on stock performance: A comparative study. *Information and Computer Security*, 26(5), 637–652. https://doi.org/10.1108/ICS-05-2018-0060.

Vakulyk, O., Petrenko, P., Kuzmenko, I., Pochtovyi, M., & Orlovskyi, R. (2020). Cybersecurity as a component of the national security of the state. *Journal of Security & Sustainability Issues*, 9(3). 775–784. https://doi.org/10.9770/jssi.2020.9.3(4)

Vargo S. L., & Lusch R. (2016). Institutions and axioms: An extension and update of service-dominant logic. Journal of the Academy Marketing Sciences (2016) 44: p. 5–23. DOI 10.1007/s11747-015-0456-3

U.S. DOE (2017). The Department of Energy's Unclassified Cybersecurity Program – 2017. https://www.oversight.gov/reports/department-energys-unclassified-cybersecurity-program-2017

Yates, A. (2014). A framework for studying mortality arising from critical infrastructure loss. *Journal of Critical Infrastructure Protection*, 7(2), 100–111. https://doi.org/10.1016/j.ijcip.2014.04.002.

Zio, E. (2016). Challenges in the vulnerability and risk analysis of critical infrastructures. *Reliability Engineering & System Safety, 152,* 137–150. https://doi.org/10.1016/j.ress.2016.02.009.

Zio, E. (2018). The future of risk assessment. *Reliability Engineering & System Safety, 177,* 176–190. https://doi.org/10.1016/j.ress.2018.04.020.

Zio, E., & Duffey, R. B. (2021). The risk of the electrical power grid due to natural hazards and recovery challenge following disasters and record floods: What next? In A. Fares (Ed.), *Climate Change and Extreme Events* (pp. 215–238). Elsevier. https://doi.org/10.1016/B978-0-12-822700-8.00008-1.

Zio, E., & Sansavini, G., & (2011). Modeling cascading failures in "systems of systems" with uncertain behavior. *Hal Open Science,* 1858–1866. https://centralesupelec.hal.science/hal-00658101/file/anno_2011_12.pdf.

The dawn of disruptive technology-driven future government

by M. Jae Moon, Seulgi Lee, Seungkyu Park, and Ire Park

1. Introduction

Digital technologies are increasingly utilised across many sectors of government, markets, and society, creating new value in previously unexplored ways. Disruptive technologies are already being used in everyday life, and, to various extents, significant disruptive technologies are functioning as critical components across different sectors. In articular, it is compelling to prepare for the future by considering how rapidly evolving technologies like artificial intelligence (AI) will be utilised in government operations, policy decisions, and public service delivery, while contemplating their positive outcomes and associated risks (Choi and Moon, 2023).

Recognising its extensive potential impacts on society, AI has been increasingly considered as a key driver of social change and economic growth as well as public sector innovations. While the benefits of AI are often celebrated, many experts often raise the potential risks and negative consequences, such as unemployment, inequality, and inhumanities (Moon, 2023). Public Administration scholars have begun to explore various aspects of AI applications in the public sector (Ahn and Chen, 2020) often highlighting the changing nature of bureaucracy and decision-making like robotic bureaucracy (Bozeman and Youtie, 2020), algorithmic bureaucracy (Kim et al., 2022), and AI-Gov (Straub et al., 2023). Critical issues of management, public values, and governance have been also explored in the literature, including the legitimacy of algorithmic decisions (Grimmelikhuijsen and Meijer, 2022), AI accountability (Busuioc, 2021), public trust in AI (Harrison and Luna-Reyes, 2022), the alignment of public values with algorithms (Andrew, 2019), public value failure in government AI adoption (Schiff et al., 2021), and inclusive AI governance for social good (Moon, 2023). Based on a systemic literature review, Zuiderwijk et al. (2021) assert that there is an increasing need for further systemic and comprehensive research concerning the use of AI in public governance given the continued advancement of AI technologies and expansion of AI applications in the public sector.

This chapter aims to forecast and present the future government model based on human–AI collaboration, analysing both the positive and negative effects, and suggests construction and operational methods for an intelligent government based on this collaboration. The digital transformation is expected to shift existing administrative systems into a cooperative form between civil servants and AI, necessitating the exploration of various issues and the proposition of appropriate responses.

The advancement of digital technology not only impacts societal development but also plays a significant role in various governmental functions. Civil servants managing government operations are aware of the importance of digital technology, and AI is already being used significantly. Following the COVID-19 pandemic, about 61% of high-ranking officials of government organizations answered that they have begun to actively utilise AI technologies for various administrative functions according to a KPMG survey (2021).

Furthermore, human–AI collaboration is expected to significantly alter the design and delivery of public services, policy decisions and implementations, and methods of citizen engagement. To understand these changes and responses concretely, this chapter explores human–AI collaboration largely based on the survey collected from both citizens and government officials in South Korea.

2. Disruptive technologies, AI, and future government

Future government operations are expected to undergo transformative changes through the adoption of various disruptive technologies (Choi and Moon, 2023), particularly digital technologies, as noted by Fang (2002) and Gil-Garcia et al. (2018). Specifically, advancements in AI are expected to revolutionise government services by facilitating hyperconnectivity and hyper-convergence, and enhancing decision-making processes (Mehr, 2017; Zheng et al., 2018). Effective utilisation of AI in future governments will require robust digital technology support (Khoury et al., 2022). For this, high-quality connectivity infrastructure like 5G is critical to boosting generation, collection, management, and utilisation of data. Many routine and repetitive administrative tasks have been and will further be assisted and replaced by automation like robotic process automation (RPA), while more sophisticated tasks like policy decisions are expected to be handled via human–AI collaborative modes in future.

According to a survey conducted by Yonsei University's Institute of Future Government on the future government in a hyper-changing society, 50.8% of respondents believed that digital technologies like AI would significantly impact financial oversight and cost-saving (IFG, 2021). Similarly, 52.2% responded that digital technology would greatly influence precise policy execution through future predictions. These results suggest that ordinary citizens view the development of digital technologies and AI as crucial for the future management of government operations.

As expected by citizens, the digital transformation of the government will lead to significant changes and innovations in governmental operations. Similar to past experiences with the introduction of e-government, technological advancements are expected to increase the efficiency of government procedures and processes. New digital and automation technologies, such as RPA and intelligent automation, will significantly transform the government using algorithms and AI, applying variably according to the characteristics and conditions of each area of government work.

The concrete changes in the government due to digital transformation and the advancement of AI will manifest in policy decision-making, organisational operation methods, public service paradigms, etc. (National Assembly Futures Institute, 2019). AI technologies are expected to bring about changes in decision-making methods, bureaucratic structures, and public sector work methods in the future, and public services will also be provided by robots operating with AI. By collecting and processing data and making actual decisions in this process, AI can cause significant changes not only in the activities of the government but also in the internal operations of the government. The division of roles between the central government and local governments may also change significantly due to AI, and these changes may enhance the independent role of local governments in public services.

The functions of future government are innovative in various aspects, such as public service delivery, policy decision-making, operational methods, and government regulation. A brief look at the examples of future government functions suggested by Canning et al. (2020) posits an anticipatory, human-centric, and resilient government in which disruptive digital technologies are widely applied (Canning et al., 2020). Key drivers for future government include: (a) cognitive automation propelled by large language models (LLMs), text analytics, etc.; (b) predictive analytics; (c) human–machine teaming; (d) quantum computing; (e) cybersecurity; (f) an open talent economy; (g) digital automation; (h) cloud computing; (i) growing debt; and (j) big data. These will eventually lead to major changes in various dimensions of government, including service delivery, policy and decision-making, government operations, regulations and enforcement, and the workforce, as summarised in Table 1 (for more details, see Canning et al., 2020).

Table 1. Comparison of legacy/current government and future government

Domains	Characteristics of Legacy/ Current Government	Characteristics of Future Government
Public Service Delivery	Standardised One-stop government Multichannel delivery User-informed Citizen experience/trust	Government of one No-touch government Once-only government Omnichannel delivery Life events
Policy and Decision-making	Cost–benefit analysis Stakeholder consultation Randomised control trials Implementation viability analysis	Anticipatory government Crowdsourced and distributed policymaking Government by simulation AI-based scenario analysis Self-correcting government Evidence-based policymaking
Operations	Shared services Automation Competitive outsourcing Efficiency in-house processes	Integrated centre office As-a-service acquisition Public sector digital factories Cognitive automation
Regulations and Enforcement	Cost–benefit analysis One-in, one-out/regulatory offsetting	Risk-based regulation Positive enforcement strategies Legislation as code RegTech for regulators Touchless compliance
Workforce	Lifetime civil service One-dimensional workforce Rigid job classifications Human versus machine	Talent cloud Human–machine collaboration Just-in-time civil service Open talent spectrum Adaptive workplaces

Adapted from Canning et al., 2020, p. 10.

The concept of a 'one-stop government', which involves a seamless policy design and service delivery, has been introduced in a digital government where a digital unity is expected to enhance communication between the government and citizens that then allows for the provision of personalised services (Canning et al., 2020). This will be increasingly shifted to the 'no-touch government', which provides digital, automated services without direct visits or requests from citizens. This will even evolve to a future form of government that offers diverse public services to citizens, even without being requested, throughout their lifecycle (Canning et al., 2020). Proposing a digital platform government, for example, the South Korean government aims to build a digital platform through which it not only offers customised information on eligibility for social benefits to individual citizens, but also provides various public services. Of course, this requires seamless integration and utilisation of data collected and managed by various government agencies, courts, healthcare organisations, and financial institutions, among others.

As Table 1 (Canning et al., 2020) shows, future government is also expected to use AI-based scenario analysis and a self-correcting government as mechanisms for policy decision-making where machine learning techniques and other AI-based systems will be widely used for various wicked problems in the future. For government operations, the application of cognitive automation is expected to be used through advanced AI-based systems like large language models (LLMs). Governments also need to refer to technological solutions for regulations by promoting RegTech, which uses digital technology-based tools to ensure and facilitate regulatory compliance. Going beyond conventional bureaucratic systems, it is also expected that the future government will need to be more flexible in recruiting technologically-savvy talent to the workforce (i.e. talent cloud) in a highly uncertain and technologically transformative era.

3. Human–AI collaborative government for the future

Although AI technology is rapidly advancing, currently AI is used as an auxiliary means or not systematically used in government operations, except for administrative automation, such as RPA and chatbot services, among others. AI simply plays a role in processing and providing information required by humans through fast information search and processing capabilities, or in searching for objective evidence that supports human judgements previously considered intuitive.

However, due to the exponential growth rate of AI technology, the expected arrival of superintelligence, that is, the singularity, is being brought forward, and thus AI is expected not to remain just an auxiliary tool for humans but has been becoming a compelling driver for changes and innovations not only in the private but also in the public sector. The surprising performance of ChatGPT in fact drew much attention to the compelling potential and impacts of AI in society. In fact, the development of AI holds the potential to bring transformative changes across society. AI surpassing human intelligence in terms of information processing, logical thinking, and from the perspectives of objectivity and rationality is not far off. However, in terms of creativity and critical thinking, human intelligence remains superior to AI and will continue to do so for a considerable period even after the singularity.

The combination of strengths through collaboration between humans and AI will clearly yield better results than keeping them separate. If AI can handle tasks that are difficult and time-consuming for humans and humans can complement the areas where AI is lacking, such as creativity and social skills, then the collaboration between humans and AI can produce superior outcomes compared to when they operate separately.

Collaboration between humans and AI is already underway. The industrial sector is seeking innovation through the intelligent application of AI. The private sector has been already experiencing or undergoing human–AI collaboration at different levels in the name of automation or intelligentisation via AI smart factories (Park et al., 2023). There are different levels and phases in human–AI collaboration. For example, Sowa et al. (2021) suggested four different levels of human–AI collaboration, progressing from separation of humans and AI (working separately), to a supplementary working relationship between humans and AI (supplementing each other), to interdependence of humans and AI (interdependent on each other), and finally to a hybrid of humans and AI.

Figure 1. Levels of proximity of humans to AI at work

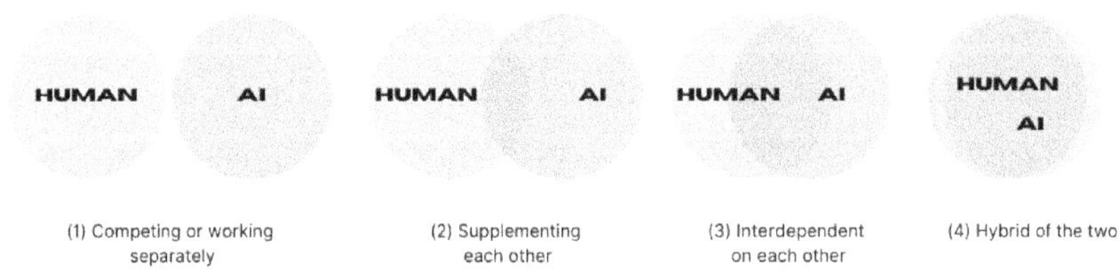

(1) Competing or working separately
(2) Supplementing each other
(3) Interdependent on each other
(4) Hybrid of the two

Source: Sowa et al., 2021, p. 136.

Similarly, Eggers et al. (2019) propose seven evolutionary phases, namely shepherding ("a human manages a group of machines, amplifying their productivity"), extending ("a machine augments human work"), guiding ("a machine prompts a human to help the human gain knowledge"), collaborating ("a problem is identified, defined, and solved via human-machine collaboration"), splitting-up ("work is broken up and parts are automated"), relieving ("machines take over routine or manual tasks"), and replacing ("machines completely perform a task once done by humans"). These phases basically represent the degree of automation. For example, the shepherding stage involves humans (e.g. civil servants) making decisions based on data provided by AI, while the final replacing phase refers to most of the tasks traditionally performed by humans (civil servants) being replaced by AI-driven decision-making. In practice, the collaborating phase, which is in the middle of the evolutionary process, is a plausible option. The collaborating phase refers to tight cooperation between humans (civil servants) and AI in decision-making focused on specific areas. The next section will discuss positive and negative perspectives on human–AI collaborative intelligent government.

Having studied 1,500 private companies in relation to human–AI collaboration and its impact on performance, Wilson and Daugherty (2018) find that companies could achieve a higher level of productivity as they make more systemic efforts to promote human–AI collaboration by putting core principles of human–AI collaboration into practice: (a) reimagining business processes; (b) embracing experimentation/employee involvement; (c) actively directing AI strategies; (d) responsibly collecting data, and (e) redesigning work to incorporate AI and cultivating related employee skills. This positive association between human–AI collaboration and performance is also expected to be found in government organisations.

4. Expected positive and negative changes in a human–AI collaborative intelligent government

This section discusses potential positive and negative changes that could emerge in a human–AI collaborative intelligent government based on the survey data collected from citizens and public servants in South Korea. The survey was conducted by the Institute of Future Government of Yonsei University in 2022.

With respect to the expected positive changes in human–AI collaborative intelligent government, among citizens the statement with the highest perceived likelihood of positive change was "ICT technologies such as CCTV will evolve to AI-based intelligent devices for public services" with 76.9% of respondents. Other highly probable positive changes included applications of AI technologies for predicting various risks of disasters, accidents, and crimes (74%), applications of AI-based intelligent robots for handling fires, natural disasters, etc. (72.8%), expansion of public data by using AI technologies for information resource management (71.3%), and applications of AI for consultation, requests and issuing public documents, and other simple services (63.5%). Conversely, the most likely negative change identified was "issues with accountability in AI decisions", with a response rate of 64.5%. Other potential negative changes included violation of information privacy protection (47.4%), malfunctions of the government's AI-based systems (39.4%), and the emergence of underserved groups in the provision of administrative services (35.2%).

The survey of public servants showed similar results, although with more positive view than ordinary citizens about the potential of AI applications in governments. For example, the positive result most expected by public servants was applications of AI technologies for predicting various risks of disasters, accidents, and crimes (82.8%). This was followed by evolution of ICT technologies such as CCTV to AI-based intelligent devices for public services (80.5%), expansion of public data by using AI technologies for information resource management (80.0%), and applications of AI-based intelligent robots for handling fires, natural disasters, etc. (78.3%). The most likely negative change perceived by public servants, as seen by the general public, was "problems with accountability in AI decisions", with 71.7%. Additional possible negatives included violation of information privacy protection and information leakage (47.5%), malfunctions of the government's AI-based systems (41.8%), accidents in the government's AI-based systems (41.8%), and the emergence of underserved groups (33.0%).

Overall, both citizens and public servants generally agree on the potential positive and negative changes, although public servants are more positive than ordinary citizens about the improvement of public services and anticipatory/preventive government operations, particularly in disaster management. Both citizens and public servants agree that accountability problems when AI-based decision-making systems do not work appropriately are the most compelling risk relating to AI applications in governments.

Expected changes in work practices in a human–AI collaborative intelligent government

To directly gauge changes in the human–AI collaborative intelligent government, we explored what citizens and public servants expect in terms of the extent to which humans and AI will work together in decision-making processes in governments. In order to examine this, we asked both citizens and public servants about whether human-centred decisions, human–AI collaborative decision-making or AI-centred decision-making is expected in future governments. We found both similarities and differences in perceptions between citizens and public servants. As Table 2 shows, citizens showed the highest degree of agreement with the statement about close collaboration between public servants and AI in decision-making (53.0%), while public servants most agreed with "public servants primarily conducting decision-making" (60.0%). The biggest perception gap between the groups was on the statement "AI will replace most of the tasks currently performed by public servants", with 42.3% of public respondents agreeing versus only 28.3% of public servants.

Table 2. Perceptions of citizens and public servants on human–AI collaboration

Citizens			Mode of Human-AI Collaboration	Public Servants		
Disagree	Neutral	Agree		Disagree	Neutral	Agree
13.3	36.6	50.1	Public servants play a primary role in policy decisions based on the data assisted by AI (public servant-centred decision-making)	9.3	30.7	60.0
11.7	35.3	53.0	Public servants and AI play equal role in decision-making policy in specific policy areas	9.7	33.0	57.3
19.6	38.1	42.3	AI replaces many roles played by public servants in decision-making process (AI-centred decision-making)	39.5	32.2	28.3

Source: Institute for Future Government (2022).

Comparing the responses from citizens and public servants, citizens responded somewhat equally, whereas public servants favoured human-centred decision-making and disagreed with the scenario of AI replacing public servants, though to a lesser extent.

In order to measure the level of trust in human–AI collaborative decision-making in different policy contexts, we presented three hypothetical scenarios for human–AI collaboration in decision-making to see which types of policy decisions citizens and public servants would trust more or less. The hypothetical scenarios were that AI systems and human experts would propose different policy alternatives to three policy contexts. Scenario 1 was the different policy responses proposed by AI and policy analysts to a serious new pandemic situation after COVID-19. Scenario 2 was that an AI-based judicial system and the judge took different positions on the appropriate sentence to give a particular criminal convicted of a serious crime. Scenario 3 was that an AI system providing climate solutions and the government Taskforce (TF) for climate change response proposed different solutions to a natural disaster caused by climate change.

Table 3. Trust in human and AI decisions in different scenarios

Scenarios	Subjects	Trust in AI Decision	Trust in Human Decision	No Trust in Either
Scenario 1 Pandemic	Citizens	30.8	45.9	23.3
	Public Servants	35.0	52.7	12.3
Scenario 2 Judicial Sentencing	Citizens	36.9	41.6	21.5
	Public Servants	41.3	48.7	10.0
Scenario 3 Response to Natural Disaster	Citizens	46.3	33.4	20.3
	Public Servants	52.2	39.3	8.5

Source: Institute for Future Government (2022).

As summarised in Table 3, the survey results showed that in Scenario 1, both citizens and public servants trusted human decisions more (citizens 45.9%, public servants 52.7%) than AI-based decisions. Similar results were observed in Scenario 2, with citizens and public servants showing a high level of trust in human decisions (citizens 41.6%, public servants 48.7%). Overall, trust in human decisions was higher than trust in AI in both scenarios across both groups. However, public servants showed a higher level of trust in human decisions compared to citizens. In addition, the level of distrust in both human and AI decisions was lower among public servants, indicating a general trust in decisions regardless of the decision-maker. In Scenario 3, both groups trusted AI decisions more (citizens 46.3%, public servants 52.2%) than human decisions. However, public servants showed a higher level of trust in AI decisions, indicating that the trust in decision-making could vary by the specific area of application.

We also explored how citizens and public servants prefer to allocate decision-making authority (weight) between humans and AI when both humans and AI collaborate in making policy decisions. 44.8% of citizen respondents felt it was most important to prioritise human decision-making while incorporating AI input. On the other hand, giving equal authority to both humans and AI was supported by 26.2% of respondents, and prioritising AI decisions while incorporating human input as supplementary was favoured by 23.3%. Granting full decision-making authority to either AI or humans was seen as least desirable, with only 6.2% supporting it.

Table 4. Preference for assigning decision authority in human–AI collaborative intelligent government

Subject	Full Decision Authority to AI	More Decision Authority to AI Systems while Incorporating Human's View	Equal Decision Authority to AI and Humans	More Decision Authority to Humans while incorporating AI's View	Full Decision Authority to Humans
Citizens	1.2	23.3	26.2	44.8	4.5
Public Servants	1.0	27.3	15.2	51.8	4.7

Source: Institute for Future Government (2022).

As for public servants, 51.8% agreed that human decision-making should be prioritised while incorporating AI opinions. However, unlike the citizen respondents, only 15.2% of public servants agreed that an equal partnership in decision-making between humans and AI was desirable, showing a significant difference from the 26.2% of public respondents who supported this view.

Overall, both citizens and public servants currently favour a human-led approach to decision-making, though the public show some agreement with the concept of equal decision-making authority for humans and AI, which is less supported by public servants.

In conclusion, the trustworthiness of AI's decisions varies depending on the domain. For instance, while human decisions were trusted more in the first two scenarios, AI's decisions were trusted more in the last scenario. Additionally, both citizens and public servants showed a need for some form of collaboration between humans and AI, regardless of the specific area, confirming that human–AI collaboration itself is essential and significant.

Perceived obstacles to building a human–AI collaborative intelligent government

This section surveyed general citizens and public servants on perceived obstacles to constructing a human–AI collaborative intelligent government. The survey asked about pressing issues that need to be addressed for the success of such a government, with items including lack of technical understanding among public servants, threats to personal data protection, lack of inter-departmental collaboration in data-sharing, and ambiguity in responsibility when issues arise in human–AI collaboration.

The results indicated that citizens believe institutional preparations are necessary to address threats such as personal data protection (74.9%). The next most pressing issue recognised was the ambiguity in responsibility when problems occur during human–AI collaboration (72.8%). Other urgent issues included lack of inter-departmental collaboration in data-sharing (69.6%) and lack of technical understanding among public servants (67.6%).

Table 5. Obstacles to human–AI collaborative intelligent government

	Citizens				Public Servants	
Low Urgency	Medium Urgency	High Urgency	Obstacles	Low Urgency	Medium Urgency	High Urgency
5.7	26.7	67.6	Lack of digital literacy of public servants' understanding of emerging technologies	7.0	28.8	64.2
5.9	19.2	74.9	Lack of institutional and legal preparation for threats to information privacy protection	2.7	20.8	76.5
5.3	25.1	69.6	Lack of inter-agency collaboration in data-sharing	3.7	23.7	72.7
5.4	21.8	72.8	Lack of accountability mechanism in human–AI collaboration	5.0	17.7	77.3

Public servant responses highlighted the ambiguity in responsibility in the context of human–AI collaboration as the most urgent issue (77.3%), followed by insufficient regulatory measures for data protection (76.5%). While the priorities were somewhat different, both citizens and public servants saw the ambiguity in responsibility and the insufficiency of regulatory measures for threats related to human–AI collaboration as the most urgent issues to be addressed.

The survey also asked about important factors to consider for the construction of a human–AI collaborative intelligent government, including data collection and quality management, selection of AI implementation areas, the role of top policymakers, and ensuring democratic accountability. The highest importance was given to data collection and quality management (citizens 79.2%, public servants 82.5%). Following this were decisions on AI implementation areas (citizens 70.2%, public servants 78.0%), ensuring democratic accountability (citizens 70.0%, public servants 71.8%), and the role of top policymakers such as chief information officers (CIOs) or chief technology officers (CTOs) (citizens 65.8%, public servants 70.5%).

Overall, public servants placed relatively higher importance on each element than citizens. However, the order of significance among the four factors was consistence across both citizen and public servant surveys.

5. Discussion and conclusion

Advancement of AI technologies and their applications appear inevitable in future government. In fact, there have already been preliminary applications in a number of areas, including chatbot services, predictive policing (PredPol) in crime prevention, and disaster management, among others. However, the potential risks and negative consequences still need to be be continuously addressed via AI ethical guidelines, regulations (e.g. the EU's risk-based regulation), AI impact assessments, etc. In order to have trustworthy and reliable applications of AI in public services, particularly for social good, the government needs to form and use institutional arrangements for inclusive AI governance, through which it can ensure the positive utility of AI while minimising or at least managing the potential risks (Moon, 2023).

In planning human–AI collaborative government, governments also need to examine what citizens and public servants consider and expect the nature, prospects, and risks of AI applications in governments to be. We learn from the survey results that both citizens and public servants generally have a positive perception of a human–AI collaborative intelligent government and recognise its feasibility and potential benefits for the quality of public services and government, while simultaneously having concerns about the risks.

Both citizens and public servants also expect AI to be well utilised in providing simple services and predicting and analysing future risks. Additionally, they believe the introduction of a human–AI collaborative intelligent government would contribute significantly to solving problems in areas such as natural disasters and environmental safety. Proactively using human–AI collaboration systems to predict and respond to future disasters and environmental changes could enable a gradual expansion and adoption of such systems.

Secondly, both groups looked forward to the positive changes that collaboration between humans and AI could bring about, but also expressed concerns about AI's involvement in significant government decision-making. Overall, when considering the distribution of decision-making authority, both citizens and public servants largely agreed with a human-led decision-making approach. There were differences, with citizens being more positive about equal decision-making between humans and AI, while public servants showed a more negative attitude. Despite this perceptual difference, the survey results indicate that both citizens and public servants recognise the need for some form of collaboration between humans and AI, rather than giving full decision-making authority to one party. Consequently, the specific form of human–AI collaboration may vary depending on the area in which it is applied, but the collaboration itself is deemed essential.

Thirdly, citizens also showed high expectations that a human–AI collaborative intelligent government would predict and proactively respond to future issues. They anticipated that such a government could decide on efficient and effective responses to policy challenges such as environmental changes and pandemics. Therefore, it is necessary to raise public awareness that a human–AI collaborative intelligent government could address issues beyond future predictions and costs savings, such as quality of life and social integration.

Fourthly, regarding the problems and obstacles associated with human–AI collaboration, there were some differences in the specific level of agreement between citizens and public servants, but both groups generally recognised the issue of responsibility in human–AI collaboration and the lack of regulatory measures covering the risks of collaboration as the most urgent issue to be resolved. In other words, for human–AI collaboration to function effectively, a clear definition of who is responsible when issues or accidents occur during the collaboration must be established. This goes beyond merely assigning responsibility to include legal and regulatory preparations for the degree and locus of responsibility and subsequent measures. The lack of preparedness in law and regulation is more pronounced in survey questions targeted at public servants. As public servants also consider post-management and legal frameworks arising from AI implementation as important preparatory elements, prioritising legal and regulatory adjustments for a human–AI collaborative intelligent government is necessary.

It should be also noted that AI applications should not be considered a panacea for future government, but concerted efforts should nevertheless be made to take advantage of AI's potential for improving the quality of public services and enhancing administrative efficiency. Taking a cautious position about a technology-deterministic perspective, we might need to go back to basics like accountability, coordination, collaboration, and transparency in the course of pursuing healthy, constructive, and sustainable human–AI collaboration in future government. As we introduce AI-based systems in governments, ironically the human role might become more significant, meaning that it is important to prepare public servants as empowered and competent users of various AI-based by upskilling and reskilling them in the age of human–AI collaboration at work.

References

Ahn, M. J., & Chen, Y.-C. (2020). Artificial Intelligence in government: Potentials, challenges, and the future. In S.-J. Eom, and J. Lee (Eds.), *The 21st Annual International Conference on Digital Government Research*. Association for Computing Machinery. https://doi.org/10.1145/3396956.3398260.

Andrew, L. (2019). Public administration, public leadership, and the construction of public value in the age of algorithm and big data. *Public Administration, 97*(2), 296–310. https://doi.org/10.1111/padm.12534.

Bozeman, B., & Youtie, J. (2019). Robotic bureaucracy: Administrative burden and red tape in university research. *Public Administration Review, 80*(1), 157–162. https://doi.org/10.1111/puar.13105.

Canning, M., Eggers, W. D., O'Leary, J. & Chew B. (2020). Creating the government of the Future: Uncovering the building blocks of change to become more anticipatory, human-centered and resilient. Deloitte Insights. https://www2.deloitte.com/us/en/insights/industry/public-sector/government-of-the-future-evolution-change.html.

Choi, S. M., & Moon, M. J. (2023). Disruptive technologies and future societies: Perspectives and forecasts based on Q-methodology. *Futures, 145*, 1–15. https://doi.org/10.1016/j.futures.2022.103059.

Eggers, W. D., Datar, A., Parent, D., & Gustetic, J. (2019). *How to redesign government work for the future*. Deloitte Insights. https://www2.deloitte.com/content/dam/insights/us/articles/5120_redesign_government_work/DI_redesign-govt-work.pdf.

Gil-Garcia, J. R., Dawes, S. S., & Pardo, T. A. (2018). Digital government and public management research: Finding the crossroads. *Public Management Review, 20*(5), 633–646. https://doi.org/10.1080/14719037.2017.1327181.

Grimmelikhuijsen, S., & Meijer, A. (2022). Legitimacy of algorithmic decision-making: Six threats and the need for a calibrated institutional response. *Perspectives on Public Management and Governance, 5*(3), 232–242. https://doi.org/10.1093/ppmgov/gvac008.

Harrison, T. M., & Luna-Reyes, L. F. (2022). Culitivating trustworthy artificial intelligence in digital government. *Social Science Computer Review, 40*(2), 494–511. https://doi.org/10.1177/0894439320980122.

Institute of Future Government (IFG) (2019). *National Survey on Disruptive Technology and Social Impact*. Yonsei University.

Institute of Future Government (IFG) (2022). *National Survey on Hyper-changing and Hyper-Intelligent Society*. Yonsei University.

Khoury, R., Alnesayan, R., Nel, S., & Ezzedine, M., (2022, February). *The government of the future*. Arthur D Little. https://www.adlittle.com/fr/node/23980.

Kim, S., Andersen, K. N., & Lee, J. (2021). Platform government in the era of smart technology. *Public Administration Review*, 82(2), 362–368. https://doi.org/10.1111/puar.13422.

KPNG (2021). *Thriving in an AI world: Unlocking the value of AI across seven key industries*. KPMG. https://assets.kpmg.com/content/dam/kpmg/tw/pdf/2021/05/tw-thriving-in-an-ai-world-2021.pdf.

Mehr, H., (2017). *Artificial Intelligence for Citizen Services and Government*. Harvard Kennedy School, Ash Center for Democratic Governance and Innovation.

Moon, M. J. (2023). Searching for inclusive artificial intelligence for social good: Participatory governance and policy recommendations for making AI more inclusive and benign for society. *Public Administration Review*, 83(6), 1496–1505. https://doi.org/10.1111/puar.13648.

National Assembly Futures Institute (2019). *Advancement of Disruptive Technologies and Paradigm Shift in Public Service Delivery*. Unpublished report [Korean].

Park, B., Kim, T., & Jeong, J.-P. (2023). AI-smart factory: Design and verification of Korean SME AI smart factory using level diagnosis system. *Procedia: Computer Science*, 224, 169–179. https://doi.org/10.1016/j.procs.2023.09.025.

Schiff, D. S., Schiff, K. J., & Pierson, P. (2021). Assessing public value failure in government adoption of artificial intelligence. *Public Administration*, 100(3), 653–673. https://doi.org/10.1111/padm.12742.

Sowa, K., Przegalinska, A., & Ciechanowski, L., (2021). Cobots in knowledge work: Human-AI collaboration in managerial professions. *Journal of Business Research*, 125, 135–142. https://doi.org/10.1016/j.jbusres.2020.11.038.

Straub, V. J., Morgan, D., Bright, J., Magetts, H., & (2023). Artificial Intelligence in Government: Concepts, standards, and a unified framework. *Government Information Quarterly*, 40(4), 1–16. https://doi.org/10.1016/j.giq.2023.101881.

Wilson, H. J., & Daugherty, P. (2018, July/August). Collaborative intelligence: Humans and AI are joining forces. *Harvard Business Review*. https://hbr.org/2018/07/collaborative-intelligence-humans-and-ai-are-joining-forces.

Zheng, Y., Yu, H., Cui, L., Miao, C., Leung, C., Yang, Q. (2018). SmartHS: An AI Platform for improving government service provision. *Proceedings of the AAAI Conference on Artificial Intelligence*, 32(1). https://doi.org/10.1609/aaai.v32i1.11382.

Zuiderwijk, A., Chen, Y., Salem, F., & (2021). Implications of the use of artificial intelligence in public governance: A systematic literature review and a research agenda. *Government Information Quarterly*, 38(3), 1–19. https://doi.org/10.1016/j.giq.2021.101577.

The digital transformation as a double governance challenge

by Albert Meijer

1. Introduction

A new wave of digital technologies is currently rapidly changing our economies and societies (Van Dijck et al., 2018; Zuboff, 2019; Strømmen-Bakhtiar, 2020). The combination of platform technologies and artificial intelligence is radically transforming economic relations and also societal patterns. Social media and digital platforms have rapidly changed the ways in which we consume, meet partners, and organise both work and leisure. The current fascination with – and fear of – general artificial intelligence highlights the current focus on technology as a key driving factor of change in our modern societies.

This digital transformation generates a host of questions in society related to topics as diverse as fake news, new labour conditions, stress among children, and new forms of crime (Trittin-Ulbrich et al., 2021). For this reason, the digital transformation is not a topic for only the information technology specialists in government but touches upon all policy domains. Government policies for sectors as diverse as social security, policing, sustainability, healthcare, and culture and arts are all influenced by the digital transformation.

Further increasing the complexity of the issue, the digital transformation of society needs to be understood as a double challenge for governments. On the one hand, governments need to provide answers to new challenges such as the reorganisation of labour, fake news, and digital crime (Van Dijck et al., 2018; Strømmen-Bakhtiar, 2020). On the other hand, governments themselves are rapidly transforming through the incorporation of new technologies in their internal and external processes (Mergel et al., 2019).

This chapter will explore the governance of the digital transformation as a double challenge: a challenge to the organisation of government and a challenge to the role of government in society. One could also argue that this is an issue of a new form of alignment: the institutional form of government needs to be re-aligned with the structure of society. I will discuss the nature and pervasiveness of the broad societal and governmental trend of digital transformation, the key challenges for governance, and the types of responses that are being developed in the form of hard and soft rules, and various strategic responses. I will end with a brief research agenda and basically a call for Public Administration scholars to engage in multidisciplinary research on these topics. Our expertise is needed to ensure that the digital transformation will indeed bring us a better world.

2. Digital transformation

New digital technologies, most importantly artificial intelligence, are rapidly transforming our societies. The concept of digital transformation comes from the private sector and refers to the radical reorganisation of markets, business processes, and customer relations through the introduction of new digital technologies (Vial, 2019). A key example of a company that failed to understand the importance of the new technologies is Kodak (Lucas and Goh, 2009). Other companies are still in business but have lost a large part of their market share to new companies, and various other types of companies, such as travel agencies, taxis, and tax consultants, are threatened in their existence. Currently, the leading companies in the world are no longer traditional industrial companies such as General Motors and Siemens but high-tech companies such as Alphabet and Meta.

More recently, the concept of digital transformation has also been introduced to refer to rapid processes of socio-technical changes in the public sector. In this case, there is usually no direct threat such as losing market share going out of business; rather the promise of a more effective and efficient government and the threat of the erosion of citizen trust and legitimacy are key drivers to transform government through new technologies.

The term 'digital transformation' has been translated to the public sector. On the basis of a thorough exploration of both the literature and emerging empirical practices, Mergel et al. (2019, p. 12) define digital transformation as follows:

> Digital transformation is a holistic effort to revise core processes and services of government beyond the traditional digitization efforts. It evolves along a continuum of transition from analog to digital to a full stack review of policies, current processes, and user needs and results in a complete revision of the existing and the creation of new digital services. The outcome of digital transformation efforts focuses among others on the satisfaction of user needs, new forms of service delivery, and the expansion of the user base.

This definition clearly positions the digital transformation as a socio-technical process: the introduction of new technologies plays a key role but does not determine the digital transformation. Various social, political, and policy responses, such as rules, policies, trainings, professional roles, etc., form part of the process of digital transformation (see also Grimmelikhuijsen and Meijer, 2022).

The term 'digital transformation' is also used in a broader sense and then refers to fundamental socio-technical changes in economy and society triggered by the development of new technologies (Strømmen-Bakhtiar, 2020). The digital transformation radically changes policy domains and economic sectors in society. A key example is healthcare. The digital transformation has transformed the nature of medical processes through the use of artificial intelligence for processes as diverse as breast cancer screening, streamlining doctor–patient communication, and reorganising the work of nurses. It has also resulted in much more emphasis on information as a key resource for public health programmes. Recently, the COVID-19 pandemic has highlighted the primary role of digital technologies in finding proper responses to health threats (Meijer and Webster, 2020).

Another example is transport. The rise of alternative mobility options, such as car sharing, flexible bicycle options, and platform services for taxis like Uber and Lyft, have transformed mobility in urban environments. E-scooters may create convenient and sustainable transport options but they may also have undesirable side effects such as blocking pavements and complicating cycling courtesy rules. In addition, the availability of routing systems limits government options for redirecting traffic to ensure that it does not negatively affect the livability of cities. And the collection of data about mobility strengthens the power position of tech companies since they know more about usage patterns than governments.

A final example is the media sector. Whereas in many countries national broadcasting companies and national newspapers formerly controlled professional standards for news provision, the sector is now controlled by big tech companies such as Alphabet (YouTube) and Meta (Facebook, Instagram). Many people, especially young people, get their news through social media networks rather than through the 'old' mass media channels. The dependence on these types of public information has resulted in concerns about polarisation and influence on voter behaviour.

The digital transformation results in drastic rearrangements of all (public and private) sectors in terms of mechanisms, value, and power positions and thus creates enormous challenges for governments in different domains. How can governments regulate public health when international high-tech companies have more healthcare data than governments? How can governments ensure high-value transport options when cheap transport platforms erode citizen support for public transportation? What can governments do to ensure that citizens are well informed about public issues and protect them against misinformation spread by many platforms?

3. Governance of the digital transformation: a variety of challenges

The digital transformation offers great opportunities, such as better government services, more effective government, more prosperous societies, and better responses to wicked problems, but also comes with a variety of risks, such as erosion of trust, increased inequalities, and power imbalances (Pappas et al., 2019). The digital transformation of government and society is often promoted using the argument that it can bring us all kinds of benefits, such as a more prosperous society and effective government. The digital transformation is also regarded a key element in all kinds of solutions to wicked problems facing societies, such as poverty, climate change, and unsafety. These hopeful narratives drive the digital transformation, but at the same time numerous challenges related to the digital transformation have been mentioned in the literature. Various authors have expressed concerns about the digital transformation and the new type of society that it will bring us (O'Neil, 2016; Eubanks, 2017).

The opportunities and risks can be understood as a double challenge: an internal and external challenge for governance. The governance of the digital transformation is firstly an external challenge. Governments face the task of channelling the variety of issues and problems related to the digital transformation in all these sectors in a desirable direction. Meijer et al. (2020) investigated three cases of the digital transformation – automatic number-plate recognition, the gig economy, and 5G networks – and conclude that the governance of these sectors is complicated for four reasons:

- *Technical complexity of digital systems.* Digital systems such as algorithms, platforms, and networks are complex in themselves and their complexity is compounded by the fact that they rely on other systems – i.e. infrastructures or databases – and this results in complex technological assemblages.
- *Social complexity.* The digital systems that were analysed are directly connected to changing social practices. In Meijer et al.'s (2020) analysis, this was most concrete for the gig economy, since this has resulted in new consumer practices and also new work relations between employees and companies.

- *Institutional complexity.* The analysis of the three cases by Meijer et al. (2020) also highlighted the institutional complexity. This became specifically clear for 5G networks, since the introduction of these networks is closely connected not only to rules for technology use but also to spatial planning, health guidelines, and rules for international security.
- *Value complexity.* Finally, the values that are involved in the governmental and societal use of new technological systems are manifold (Meijer et al., 2020). While this was relatively simple for automatic number-plate recognition (security versus privacy), it is much for complicated for the changing labour relations in the gig economy and the dependence on infrastructures for 5G networks.

Secondly, the governance of digital transformation is an internal challenge: the transformation of government through the use of digital technologies for a variety of processes is a governance challenge in and of itself. Meijer and Grimmelikhuijsen (2021) highlight that this process of digital transformation entails not only the introduction of new technologies in government organisations but also changes in expertise (such as data scientists in government), information relations (for example between tax departments and banks), organisational structure (such as the introduction of a CIO office), organisational policy (for proper use of new technologies), and monitoring and evaluation (for continuous learning). All these elements need to be aligned to ensure that the digitalisation contributes to organisational performance (Henderson and Venkatraman, 1993). This challenge is even more complicated since governments increasingly collaborate in information networks with a variety of government, private, and non-profit organisations and therefore the different elements of the transformation process also need to be negotiated and adjusted in these inter-organisational networks (Homburg, 2008). In the Netherlands, the Province of South-Holland has even initiated a learning process around the question whether government could become a platform ('government-as-a-platform') and thus have a radically different relation towards societal partners.[1] In empirical work, this radical shift has not yet been observed, but various authors have highlighted that the position of government, which was developed in the age of the steam engine, needs to be urgently updated to the information age (Cordella and Paletti, 2019; Eom and Lee, 2022).

The internal and external challenges of the digital transformation should not be understood as separate challenges: they are highly connected. The internal transformation is about realising a type of (networked) government that aligns with what is needed from government in view of the external challenges. An example of the connection between the digital transformation of society and the digital transformation of government is the regulation of algorithms through algorithms (Lorenz et al., 2022). The basic argument about this form of regulation is that the way in which companies use algorithms, for example for banking or advertisement, is so complex that regulators will only be able to do their work if they use algorithms for regulatory purposes. Regulation then basically becomes an arms race between companies that use algorithms for their commercial purposes and regulators that use algorithms to inspect whether this usage by companies conforms with legal requirements.

4. A theoretical understanding of the digital transformation challenges

To obtain a theoretical understanding of the challenges of the digital transformation, they can be organised on the basis of two dimensions. First, a distinction can be made between internal challenges – challenges related to the use of digital technologies by government organisations – and external challenges – challenges related to the use of digital technologies in the economy and society (most importantly: big tech). Second, a distinction can be made between challenges that are related to what Scharpf (1999) refers to as the input and output dimensions of legitimacy. The input dimension refers to 'legitimate power': the positions and responsibilities of key actors, mechanisms for empowerment, and their checks and balances. The output dimension refers to the production of outputs for society in the form of public values and how these are distributed.[2]

On the basis of these two dimensions, we can develop the following overview of the main challenges for governing the digital transformation:

Table 1. Main challenges for governing the digital transformation

	Digital transformation of government	Digital transformation of society
Legitimate power	Legitimate use of digital technologies by government	Legitimate power positions of big tech in society
Public values	Government use of digital technologies contributes to public values	Use of digital technologies by big tech contributes to public values

There is a substantial amount of research on each of these four cells. In the context of this chapter, I would like to highlight the main issues mentioned in the literature to sketch the fundamental nature of these challenges.

Legitimate use of digital technologies by government

A key concern in the literature is that use of digital technologies by government can result in a lack of accountability and consequently a decline in citizen trust in government. Busuioc (2021) concludes:

> Such transformations are taking place insidiously rather than in a deliberate and considered manner, with bureaucratic actors losing the ability to understand, scrutinise, and exercise meaningful control. These concerns are compounded by the fact that these developments increasingly impact non-routine, high-stakes areas (such as criminal justice) where the exercise of human discretion and expertise has been regarded as critical to their implementation. The twin foundations of bureaucratic legitimacy – bureaucratic expertise and accountability – are being simultaneously diminished.

In a systematic assessment of the legitimacy threat of algorithms, Grimmelikhuijsen and Meijer (2022) make similar observations and highlight the following key issues related to the legitimate use of digital technologies by government: erosion of democratic control, limited responsiveness, violated procedural responsiveness, and lack of checks and balances.

Government use of digital technologies contributes to public values

The current debate focuses mainly on possible negative effects of key values such as non-discrimination and equity; however, various authors have highlighted that analyses should also focus on the positive outcomes that can be realised for values such as effectiveness and efficiency, and maybe also for equity and non-discrimination. The issue of public values produced by governments using digital technologies has been discussed extensively by Bannister and Connolly (2014) and they emphasise that information and communication technologies can and do have transformative effects on public values, for better and for worse. More specifically, Selten and Meijer (2021) analyse the available literature and use Hood's (1991) distinction of clusters of public values to analyse (expected) effects of the use of AI on public values. They conclude that algorithms can strengthen organisational performance (sigma values) but generate risks for fairness and transparency (theta values), while there has been little attention paid to the ability of organisations to be adaptive and robust (lambda values).

Legitimate power positions of big tech in society

There have been many important analyses of the growing role of big tech in society and the risks that this brings with it in terms of the concentration of unchecked power in a limited number of big companies (see also Gerbrandy and Phoa, 2022, on what they call "modern bigness"). A key contribution to the debate on the power of big tech is Shoshana Zuboff's (2019) *The age of surveillance capitalism*. In this rich analysis of the fundamental changes to capitalism, Zuboff highlights that surveillance is a key feature of modern capitalist societies and a key source of profit. Her analysis highlights that, similar to the need to regulate labour conditions in the Industrial Revolution, this transformation of the capitalist mode of production requires a strong state to counter the concentration of enormous information powers in the hands of big tech industries.

Use of AI by big tech contributes to public values

The risk that the use of digital technologies may have a negative influence on public values in society has been discussed in great detail by Van Dijck et al. (2018). They analyse the changing dynamics through the introduction of various platforms in four sectors – news, urban transport, healthcare, and education – and assess these changes in terms of their consequences for public values. This results in a host of specific insights. Even though they acknowledge that platforms can make a positive contribution to these four sectors, they also identify a wide variety of risks. For news, the risks to journalistic independence and accurate and comprehensive news coverage are identified. For transport, the authors highlight the risks of labour conditions (for example for Uber drivers) and the erosion of public infrastructures. For healthcare, not only are individuals' rights to control their data threatened, but also the whole idea of health as a public rather than a private good. For education, they conclude that there is not only a threat to privacy but also to pedagogical autonomy and the quality of education. An overarching concern is that comprehensive public values in all these sectors – reliable news, mobility for everyone, accessible healthcare, and high-quality education – will be eroded by a focus on partial (commercial) interests of platforms.

5. Responses to the challenges of digital transformation

In current literature, there is an emphasis on the need to limit perverse outcomes of the digital transformation. At the same time, less attention has been paid to a more strategic perspective on the new position of government in society.

Regulating the digital transformation

Both in the academic world and in the public sector, responses to the digital transformation can roughly be grouped into two types: 'hard rules' in the form of legislation or organisational rules; and 'soft rules' such as rules for responsible coding and reflection tools for organisations (Blomqvist, 2018). These two are of course complementary, but they present a different emphasis.

The digital transformation takes place within a broad set of legal requirements for data security, privacy, transparency, and other key legal principles. These requirements have been established over time in response to the various technological developments. Currently, there is much concern regarding the rapid development and pervasiveness of AI and platforms resulting in new legal frameworks. The best-known current example of hard rules for the digital transformation is the European AI Act (AIA, which has been formally approved by the European Parliament and the European Council in 2024, and which will start applying in 2026. The AIA presents a risk-based approach to regulating both single-purpose AI systems and general-purpose AI systems and models such as ChatGPT. The AIA is a key example of regulation both for the digital transformation in government and the digital transformation in society. Specifically as regards the external transformation, important academic work is being done by legal scholars investigating new forms of competition law. Gerbrandy and Phoa (2022) argue that the power of big tech should be understood not only as market power but as a combination of instrumental power, structural power, and discursive power that manifests itself in economies as well as in political and personal domains. For this reason, they highlight that competition law needs to be amended to fit the new reality.

While hard rules, especially the European AIA, have received most attention in the media and also in the academic literature, quite a bit of attention has also been paid to soft rules. In view of the complexity and speed of technological developments, formal rules will never be able to capture all practices; hence, rules that emphasise the responsibility of organisations and professionals are important complements to formal rules (Hagemann et al., 2018).

A first group of soft rules are the various reflection instruments that are being developed to assist organisations in making deliberate choices – choices that guarantee public values when digital technologies are introduced. One of these reflection tools is the Code for Good Digital Governance, which has been developed for the Netherlands Ministry of the Interior to structure reflection on good governance in a digital age. This Code emphasises the need to reflect on the risks that digital systems may create for 30 key values for good governance, clustered around key values of democracy, rule of law, and government competence. Another instrument is the Fundamental Rights Impact Assessment (FRIA), which focuses on analysing the impact of the use of artificial intelligence on human rights. This reflective tool is directly connected to hard rules since a FRIA is compulsory for all high-risk AI.

A second group of soft rules is called 'responsible coding', which builds upon the idea of professional standards. Standards for developers of complex technological systems need to be drafted and professional coders are expected to be trained in and adhere to these standards. These guidelines are still being developed and their nature and focus is discussed in a growing number of publications on ethics and data science (for an overview see Saltz and Dewar, 2019). These discussions also have direct implications for training programmes for data scientists. Lewis and Stoyanovich (2022) highlight the importance of teaching data scientists not only technical skills but also ethical issues in AI, legal compliance, data quality, algorithmic fairness and diversity, transparency of data and algorithms, privacy, and data protection.

Strategic responses to the digital transformation

While regulation is of key importance, there is more to governance than regulation. Strategic government responses to the digital transformation entail more than avoiding perverse effects: these responses refer to aligning the internal and external digital transformations. Governments need to make a strategic analysis of what is needed from digital government in an age where society is also transforming. This strategic analysis covers the functions, structures and position of government in society and some key domains for strategic responses are highlighted here.

A first set of responses concerns the strategic build-up of informational capacities for the state (Lember et al., 2018). While governments have been focusing on developing the information capacities they need for public services, internal processes, policy development, and regulation, they need to realise that information capacities are required that connect all these functions and enable governments. They need to take the step from a fragmented perspective to a holistic perspective on informational capacities. Governments need to step up their game to prevent a huge information asymmetry between government and big tech which might effectively make government powerless. This will be a key challenge for all governments, but especially for weaker states.

A second domain of action is the development of public infrastructures (Ianacci, 2010). Building infrastructures has been a key activity for governments, but processes of privatisation have resulted in a more limited role. In view of the key importance of digital infrastructures in control over societal processes, there is a need for governments to step back in and assume some form of control over public infrastructures. Current EU efforts to develop public cloud facilities are urgently needed (Geilenberg et al., 2024), but the experiences with Gaia X also highlight how difficult it is for governments to take a position in this complex field, especially since the investment capacities of big tech companies are so incredibly high.

A third domain is the strategic support and facilitation of civic tech. Following Chatwin and Mayne, 2020, p. 215), I define civic tech as an ecosystem of stakeholders which centres the use of boundary-spanning data, design, and technology to support the interaction of democratic institutions with citizens. This strategic domain is about building new relations with online communities to strengthen their capacity to address a variety of social issues and engage in innovation and learning for developing innovative solutions (Mačiulienė and Skaržauskienė, 2020). These new connections to a rapidly expanding online civil society presents an important new strategic potential for governments that need to respond to the digital transformation of society.

In addition, there is the broad domain of (international) security. This will obviously be a key challenge for government and requires a host of responses (Dunn Cavelty and Wenger, 2020). This topic, however, requires a separate discussion (see also the chapter by Greta Nasi in this book).

6. Research agenda

The governance of the digital transformation is currently emerging as a key topic in Public Administration research. Whereas previously most research on this topic was published in specialised journals such as *Government Information Quarterly* and *Information Polity*, many papers on this topic are now also published in key journals in the field such as *Public Administration Review, Public Management Review*, and *Public Administration*. Nearly two decades ago, I complained that mainstream Public Administration scholars were failing to listen to researchers who highlighted the importance of digitalisation

(Meijer, 2007), but this has now completely changed. This means that the digital transformation is no longer viewed in isolation but is connected to other debates about the future of Public Administration focusing on the expertise, autonomy, and structure of government.

Research into the governance of the digital transformation is rapidly expanding (Meijer, 2018; Andrews, 2019; Busuioc, 2021), but much of the research still focuses on technological and organisational processes. There is an urgent need for rigorous research that assesses the extent to which the digital transformation can actually provide new answers to the grand societal challenges such as security, poverty, social inclusion, and sustainability. The promise of technology is presented by a range of 'believers' but the extent to which this promise can be realised with the new technologies requires an in-depth evaluation and large-scale comparative research that does not focus on the output – functioning technological systems – but on the outcome – implications for public values such as sustainability, democracy, education, security, and health.

Recently, we have seen that the need to establish hard and soft rules to tackle the risks connected to the digital transformation have been proposed and also implemented in various forms, such as the AIA, codes for good digital governance, and ethical standards for professional data scientists. As academics, we need to assess whether the variety of rules that have been proposed actually helps to tackle risks and ensure digital practices that are legitimate and contribute to public values. In essence, this means that traditional approaches from Public Administration research focusing on evaluating policy plans and regulatory efforts are needed. This requires scholars in our field to work in interdisciplinary teams with information scientists, legal scholars, media scientists, and academics from other fields. Our expertise is needed in these interdisciplinary teams to help societies and make sure that the digital transformation will indeed bring us a better world.

Finally, the strategic implications of the digital transformation for government have hardly received any systematic attention in the literature. Strategic capacities are crucial for aligning the internal and external digital transformations. There is some work on the building up informational capacities, limited work on the role of government in the realisation of public infrastructures, and some work on civic tech, but this is still at a very preliminary stage. There is a need to combine our knowledge about strategising (Ferlie and Ongaro, 2022) with research into the digital transformation to provide new insights. As a final note, we as a community of scholars should not be afraid to extend our knowledge outputs from good empirical and theoretical work to more prospective and futuring work. The future is being shaped now and we should engage to ensure that this shaping does not result in a scary technocracy but in a legitimate form of government that produces the public values that society desires.

Notes

1. https://www.zuid-holland.nl/onderwerpen/digitaal-zuid-holland/vervolg-expeditie-publieke-platformen/.
2. Vivienne Schmidt (2013) has highlighted the relevance of throughput legitimacy, and this was translated by Grimmelikhuijsen and Meijer (2022) to the digital transformation of government. This throughput dimension provides an important nuance but for this chapter I have chosen to focus on the main argument provided by Scharpf (1999).

References

Andrews, L. (2018). Public administration, public leadership, and the construction of public value in the age of algorithm and big data. *Public Administration, 97*(2), 296–310. https://doi.org/10.1111/padm.12534.

Bannister, F., & Connolly, R. (2014). ICT, public values and transformative government: A framework and programme for research. *Government Information Quarterly, 31*(1), 119–128. https://doi.org/10.1016/j.giq.2013.06.002.

Blomqvist, P. (2018). Soft and hard governing tools. In C. Ansell & J. Torfing (Eds.), *Handbook on Theories of Governance* (pp. 267–278). Edward Elgar Publishing. https://doi.org/10.4337/9781800371972.00035.

Busuioc, M. (2020). Accountable artificial intelligence: Holding algorithms to account. *Public Administration Review, 81*(5), 825–836. https://doi.org/10.1111/puar.13293.

Chatwin, M., & Mayne, J. (2018). Improving monitoring and evaluation in the civic tech ecosystem: Applying contribution analysis to digital transformation. *JeDEM-eJournal of eDemocracy and Open Government, 12*(2), 216–241. https://doi.org/10.29379/jedem.v12i2.598.

Cordella, A., & Paletti, A. (2019). Government as a platform, orchestration, and public value creation: The Italian case. *Government Information Quarterly, 36*(4), 1–15. https://doi.org/10.1016/j.giq.2019.101409.

Dunn Cavelty, M., & Wenger, A. (2019). Cyber security meets security politics: Complex technology, fragmented politics, and networked science. *Contemporary Security Policy, 41*(1), 5–32. https://doi.org/10.1080/13523260.2019.1678855.

Eom, S. J., & Lee, J. (2022). Digital government transformation in turbulent times: Responses, challenges, and future direction. *Government Information Quarterly, 39*(2), 1–9. https://doi.org/10.1016/j.giq.2022.101690.

Eubanks, V. (2018). *Automating Inequality: How High-Tech Tools Profile, Police, and Punish the Poor*. St. Martin's Press.

Ferlie, E., & Ongaro, E. (2022). *Strategic Management in Public Services Organizations: Concepts, Schools and Contemporary Issues* (2nd ed.). Routledge. https://doi.org/10.4324/9781003054917.

Geilenberg, V., Kleis, H., Mize, J., & Schulz, W. H. (2022). From self-descriptions (SD) to self-recommendations (SR): Evolving Gaia-X for the future European economy. *International Journal of Information Management Data Insights*, 4(2), 1–9. https://doi.org/10.1016/j.jjimei.2024.100249.

Gerbrandy, A., & Phoa, P. (2022). The power of big tech corporations as modern bigness and a vocabulary for shaping competition law as counter. In M. Bennett, H. Brouwer, & R. Claassen (Eds.), *Wealth and Power: Philosophical Perspectives* (1st ed., pp. 166–185). Routledge. https://doi.org/10.4324/9781003173632-11.

Grimmelikhuijsen, S., & Meijer, A. (2022b). Legitimacy of algorithmic decision-making: Six threats and the need for a calibrated institutional response. *Perspectives on Public Management and Governance*, 5(3), 232–242. https://doi.org/10.1093/ppmgov/gvac008.

Hagemann, R., Huddleston Skees, J., & Thierer, A. (2016). Soft law for hard problems: The governance of emerging technologies in an uncertain future. *Colorado Technology Law Journal*, 17(1), 37–130. https://ctlj.colorado.edu/wp-content/uploads/2019/03/3-Thierer_3.18.19.pdf.

Henderson, J. C., & Venkatraman, N. (1993). Strategic alignment: Leveraging information technology for transforming organizations. *IBM Systems Journal*, 32(1), 4–16. https://doi.org/10.1147/sj.382.0472.

Homburg, V. (2008). *Understanding e-government: Information systems in public administration* (1st ed.). Routledge. https://doi.org/10.4324/9780203885642.

Hood, C. (1991). A public management for all seasons? *Public Administration*, 69(1), 3–19. https://doi.org/10.1111/j.1467-9299.1991.tb00779.x.

Iannaci, F. (2010). When is an information infrastructure? Investigating the emergence of public sector information infrastructures. *European Journal of Information Systems*, 19(1), 35–48. https://doi.org/10.1057/ejis.2010.3.

Lember, V., Kattel, R., & Tõnerist, P. (2016). Technological capacity in the public sector: The case of Estonia. *International Review of Administrative Sciences*, 84(2), 214–230. https://doi.org/10.1177/0020852317735164.

Lewis, A., & Stoyanovich, J. (2022). Teaching responsible data science: Charting new pedagogical territory. *International Journal of Artificial Intelligence in Education*, 32, 783–807. https://doi.org/10.1007/s40593-021-00241-7.

Lorenz, L., Van Erp, J., & Meijer, A. (2022). Machine-learning algorithms in regulatory practice: Nine organisational challenges for regulatory agencies. *Technology and Regulation*, 2022, 1–11. https://doi.org/10.26116/techreg.2022.001.

Lucas Jr, H. C., & Goh, J. M. (2009). Disruptive technology: How Kodak missed the digital photography revolution. *The Journal of Strategic Information Systems*, 18(1), 46–55. https://doi.org/10.1016/j.jsis.2009.01.002.

Mačiulienė, M., & Skaržauskienė, A. (2020). Building the capacities of civic tech communities through digital data analytics. *Journal of Innovation & Knowledge*, 5(4), 244–250. https://doi.org/10.1016/j.jik.2019.11.005.

Meijer, A. (2007). Why don't they listen to us? Reasserting the role of ICT in public administration. *Information Polity*, 12(4), 233–242. https://doi.org/10.3233/IP-2007-0127.

Meijer, A. (2018). Datapolis: A public governance perspective on "smart cities". *Perspectives on Public Management and Governance, 1*(3), 195–206. https://doi.org/10.1093/ppmgov/gvx017.

Meijer, A., & Grimmelikhuijsen, S. A. (2020). Responsible and accountable algorithmization: How to generate citizen trust in governmental usage of algorithms. In M. Schuilenburg, & R. Peeters (Eds.), *The Algorithmic Society: Technology, Power, and Knowledge* (1st ed., pp. 53–66). Routledge. https://doi.org/10.4324/9780429261404-5.

Meijer, A., & Webster, C. W. R. (2020). The COVID-19-crisis and the information polity: An overview of responses and discussions in twenty-one countries from six continents. *Information Polity, 25*(3), 243–274. https://doi.org/10.3233/IP-200006.

Meijer, A., Ruijer, E., & Dekker, R. (2020). *Navigatiestrategie. Lessen uit drie casusstudies over de kennispositie van de Tweede Kamer op het gebied van digitalisering.* USBO Advies. https://www.uu.nl/sites/default/files/Rapport%20USBO%20Advies%20voor%20TCDT.pdf

Mergel, I., Edelmann, N., & Haug, N. (2019). Defining digital transformation: Results from expert interviews. *Government Information Quarterly, 36*(4), 1–16. https://doi.org/10.1016/j.giq.2019.06.002.

Trittin-Ulbrich, H., Scherer, A. G., Munro, I., & Whelan, G. (2021). Exploring the dark and unexpected sides of digitalization: Toward a critical agenda. *Organization, 28*(1), 8–25. https://doi.org/10.1177/1350508420968184.

O'Neil, C. (2016). *Weapons of Math Destruction: How Big Data Increases Inequality and Threatens Democracy.* Crown.

Pappas, I. O., Mikalef, P., Dwivedi, Y., Jaccheri, L., Krogstie, J., & Mäntymäki, M. (2019). *Digital Transformation for a Sustainable Society in the 21st Century* (1st ed.). Springer Cham. https://doi.org/10.1007/978-3-030-39634-3.

Saltz, J. S., & Dewar, N. (2019). Data science ethical considerations: A systematic literature review and proposed project framework. *Ethics and Information Technology, 21*, 197–208. https://doi.org/10.1007/s10676-019-09502-5.

Scharpf, F. W. (1999). *Governing in Europe: Effective and Democratic?* Oxford University Press. https://doi.org/10.1093/acprof:oso/9780198295457.001.0001.

Schmidt, V. A. (2013). Democracy and legitimacy in the European Union revisited: Input, output and "throughput". *Political Studies, 61*(1), 2–22. https://doi.org/10.1111/j.1467-9248.2012.00962.x.

Selten, F., & Meijer, A. (2019). Managing algorithms for public value. *International Journal of Public Administration in the Digital Age, 8*(1), 1–16. https://doi.org/10.4018/IJPADA.20210101.oa9.

Strømmen-Bakhtiar, A. (2019). *Introduction to Digital Transformation and its Impact on Society.* Informing Science Press.

Van Dijck, J., Poell, T., & De Waal, M. (2018). *The platform society: Public values in a connective world.* Oxford University Press. https://doi.org/10.1093/oso/9780190889760.001.0001.

Vial, G. (2019). Understanding digital transformation: A review and a research agenda. *The Journal of Strategic Information Systems, 28*(2), 118–144. https://doi.org/10.1016/j.jsis.2019.01.003.

Zuboff, S. (2019). *The Age of Surveillance Capitalism: The Fight for a Human Future at the New Frontier of Power.* Profile Books.

PART 3
FUTURES OF CITIZEN-STATE INTERACTIONS

The rise of sceptical citizens about public administration communication

by María José Canel

Addressing citizens with trustworthy and reliable messages is becoming one of the most challenging issues public administrations are facing nowadays across the world (Bjørnå and Salomonsen, 2016; Canel and Luoma-aho, 2019; Luoma-aho and Canel, 2020; Overman et al., 2020; De Boer, 2020; Boon and Salomonsen, 2020). According to both research and survey data (see below), citizens are increasingly showing more reluctant and sceptical attitudes towards governments' communication about public policies and issues, and this is forcing policymakers to rethink and reflect about their communications, as well as to look for new ways of approaching citizens.

This chapter explores this trend of sceptical citizens in connection with recent developments in the field of communication research. By connecting public administration sciences and communication sciences, this chapter provides insights into how convergences between these two fields could improve our understanding of how public administrations work.

The structure is as follows. First, the conceptual approach to defining the trend is presented, followed by its supporting data. Negative and positive consequences are discussed, and finally lines of development and the research agenda are defined.

1. Conceptual approach to presenting the trend of more sceptical citizens

Three concepts are relevant for articulating the description of this trend. First is the concept of communication in relation to public administration. The more explicit term provided by literature is that of 'public sector communication', defined as:

> goal-oriented communication inside organizations and between organizations and their stakeholders that enables public sector functions, within their specific cultural/political settings, with the purpose of building and maintaining the public good and trust between citizen and authorities. (Canel and Luoma-aho, 2019, p. 33)

Two aspects of this definition are of interest for the purposes of this chapter. First, communication must be geared towards enabling public sector functions, which means that messages and narratives must be supported by real behaviours and achievements; and second, the goal of maintaining the public good and trust entails long-term approaches in order to build longstanding relationships between public sector organisations and stakeholders.

The second concept is that of 'post-truth', a term which was incorporated into dictionaries in the year 2016, after the Trump and Brexit campaigns triggered the use of this word (Flood, 2016; Jeffries, 2017). The Oxford Dictionary defines post-truth as: "Circumstances in which objective facts are less influential in shaping public opinion than appeals to emotion and personal belief" (Oxford English Dictionar, 2016). Based on a review of research that explores the concept (Russo, 2017; Wilber, 2017; d'Ancona, 2017; McIntyre, 2018; Waisbord, 2018; Ihlen et al., 2019), post-truth could be described as follows. 'Post-truth' indicates a condition of current societies by which feelings have more weight than evidence in public discourse and, as a consequence, falsehoods are presented even when there is evidence to the contrary. Post-truth has changed the way people relate to facts (Waisbord 2018), as it involves 'alternative facts' that replace actual ones (McIntyre 2018). Referring to this concept, Gil and Jiménez state that post-truth has "given way to a society without truth, or, as it would be translated in German, to a society that had left facts behind (*postfaktisch*)" (Gil and Jiménez, 2019, p. 251).

Since 2016 scholars have explored the notion and consequences of post-truth, and literature shows a certain consensus about the fact that it does not refer to a new way of handling the truth (see for instance Harsin, 2015; Lockie, 2017; Macnamara, 2018; Gil and Jiménez, 2019; Ihlen et al., 2019). For the purposes of this chapter, a specific characteristic is stressed here in order to categorise the trend under analysis in relation to public administration. Post-truth is not just and merely a denial of the factual, but refers to the relevance given to emotions that gives rise to a condition of "a certain relativism where personal values, beliefs and emotions take precedence" (Ihlen et al., 2019, p. 2). What counts are not facts but "the feelings that are generated by the news and the attitudes of the recipient who follows it" (Gil and Jiménez, 2019, p. 251).

This 'post-truth condition' of today's societies, by which emotions are overweighted to the detriment of facts, challenges public administrations to overcome citizens' scepticism towards their messages and communication. To the extent that the truth and veracity of facts and data lose relevance, shared references are weakened and it becomes more difficult to keep a common ground when communicating. This leads to the third and last aspect of the present conceptual approach.

The term 'post-communication' has been coined in the field of corporate communication to refer to the non-real communication that is associated with the 'post-truth condition' (Waisbord, 2018; Macnamara, 2018). Post-truth derives from a change in the conditions in which communication unfolds today; as a result of that change, shared evaluations of realities have become more difficult. Audiences tend to base their judgements less on facts and instead to consume the pieces of information that are in line with and reaffirm their prejudices and biases. As a consequence, factual data are put at the service of narratives by blurring the border between fact and fiction, between truth and lies. Ultimately, what is right and what is wrong is no longer relevant (Ihlen et al., 2019, p. 2).

Referring to the communication that organisations undertake to address their stakeholders, 'post-communication' is a one-way, propagandistic, top-down form of communication that aims not at mutual benefit but at the interests of the communicating organisation (Macnamara, 2018). Communication therefore is no longer oriented towards the establishment of longstanding relationships, but rather it becomes easier for audiences to perceive governments and public administrations with scepticism, reluctance, and distrust (Sanders and Canel, 2013).

2. Supporting data

This chapter does not deal with citizen distrust or with discontent, but rather with the scepticism with which citizens see governmental messages and communication about public policies and policy issues. Scholarly literature considers that citizens' perceptions about public policy communication are shaped by the extent to which governments are seen as being transparent (transparency), providing accessible information (accessibility), facilitating opportunities for citizen input (responsiveness), and being honest (integrity) in their communication practices (see for instance He and Ma, 2020; Piotrowski et al., 2019; Dreshpak et al., 2020; Moreno et al., 2020; Hyland-Wood et al., 2021; Sauer et al., 2021; Mansoor, 2021). What follows is a collection of recent data related to these factors, and which are provided by surveying companies as well as by institutes that conduct research on social trends. Disregarding that the following data do not include an analysis of an evolution over time, they allow us to state that citizens' scepticism towards governmental messages deserves the attention of both scholars and practitioners of public administration.

Amongst the data referring to *transparency*, recent global barometers find that about half of respondents (46%) think that the government is a source of false or misleading information (versus 39% who think it is a reliable source of trustworthy information) (Edelman Trust Institute, 2023). There is no series data on this, but since 2018, when the Edelman Trust Institute titled its report *The Battle for Truth*, this entity has been reporting an increase in scepticism of citizens towards information: 70% of those surveyed are worried about false information or fake news being used as a weapon (2018), a figure that increased to 73% in 2019, and 76% in 2022. Regarding US citizens specifically, nearly two-thirds of adults find it hard to tell what is true when elected officials speak (Pew Research Center, 2019).

As regards *accessibility*, only 50 out of the 142 countries (about one-third) included in the World Justice Project Rule of Law Index score over 0.6 on a 0–1 scale, with 1 indicating the strongest adherence to the rule of law. This index is comprised of factors which indicate features relating to the trend looked at in this chapter. One factor measures whether publicised laws and government data are presented in plain language, as well as whether administrative regulation, drafts of legislation, and high court decisions are made accessible to the public in a timely manner. The factor 'right to information' measures whether requests for information held by a government agency are granted, whether these requests are granted within a reasonable time period, whether the information provided is pertinent and complete, whether requests for information are granted at a reasonable cost and without having to pay a bribe, and whether relevant records are accessible to the public upon request. Finally, the 'civic participation' factor measures the openness of government, defined by the extent to which a government shares information, empowers people with tools to hold the government accountable, and fosters citizen participation in public policy deliberations (World Justice Project, 2023). Regarding US citizens specifically, the Pew Research Centre reported in 2019 that 69% of them say the federal government intentionally withholds important information from the public that it could safely release (Pew Research Center, 2019). This figure is slightly higher (71%) in the year 2022 (Pew Research Centre, 2022a).

Not much data is available about how governments facilitate opportunities for citizen input (*responsiveness*). Only one in three of surveyed EU citizens think the political system allows people to have a say in what government does (European Social Survey, 2020). In the case of the US, only 8% describe the government as being responsive to the needs of ordinary Americans, and 65% think political candidates run for office to serve their own personal interests rather than their communities' (Pew Research Center, 2022b). At a more global level, the Edelman Trust Institute reports that listening is a top trust-building action for citizens: 82% of respondents agree that the factor "'hear our concerns and let us ask questions' is important to earning or keeping their trust in the governments to be good managers of change" (Edelman Trust Institute, 2024).

As regards *integrity*, the Edelman Trust Barometer reports that governments are seen as far less competent and ethical than business (52 points less), and 63% of respondents think that government leaders are purposely trying to mislead people by saying things they know are false or gross exaggerations (Edelman Trust Institute, 2024). For its part, Ipsos has been conducting a survey since 1983 to measure trust in 31 professions. In 2023 the Ipsos Veracity Index (measuring whether professionals are generally trusted to tell the truth) reveals that the proportions of people who say they trust politicians and government ministers to tell the truth have reached their lowest scores since the survey began. Government ministers is one of the five least trusted professions (with a score of 10%), along with "politicians generally" (9%). It should be mentioned, however, that civil servants are at the middle of the table with a score of 51% (Ipsos Veracity Index, 2023).

3. Is this a desirable trend? What will be the positive/negative effects?

For an overall assessment of this trend of citizens' scepticism towards government and public administration messages, Ihlen et al.'s (2019) assertion bluntly indicates negative effects: "the post-truth condition is detrimental to democratic societies" (p. 3). In the same vein, d'Ancona (2017) states that, in post-truth, "the art of lying is shaking the very foundations of democracy" (p. 1). However, exploring the negative effects in detail allows us to identify associated positive effects, and this is what is dealt with in this section.

Negative effects of more sceptical citizens

The negative effects of the increase in citizens' scepticism towards messages about public policies associated with the post-truth condition of today's societies have been widely addressed by literature, and there are three major effects referred to.

The first has to do with how audiences are changing *in how they relate to facts*. The post-truth condition of today's societies is characterised by this in the sense that facts have become less relevant. The negativeness of this effect becomes particularly visible in the attitude towards scientific evidence: a significant part of the debate about post-truth revolves around denialist discourse on climate change. This discourse, according to critics, downplays scientific evidence in order to advance a specific ideological position (Murphy, 2016; Lockie, 2017; Ihlen et al., 2019). Post-truth ignores the science developed in relation to topics which are crucial for the development of societies (e.g. sustainability), and lowering the relevance of true facts may make it more difficult to reach agreements between the different sides and actors involved in a policy issue.

The second negative effect is the *upsurge of populism*. Literature has extensively explored he relationship between post-truth and populism, stating that the upsurge of populist politics is symptomatic of the consolidation of post-truth communication as a distinctive feature of contemporary politics (Waisbord, 2018). Despite its length, I am including the following quote because it is representative of this negative effect of the post-truth condition:

> [Populist politics] stands in opposition to the possibility of truth-telling as a collective effort to produce agreed-upon facts and reach consensus on the correspondence between assertions and reality, and it thrives in the context of wide-ranging challenges to elite definition of truth and reality. Populism opposes fundamental principles of democratic communication such as the need for fact-based, reasoned debate, tolerance, and solidarity; it rejects key principles of public communication, including the role of watchdog journalism, unfettered speech, state protection of speech rights, citizens' access to public information, and the centrality of deliberation across difference. (Waisbord, 2018, pp. 17–18)

The last identified negative effect is the *increased fragmentation of societies*. According to Waisbord (2018, p. 4), "[p]ost-truth denotes shifts in the structural conditions for public communication that are needed for truth-telling as agreements on the representation of reality. Truth-telling demands that publics share norms and judgments in the understanding of reality". If that sharing is lacking, communication becomes more difficult. In post-truth communication, truth becomes an illusion, "or at least so relative as to be stretched beyond any boundaries of reality" (Russo, 2017, p. 3). As a consequence, the possibilities of identifying and preserving common grounds are diminished, and the fragmentation of opinions about shared values increases. The epistemic foundation of societies "becomes more polarized, fragmented, uncertain, and fluid, grasping the ways in which organizations communicate becomes important to understand what contributes to an increase or decrease in social fragmentation" (Ihlen et al., 2019, p. 4). This fragmentation of societies makes it more difficult for dialogue to be developed between the public administration and its audiences; when common grounds are blurred in the public debate, consensus is hindered.

Are there positive effects associated with more sceptical citizens?

One possible positive effect is that more sceptical citizens become more demanding about policymakers supporting their messages in deeds and actual behaviours. More sceptical citizens tend to increase pressure on governments, expecting more facts and achievements from their words. Research on communication about public administration reforms has shown that the more the making and the telling come together in communication, the higher the chances of civil society being able to collaborate with the public administration (Bouckaert et al., 2023). How to apply this to the communication of public policy and administration needs to be explored.

A related positive effect of this trend is an increased demand from stakeholders for public sector organisations to be authentic. Research has been developed around the notion of authenticity in relation to corporate social responsibility and corporate social advocacy (see for instance Molleda, 2010; Carroll and Wheaton, 2009; Parcha and Kingsley, 2020; Lim and Jiang, 2021), which may inspire developments in public administrations.

Authenticity refers to the quality of being true in substance, and Molleda (2010) suggests that "the construct of authenticity" represents "the consistency between the genuine nature of corporate offerings and their communication" (p. 233). Applying the concept of authenticity to public administrations would entail addressing not only the challenge of being genuine in its commitments, but also the challenge of communicating practices in an authentic manner, an issue I turn to next.

4. What should be done to respond to the trend of sceptical citizens?

Five major lines of development are identified here to address the trend under analysis.

Authentic communication versus post-truth communication

Scholarly research on public relations and communication emphasises that quality relationships between organisations and the public derive from the practice of authentic communication that reflects the character, values, and heritage of an organisation (Carroll and Wheaton, 2009; Molleda, 2010; Lim and Liang, 2021).

The conclusions of a previous study on how a public sector organisation (a provincial government) used communication to encourage collaboration among different actors to advance social policies (Bouckaert et al., 2023) can be applied to what should be done to address the 'post-communication' typical of a 'post-truth society'. This study showed that communicating in order to engage audiences in collaboration goes beyond crafting messages to 'sell' policies, and requires both 'walking the talk and talking the walk' (Bouckaert et al., 2023, p. 233). This is related to the challenge of combining substance with presentation. More specific case studies and analyses are needed to inspire both the study and the practice of public administration communication.

Advancing the definition and projection of a public administration's identity

Crafting and communicating authenticity entails going beyond a plan, a programme, or a campaign. Being authentic has to do with portraying the essence of what an entity or an organisation fundamentally is, including permanent associations with its actions, decisions, and philosophy of living up to its own and others' expectations and needs (Molleda, 2010, p. 224). Work needs to be done in order to advance the definition and projection of the public administration's identity, which includes better and more clearly identifying the list of attributes that should be attributed to it by its audiences. Attempts such as those of Canel (2014, 2018), Carpenter (2014), Waeraas and Maor (2014), Carpenter and Krause (2012), da Silva and Batista (2007), Castilla (2006), and Garnett (1997) are contributions upon which to build.

This endeavour should take into account what research has achieved regarding corporate identity in the private sector (Whetten, 1997; Deephouse, 1999; King and Whetten, 2008; Koschmann et al., 2012; Olins, 1990; Suchman, 1995).

Research has shown that the communication of an organisation is perceived as authentic when it is connected to the existential essence of the organisation as claimed, and when there is a high degree of concordance between a company's espoused identity as reflected in its communication and its identity as conceived by stakeholders (Lim and Liang, 2021). Practitioners and scholars should work together to identify the gaps between public administrators' definitions of identity and audiences' perceptions of the latter, explore the causes of these gaps, and define actions to address gaps (Canel, 2018).

Building upon Carroll and Wheaton's work (2009) on the projection of an organisation identity, the following could be taken as clues to work on the projection of the identity of the public administration. Projecting authenticity requires: (a) an identity claim be visibly projected; (b) the purported identity be credible; and (c) the identity to be perceived as reflecting the meaning of authenticity in question.

Authenticity is projected more credibly when it is organisationally constructed. By organisational construction, what is meant is "that a specific lasting feature of the organization (usually part of its structure or operations) radiates the symbolic meaning about authenticity that lies at the heart of the appeal of the producer and its products or services" (Carroll and Wheaton, 2009, p. 274). Public administrations should work on what 'organisational construction' is needed to portray authentic purpose when communicating public policies. This includes choosing the attributes that best fit the policy context, making them visible in the organisational structures, and guaranteeing these attributes' durability.

Dealing with the fragmentation of values by communication aimed at finding common ground

In addressing the post-truth condition of today's societies, several authors call for using communication to search for what we have in common (Russo, 2017; Macnamara, 2018; Ihlen et al., 2019; Waisbord, 2018; López and Monfort 2017). In this regard, what Macnamara (2018) notes about the word 'communicate' itself is meaningful: it comes from the Latin *communis* ('community' or 'commonness') and from the Latin verb *communicare* ('create' or 'build'), and thus "communication is by definition a *two-way* interactive process aimed, not only at persuasion, but at coming together to share meaning and understanding – not necessarily agreement, but understanding, accommodation, adaptation, co-orientation" (Macnamara, 2018, p. 12). Both the study and the practice of public administration must work on how communication can help by making it explicit what the common grounds and values are to different actors who are working together for the common good.

Advancing public sector communication by learning from 'real world laboratories'

The above-mentioned analysis of the development of a collaborative governance programme in the Basque region of Gizpukoa (Barandiarán et al., 2023) concluded by identifying several mechanisms and conditions for collaboration between the public sector and civil society to happen. Several of them include learnings about communication practice.

One of those conditions refers to listening and learning as part of communication, and states that "the higher the levels of internal and of external active collaborative listening and learning, the higher the chances of collaborative governance" (Bouckaert et al., 2023, p. 242). Listening and learning is about feedback mechanisms, which should impact and improve public administration processes. Public administrations need to work on ways of systematising organisational listening and learning in order to put citizens at the core of policymaking (Macnamara, 2017, 2019).

Another identified mechanism for collaborative governance is related to forms and segmentation of communication, and states that "the more different forms of communication for different purposes and different target groups, the higher the chances of collaborative governance" (Bouckaert et al., 2023, p. 242). Since public administrations are being challenged to establish relationships with new, diverse, and probably mutually contradicting audiences, it appears to be key to segment the public, as well as to craft and channel the message accordingly.

A key challenge that emerges when observing real cases of public administration reforms is that of combining actions with messages. "Communicating collaborative governance is more about acting together than about sending messages" (Bouckaert et al., 2023, p. 242). Communicating public policies requires combining substance with presentation. In other words, emphasis not only has to be placed on actions, facts, and actual performance, but also on staging and making this visible.

5. The impact on the research agenda

Considering the challenges and opportunities that are entailed by more sceptical citizens associated with the post-truth condition of today's societies, the impact on the research agenda can be set out in the following terms.

There are several aspects of communication practice that require a scholarly contribution to address sceptical citizens. Knowledge is needed to: manage stakeholders' expectations to better adjust public policies to what is both needed and possible; develop solid narratives for aligning different audiences around common goals; combine distributed and shared power with the necessary consistent coordination of communication among different and sometimes divergent actors; engage the media's attention with policies which are mainly based on intangible aspects; and better address the suspicion in message receivers, which derives from the instrumentalisation of policies through self-promoting communication (Sanders and Canel, 2013; Canel and Luoma-aho, 2019; Luoma-aho and Canel, 2020; Wæraas and Byrkjeflot, 2012).

At the theory, conceptual, and disciplinary level, more interdisciplinary links between studies and the science of communication and of Public Administration should be developed. In the face of the challenges ahead, it can be stated that the future of Public Administration should embrace communication science for several reasons, from which the following are identified.

The first reason relates to the crucial role that communication plays in the successful implementation of public policies (Canel, 2018, 2007; Canel and Luoma-aho, 2019; Luoma-aho and Canel, 2020). By applying concepts, theories, and methodologies from the field of communication, clearer and more concise communication strategies can be developed for more efficient and effective policies.

Second, advancing the development of Public Administration increasingly entails and requires engaging citizens in collaboration, and communication science provides valuable insights into how to engage and communicate with diverse stakeholders. This is particularly the case in relation to the collaboration that is at the basis of the development of the SDGs from the 2030 Agenda. Public administrations can leverage communication strategies to foster meaningful dialogue, collaboration, and participation in decision-making processes (Luoma-aho and Canel, 2020; Piqueiras et al., 2020; Bouckaert et al., 2023). The question about what drives authenticity and perceptions of authentic policies is also relevant, as well as the connections between these drivers and trust in public administration. This entails exploring what is "authentically trustworthy" (Molleda, 2010) in public administration.

Third, in times of uncertainty and turbulence, effective communication has shown to be critical for managing risks and crises and coordinating response efforts. By integrating communication science, Public Administration can develop crisis communication plans and strategies to effectively communicate with the public during risks and emergencies (Frandsen and Johansen, 2020). Studies around the role of communication in addressing the consequences of the pandemic caused by COVID-19 (see for instance Hyland-Wood et al., 2012; Sauer et al., 2021) show how communication can help the public sector to fulfil its functions.

Fourth, communication plays an important role in developing intangible resources such as citizen engagement, reputation, legitimacy, social responsibility, and trust. Research has shown the crucial relevance of intangible capital for the sustainable and inclusive social and economic development of countries (Secundo et al., 2020; Massaro et al., 2018; Suciu and Năsulea, 2019). Building intangible resources has become a decisive factor for a more sustainable society (Matos et al., 2019), showing that the human, structural, and relational dimensions of intangible capital are interrelated with the maximisation of sustainable performance. Intangible capital, resources, and practices, in both private and public sector organisations, are cross-cutting factors to shape the cultural change of organisations and civil society and foster a solid commitment to sustainable reforms in public administration.

Of particular relevance is the intangible value that is developed in the form of social capital, which is a relational capital as it resides in the relations among individuals and organisations (Barandiarán et al., 2022; Johnston and Lane, 2018; Maak, 2007; Yang and Taylor, 2013). Through building and maintaining relationships, and facilitating communication among different actors, communication contributes to the accumulation of social capital, and this social capital will be paramount as a pre-condition for the development of alliances among public administrations and diverse actors to address the challenges ahead.

Fifth and finally, communication science emphasises the importance of feedback and evaluation in communication processes, and this information can be used by public administrations to assess the effectiveness of their communication strategies, gather feedback from stakeholders, and make data-driven improvements to communication practices (Macnamara, 2020a; Macnamara, 2020b). This feedback information from stakeholders is particularly helpful for identifying gaps that might exist between public administrations' achievements and their messages, as well as between the latter and what their audiences perceive (Canel, 2018).

On the whole, communication science may help in understanding and improving how public administrations function, and also how they can better serve the needs of citizens in an increasingly complex and interconnected world.

References

Boon, J., & Houlberg Salomonsen, H. (2020). Public sector organizations and reputation. In V. Luoma-aho, & M.-J. Canel (Eds.), *The Handbook of Public Sector Communication* (pp. 215–227). John Wiley & Sons. https://doi.org/10.1002/9781119263203.ch14.

Barandiarán, X., Murphy, A., & Canel, M. J. (2022). Qué aporta la escucha al capital social? Lecciones de un proceso de aprendizaje de líderes públicos. *Gestión y Política Pública, 31*(1), 1–30. https://doi.org/10.29265/gypp.v31i1.1011.

Barandiarán, X., Canel, M.J., & Bouckaert, G. (Eds.) (2023), *Building Collaborative Governance in Times of Uncertainty. Pracademic Lessons from the Basque Gipuzkoa Province.* Leuven University Press. https://doi.org/10.11116/9789461665058.

Bouckaert, G., Canel, M. J., & Barandiarán, X. (2023). Conclusions: Pracademic lessons learned. In X. Barandiarán, M. J. Canel, & G. Bouckaert (Eds.), *Building Collaborative Governance in Times of Uncertainty: Pracademic Lessons from the Basque Gipuzkoa Province* (pp. 229–244). Leuven University Press. https://doi.org/10.2307/j.ctv35r3v4r.16.

Bjørnå, H., & Houlberg Salomonsen, H. (2016). Reputation and brand management in Scandinavian municipalities. *Scandinavian Journal of Public Administration, 20*(2), 3–5. https://doi.org/10.58235/sjpa.v20i2.14950.

Canel, M.-J. (2007). *Comunicación de las Instituciones Pública.* Editorial Tecnos.

Canel, M.-J. (2014). Reflexiones sobre la reputación ideal de la Administración Pública. In M. Herrero López, A. Cruz Prados, R. Lázaro, & A. Martínez Carrasco (Eds.), *Escribir en las almas. Estudios en honor de Rafael Alvira* (pp. 69–88). Eiunsa. https://mariajosecanel.com/pdf/lareputacionidealdelaadmonpublica.pdf.

Canel, M.-J. (2018). *La Comunicación de la Administración Pública: Para Gobernar con la Sociedad.* Fondo de Cultura Económica.

Canel, M.-J., & Luoma-aho, V. (2019). *Public Sector Communication. Closing Gaps between Citizens and Organization.* John Wiley & Sons. https://doi.org/10.1002/9781119135630.

Carpenter, D. (2014). *Reputation and Power: Organizational Image and Pharmaceutical Regulation at the FDA.* Princeton University Press. https://muse.jhu.edu/book/31134.

Carpenter, D. P., & Krause, G. A. (2011). Reputation and public administration. *Public Administration Review, 72*(1), 26–32. https://doi.org/10.1111/j.1540-6210.2011.02506.x.

Carroll, G., & Wheaton, D. (2009). The organizational construction of authenticity: An examination of contemporary food and dining in the US. *Research in Organizational Behavior, 29*, 255–282. https://doi.org/10.1016/j.riob.2009.06.003.

Castilla, J. I. M. (2003). Valor y valores de una administración al servicio público. *Auditoría Pública: Revista de los Organos Autónomos de Control Externo, 38*, 25–34. https://asocex.es/wp-content/uploads/PDF/200604_38_25.pdf.

D'Ancona, M. (2017). *Post-Truth: The New War on Truth and How to Fight Back.* Ebury Press.

da Silva, R., & Batista, L. (2007). Boosting government reputation through CRM. *International Journal of Public Sector Management, 20*(7), 588–607. https://doi.org/10.1108/09513550710823506.

De Boer, N. (2020). How do citizens assess street-level bureaucrats' warmth and competence? A typology and test. *Public Administration Review, 80*(4), 532–542. https://doi.org/10.1111/puar.13217.

Deephouse, D. L. (1999). To be different, or to be the same? It's a question (and theory) of strategic balance. *Strategic Management Journal, 20*(2), 147–166. https://doi.org/10.1002/(sici)1097-0266(199902)20:2<147::aid-smj11>3.0.co;2-q.

Dreshpak, V. M., Kovalov, Babachenko, N. V., V. G., & Pavlenko, E. M. (2020). Communicative policy of public authorities in European countries: Comparative analysis. *International Journal of Management, 11*(6), 529–543. https://doi.org/10.34218/IJM.11.6.2020.046.

Edelman Trust Institute (2022). *2022 Edelman Trust Barometer: Global Report*. Edelman Trust Institute. Retrieved July 2, 2024, from https://acortar.link/OghpK1.

Edelman Trust Institute (2023). *2023 Edelman Trust Barometer Global Report*. Edelman Trust Institute. Retrieved July 2, 2024, from https://acortar.link/1niAbt.

Edelman Trust Institute (2024). *2024 Edelman Trust Barometer. Innovation in Peril*. Edelman Trust Institute. Retrieved July 2, 2024, from https://www.edelman.com/sites/g/files/aatuss191/files/2024-02/2024%20Edelman%20Trust%20Barometer%20Global%20Report_FINAL.pdf.

European Social Survey (2022). *Democracy, Digital Social Contacts*. ESS Data Portal. Retrieved July 9, 2024, from https://ess.sikt.no/en/?tab=overview.

Flood, A. (2016). "Post-Truth" named Word of the Year by Oxford Dictionaries. *The Guardian*. https://www.theguardian.com/books/2016/nov/15/post-truth-named-word-of-the-year-by-oxford-dictionaries.

Frandsen, F., & Johansen, W. (2020). Public sector communication: Risk and crisis communication. In V. Luoma-aho, & M.-J. Canel (Eds.), *The Handbook of Public Sector Communication* (pp. 229–244). Wiley Blackwell. https://doi.org/10.1002/9781119263203.ch15.

Garnett, J. L. (1997). Administrative communication: Domain, threats, and legitimacy. In J. L. Garnett & A. Kouzmin (Eds.), *Handbook of Administrative Communication* (1st ed., pp. 1–20). Marcel Dekker, Inc.

Gil, A., & Jiménez Cataño, R. (2019). Special issue on post-truth. *Church, Communication and Culture, 4*(3), 251–254. https://doi.org/10.1080/23753234.2019.1664919.

Harsin, J. (2015). Regimes of Posttruth, Postpolitics, and Attention Economies. *Communication, Culture and Critique, 8*(2), 327–333. https://doi.org/10.1111/cccr.12097.

He, A. J., & Ma, L. (2021). Citizen participation, perceived public service performance, and trust in government: Evidence from health policy reforms in Hong Kong. *Humanities and Social Sciences Communications, 44*(3), 471–493. https://doi.org/10.1080/15309576.2020.1780138.

Hyland-Wood, B., Gardner, J., Leak, J., & Ecker, U. K. H., (2021). Toward effective government communication strategies in the era of COVID-19. *Humanities and Social Sciences Communications, 8*(1), 1–11. https://doi.org/10.1057/s41599-020-00701-w.

Ihlen, Ø., Gregory, A., Luoma-aho, V., & Buhmann, A. (2019). Post-truth and public relations: Special section introduction. *Public Relations Review, 45*(4), 1–4. https://doi.org/10.1016/j.pubrev.2019.101844.

IPSOS (2021). *Ipsos Veracity Index 2023: Trust in Professions Survey*. IPSOS. Retrieved June 20, 2024, from https://www.ipsos.com/sites/default/files/ct/news/documents/2023-12/ipsos-trust-in-professions-veracity-index-2023-charts.pdf.

Jeffries, S. (2017). "Bullshit is a Greater Enemy than Lies" – Lessons from Three New Books on the Post-Truth Era. *The Guardian*. https://www.theguardian.com/us-news/2017/may/22/post-truth-era-trump-brexit-lies-books.

Johnston, K. A., & Lane, A. (2018). Building relational capital: The contribution of episodic and relational community engagement. *Public Relation Review, 44*(5), 633–644. https://doi.org/10.1016/j.pubrev.2018.10.006.

King, B. G., & Whetten, D. A. (2008). Rethinking the relationship between reputation and legitimacy: A social actor conceptualization. *Corporate Reputation Review, 11*(3), 192–207. https://doi.org/10.1057/crr.2008.16.

Koschmann, M. A., Kuhn, T. R., & Pfarrer, M. D. (2012). A communicative framework of value in cross-sector partnerships. *Academy of Management Review, 37*(3), 332–354. https://doi.org/10.5465/amr.2010.0314.

Lim, J. S., & Jiang, H. (2021). Linking authenticity in CSR communication to organization-public relationship outcomes: Integrating theories of impression management and relationship management. *Journal of Public Relations Research, 33*(6), 464–486. https://doi.org/10.1080/1062726X.2022.2048953.

Lockie, S. (2017). Post-truth politics and the social sciences. *Environmental Sociology, 3*(1), 1–5. https://doi.org/10.1080/23251042.2016.1273444.

López Vazquez, B., & Monfort, A. (2017). Creating shared value in the context of sustainability: The communication strategy of MNCs. In O. L. Emeagwali (Ed.), *Corporate Governance and Strategic Decision Making*. Intech Open. https://doi.org/10.5772/intechopen.70177.

Luoma-aho, V., & Canel, M. J. (2020). *The Handbook of Public Sector Communication*. John Wiley & Sons, Inc. https://doi.org/10.1002/9781119263203.

Maak, T. (2007). Responsible leadership, stakeholder engagement, and the emergence of social capital. *Journal of Business Ethics, 74*(4), 329–343. https://doi.org/10.1007/s10551-007-9510-5.

Macnamara, J. R. (2017). *Creating a "democracy for everyone": Strategies for increasing listening and engagement by government*. The London School of Economics and Political Science and University of Technology Sydney. https://www.lse.ac.uk/media-and-communications/assets/documents/research/2017/MacnamaraReport2017.pdf.

Macnamara, J. R. (2018). Public relations and post-communication: Addressing a paradox in public communication. *Public Relations Journal, 11*(3), 1–20. https://opus.lib.uts.edu.au/bitstream/10453/122293/1/PR%20and%20Post-Communication.pdf.

Macnamara, J. R. (2019). Explicating listening in organization–public communication: Theory, practices, technologies. *International Journal of Communication, 13*, 5183–5204. https://ijoc.org/index.php/ijoc/article/view/11996/2839.

Macnamara, J. R. (2020a). New developments in best practice evaluation: Approaches, frameworks, models, and methods. In V. Luoma-aho, & M.-J. Canel (Eds.), *The Handbook of Public Sector Communication* (pp. 435–454). Wiley Blackwell. https://doi.org/10.1002/9781119263203.ch28.

Macnamara, J. R. (2020b). Public sector communication measurement and evaluation. In V. Luoma-aho, & M.-J. Canel (Eds.), *Handbook of Public Sector Communication* (pp. 361–365). John Wiley & Sons, Inc. https://doi.org/10.1002/9781119263203.part5.cM

Mansoor, M. (2021). Citizens' trust in government as a function of good governance and government agency's provision of quality information on social media during COVID-19. *Government Information Quarterly, 38*(4), 1–14. https://doi.org/10.1016/j.giq.2021.101597.

Massaro, M., Dumay, J., Garlatti, A., & Dal Mas, F., (2018). Practitioners' views on intellectual capital and sustainability: From a performance-based to a worth-based perspective. *Journal of Intellectual Capital, 19*(2), 367–386. https://doi.org/10.1108/JIC-02-2017-0033.

Matos, F., Vairinhos, V., Selig, P. M., & Edvinsson, L. (2019). *Intellectual Capital Management as a Driver of Sustainability: Perspectives for Organizations and Society*. Springer International Publishing. https://doi.org/10.1007/978-3-319-79051-0.

McIntyre, L. (2018). *Post-Truth*. MIT Press. https://doi.org/10.7551/mitpress/11483.001.0001.

Molleda, J. C. (2010). Authenticity and the construct's dimensions in public relations and communication research. *Journal of Communication Management, 14*(3), 223–236. https://doi.org/10.1108/13632541011064508.

Moreno, Á., Fuentes-Lara, C., & Navarro, C. (2020). Covid-19 communication management in Spain: Exploring the effect of information-seeking behavior and message reception in public's evaluation. *Profesional de la Información, 29*(4), 1–16. https://doi.org/10.3145/epi.2020.jul.02.

Murphy, R. (2016). Conceptual lenses to bring into focus the blurred and unpack the entangled. *Environmental Sociology, 2*(4), 333–345. https://doi.org/10.1080/23251042.2016.1229592.

Olins, W. (1990). *Corporate identity: Making business strategy visible through design*. Harvard Business School Press.

Overman, S., Wood, M., & Busuioc, M. (2020). A multidimensional reputation barometer for public agencies: A validated instrument. *Public Administration Review, 80*(3), 415–425. https://doi.org/10.1111/puar.13158.

Oxford English Dictionary (2016). Post-Truth. https://www.oed.com/dictionary/post-truth_adj?tl=true.

Parcha, J. M., & Kingsley Westerman, C. Y. (2020). How corporate social advocacy affects attitude change toward controversial social issues. *Management Communication Quarterly, 34*(3), 350–383. https://doi.org/10.1177/0893318920912196.

Pew Research Center (2019, June 5). *Many Americans Say Made-Up News Is a Critical Problem That Needs To Be Fixed*. Retrieved July 2, 2024, from https://www.pewresearch.org/journalism/2019/06/05/many-americans-say-made-up-news-is-a-critical-problem-that-needs-to-be-fixed/.

Pew Research Center (2022a, June 6). *Americans' Views of Government: Decades of Distrust, Enduring Support for Its Role: 1. Public Trust in Government*. Retrieved July 2, 2024, from https://ur0.jp/d8lrF.

Pew Research Center (2022b, June 6). *Americans' Views of Government: Decades of Distrust, Enduring Support for Its Role: 2. Public views about the federal government*. Retrieved July 3, 2024, from https://acortar.link/CgaGze.c

Pew Research Center (2024, June 24). *Public Trust in Government: 1958–2024*. Retrieved July 2, 2024, from https://ur0.jp/t3lN9.

Piotrowski, S., Grimmelikhuijsen, S., & Deat, F., (2019). Numbers over narratives? How government message strategies affect citizens' attitudes. *Public Performance & Management Review, 42*(5), 1005–1028. https://doi.org/10.1080/15309576.2017.1400992.

Piqueiras, P., Canel, M.-J., & Luoma-aho, V. (2020). Citizen engagement and public sector communication. In V. Luoma-aho & M.-J. Canel (Eds.), *Handbook of Public Sector Communication* (pp. 277–287). John Wiley & Sons. https://doi.org/10.1002/9781119263203.ch18.

Russo, G. (2017, May 18). Donald Trump and the Era of Post-Truth. *La Voce Di New York*. http://www.lavocedinewyork.com/en/news/2017/05/18/donald-trump-and-the-era-of-post-truth/.

Sauer, M. A., Truelove, S., Gerste, A. K., & Limaye, R. J. (2021). A failure to communicate? How public messaging has strained the COVID-19 response in the United States. *Health Security, 19*(1), 65–74. https://doi.org/10.1089/hs.2020.0190.

Secundo, G., Ndou, V., Del Vecchio, P., & De Pascale, G., (2020). Sustainable development, intellectual capital and technology policies: A structured literature review and future research agenda. *Technological Forecasting and Social Change, 153*, 1–21. https://doi.org/10.1016/j.techfore.2020.119917.

Suchman, M. C. (1995). Managing legitimacy: Strategic and institutional approaches. *Academy of Management Review, 20*(3), 571–610. https://doi.org/10.2307/258788.

Suciu, M. C., & Năsulea, D.-F. (2019). Intellectual capital and creative economy as key drivers for competitiveness towards a smart and sustainable development: Challenges and opportunities for cultural and creative communities. In F. Matos, V. Vairinhos, P. M. Selig, & L. Edvinsson, (Eds.), *Intellectual capital management as a driver of sustainability: Perspectives for organizations and society* (pp. 67–97). Springer International Publishing. https://doi.org/10.1007/978-3-319-79051-0_5.

Wæraas, A., & Byrkjeflot, H. (2012). Public sector organizations and reputation management: Five problems. *International Public Management Journal, 15*(2), 186–206. https://doi.org/10.1080/10967494.2012.702590.

Wæraas, A., & Maor, M. (Eds.) (2014). *Organizational Reputation in the Public Sector*. Routledge.

Waisbord, S. (2018). The elective affinity between post-truth communication and populist politics. *Communication Research and Practice, 4*(1), 17–34. https://doi.org/10.1080/22041451.2018.1428928.

Whetten, D. A. (1997). Part II: Where do reputations come from? Theory development and the study of corporate reputation. *Corporate Reputation Review, 1*(1), 25–34. https://doi.org/10.1057/palgrave.crr.1540011.

Wilber, K. (2017). *Trump and a Post-truth World*. Shambhala Publications.

World Justice Project (2023). *World Bank Leader: Rule of Law is "Essential" to Sustainable Development*. Retrieved July 2, 2024, from https://acortar.link/c4C8SB.

Yang, A., & Taylor, M. (2012). The relationship between the professionalization of public relations, societal social capital and democracy: Evidence from a cross-national study. *Public Relations Review, 39*(4), 257–270. https://doi.org/10.1016/j.pubrev.2013.08.002.

Politicisation and populism: The future of the frontline of public services

by Gabriela Lotta

1. The trend of politicisation and populism

"There is confusion between ideological preferences and functional duties of police officers […] It is in the nation's interest that all public servants fulfil their duties." This phrase was uttered by Flavio Dino, the Brazilian Minister of Justice of the new Lula government, on 8 January 2023, when a group of Bolsonaro's supporters attacked and invaded the Supreme Court, National Congress, and Presidential Palace. The lack of a police reaction was the primary explanation for why institutions could be invaded. Videos from the invasion showed that many police officers helped the attackers. This frightening situation is evidence of a process of ideological radicalisation of the police that has been experienced in Brazil in recent years during Bolsonaro's government, a period when the country faced a process of democratic backsliding. However, it is also an example of how politicisation around policies can affect street-level bureaucrats' abilities to implement policies and comply with their official duties.

Numerous countries have witnessed a recent upsurge in authoritarian populism and democratic backsliding (Bauer et al., 2021). Unlike the military coups and interventions of the past, the current processes are more subtle and generally involve the arrival in office of elected presidents who change the country's institutions from within (Yesilkagit, 2018), as has occurred, for example, in Hungary, Turkey, Mexico, Brazil, and in the United States under Trump. This new authoritarian populism, many times reinforced by New Public Management reforms that have weakened the institutions (Peters and Pierre, 2022), exploits the considerable potential for institutional contagion and democratic backsliding (Levitsky and Ziblatt, 2018). Recent studies have shown how these authoritarian populist leaders deal with the public administration and, mainly, the state bureaucracy (Peters and Pierre, 2021; Rockman, 2021), highlighting practices such as co-option, loyalty, and sidelining (Bauer et al., 2021). However, these studies have generally focused on middle- and senior-ranking bureaucrats, who are more directly affected by presidential decision-making. Few studies have examined the effects of this new authoritarian populism at the street level.

Street-level bureaucrats are responsible for implementing policies and directly affecting the image of the state and the services and rights received by the population (Lipsky, 2010). Although distant from the decision-making centre, street-level bureaucrats are crucial to politicians because they can alter the direction of public policies and government agendas (Hassan, 2021). Therefore, these authoritarian leaders tend to pressure street-level bureaucrats to implement the populist agenda, even if it goes against official duties or their own will (Eiró, 2022). Understanding how this process occurs remains a theoretical lacuna.

Although street-level bureaucrats possess extensive discretionary powers, they are embedded in institutional, cultural, and organisational environments that influence their decisions (Brodkin, 2021; Maynard-Moody and Musheno, 2003). Therefore, populist government contexts are expected to affect the behaviour of street-level bureaucrats in different ways. Populist politicians can politicise and polarise the context of policy implementation by carrying out institutional changes, pressuring street-level bureaucrats through discourse, or even creating conflicts between citizens and street-level bureaucrats (Lotta et al., 2024). Understanding the work of street-level bureaucrats in these contexts thus contributes to a more specific agenda of studying authoritarian populism and democratic backsliding and a research agenda on polarisation and politicisation at the street level (Piotrowska, 2022). Moreover, understanding this process enables us to comprehend how service delivery can be affected in contexts of populism, generating consequences for citizens and their access to public rights.

This chapter aims to contribute to these themes by examining the relationship between authoritarian populist governments and street-level bureaucrats. Moreover, we intend to observe this process over time. We contend that authoritarian populists influence the work of street-level bureaucrats not only during their time in government but also when out of power by crafting narratives and generating tensions between citizens and workers on policy issues. Therefore, understanding this process is crucial not just for nations already under populist governments but also for other countries experiencing a rise in populist and authoritarian discourses within society.

For that, we explore in this chapter how the context of polarisation and politicisation during and after the populist authoritarian government affected the perceptions and behaviours of street-level bureaucrats when implementing policies under their responsibility. Based on findings from different papers and research, we present here the main consequences of the politicisation on street-level bureaucracy work.

2. What is the evidence?

Given the increase in authoritarian populist governments worldwide in recent years (Levitsky and Ziblatt, 2018), many scholars have focused on understanding how these politicians deal with public administration in general and public bureaucracies in particular (see, for example, Bauer et al., 2021; Peters and Pierre, 2022, 2020; Rockman, 2019; Moynihan, 2022; Story et al., 2023). Given the plurality of definitions, we employ the concept of populism proposed by Mudde and Rovira Kaltwasser as follows:

> A thin-centered ideology that considers society to be ultimately separated into two homogenous and antagonistic groups, 'the pure people' and the 'corrupt elite,' and which argues that politics should be an expression of the volonté générale of the people (general will of the people). (Mudde and Rovira Kaltwasser, 2017, p. 6)

Central to this concept is the idea that authoritarian populists govern by fomenting antagonism between social groups and adopting an anti-pluralistic approach that refuses to accept different ideas. Furthermore, the agendas of populist leaders are conceived to centre on an attempt to express what they consider a general will. Therefore, they tend to polarise and politicise many policy issues, creating the idea of what is good or bad for their supporters and which are good citizens. At the same time, since they wish to maintain their power, they must effectively deliver an agenda recognised by their supporters and fight against what they consider antagonists. This explains why these politicians rely on bureaucracy, given that the agenda has to be implemented by the public administration and its bureaucrats.

Consequently, populist politicians have conflictual and mutually dependent relationships with bureaucrats. On the one hand, they need them to implement their agenda, which is when politicians try to win their loyalty (Hajnal and Boda, 2021) or empower them (Peters and Pierre 2019). But on the other hand, bureaucrats may impose barriers to the implementation of new agendas (Eiró, 2022), either because they do not believe in new agendas or because the new agendas are illiberal or even illegal. In these cases, as a reaction, populist politicians categorise bureaucrats as among their enemies and attempt to sideline them:

> As public administration has become a pluralist institution in modern democracies, populists will need to address it in their quest to 'rewrite the operational manual of the state in their favor' (Müller 2016:56); that is, they need to mold and steer it according to their ideological needs. (Bauer and Becker, 2020, p. 20)

Studies highlight how the New Public Management reforms increased this process as, in weakening public institutions and the bureaucracies, populist politicians find more space to change the institutions from inside and to attack or co-opt bureaucrats, imposing their new agendas (Peters and Pierre, 2022). On the other side, studies have also shown that bureaucrats may respond to these processes in different ways. They may become loyal or may resist, using different strategies, such as voice, exit, and sabotage (Guedes-Neto and Peters, 2021; O'Leary, 2017; Lotta et al., 2023). The outcome of this war, in which populists attempt to seize control and bureaucrats offer resistance, depends on the capacity of both types of actors to use effective strategies (Lotta et al., 2023). Despite these recent advances in the literature, most studies have analysed this process by observing high- and mid-ranking bureaucrats who are closer to politicians.

However, while high- and mid-level bureaucrats can pose many barriers to authoritarian populists, it is at the street level that conflict can be most critical. These politicians require street-level bureaucrats to maintain their popularity by implementing agendas that appeal to their constituencies. Street-level bureaucrats are defined as actors who implement policies in daily relations with citizens (Lipsky, 2010). They are the faces of the state (Dubois, 1999) and, simultaneously, gatekeepers of public services (Brodkin, 2011). Street-level bureaucrats are recognised by a high degree of decision-making autonomy (Cohen and Golan Nadir, 2020) and lack of control (Lipsky, 2010). However, the use of discretionary powers is neither unique nor random (Rutz et al., 2017) and is strongly regulated and influenced by the institutional environment (Huising and Silbey, 2011; Piore, 2011; Davidovitz and Cohen, 2020; Gofen, 2014), as it is permanently embedded in political, organisational, and policy contexts (Rutz et al., 2017, Baviskar and Winter, 2017; Brodkin, 2011). This means that changes in the political context may affect street-level behaviour (Eiró, 2022). Moreover, street-level bureaucrats may suffer political pressure (Hassan, 2021; Hinterleitner and Wittwer, 2022; Davidovitz and Cohen, 2021) to change how they act (Eiró, 2022). On the other side, street-level bureaucrats may react in different ways to this process, depending on their values and on the resources they have.

Therefore, despite being far from the centre of power, street-level bureaucrats are extremely important for politicians since the latter need the compliance of street-level bureaucrats to implement their agenda (Hassan, 2021). This explains why politicians usually need to convince, co-opt, or coerce street-level bureaucrats to ensure the implementation of their projects at the local level (Hassan, 2021).

The pressure to guarantee that street-level bureaucrats comply with and implement the politician's agenda is a common issue in a democracy (Gofen, 2014). However, the purposes and instruments to do it are different in the context of authoritarian populism, where the rule of law and the checks and balances systems are under attack (Story et al., 2023; Lotta et al., 2023). Moreover, they may also be affected by the institutional capacities of each country that may, or may not, be affected by New Public Management reforms (Peters and Pierre, 2022). In this way, we have to consider that both the attack on street-level bureaucrats and the instruments to do it are part of the authoritarian populist agenda. Understanding how street-level bureaucrats work in these contexts and the consequences of this process are yet to be explained and central to advancing a theory about street-level bureaucracy and democracy.

Looking at previous studies, there are different ways through which authoritarian populist politicians can try to enforce their agenda. First, they can try to co-opt street-level bureaucrats, using resources or instruments of punishment and incentives (Eiró, 2022; Piotrowska, 2022). The literature about patronage provides rich examples of how this works (see Peeters and Campos, 2022 and Kopecký et al., 2016 for more).

However, when they cannot co-opt street-level bureaucrats, politicians try to sideline and attack them, transforming them into one more enemy (Eiró, 2022). In this process, cutting resources and trying to change policy design is usually not enough, as street-level bureaucrats can develop forms of resistance (Lotta et al., 2022). Therefore, another strategy politicians use is to attack the very foundation of street-level bureaucrats and what legitimises their work, their bureaucratic ethos and professionalism, bashing bureaucrats (Caillier, 2018) and questioning their expertise (Lotta et al., 2021).

However, this process is not unilateral and street-level bureaucrats may change and adapt their implementation agenda to deal with the authoritarian populist. Considering what we know about street-level bureaucrats' behaviour, we expect them to react, handle, and cope with this context differently. For example, previous research shows how they can collaborate with politicians

(Eiró, 2022; Hassan, 2021; Piotrowska, 2022). However, they can also diverge and refuse to implement (Gofen, 2014), developing practices of sabotage or resistance (Eiró, 2022). They can try to moderate conflicts, counterbalance (Eiró, 2022), or 'voice'.

Despite some exploratory discussions about what happens to street-level bureaucrats working under authoritarian populist regimes, we are still missing a more systematic understanding of this process. In this chapter, we aim to contribute to the literature by understanding how politicians affect street-level bureaucrats, how these bureaucrats react to it, and which factors explain the reactions. For that, we analyse the Brazilian context under and after Bolsonaro's government, considered by the literature as a case of authoritarian populism that affected the work of bureaucrats (Peci, 2021; Peter and Pierre, 2022; Lotta et al., 2023; Lotta et al., 2024; Story et al., 2023).

3. Consequences of the trend: politicisation at the street level

To analyse the effects of the politicisation on street-level bureaucrats, we looked at recent studies published about Brazil under and after Bolsonaro's government. We also analysed 10 interviews carried out with teachers in December 2023 – one year after Bolsonaro's government – that are part of a broader research project to analyse the effects of the populism over time. We found essentially four consequences of the politicisation on street-level bureaucrats, detailed and exemplified below.

Conflicts and frictions at the street level

Political actions have the potential to render policies more conflictual and ambiguous, thereby undermining the capacity of street-level bureaucrats to implement them effectively (Matland, 1995). As populist discourses are based on the narrative of 'us versus them', it can significantly escalate conflicts and frictions at the street level, exerting detrimental effects at the street level.

The politicised environment can generate friction between street-level bureaucrats and their clients (Eiró, 2022). Citizens, expecting the implementation of policies or measures promised by politicians, may be frustrated or disappointed when these expectations are unmet by street-level bureaucrats. For instance, research on health and social workers highlighted how polarisation around the COVID-19 pandemic led to conflicts and even violence between street-level workers and citizens (Lotta et al., 2021).

Moreover, politicians aligned with populist agendas can erode citizens' trust in street-level bureaucrats, especially when these bureaucrats are portrayed as adversaries by the populist government. As trust is a cornerstone of street-level work (Davidovitz and Cohen, 2022a), its erosion can have profound implications for interactions between street-level bureaucrats and citizens, potentially escalating instances of violence (Davidovitz and Cohen, 2022b; Spink et al., 2021), as also found in Brazilian context (Bittencourt et al., 2021).

Moreover, these effects on trust may remain over time, even with changes in the government, as exemplified by this excerpt from an interview with a teacher one year after Bolsonaro's government:

> Just yesterday, I spoke with two mothers who were shocked by the art class where the teacher was discussing different religions. They complained that they didn't want Afro-religions in the classroom. We have been witnessing a significant ethical setback. There's always a family that says, 'You teachers are all abortionists, communists!' And everything we do is based on the curriculum and the rules!

Undermining street-level bureaucrats

Populist governments can significantly undermine the capacity of street-level bureaucrats to effectively carry out their responsibilities. One primary reason is that the actions implemented by politicians can personally target street-level bureaucrats, adversely affecting both their well-being and their motivation to implement policies.

Recent research conducted during Bolsonaro's government revealed a substantial decline in the self-efficacy of street-level bureaucrats, particularly in the context of the politicisation surrounding the COVID-19 pandemic (Lotta et al., 2024). The findings highlight how the populist approach interfered with the technical work of health workers, as encapsulated by a statement from one health worker: "Politicians are interfering in our technical work; we do not know whom to trust. Politicization is confusing people; we do not know how to make decisions, we do not know which way to go, and we must face a pandemic."

This example demonstrates that when politicians target street-level bureaucrats personally and subject them to political interference, it creates an atmosphere of confusion, eroding trust and self-confidence. Other research shows how the continuous bashing and criticism of teachers affects their physical and emotional ability (Ceballos and Carvalho, 2021). The environment of conflict created by populist discourses not only hampers street-level bureaucrats' ability to make effective decisions but also poses significant challenges to their overall well-being, ultimately undermining their capacity to carry out policies effectively.

Non-compliant behaviour (sabotage)

Another consequence of the politicisation of street-level bureaucracy is that it may change street-level bureaucrats' behaviour, leading to non-compliance with established rules or the adoption of a guerrilla-like approach in response to political pressures.

Regarding the first element, studies reveal that the expectations set by politicians regarding policy implementation can prompt street-level bureaucrats to deviate from established rules or resist complying with the agenda dictated by politicians. For instance, a study on police officers in Brazil highlighted how Bolsonaro's speeches influenced their decisions not to implement measures enforcing physical distancing or the use of masks during the pandemic (Alcadipani et al., 2021). This non-compliance with public health guidelines illustrates the direct impact of populist narratives on the behaviour of street-level bureaucrats, particularly in roles that involve enforcing regulations.

Regarding the second element, research on social workers has demonstrated a shift in behaviour as a form of resistance against changes proposed by Bolsonaro's government (Eiró, 2022). This resistance can manifest as a form of guerrilla behaviour, where street-level bureaucrats, motivated by disagreement with political agendas, intentionally modify their approach to align with their own professional values or counteract perceived detrimental policies.

In both cases, studies suggest that the influence of populist governments on street-level bureaucrats can lead to a divergence from established rules and the adoption of resistant or guerrilla-like behaviours, driven by a combination of political pressure and a desire to uphold professional integrity in the face of policies they perceive as harmful or contrary to their mission.

Inequalities in service delivery

Finally, another potential consequence of the politicisation is to generate new (or reproduce existing) inequalities in service delivery. The populist discourse of 'us versus them' may pressure street-level bureaucrats to take care of only 'good citizens' and not prioritise those considered 'enemies'. This selective provision of services can lead to the exclusion of others who may not share the same political views or align with the populist narrative. In essence, street-level bureaucrats may be compelled to favour individuals who endorse the populist ideologies, thus contributing to unequal access to services based on political alignment. This may even be reinforced in contexts where New Public Management reforms have already created divisions between 'good' and 'bad' citizens, or 'deserving' and 'non-deserving' ones. This type of inequality was found by previous research in Brazil showing how Bolsonaro encouraged civil servants to prioritise only those he considered 'good citizens' (*cidadão do bem*), meaning those who are not part of minorities and who do not support leftist agendas.

Another example comes from a recent interview with a teacher, one year after Bolsonaro's government. She says that:

> Engaging with students means engaging with the LGBTQIA+ community, and I have families who are against including gender issues in school. However, I have transgender students, and I need to discuss what they experience and respect their struggles. Yet we have been receiving many attacks from families complaining about what we do. I tell them: we have to include everyone; everyone is welcome, everyone should be accepted. But they continue not to accept. I see the issue with Black students now as well: there are students who now think they can call a Black person a monkey, thinking it's a joke. If we don't have discussions about these issues in school, we are accepting that one person humiliates another. However, it's very challenging to face the criticism from families and the attacks from churches.

This excerpt shows how emphasis on serving only a specific demographic aligned with the populist narrative, at the expense of others, underscores how populist governments can directly contribute to the exacerbation of inequalities through the actions and decisions of street-level bureaucrats. This selective favouritism not only reinforces existing disparities but also introduces new dimensions of inequality based on political alignment and who gets to be perceived as the deserving ones (usually aligned with populist ideas).

4. What should we do about it?

The four consequences presented here evidence how the politicisation of street-level bureaucracy may have many harmful consequences for policy implementation. It can, on the one hand, reduce policy outputs and outcomes, and at the same time increase existing inequalities. Therefore, understanding this process better and proposing solutions to reduce the politicisation may be crucial for the future of service delivery and welfare states.

In this sense, besides proposing a research agenda in the next section, we suggest here some basic measures that should be addressed in the future to prevent situations like those evidenced here. The cases reported in the literature show the importance of having a professional street-level bureaucracy that, based on their expertise and professional support, is strong enough to impose barriers to political interference. In this sense, it is important to invest in the professionalisation of street-level bureaucracy, especially in countries of the Global South where many bureaucracies are not professionalised (Peeters et al., 2024). Institutional protection may also come from strengthening the teams and the support that managers may give to street-level bureaucrats (Lotta et al., 2024).

It is also important to reinforce street-level bureaucracy protocols that may create more stabilised and protected practices of policy implementation, protecting the discretion and the directives that should guide them. This may also limit the political interference and the changes proposed by populist governments.

Public campaigns to valorise and protect street-level bureaucrats and to promote policies are also a potential solution to reduce the frictions on the ground, especially considering contexts in which populist governments get into public disputes over narratives or into practices of bashing.

Finally, it is important to anticipate the potential inequalities produced by populist governments in order to design policies that protect the most vulnerable groups. Policies with a clear aim to reduce inequalities and to guarantee access to the most vulnerable groups have to be clear about the priorities and the protocols that deal with inequalities.

5. Future studies on politicisation of street-level bureaucracy

As the literature review suggests, there are different ways in which authoritarian populism affects street-level bureaucrats and how they react to this process. Future research should further explore these issues for an understanding of what explains these differences. We propose here some dimensions to be explored by future work.

Professionalism: The literature on street-level bureaucracy has shown how professional status influences behaviour, identity, and the way street-level bureaucrats use their discretion (see, for example, Evans, 2010; Møller, 2021;

Cecchini and Harrits, 2021; Harrits, 2019; Malandrino and Sager, 2021). The literature also proposes how expertise and training, which are connected to professions, are essential components of the bureaucratic ethos (Møller et al., 2022). Future research should analyse whether and how professional identities and professionalism explain different reactions. Future work should for example test whether street-level bureaucrats with stronger professional identity are better able to resist the populist discourse, maintaining their professional practices.

Vocation: Street-level bureaucrats are a specific group of people subject to specific types of demands, forms of action, moral dimensions, and ethics related to what it is to be a street-level bureaucrat (Møller et al., 2022). To work in accordance with their expectations and roles, they have to be "committed to specific and historical patterns of moral qualities and skills in polytheistic organizational contexts with a variation of value-rational action specific to their office and its primary task" (p. 156). Similar discussions have been proposed by the literature about public service motivation, which analyses the connection between the desire of individuals to serve the public and the overall public interest. Future research should explore better the idea of vocation and how much it explains the capacity to react to populist discourses. It could test, for example, whether workers with high levels of vocation or or Public Service Motivation (PSM) are more able to resist changes proposed by authoritarian populist discourses.

Organisational environment: Street-level bureaucrats are highly influenced by the organisational environment (Brodkin, 2011; May and Winter, 2009; Hupe and Buffat, 2014), including culture (Cohen, 2018) and their relationships with peers and managers (Oberfield, 2014; Gassner and Gofen, 2018; Oberfield and Incantalupo, 2021; May and Winter, 2009). Previous research has shown how mid-level bureaucrats' reactions to authoritarian populists can be influenced by the organisational environment (Story et al., 2023). Future research should explore this issue at the street level, testing how much the support from peers and managers explains street-level bureaucrats' reactions to the populist discourse and if organisational autonomy influences these reactions.

Embeddedness: Street-level bureaucrats may have different levels of embeddedness in their communities. Embeddedness is defined as having strong ties to the citizens they interact with (Bhavnani and Lee, 2018; Pepinsky et al., 2018; Lotta and Marques 2020). Embeddedness improves policy implementation (Pepinsky et al., 2018), as it diminishes transaction costs in service distribution (Hassan, 2021), improves trust (Bhavnani and Lee, 2018), and increases the legitimacy of street-level bureaucrats (Lotta and Marques, 2020). Moreover, embeddedness can increase casuistry, meaning the "practical wisdom needed to deal prudently with individual cases" (Møller et al., 2022). Future research should explore how embeddedness in the community influences street-level bureaucracy responses to populist discourse. On the one hand, we might expect that street-level bureaucrats who are more embedded in the community where they work will be better able to impose barriers on the populist agenda as they are supported by the community. On the other hand, we might also expect embeddedness to play the opposite role, making street-level bureaucrats more sensitive to pressure from communities that are more aligned with the populist agenda. Future work should explore these issues.

6. Conclusion

This chapter has proposed an exploratory analysis of the complex relationship between authoritarian populism and street-level bureaucrats. Based on recent research on Bolsonaro's government, the chapter shows the multifaceted consequences of politicisation of public services. From heightened conflicts and frictions at the street level to the erosion of bureaucratic capacity, non-compliant behaviours, and perpetuation of inequalities in service delivery, the chapter captures the enduring impact of populist discourses on service delivery. This discussion contributes to scholarly discussions on authoritarian populism and populism in general, but it also has practical implications for policymakers. By shedding light on the complexities of political ideologies influencing public service delivery, the study informs strategies to uphold the integrity of street-level bureaucrats and fortify democratic institutions against populist challenges. As future research explores dimensions like professionalism, vocation, organisational environment, and embeddedness, a more nuanced understanding of bureaucrats' responses to populist discourses can emerge, offering valuable insights for both academia and practical governance.

References

Alcadipani, R., Cabral, S., Fernandes, A., & Lotta, G. (2020). Street-level bureaucrats under COVID-19: Police officers' responses in constrained settings. *Administrative Theory & Praxis*, 42(3), 394–403. https://doi.org/10.1080/10841806.2020.1771906.

Baviskar, S., & Winter, S. C. (2017). Street-level bureaucrats as individual policymakers: The relationship between attitudes and coping behavior toward vulnerable children and youth. *International Public Management Journal*, 20(2), 316–353. https://doi.org/10.1080/1096749 4.2016.1235641.

Bauer, M. W., Peters, B., Pierre, J., Yesilkagit, & K. Becker, S. (Eds.) (2021). *Democratic Backsliding and Public Administration: How Populists in Government Transform State Bureaucracies.* Cambridge University Press. https://doi.org/10.1017/9781009023504.

Bauer, M. W., & Becker, S. (2020). Democratic backsliding, populism, and public administration. *Perspectives on Public Management and Governance, 3*(1), 19–31. https://doi.org/10.1093/ppmgov/gvz026.

Bhavnani, R. R., & Lee A. (2018). Local embeddedness and bureaucratic performance: Evidence from India; *The Journal of Politics, 80*(1), 71–87. https://doi.org/10.1086/694101.

Bitencourt, María R., Alarcão, A. C. J., Silva, L. L., De Carvalho Dutra, A., Caruzzo, N. M., Roszkowski, I., Bitencourt, Marcos R., Marques, V. D., Pelloso, S. M., & De Barros Carvalho, M. D., (2021). Predictors of violence against health professionals during the COVID-19 pandemic in Brazil: A cross-sectional study. *PLOS ONE, 16*(6). https://doi.org/10.1371/journal.pone.0253398.

Brodkin, E. Z. (2011). Policy work: street-level organizations under new managerialism. *Journal of Public Administration Research and Theory, 21*(2), 253–277. https://doi.org/10.1093/jopart/muq093.

Brodkin, E. Z. (2021). Street-level organizations at the front lines of crises. *Journal of Comparative Policy Analysis: Research and Practice, 23*(1), 16–29. https://doi.org/10.1080/13876988.2020.1848352.

Cecchini, M., & Harrits, G. (2022). The professional agency narrative: Conceptualizing the role of professional knowledge in frontline work. *Journal of Public Administration Research and Theory, 32*(1), 41–57. https://doi.org/10.1093/jopart/muab021.

Cohen, N., & Golan-Nadir, N. (2020). Why do street-level bureaucrats risk themselves for others? The case of Israeli police officers. *Australian Journal of Public Administration, 79*(4), 480-494. https://doi.org/10.1111/1467-8500.12417.

Davidovitz, M., & Cohen, N. (2020). Playing defence: The impact of trust on the coping mechanisms of street-level bureaucrats. *Public Management Review, 24*(2), 279–300. https://doi.org/10.1080/14719037.2020.1817532.

Davidovitz, M., Cohen, N. (2021). Frontline social service as a battlefield: Insights from street-level bureaucrats' interactions with violent clients. *Social Policy & Administration, 56*(1), 73–86. https://doi.org/10.1111/spol.12756.

Davidovitz, M., Cohen, N., & Gofen, A. (2020). Governmental response to crises and its implications for street-level implementation: policy ambiguity, risk, and discretion during the COVID-19 pandemic. *Journal of Comparative Policy Analysis: Research and Practice, 23*(1), 279–300. https://doi.org/10.1080/13876988.2020.1841561.

Davis, K. C. (1969). *Discretionary justice: A preliminary inquiry.* Louisiana State University Press.

De Ceballos, A. G. C., & Carvalho, F. M. (2021). Violence against teachers and work ability: A Cross-sectional study in northeast Brazil. *Journal of Interpersonal Violence, 36*(19–20). https://doi.org/10.1177/0886260519881002.

De Sá e Silva, M. M. (2020). Once upon a time, a human rights ally: The state and its bureaucracy in right-wing populist Brazil. *Human Rights Quarterly, 42*(3), 646–666. https://doi.org/10.1353/hrq.2020.0036.

Dubois, V. (1999). *La vie au guichet. Administrer la misère* (2nd ed.). Economica.

Dussauge-Laguna, M. (2022). The promises and perils of populism for democratic policymaking: The case of Mexico. *Policy Sciences*, 55, 1–27. https://doi.org/10.1007/s11077-022-09469-z.

Eiró, F. (2022). Translating politics into policy implementation: Welfare frontline workers in polarized Brazil. *International Journal of Law in Context*, 18(3), 303–316. https://doi.org/10.1017/S1744552322000258.

Evans, T. (2010). Professionals, managers, and discretion: Critiquing street-level bureaucracy. *The British Journal of Social Work*, 41(2), 368–386. https://doi.org/10.1093/bjsw/bcq074.

Gassner, D., & Gofen, A. (2018). Street-level management: A clientele-agent perspective on implementation. *Journal of Public Administration Research and Theory*, 28(4), 551–568. https://doi.org/10.1093/jopart/muy051.

Gofen, A. (2014). Mind the gap: Dimensions and influence of street-level divergence. *Journal of Public Administration Research and Theory*, 24(2), 473–493. https://doi.org/10.1093/jopart/mut037.

Guedes-Neto, J. V., & Peters, G. (2021). Working, Shirking, and sabotage in times of democratic backsliding: An experimental study in Brazil. In M. W. Bauer, B. G. Peters, J. Pierre, K. Yesilkagit, & S. Becker (Ed.), *Democratic Backsliding and Public Administration: How Populists in Government Transform State Bureaucracies*, Cambridge University Press. 221–45. https://doi.org/10.1017/9781009023504.011.

Hajnal, G., & Boda, Z. (2021). Illiberal transformation of government bureaucracy in a fragile democracy: The case of Hungary. In M. W. Bauer, B. G. Peters, J. Pierre, K. Yesilkagit, & S. Becker, (Eds.), *Democratic Backsliding and Public Administration* (pp. 76–99). Cambridge University Press. https://doi.org/10.1017/9781009023504.005.

Harrits, G. S. (2019). Stereotypes in context: How and when do street-level bureaucrats use class stereotypes? *Public Administration Review*, 79(1), 93–103. https://doi.org/10.1111/puar.12952.

Hassan, M. (2021). *Regime Threats and State Solutions: Bureaucratic Loyalty and Embeddedness in Kenya*. Cambridge University Press. https://doi.org/10.1017/9781108858960.

Hassan, M. S., Ariffin, R., Mansor, N. , & Al Habusi, H. (2021). The moderating role of willingness to implement policy on street-level bureaucrats' multidimensional enforcement style and discretion. *International Journal of Public Administration*, 46(6), 1–15. https://doi.org/10.1080/01900692.2021.2001008.

Hinterleitner, M., & Wittwer, S. (2022). Serving quarreling masters: Frontline workers and policy implementation under pressure. *Governance*, 36(3), 759–778.

Huising, R., & Silbey, S. (2011). Governing the gap: Forging safe science through relational regulation. *Regulation & Governance*, 5(1), 14–42. https://doi.org/10.1111/j.1748-5991.2010.01100.x.

Hupe, P., & Buffat, A. (2014). A public service gap: Capturing contexts in a comparative approach of street-level bureaucracy. *Public Management Review*, 16(4), 548–569. https://doi.org/10.1080/14719037.2013.854401.

Kopecký, P., Meyer Shaling, J.-H., Panizza, F., Scherlis, G., Schuster, C., & Spirova, M. (2016). Party patronage in contemporary democracies: Results from an expert survey in 22 countries from five regions. *European Journal of Political Research*, 55(2), 416–431. https://doi.org/10.1111/1475-6765.12135.

Levitsky, S., & Ziblatt, D. (2018). *How Democracies Die*. Broadway Books.

Lipsky, M. (2010). *Street-Level Bureaucracy: Dilemmas of the Individual in Public Service*. Russell Sage Foundation. https://www.jstor.org/stable/10.7758/9781610447713.

Lotta, G., & Marques, E. C., (2020). How social networks affect policy implementation: An analysis of street-level bureaucrats' performance regarding a health policy. *Social Policy & Administration*, 54(3), 345–360. https://doi.org/10.1111/spol.12550.

Lotta, G., Coelho, V., & Brage, E. (2021). How Covid-19 has affected frontline workers in Brazil: A comparative analysis of nurses and community health workers. *Journal of Comparative Policy Analysis: Research and Practice*, 23(1), 63–73. https://doi.org/10.1080/13876988.2020.1834857.

Lotta, G., Thomann, E., Fernandez, M., Vogler, J., Leandro, A., & Corrêa, M. G. (2024). Populist government support and frontline workers' self-efficacy during crisis. *Governance*, 37(S1), 101–125. https://doi.org/10.1111/gove.12851.

Malandrino, A., & Sager, F. (2021). Can teachers' discretion enhance the role of professionalism in times of crisis? A comparative policy analysis of distance teaching in Italy and Switzerland during the COVID-19 pandemic. *Journal of Comparative Policy Analysis: Research and Practice*, 23(1), 74–84.

Matland, R. E. (1995). Synthesizing the implementation literature: The ambiguity-conflict model of policy implementation. *Journal of public administration research and theory*, 5(2), 145-174. https://doi.org/10.1093/oxfordjournals.jpart.a037242.

May, P. J., & Winter, S. C. (2019). Politicians, managers, and street-level bureaucrats: Influence on policy implementation. *Journal of Public Administration Research and Theory*, 23(1), 95–108. https://doi.org/10.1093/jopart/mum030.

Maynard-Moody, S. W., & Musheno, M. C. (2022). *Cops, Teachers, Counselors: Stories from the Front Lines of Public Service: Stories from the Front Lines of Public Service*. University of Michigan Press. https://doi.org/10.3998/mpub.12247078.

Møller, A. M., Pedersen, K. Z., & Pors, A. S. (2022). The bureaucratic ethos in street-level work: Revitalizing Weber's ethics of office. *Perspectives on Public Management and Governance*, 5(2), 151–163. https://doi.org/10.1093/ppmgov/gvac001.

Møller, M. O. (2021). The dilemma between self-protection and service provision under Danish COVID-19 guidelines: A comparison of public servants' experiences in the pandemic frontline. *Journal of Comparative Policy Analysis: Research and Practice*, 23(1), 95–108. https://doi.org/10.1080/13876988.2020.1858281.

Moynihan, Donald P. 2022. Public management for populists: Trump's Schedule F executive order and the future of the civil service. *Public Administration Review* 82(1), 174–8. https://doi.org/10.1111/puar.13433.

Mudde, C., & Rovira Kaltwasser, C. (2017). *Populism: A Very Short Introduction*. Oxford University Press. https://doi.org/10.1093/actrade/9780190234874.001.0001.

Oberfield, Z. W. (2012). Public management in time: A longitudinal examination of the full range of leadership theory. *Journal of Public Administration Research and Theory*, 24(2), 407–429. https://doi.org/10.1093/jopart/mus060.

Oberfield, Z. W., & Incantalupo, M. (2021). Racial discrimination and street-level managers: Performance, publicness, and group bias. *Public Administration Review*, 81(6), 1055–1070. https://doi.org/10.1111/puar.13376.

O'Leary, R. (2017). The ethics of dissent: Can President Trump survive guerrilla government? *Administrative Theory & Praxis*, 39(2), 63–79. https://doi.org/10.1080/10841806.2017.1309803.

Peci, A. (2021). Populism and bureaucratic frictions: Lessons from Bolsonarism. *Journal of Policy Studies*, 36(4), 27–35. https://doi.org/10.52372/kjps36403.

Peeters, R., & Campos, S. A. (2022). Street-level bureaucracy in weak state institutions: A systematic review of the literature. *International Review of Administrative Sciences, 89*(4), 977–995. https://doi.org/10.1177/00208523221103196.

Peeters, R., Lotta, G. S., & Nieto-Morales, F. (Eds.) (2024). *Street-Level Bureaucracy in Weak State Institutions* (1st ed.). Policy Press. https://doi.org/10.2307/jj.9692611.

Pepinsky, T. B., Pierskalla, J. H., & Sacks, A. (2017). Bureaucracy and service delivery. *Annual Review of Political Science, 20*, 249–268. https://doi.org/10.1146/annurev-polisci-051215-022705.

Peters, B. G., & Pierre, J. (2019). Populism and public administration: Confronting the administrative state. *Administration & Society, 51*(10), 1521–1545. https://doi.org/10.1177/0095399719874749.

Peters, B. G., & Pierre, J. (2020). A typology of populism: Understanding the different forms of populism and their implications. *Democratization, 27*(6), 928–946. https://doi.org/10.1080/13510347.2020.1751615.

Peters, B. G., & Pierre, J. (2022). The politicisation of the public service during democratic backsliding: Alternative perspectives. *Australian Journal of Public Administration, 81*(4), 629–639. https://doi.org/10.1111/1467-8500.12561.

Piore, M. J. (2011). Beyond markets: Sociology, street-level bureaucracy, and the management of the public sector. *Regulation & Governance, 5*(1), 145–164. https://doi.org/10.1111/j.1748-5991.2010.01098.x.

Piotrowska, B. (2022). Democratic backsliding and street-level bureaucracy in Hungary and Poland. [Paper]. European Consortium for Political Research General Conference 2022. https://ecpr.eu/Events/185.

Rockman, B. A. (2020). Bureaucracy, power, policy, and the state. In L. B. Hill (Ed.), *The State of Public Bureaucracy* (1st ed.). Routledge. https://doi.org/10.4324/9781315288536-6.

Rutz, S., Mathew, D., Robben, P., & De Bont, A., (2017). Enhancing responsiveness and consistency: Comparing the collective use of discretion and discretionary room at inspectorates in England and the Netherlands. *Regulation & Governance, 11*(1), 81–94. https://doi.org/10.1111/rego.12101.

Sager, F., & Gofen, A. (2022). The polity of implementation: Organizational and institutional arrangements in policy implementation. *Governance, 35*(2), 347–364. https://doi.org/10.1111/gove.12677.

Schmidt, F. (2022). Presença de militares em cargos e funções comissionadas do executivo federal: Nota Técnica n. 58. In *Repositório do Conhecimento do Ipea* (Vol. 58). IPEA.

Story, J., Lotta, G., & Tavares, G. (2023). (Mis)Led by an outsider: Abusive supervision, disengagement, and silence in politicized bureaucracies. *Journal of Public Administration Research and Theory, 33*(4), 549–562. https://doi.org/10.1093/jopart/muad004.

Thomann, E., Van Engen, N., & Tummers, L. (2018). The necessity of discretion: A behavioral evaluation of bottom-up implementation theory. *Journal of Public Administration Research and Theory, 28*(4), 583–601. https://doi.org/10.1093/jopart/muy024.

Yesilkagit, K. (2018). Bureaucracy under authoritarian rule: Autonomy and resilience of administrative institutions in divided times. [Paper] in *Structure and Organization of Government. 2018 Conference: "Bureaucracy in Divided Times"*. University of Potsdam.

Zacka, B. (2017). *When the State Meets the Street*. Harvard University Press.

PART 4
FUTURES OF ADMINISTRATING THE STATE

The transformation of the regulatory state?

by Martin Lodge

Thirty years ago, in 1994, Giandomenico Majone proclaimed that we were witnessing the rise of a regulatory state in Europe (Majone, 1994). That argument was largely focused on the rise of regulation as a policy tool to enhance the European Commission's influence over policy content in the absence of discretionary budgetary resources. Subsequently, the coming of the 'age of the regulatory state' was widely diagnosed (Majone, 1997), whether it was in the emergence of regulatory agencies, public services witnessing a shift towards more private or market-style arrangements, and the growing codification of relations between governmental agencies and individuals. The rise of regulatory agency was first diagnosed in the context of the regulation of infrastructures and then extended into further areas, such as the rise of ethics watchdogs and value-for-money watchers such as audit offices. Beyond a general policy consensus advocating the separating out of control functions from ministerial departments to freestanding agencies, there was a consensus towards a set of regulatory strategies that supposedly overcame the limits of 'market', 'regulatory', and 'government' failure. In particular, these strategies were to incentivise regulated entities to regulate themselves in a system of enforced self-regulation. Politically, too, such a promise appeared to be highly attractive, offering a managerialist and technocratic 'third way' of delegated governing that combined the supposedly 'best' worlds between state and markets.

From the viewpoint of the mid-2020s, the record of the 1990s regulatory state appears somewhat problematic. Some observers, such as Roberts (2009), noted over a decade ago that the 'logic of discipline' was giving way to a different 'logic of politics'. In the context of the UK (and over two decades ago), Michael Moran noted that the logic of the regulatory state represented a political movement of 'high modernism' that reinforced social dynamics away from old-style informal club government (Moran, 2003). However, this overall trend had remained incomplete, clashing with persistent 'club government' logics of governing that dominated political life.

The financial crisis of the late 2000s/early 2010s illustrated the limits of the supposedly high-intelligence world of regulation. Whether regulatory responses post-crisis were appropriate remained a matter of debate, especially in view of largely untested banking resolution regimes (see Cabane and Lodge, 2024). The rise of 'populism', the climate crisis and growing geopolitical considerations changed the 'habitat' in which much of the regulatory state of the 1990s has been set (Bauer et al., 2021; Besselink and Yesilkagit, 2001). Indeed, by the mid-2020s, the promises of the regulatory state in developing (privately run and financed) infrastructures had come undone. For example, in the context of the British regulatory state, hardly a week went by without another story of cash-stripped private water companies facing insolvency,[1] poorly designed railway franchising contracts,[2] debates about school inspection regimes,[3] or the implications for building regulation from the death of 72 people in a fire in a tower block in west London in 2017.[4] It was therefore also not surprising that among the key issues identified on the 'risk register' of the UK Labour Party before the 2024 election, challenges for regulation and existing regulatory regimes featured strongly.[5]

At the same time, despite these signs of cumulative disappointment with the performance of the 1990s-style regulatory state, issues of control and regulation remained central for the running of public services. The ideas that underpinned the regulatory state of the late 20th century continued to be relevant: regulation continued to be a preferred policy tool. Examples, again from the English context, included the proposed creation of a 'football regulator' in England or the heated debates surrounding one regulator in English higher education, the 'Office for Students' (for example, in the way in which 'freedom of speech' at higher education institutions was to be overseen). Regulation therefore represented both a problem and a solution in contemporary policy discourse.

So, three decades later, what can one say about the 'regulatory state' in the 2020s? If it is agreed that the habitat of the regulatory state has witnessed a transformation, have the characteristics of the regulatory state witnessed adaptation in view of cumulative 'misfit' with the political environment and growing policy disappointment? Or has the trend been one of decline and inevitable extinction? After all, policy change is supposedly reactive, based on growing 'surprises' and disappointment that generate a drumbeat of support for alternative policy arrangements. To explore this question, and following the overall direction of this volume, this chapter develops its argument in four steps. First, it illustrates the key features of the regulatory state that emerged in the last two decades of the 20th century. Second, it identifies the contemporary challenges and trends that impact on the regulatory state.

Third, the chapter points to a range of potential futures, before, finally, the chapter turns to potential implications for practice and research. In conclusion, this chapter points to a continuous hybridisation of regulatory logics that inevitably will lead to further policy instability.

1. The rise of the regulatory state: it could only get better?

The emergence of a particular style of regulation as an attractive policy proposition has been linked to a range of sources. First, an age of depleted national budgets reduced governments' opportunities to engage in publicly financed infrastructure expansion (Lodge, 2008). Given the resultant dependence on private sector finance, state organisations had to provide these private funders of public services and infrastructures with 'predictability and 'consistency' to signal that their private investment was secure. Contracts, licences and regulatory agencies were to signal 'credible commitment' that governments would abstain from short-term 'cheating'. Given that countries were said to be in an international race for private finance, they were also in a race to adopt seemingly similar institutional solutions, whether to please international funding organisations or appear 'appropriately modern' in front of their peers (Lodge and Stirton, 2006). Third, regulation also became a prominent policy tool in that it shifted the costs of implementation to third parties. Politicians and bureaucracies could govern, in seemingly costless ways (at least to the taxpayer rather than the consumer), by dictating policy substance.

The regulatory state as in the 1990s was said to address two types of challenges that characterised regulatory arrangements in the previous age. One fundamental challenge concerned the degree of rule intensity, namely one that regarded regulation as being 'too prescriptive', whilst others were concerned about the lack of regulatory guidance. The second challenge concerned the appropriate level of regulatory distance between regulator and regulatee, with some arguing that relationships were 'too close', proclaiming an ideal of shared professional outlook whilst, in reality, seeking to minimise external accountability. In contrast, others argued that regulation was 'too distant'.

Bringing these two dimensions together allows for the identification of four problems that the 1990s-style regulatory state was supposed to address. These four types of problems can be characterised as problems of *paternalism, professionalism, business self-regulation* and *formalism*. In terms of *formalism*, one of the standard criticisms of regulation, in the US and elsewhere, has been the 'going by the book' form of adversarial formalism, as noted by Bardach and

Kagan (1982). Accordingly, resource-poor regulators are resigned to conducting their business without any responsiveness to the needs of the regulated entity. Regulation takes place without any 'professional conversation' and use of responsible discretion, on either the regulatory or regulated side. Instead, there is a reliance on rigid formalism. In terms of *paternalism*, the regulators were accused of following close political instructions, erring on the side of the politically powerful in precautionary rather than 'resilience'-based ways. In terms of problems of *business self-regulation*, the standard concern has been with 'capture' and the unwillingness of business to be regulated, whether it is because of a lack of capacity or due to a lack of motivation. Finally, problems with *professionalism* occurred in areas dominated by professional self-regulation, such as in accounting or medicine. Here the concern was the limited external accountability of such systems, especially in view of a growing awareness of professional misconduct, whether this involved medical negligence or corporate governance scandals. Table 1 illustrates these concerns (which still feature prominently in any discussion of 'better regulation').[6]

Table 1. Problems searching for the regulatory state solution

	High regulatory distance	Low regulatory distance
High regulatory rule intensity	Problem of formalism Diagnosed problem of ill-considered application of rules without professional judgement	Problem of paternalism Diagnosed problem with rule prescriptiveness and close entanglement with state interest
Low regulatory rule intensity	Problem of business self-regulation Diagnosed problem of lack of professional discipline and absence of understood rules	Problem of professionalism Diagnosed problem with dominance of in-group deliberation without external accountability

These four problems did not occur in all areas of economic and social life across countries. However, the 1990s answer was institutionally rather similar across the Global North and South – involving codification, free-standing oversight/regulatory bodies and an emphasis on performance- and management-based standards which emphasised the importance of 'enforced self-regulation' that placed regulated entities at the heart of regulation.

The age of the regulatory state was therefore both about machinery of government changes and about a normative shift in the overall objective of the state vis-à-vis its citizens. In terms of machinery of government changes, the rise of 'regulatory agencies' as free-standing entities, decoupled from direct operational control by their ministerial departments, was seen as a significant part of a wider 'hollowing out' of the state. In terms of the overall normative direction of the state, the regulatory state was associated – similar to ideas linked to the 'New Public Management' (Hood, 1991) – with a dominance of 'efficiency' over other administrative values such as redistributive fairness or continuity of service. The latter was seen as largely unproblematic in view of a diagnosed (or alleged) inheritance of 'gold plating' by engineer-dominated state-owned enterprises. In terms of fairness, the emphasis was less on directly redistributing resources to different groups in the population. Instead, consumers were to be enabled to conduct informed choice on the market (in other words, the dominant administrative doctrine moved towards 'consumer sovereignty'-type arguments).

The dominant justification for regulatory intervention during this period was 'market failure' rather than an appeal to social solidarity (Prosser, 2006), usually on the basis of trying to reduce market power or addressing 'information asymmetries'. In turn, regulatory instruments were preferred that were supposed to be 'incentive-based'. On the one hand, 'incentive-based' regulation was utilised for regulated companies in infrastructure sectors, such as in the form of 'price caps' in the regulation of monopolies (known as 'RPI-X'). On the other hand, incentive-based regulation was introduced by establishing market-type mechanisms (such as emissions trading). Overall, there was a move away from prescription towards a model that sought to appeal to companies' motivations to 'do the right thing', leading to the advocacy of 'enforced self-regulation'. According to this idea, rather than relying on 'direct command and control', superior regulatory outcomes are achieved by granting regulated entities the discretion to develop their own paths to achieve regulatory objectives. Superior problem-solving was said to lie with those at the 'frontline', namely regulated entities, rather than with 'the state' as such.

This idea of 'high-intelligence' regulation that would encourage an entity to self-regulate was also endorsed by socio-legal and regulatory scholars (Ayres and Braithwaite, 1992). Building on Teubner's 'regulatory trilemma', according to which regulatory interventions are rarely likely to achieve their intended outcome but threaten to lead to futility, 'capture' (the dominance of entity interests), or disruption and displacement, the emphasis was on encouraging 'reflexivity' among regulated entities (Teubner, 1984). Through contextual steering or 'meta-regulation', entities could be made to self-regulate in ways that would combine self-interest with broader public-interest goals. As a result, the idea of 'enforced self-regulation' was one of the central aspects of the regulatory state of the late 20th and early 21st centuries, as encapsulated in concepts such as principles-based (rather than rules-based) regulation, and the advocacy of outcome-based regulation (such as in 'performance-based regulation') and management-based regulation.

2. The future once? The transforming nature of the regulatory state

Thirty years later, none of the criticisms noted above have entirely gone away. The financial crisis revealed that financial institutions had neither the capacity nor the motivation to regulate themselves. In addition, financial regulators were said to be intellectually and relationally 'too close' to the regulated industry as well as guided by political masters keen to signal 'light-touch' regulatory approaches (on the concept of 'regulatory capture' more generally, see Carpenter and Moss, 2013). During crises, such as the financial crisis and the COVID-19 pandemic, regulators were said to amass regulatory authority without much political oversight (Tucker, 2019). In energy, transitions towards 'net zero' as well as geopolitical conflicts highlighted the need for policy competence at the centre of government to make central redistributive decisions that could not be left to regulators and markets alone as they involved large-scale infrastructure planning decisions. Emission scandals, such as in the car industry (e.g. the widespread use of manipulated air emission tests by car manufacturers, most prominently by Volkswagen), as well as in building and aeroplane safety (e.g. Boeing), highlighted the limitations of relying uncritically on industry self-certification. Food scandals similarly pointed to problems with regulatory resources and strategies (Lodge and Wegrich, 2011; Lodge et al., 2010). Finally, diagnosed changes in geopolitical constellations also encouraged a reconsideration of dominant ideas regarding 'economic security' which sat uneasily with the dominance of economic ideas.

What, then, accounts for this trend towards growing disappointment with the regulatory state? Three factors can be put forward to account for the disappointment with the 1990s model of the regulatory state, over-confidence, blind spots and Achilles' heels, and institutional strangulation (see also Bach and Wegrich, 2019).

Problems of 'over-confidence' point to at least two phenomena. One is that the instruments of the regulatory state would identify and address risks and crises in appropriate ways. The various crises noted in this chapter pointed to regulatory outcomes: the supposedly high-intelligence world of regulatory intervention could not clearly be shown to directly contribute to desired outcomes, especially as the field of regulatory objectives continued to multiply. A second problem with 'over-confidence' was the ever-growing scope of regulatory activity. Regulation might have been seen as a highly attractive programmatic idea based on the supposedly robust technologies of economic analysis (Power, 1998). However, not only did the technologies prove themselves to be more limited than advertised, the ever-further expansion into different policy domains made the use of regulatory language, especially when couched in the terminology of 'market failure', highly problematic. For one, justifying interventions in, for example, education in market failure terms ran the risk of not only misdiagnosing the type of 'good' that was being regulated. Consuming education, even in market terms, is not the same as purchasing tinned tomatoes. As a result, drawing on the regime for airline insolvency to deal with the potential insolvency of universities highlighted that the consumption of a plane journey was not the same as that of a degree (given differences in prestige of university, for example). Over-extension into 'inappropriate' domains, therefore, further increased the likelihood of failure and criticism.

In terms of blind spots and Achilles' heels, the regulatory state revealed, as any organisation, systematic vulnerabilities. In terms of Achilles' heels, the regulatory state of the 1990s had a number of 'known' weaknesses. These were 'accepted' because of the perceived superiority of an emphasis on efficiency and choice. Once-alternative public service goals, such as fairness and redundancy, became increasingly prominent. First, there was growing disappointment with challenges of fairness (especially in terms of the discovery of vulnerability of consumers that went far beyond established administrative categories of vulnerability). Second, existing regulatory instruments seemed limited in terms of devolving on investment into modernisation and additional infrastructure. Questions of fairness were always supposed to be a 'political' rather than a regulatory domain, even though the idea that regulators could pursue a path towards becoming efficiency-seeking competition watchdogs without redistributive effects was always highly problematic. Similarly, ideas of redundancy, security of supply and the need to incentivise investment into long-term infrastructures required adaptation of market-based mechanisms to encourage 'spare capacity'. These challenges were particularly problematic as companies were found to create complex ownership structures to extract value from utilities that were left with considerable debt to be serviced by domestic consumers, as was the case in the English water industry. Extending the instruments of the regulatory state in response to these developments meant ever-growing complexity of regulatory analysis.

Furthermore, the idea of 'enforced self-regulation' also suffered from some inherent vulnerabilities. In particular, 'enforced self-regulation' is built on the core idea that 'amoral calculators' can be made, through careful institutional design, to behave as if they were responsible public-interest-seeking 'honest triers'. Such a strategy depended on a careful design to encourage professional curiosity by regulators. It also required credible sanctions should continued non-compliance be observed. Both of these two pre-conditions were found to be inherently difficult to achieve, let alone sustain. Instead, extensive gaming emerged.

In terms of 'blind spots' (the 'not seeing the not seeing'), numerous examples emerged regarding the limits of regulatory information gathering. These limits were induced by the financial or legal constraints on regulators to extensively monitor industry behaviour. For example, the increasing concern with sewage in rivers and on beaches in England revealed the limited monitoring by the responsible regulatory authority, the Environment Agency, due to financial constraints and a reliance on industry self-monitoring and self-reporting. In some cases, these blind spots also emerged due to clear political steers (such as in the case of the financial crisis with the demand for regulators to be 'light touch').

Finally, a further reason for the non-responsiveness of the regulatory state to a changing policy habitat was institutional strangulation (Carpenter, 2010). Regulatory arrangements proved hard to reform. In economic regulation, the dependence on private finance meant that the inherent trade-off in regulation between sanctioning and seeking to retain 'healthy' private owners in the sector became one-sided towards the latter. Regulators themselves became advocates of policy consistency and agents of blame games, such as in the case of the regulatory blame game over who had been found to be asleep at the wheel during the financial crisis.

Put together, then, the 1990s regulatory state was found wanting on a number of dimensions. It was found wanting in terms of achieving desired policy outcomes, and it was found wanting in terms of weaknesses within the organisation of the regulatory state. Both of these were seen to be directly implicated in the non-achievement of these outcomes. As a result, the regulatory state that had once been seen as the future had become part of the problem.

3. An epitaph?

So, is this the end of the age of the regulatory state? Whether desirable or not, the regulatory state of the 1990s was shown to be ill-equipped to deal with the challenges of the contemporary age. For one, the challenges of geopolitics placed a growing emphasis on non-economic factors in the delivery of public services. Such issues ranged from global supply chains to components for critical infrastructures. Geopolitical considerations sat uneasily with organisations staffed with economics-trained regulocrats. Similarly, non-majoritarian institutions were ill-suited to address the considerable redistributional issues arising from climate change. Apart from legitimacy, the rise of 'new' wicked issues such as climate change also raised technical competency issues following decades of managerialism and a political emphasis on placing problem-solving responsibilities on markets and their regulators: ministerial departments had lost their subject expertise. For example, it was difficult to imagine how an economic regulator – tasked with safeguarding private investment in an existing infrastructure – was to position itself in view of a policy context that would require a strategy of disinvestment into existing grids so as to close them down (such as debates about the future of existing gas networks for domestic heating). Furthermore, evidence that most regulatory entities were ultimately, in one way or another, 'too big to fail' suggested that regulatory regimes did not provide for credible commitment either. Furthermore, a political age characterised by a rise of populist demands regarding public services was also ill-suited for an administrative state geared towards the 'responsible' rather than 'responsive' exercise of authority (Mair, 2009). Unsurprisingly, the regulatory state had therefore witnessed considerable criticism and pressure – especially as politicians regarded regulatory arrangements no longer as solutions, but as problems (Koop and Lodge, 2020).

In view of these emerging trends, what might be said about the future of the regulatory state (see Dussauge-Laguna et al., 2024)? According to one view, the world of the 1990s-style regulatory state had come and gone: first, the institutional arrangements had proven incapable of dealing with political and policy problems and, second, the idea that efficiency should be the animating principle of regulatory intervention had been displaced by concerns about fairness and redundancy. Indeed, the broader challenge for the regulatory state was, according to this view, less the organisation and instruments of regulation. Rather, it was the growing realisation that market-based solutions were politically unpalatable, whether it was due to a reliance on user charges for public services (where fee increases were increasingly electorally unpalatable) or the lack of resources where the public management challenge was one of rationing rather than facilitating choice.

In contrast to this extinction view of the regulatory state, an alternative perspective would point to a process of institutional adjustment through ever-increasing layering and 'complexification'. In this age of complexification, there was no clear guiding policy idea as may have existed in the 1990s. The need for regulation had, after all, not declined. Dominant providers continued to require oversight (as could be seen in debates about 'big tech'), quality standards and their enforcement remained central for user reassurance, and a world of rationing might call for a different type of regulatory style, one that was increasingly based on 'improvement' rather than forcing 'exit from the market'. Similarly, the question of how to align the interests of 'principal' and 'agent' remained a central unresolved (and irresolvable) question. While it might be time to call time on 'the age of the regulatory state' in its 1990s incarnation, it was unlikely that the need to regulate as such had declined.

In view of these diverse trends, and the view that the regulatory state is witnessing a transformation in the form of complexification rather than extinction, how can we envisage the evolution of regulatory state arrangements? Table 2 highlights four potential futures of the regulatory state. It distinguishes these futures on two dimensions, namely the capacities for exercising regulation by regulatees and regulators alike.

Table 2. Regulatory state futures

	Low regulatee capacity	High regulatee capacity
High regulatory capacity	**Control state** Return of regulatory oversight to ministerial departments and more explicit state involvement	**Regulatory state 2.0** Management-based regulation with more responsive regulatory bodies
Low regulatory capacity	**Abandonment** *Ad hoc* regulatory activities without long-term commitment	**Industry self-certification state** Reliance on industry self-regulation and certification to guide consumer choice/enabling of experimentation

The 'regulatory state 2.0' age largely represents a path of incremental adaption. The institutions of the regulatory state would display considerable resilience in the face of the diagnosed challenges, whether it is because of a political reluctance to take on major political decisions with redistributive consequences, the continued dependence on private organisations and international finance to support infrastructure development, or the entrenched institutional interests of regulators that restrict major machinery of government changes. Accordingly, we would continue to witness a large-scale reliance on private investors, sovereign wealth funds, and pension funds for the investment in and management of infrastructures overseen by regulators. Regulators would continue to seek a more 'responsive' appearance towards politics and broader sectors of society, whether that would include growing consideration of 'consumer vulnerability' and/or further interest in developing 'customer engagement' processes to increase the perceived legitimacy of regulatory decision-making.

In terms of adaptation, one would observe an ever-increasing number of statutory objectives placed on regulators, with regulators becoming increasingly concerned with their appearance with the wider public. Trends such as 'customer engagement' across economic regulators did point to such a future (Haber and Heims, 2020; Heims and Lodge, 2018). Furthermore, given the irresolvable tension between 'too close' and 'too distant' relations between regulators and regulatees, it was also not unlikely that there would be a continued interest in 'enforced self-regulation'-type regulatory strategies, based on supposedly carefully calibrated risk-based frameworks.

The 'regulatory state 2.0' would represent a complexified version of the 1990s regulatory state: it is a hybridised version in that the initial dominance of 'efficiency'-based thinking is replaced by more complex considerations, involving fairness and security. Whereas the content of regulation might have changed, the broad institutional arrangements would continue.

However, other observers would suggest that the idea of the 'regulatory state' in its 1990s version is little else but a busted flush in view of the lack of future-oriented investment, growing resource shortages and rationing (rather than abundant choice), and the spectre of having to resurrect national industrial policies to deal with decarbonised supply chains (and geopolitical sensitivities). In response, one future therefore might be the reassertion of the 'control state'. According to this future, the central government would witness a reassertion of its regulatory powers, moving away from a reliance on delegation to arms-length regulated agencies and regulated entities. Instead, ministerial departments and elected politicians would return to the forefront of oversight. Such a trend may be seen, for example, in debates regarding the appropriate constitutional structure of the German railway infrastructure. In this case, despite ownership always remaining 'public', the private legal form was seen as restricting the federal government's powers of intervention in infrastructure planning and overall control. The creation of an entity supposedly dealing with the *Gemeinwohl* in 2024 was to highlight not just an assertion of central oversight powers, but also to provide for a clear indication that economic objectives were to be more explicitly balanced with supposedly 'public interest' considerations. It might equally be said that the 'decarbonisation' of infrastructures will require considerable state involvement, whether it is in regulating for the decommissioning of gas transmission networks, in the creation of different electricity and water networks and the provision of spare energy generation capacity, or in the generation of supply chains to deal with rare minerals. In this age of the 'control state', the state would therefore be centrally involved in 'picking winners'. The 'control state' is also one that would witness a return to a more security-based understanding of economic infrastructures, involving, for example, prohibitions on particular suppliers given their country of origin.

In contrast to an age of a reassertion of 'the state', one might also diagnose a conscious shift towards engaging market actors in self-regulation. Accordingly, an age of increased reliance on 'industry self-certification' would build on existing international certification regimes that have emerged as part of cooperation between non-state actors. Domestically, this would represent a reliance on industry to define its own standards and to offer consumers the kind of confidence that such industry standards would be credible. Indeed, the private regulation of supply chains might already offer more intensive regulatory oversight than any state-based inspection regime could provide. Compliance could be assessed by private parties (similar to the world of audit). Enthusiasts of such an approach would also suggest that such a world would allow for regulatory competition between standards, enabling for experimentation. This is a world that believes, at most, in the guiding hand of benchmarks and online reviews to inform customer choice and voice.

All these futures rely on the capacity and motivation of some parties to 'regulate'. However, a world of limited resources and also motivation can hardly be discounted. This age of 'abandonment' would be characterised by some rudimentary regulatory standards, but in view of limited resources neither regulators nor regulated entities would pay much attention to these standards. Attention to standards would potentially follow a few high-salience events, only for regulatory attention to evaporate in view of limited resources. Such a future might also involve the purposeful withdrawal of regulatory intervention and oversight so as to make account-holding highly complex. Politically such a strategy might offer the benefit of avoiding blame as the consequence of policy decisions might become invisible.

All of these four scenarios offer a potential future for the regulatory state. Traces of each of them can be found across contemporary states. In general, therefore, it is likely that rather than witnessing any full transformation towards one particular model of 'new' regulatory state, we might be witnessing a continued differentiation and fragmentation. In such a 'multiple worlds' future, there would therefore be no overall policy trajectory; instead, the world of regulation and regulatory agencies would be characterised by disjointedness.

4. So what?

A future of complexification might be seen as both a blessing and a curse for both the worlds of research and practice. There are no 'paradigms' to diagnose or attack. Rather, it is a world of inconsistency, incrementalism, and diversity. Regulatory dynamics would occur in largely decoupled policy domains. Such a future might be attractive for some, and unattractive to others. For the world of research, a number of central questions emerge from this discussion. One is how to classify the world of 1990s regulation. Is this a world that should be assumed to be a standard, therefore allowing for a bemoaning of closer political attention to regulatory matters? If that was the case, researchers and practitioners should be strongly concerned about explicitly political appointments, or more refined variants. One example of such subversion would be the careful selection of individuals serving on appointment panels for regulatory leadership positions.

Alternatively, one may suggest that the age of 'independence' in regulatory activities that characterised the 1990s was the exception to the rule. Accordingly, the key animating question then would be the search for answers as to what generated the conditions for the 1990s-style regulatory state. A second research question would focus on the growing tensions within the existing regulatory state institutions – and therefore explore the effects of layering. For example, this would include the interaction between regulatory systems based on the assumption of competition and attention to the performance of individual entities and regulatory systems seeking to encourage coordination in an age of rationing rather than abundant choice.

The central questions of regulation – whether it is about the appropriate levels of distance between oversight and producer, the type of rule prescriptiveness, or the appropriate level of oversight intensity are therefore unlikely to go away. How these questions are being answered, however, is likely to receive increasingly diverse responses. In short, then, the age of the regulatory state that justified its intervention on the basis of 'market failure' following a supposedly technocratic cost–benefit analysis has given way to an age of multiple logics as to the when and how of regulation. These will, in turn, produce their own side effects and disappointments, leading to further instability.

Notes

1. 'Regular plans to cut fines to help stressed water companies', *Financial Times*, https://www.ft.com/content/7dcb0a2a-da50-4032-bffd-f52a5d889522 (28 May 2024).
2. 'Ministers cut performance targets for biggest UK rail franchise', *Financial Times*, https://www.ft.com/content/16011adf-94a6-415b-8d3a-78f4cbbddc58 (9 February 2024).
3. Lucy Kellaway, 'Sweep away Ofsted grading and allow teachers to teach', *Financial Times*, https://www.ft.com/content/b23a303e-346d-4e31-805e-5b108f1ece90 (24 March 2023).
4. 'Grenfell: the anatomy of a housing disaster', *Financial Times*, https://www.ft.com/content/5381b5d2-5c1c-11e7-9bc8-8055f264aa8b (20 June 2017).
5. The list included: potential collapse of Thames Water, public sector pay negotiations, overcrowding in prisons, universities going under, NHS funding shortfall, failing local councils. Three issues in particular (Prisons, water and universities) were centrally about regulation ('Labour faces series of crises if elected, internal dossier warns', *Financial Times*, https://www.ft.com/content/b95976ff-d861-4baf-a168-fd262b4e2f95 (21 May 2024)).
6. See for example Center for European Reform, 'Better regulation in Europe', Policy Brief, 19 March 2024, https://www.cer.eu/publications/archive/policy-brief/2024/better-regulation-europe-action-plan#:~:text=The 'better regulation' agenda has, and contribute their own evidence.

References

Ayres, I., & Braithwaite, J. (1992). *Responsive Regulation*. Oxford University Press.
Bach, T., & Wegrich, K. (2019). *The Blind-Spots of Public Bureaucracy and the Politics of Non-Coordination*. Palgrave Macmillan. https://doi.org/10.1007/978-3-319-76672-0.
Bardach, E., & Kagan, R. (1982). *Going by the Book: The Problem of Regulatory Unreasonableness* (1st ed.). Temple University Press.
Bauer, M. W., Peters, B. G., Pierre, J., Yesilkagit, K., & Becker, S. (2021). *Democratic Backsliding and Public Administration*. Cambridge University Press. https://doi.org/10.1017/9781009023504.
Besselink, T., & Yesilkagit, K. (2021). Market regulation between economic and ecological values: Regulatory authorities and delimmas of responsiveness. *Public Policy and Administration*, 36(3), 304–322. https://doi.org/10.1177/0952076719827630.
Cabane, L., & Lodge, M. (2024). Un-solvable crises? Differential implementation and transboundary crisis management in the EU. *West European Politics*, 47(3), 491–514. https://doi.org/10.1080/01402382.2023.2282284.
Carpenter, D. (2010). Institutional strangulation: Bureaucratic politics and financial reform in the Obama administration. *Perspectives on Politics*, 8(3), 825–846. https://doi.org/10.1017/S1537592710002070.
Carpenter, D., & Moss, D. A. (2013). *Preventing Regulatory Capture: Special Interest Influence and How to Limit it*. Cambridge University Press. https://doi.org/10.1017/CBO9781139565875.

Dussauge-Laguna, M. I., Elizondo, A., González, C. I., & Lodge, M. (2024). Regulation and development: Theoretical contributions and empirical lessons from Latin America. *Regulation & Governance, 18*(2), 331–347. https://doi.org/10.1111/rego.12584.

Haber, H., & Heims, E. (2020). Regulating with the masses? Mapping the spread of participatory regulation. *Journal of European Public Policy, 27*(11), 1742–1762. https://doi.org/10.1080/13501763.2020.1817128.

Heims, E., & Lodge, M. (2018). Customer engagement in UK water regulation: Towards a collaborative regulatory state. *Policy & Politics, 46*(1), 3–19. https://doi.org/10.1332/030557317X15046029080815.

Hood, C. (1991). A public management for all seasons? *Public Administration, 69*(1), 3–19. https://doi.org/10.1111/j.1467-9299.1991.tb00779.x.

Koop, C., & Lodge, M. (2020). British economic regulators in an age of politicisation: from the responsible to the responsive regulatory state? *Journal of European Public Policy, 27*(11), 1612–1635. https://doi.org/10.1080/13501763.2020.1817127.

Lodge, M. (2008). Regulation, the regulatory state and European politics. *West European Politics, 31*(1–2), 280–301. https://doi.org/10.1080/01402380701835074.

Lodge, M., & Stirton, L. (2006). Withering in the Heart? In search of the regulatory state in the Commonwealth Caribbean. *Governance, 19*(3), 465–495. https://doi.org/10.1111/j.1468-0491.2006.00326.x.

Lodge, M., & Wegrich, K. (2011). Governance as contested logics of control: Europeanized meat inspection regimes in Denmark and Germany. *Journal of European Public Policy, 18*(1), 90–105. https://doi.org/10.1080/13501763.2011.520880

Lodge, M., Wegrich, K., & McElroy, G. (2010). Dodgy kebabs everywhere? Variety of worldviews and regulatory change. *Public Administration, 88*(1), 247–266. https://doi.org/10.1111/j.1467-9299.2010.01811.x.

Mair, P. (2009). *Representative versus responsible government*. MPIfG Working Paper 09/8, Max Planck Institute for the Study of Societies.

Majone, G. (1994). The rise of the regulatory state in Europe. *West European Politics, 17*(3), 77–101. https://doi.org/10.1080/01402389408425031.

Majone, G. (1997). From the positive to the regulatory state: Causes and consequences of changes in the mode of governance. *Journal of Public Policy, 17*(2), 139–167. https://doi.org/10.1017/S0143814X00003524.

Moran, M. (2003). *The British Regulatory State: High Modernism and Hyper-Innovation*. Oxford University Press. https://doi.org/10.1093/0199247579.001.0001.

Power, M. (1998). *The Audit Society: Rituals of Verification*. Oxford University Press. https://doi.org/10.1093/acprof:oso/9780198296034.001.0001.

Prosser, T. (2006). Regulation and social solidarity. *Law and Society, 33*(3), 364–387. https://doi.org/10.1111/j.1467-6478.2006.00363.x.

Roberts, A. (2009). *The Logic of Discipline: Global Capitalism and the Architecture of Government*. Oxford University Press. https://doi.org/10.1093/acprof:oso/9780195374988.001.0001

Teubner, G. (1984). After legal instrumentalism: Strategic models of post-regulatory law. *International Journal of the Sociology of Law, 12*(4), 375–400. https://hdl.handle.net/1814/17111

Tucker, P. (2019). *Unelected Power: The Quest for Legitimacy in Central Banking and the Regulatory State*. Princeton University Press. https://doi.org/10.23943/9781400889518.

Why we need more public value

by Sandra Van Thiel

The way in which governments in OECD countries have organised their public sector is about to change. In the past decades, especially since the 1980s, neoliberal ideas, instruments, and arrangements have been introduced into the Weberian bureaucracies of these countries (Pollitt and Bouckaert, 2011). And while countries have differed in the rate and intensity of adoption of these ideas, the negative side effects of these reforms are now coming to light. The trade-off between efficiency and quality of services, the fragmentation that has arisen due to hiving off various parts of the government, the loss of control, and the democratic deficit are just some examples of such effects. In addition, the focus on citizens as customers only has ignored other roles of citizens and overestimated their capabilities to receive the services they need (Van de Walle, 2016; Thomas, 2012). In several countries this has led to incidents in the provision of public services, for example the childcare benefit affair in the Netherlands, the failure of the Irish national health regulatory agency, and the NAV scandal in Norway (Van Thiel and Migchelbrink, 2023; Eriksen, 2023; HHE, 2007). In response to these negative consequences, governments are looking for new and better ways to organise the public sector and public sector organisations. Several new ideas have been proposed (Torfing et al., 2020), such as the Neo-Weberian State (Byrkjeflot et al. 2018), Whole of Government (Christensen and Lægreid, 2007a), and New Public Governance (Osborne, 2010). In this chapter I will argue why, in my opinion, the Public Value approach (Bryson et al., 2014, 2015; Meyhardt, 2009; Moore, 1997) offers the best solution and what this will look like if applied to the design of the public sector.

To this end I will first discuss the classic dilemma in organising the public sector and which ideas have been consecutively tried and tested to solve this dilemma. Next, I will explain what the Public Value approach entails, and what the implications would be – positive and negative – of its application to the design of the public sector. Finally, I will present a set of questions for future research that follow from my proposition.

1. The classic dilemma of coordination and specialisation

The traditional dilemma in the design of organisations, whether public or private, is that between coordination and specialisation (Morgan, 2006; Thompson, 2005; Williamson, 1981; Mintzberg, 1980). Coordination implies that an organisation integrates multiple aspects or tasks within its entirety, aiming for alignment to achieve a holistic performance. Specialisation refers to dividing up the different aspects or tasks into separate units, with each unit being responsible for a part of the final product or performance.

These two principles can also be applied to the design of the public sector (Bouckaert et al., 2010). Coordination then refers to the inclination of governments to take on many tasks themselves, as part of the government bureaucracy. Specialisation means the supply or delivery of policies and public services through different organisations, both within and outside of the government bureaucracy (Osborne, 2021; Christensen and Lægreid, 2007b).

The dilemma regarding these two principles is that neither offers a perfect solution for the design of organisations, or the public sector. Coordination will lead to a large span of control, which in the end will become too large, leading to inefficiencies, high costs and poor performance. Too much specialisation will lead to fragmentation and loss of control, which in the end will also negatively affect performance, creating inefficient overlap or oversights. To deal with the dilemma, we see that over time coordination and specialisation take different turns as guiding principles for the design of the public sector and individual organisations. This is visible in different sectors, and even in the case of classical government tasks like the army, as illustrated in Figure 1.

Until the 1800s in most Western countries, rulers who wanted to go to war had to hire soldiers, paying them for their temporary service in the army. Soldiers who survived returned to their regular jobs and positions after the war. Around 1800, the military draft was established in most Western (European) countries, obliging all adult men (and in some countries women) to serve for a fixed amount of time in the army, after which they could always be recalled in the event of a war. This change in 'design' of the army can be seen as going from specialisation (for hire, per war) to coordination (always present, in one organisation). After two world wars, in the mid-20th century, the military draft was abolished or postponed in most Western countries, as governments preferred a smaller, more professional army with career soldiers – moving again towards more specialisation. In some cases, governments went even further in specialisation by hiring private firms to fight in wars, like the US did in the wars in Iraq and Afghanistan (Blackwater Worldwide), and the Russian government in Ukraine (Wagner Group). It is unclear at the time of writing this chapter (2024) what the future will bring. Some countries (like Germany) are considering establishing the military draft again, returning to coordination, while there are also voices in favour of increasing EU or NATO military cooperation or even establishing one joint, professional army at international level.

Figure 1. Coordination and specialisation as guiding principles for the design of the army over time

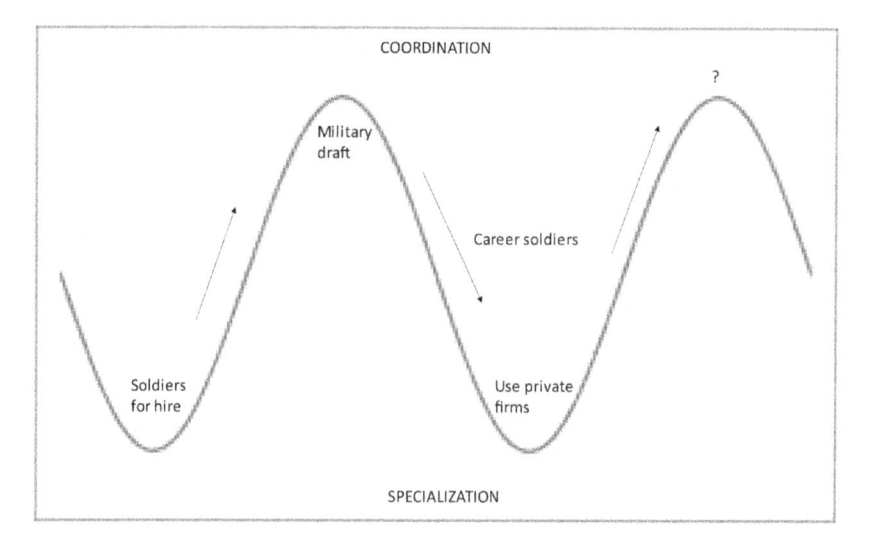

2. Different solutions to the central dilemma

A pattern of different waves of reform in organisational design, like in the example above, can be found in other parts of the public sector too (Van de Walle, 2016). Many public services, ranging from for example transport to welfare, originated privately through private companies (like the railway companies) or not-for-profit organisations (charities in the case of welfare) but were eventually taken over by governments and became part of the welfare state (De Swaan, 1988; Esping Andersen, 1990). As a result of this 'coordination', the span of control of governments increased strongly in the first half of the 20th century. Government bureaucracies increased in size, even more so as the demand for public services rose when social laws were implemented and economic decline set in, in the late 1970s. Under the influence of a new political paradigm – neoliberalism – governments turned again to specialisation as a solution for the design and performance of public sector organisations, from the early 1980s onwards. This became known under the label of New Public Management (NPM) (Pollitt and Bouckaert, 2011; Hood, 1991). Tasks and parts of the government bureaucracy were hived off, either creating single-purpose organisations with managerial autonomy, or delegating tasks to lower levels of government, or even privatising, i.e. selling off units from the government bureaucracy.

However, as argued before, specialisation is not a perfect design option either. Not only were the expected financial gains of NPM often not obtained (Overman and Van Thiel, 2016; Pollitt and Dan, 2013), new problems and challenges surfaced, including a loss of control and democratic deficits. Questions also arose whether the 'specialised' design of the public sector thwarted the realisation of public value, i.e. whether policy objectives are actually obtained, and whether citizens receive the public services they need (Bozeman, 2007).

In response to these criticisms, several new ideas have been suggested to deal with the negative effects of too much specialisation, known under the label of post-NPM (Torfing et al., 2020). Some of these ideas stay on the specialisation route of design, such as the attempts to reshuffle, merge, and reabsorb some autonomous single-purpose organisations (Flinders and Skelcher, 2013). Other solutions that are being offered, such as New Public Governance, networking, and coproduction (Osborne, 2010; Klijn et al., 2015; Pestoff, 2018; Alford, 2009), appear to lean towards restoring coordination but in a different way than before; instead of the central government taking on tasks again itself, it now has to coordinate other organisations carrying out the tasks. Whole of Government (Christensen and Lægreid, 2007a) aims to restore full coordination by re-integrating the fragmented parts of the public sector into the government bureaucracy. And the Neo-Weberian State (Byrkjeflot et al., 2018) advocates a modernised version of the traditional bureaucratic state, restoring trust in the hierarchy of government bureaucracy – which in essence has never been lost despite the pressure of NPM ideas, according to the proponents of this approach. The latter claim points to an interesting issue when looking at the consecutive waves of reform: there is no absolute pendulum swing going from one end (full coordination) to the other (full specialisation), but in fact there are always remnants of previous ideas and reforms that continue to exist even though new ideas and arrangements are being adopted (Torfing et al., 2020). This leads to a process of sedimentation or layering of ideas and principles for the design of the public sector (Lægreid and Verhoest, 2010).

In that sense, the Public Value approach (Moore, 1997; Bryson et al., 2014, 2015; Meynhardt, 2009) offers a new and different perspective than the other post-NPM ideas. Instead of promising that there is one best way or model for the design of the public sector (hierarchy, networks, market), the Public Value approach argues that there are different models, or modalities, and that it depends on the context and contingencies which model is most appropriate for a specific public sector organisation. This line of thinking fits with the practice of layering and offers a way out of the classic dilemma between coordination and specialisation. That is why I believe that the Public Value approach could be the best next approach for the design of the public sector. Below, I will explain what this entails, the possible implications, and what is necessary to make it work.

3. The Public Value approach

While increasingly popular, the Public Value approach is not a fully-fledged theoretical paradigm yet (Bryson et al., 2014). Starting with the book by Mark Moore (1997), several authors have worked on making it a more concrete approach (e.g. Bryson et al., 2014, 2015; Benington and Moore, 2010; Meynhardt, 2009) that can be used for the design of public sector organisations. However, there are still a lot of ideas that need further elaboration, testing, and research (see also the research agenda in the final section). This chapter explores what would be required if public value became the new guiding principle for designing public sector organisations and/or the public sector, based on the ideas as they are available at the time of writing (early 2024).

The basic premise of the Public Value approach is twofold. First, the design of public sector organisations should not be based on economic values like efficiency, but on the achievement of *public* value, i.e. the achievement of policy objectives and the production of public services to the benefit of all. This idea originates from the Value Chain Analysis approach as developed for the private sector by Michael Porter; organisations should be designed in such a way as to optimise the value for the customer. In the public sector this is translated into public value (Moore, 1979).

However, the definition of public value is not without problems. It should for example not be confused with public values (plural), which are the persuasions and motivations of individual behaviour of civil servants, such as integrity and accountability (Van der Wal et al., 2008; Bozeman, 2008). Public value should be seen as more in line with public *interests*, i.e. the objectives that governments pursue for society as a whole. The reader should note that there are different types of public interests, for instance substantive (e.g. safety, sustainability) and procedural (e.g. transparency, equity) interests

(Bozeman, 2008; De Bruijn and Dicke, 2006). Furthermore, public interests may change over time as new policy objectives become more important, for example due to specific events (e.g. 9/11 put counter-terrorism high on the agenda, and the war in Ukraine boosted renewable energy initiatives). A final complication regarding 'public value' as a design principle is the fact that multiple public interests can be at stake in the same situation, and these can even be conflicting with each other. The best-known example in this case is the contradiction between economic interests (e.g. building new roads) and ecological ones (e.g. preserving nature). These complications should be taken into consideration when taking public value as the basic premise for the design of public sector organisations: which public value(s) should be served? And who determines this: politicians, civil servants, citizens? We will return to these questions below.

The second premise of the Public Value approach is that there is no one best way to design public sector organisations or the public sector (Bryson et al., 2014, 2015). Depending on the situation at hand, four different organisational designs can be chosen: (a) government bureaucracy; (b) executive agencies at arm's length; (c) partnership with public and private partners; or (d) contracting out to private companies in the market. For each task, the government has to decide whether other organisations than the government bureaucracy can carry out the task more effectively and efficiently, if so whether there is a market for private parties that can be contracted or cooperated with, and how regulation or supervision by the government can be carried out, for example through monitoring and performance indicators.

The Public Value approach therefore does not make an *a priori* choice for coordination or specialisation – nor for hierarchy, markets, or networking; all modalities can be found in the public sector, at the same time. Public services can be delivered by organisations with different designs, even if they operate within the same policy field and are subordinated to the same parent department. Thus, there are no more waves of reform as described above, with one mode of design being preferred over the other during certain periods of time. Instead, there can be multiple modalities for different organisations, tasks, and sectors, fitting with the layering idea mentioned above.

While the Public Value approach seems to offer a solution for the dilemma of organisational design, it begs the question whether designing public sector organisations in this way is realistically possible. There are many implications that have to be dealt with, which I will discuss next.

4. Implications of public value as a design principle for public sector organisations

The first step in designing public sector organisations based on public value is that governments have to decide which public value has to be realised (Bryson et al., 2014, 2015; Moore, 1997). As explained before, there are different types of public interests and multiple interests can be at stake for a given task or situation. This raises questions about who decides about this, and how. In a democracy, the legislative power, i.e. the elected members of parliament, decide on the policy objectives that need to be pursued through the legislative process. However, there are many more actors involved in this process: civil servants who formulate most of the legislative proposals, using information from a variety of sources (reports, research, media, advisory bodies, think tanks); interest groups and private businesses that will lobby both the civil servants and the members of parliament to decide in their interest; citizens who can voice their concerns and wishes through elections but also through societal movements, petitions, and other means; other governments at other levels, including supranational and international; and courts that may overrule decisions or add new interpretations to existing legislation (judicial review). Decisions about which public value(s) will have to be realised can thus come about in many different ways. Governments, in this case ruling cabinets and their civil servants, will have to navigate these different actors and processes, and consider the consequences for the design of the organisation that will have to carry out the decisions after they have been taken.

The first important implication for governments is therefore that civil servants have to be familiar with all the different ways in which organisations can be designed (the four options mentioned above). Only then can they advise decision-makers about the best choice for a particular task or organisation. However, civil servants can have different preferences and competencies in this regard, also depending on their training and background (Van der Meer et al., 2023). The same implication holds for political decision-makers, by the way: they also have to know about the different modalities, and when they are called for, or not. Extant research into the motives for the creation of executive agencies shows that there are no systematic patterns in the choices made by governments and the legislature in this regard (Verhoest et al., 2012). The resulting form of public sector organisations can often be explained mostly by historical paths (Pollitt et al., 2004) and imitation (Van Thiel, 2004). Such findings do not bode well for our first implication: it can be doubted whether civil servants and political decision-makers have accurate knowledge about the different options and can make the optimal decision in a given situation.

The latter point brings us to a second important implication: politicians need to be (or become) more consistent in their choice of design, for example also after elections or during difficult times (crisis, fiscal pressure). Majone (2001) referred to 'political credibility' as a motive for choosing the design of public services in such a way that service delivery can be guaranteed even after the original decision-makers have left office (cf. also Hood, 2011, on the agency strategy to avoid blame). However, we know that politicians often keep 'meddling' with public service delivery agencies, even when these are formally at arm's length (Pollitt, 2005). Reshuffling and mergers are one of the most frequent reforms among such organisations (Wynen et al., 2020). Political aspects and political conflict can thus disturb or even undermine the political decision-making process, making it more difficult to use the Public Value approach as intended.

Third, citizens or other users of public services have to accept that there can be different modes of service delivery and they have to be able to cope with this. Research into what citizens know about how public services are designed is scarce (cf. Jakobsen et al., 2019). In a Dutch study (POC, 2012) we found that citizens know very little about the way in which public service delivery is organised, but are also not really interested in it; they only want their public services to be delivered on time and to be of good quality (cf. Hibbing and Theiss-Morse, 2002). Citizens also want the government to intervene if necessary but do not know that this is often not possible due to the way in which these services are designed, for example if services have been contracted out. Moreover, research into citizen satisfaction with public services shows several paradoxical results. Individual contacts between citizens and public service providers are always evaluated more positively than the collective public service, and public services are systematically evaluated in a more negative way than private service provision regardless of actual performance (Lee and Van Ryzin, 2020; Marvel, 2015; Hvidman and Andersen, 2015; Van Slyke and Roch, 2004). In order for public value as a design principle to work, more attention needs to be paid to the information given to citizens, but also to the match between what citizens know, want, and expect on the one hand, and the public service delivery design on the other hand.

The fourth implication of a more diversified design of public service delivery has to do with accountability. The different design modes call for different accountability mechanisms; if the government bureaucracy carries out a task, the traditional accountability requirements will apply, but if a task has for example been contracted out or there is a public private partnership involved, accountability will take on a different form (Schillemans et al., 2021; Bovens and Schillemans, 2020). Not only does this have to be arranged, but it also needs to be clear to political decision-makers and citizens that the traditional accountability forms – and hence for instance the possibilities to intervene in case of incidents – cannot be called upon (Vibert, 2007). And as the risk of differences in the quality and performance of service delivery increases as more varied organisational forms are used, the importance of accountability increases. For instance, if municipalities choose different forms for waste collection, they may also impose different tariffs on citizens, which means that it may be more expensive in one city compared to another. Such differences affect the equity and legitimacy of public service delivery (cf. Tyler and Fagan, 2008). Similarly, differences between the execution of similar tasks and delivery of similar products may arise in different policy sectors if, for example, different ministries make different design choices.

The four implications I have mentioned create complications for the application of the Public Value approach to the design of the public sector. It does not however make it *a priori* impossible, and failures in the design of individual public sector organisations do not imply a failure in the design of the public sector as a whole. After all, losing one battle does not mean losing the war.

5. Research agenda

Using the Public Value approach as a new lens for the design of public sector organisations calls for a range of new research topics and questions for Public Administration scholars in the coming years (Torfing et al., 2020), both theoretically and empirically. The first avenue for future research concerns the further theoretical elaboration of the Public Value approach. As mentioned before, it is not a full-fledged paradigm yet, and it is also not clear yet whether it will indeed become the new adage for the design of public sector organisations, replacing previous or other ideas. It is therefore important that Public Administration scholars keep working on operationalising the Public Value approach, making it suitable for use and research. Moreover, if we agree that the Public Value approach is a valuable approach for the design of public sector organisations, it has to be incorporated in the teaching programmes of our students and practitioners (Hansen et al., 2023; Bottom et al., 2022).

Second, we will need to study and monitor the trends in the design of public organisations, for example through comparative research, comparing tasks, sectors, levels of government, and countries, to determine whether there will indeed be a paradigm shift and if so which approach will become the 'new' way of working. Furthermore, the waves of reform as sketched in the introduction are typical for OECD countries (Pollitt and Bouckaert, 2011).

In other parts of the world, including transitional and developing countries, reforms have been lagging behind or have taken a different route given the political and economic situation (Randma-Liiv and Drechsler, 2017; De Vries and Nemec, 2013; Polidano, 1999). It is therefore difficult to predict when and where the Public Value approach will become the new dominant design principle for public sector organisations. More comparative research can help answer that question.

A third direction for future research concerns investigating the choices by governments regarding the different design options for different tasks, in and across policy sectors, to determine whether there are systematic patterns in the choices or not. Besides the political decisions about public sector organisations, researchers should also examine the consequences thereof, for example regarding the performance of the organisations involved, and the achievement of public value. This also calls for clearer definitions and operationalisations of the concept of public value (Bryson et al., 2014, 2015; Meynhardt, 2009).

Fourth and finally, attention should be paid in empirical studies to the implications mentioned above. This concerns a range of topics, such as the knowledge and skills of the actors involved (politicians, civil servants) to make accurate decisions about the design in specific cases, and the actual choices they make. Furthermore, researchers should carry out more research into citizens, by studying the fit of the preferred mode of design of public service delivery with the wishes and needs of citizens. And finally, attention should be paid to the rise and use of alternative forms of accountability and the effects thereof, for democracy and society.

References

Alford, J. (2009). *Engaging Public Sector Clients: From Service-Delivery to Co-Production* (1st ed.). Palgrave Macmillan. https://doi.org/10.1057/9780230235816.

Benington, J., & Moore, M. (Eds.) (2010). *Public Value: Theory and Practice* (1st ed.). Bloomsbury Publishing.

Bottom, K. A., Diamond, J., Dunning, P. T., & Elliot, I. C. (Eds.) (2022). *Handbook of Teaching Public Administration*. Edward Elgar Publishing. https://doi.org/10.4337/9781800375697.

Bouckaert, G., Peters, B. G., & Verhoest, K. (2010). *The Coordination of Public Sector Organizations: Shifting Patterns Of Public Management* (1st ed.). Palgrave Macmillan. https://doi.org/10.1057/9780230275256.

Bovens, M., & Schillemans, T. (2020). Non-majoritarian institutions and representation. In R. Rohrschneider & J. Thomassen (Eds.), *The Oxford Handbook of Political Representation in Liberal Democracies* (pp. 511–525). Oxford University Press. https://doi.org/10.1093/oxfordhb/9780198825081.013.26.

Bozeman, B. (2007). *Public Values and Public Interest: Counterbalancing Economic Individualism*. Georgetown University Press. https://doi.org/10.1353/book13027.

Bryson, J. M., Crosby, B. C., & Bloomberg, L. (2014). Public value governance: Moving beyond traditional public administration and the new public management. *Public Administration Review*, 74(4), 445–456. https://doi.org/10.1111/puar.12238.

Bryson, J. M., Crosby, B. C., & Bloomberg, L. (Eds.) (2015). *Public Value and Public Administration*. Georgetown University Press. https://www.jstor.org/stable/j.ctt18z4hhp.

Byrkjeflot, H., Du Gay, P., & Greve, C. (2018). What is the "Neo-Weberian State" as a regime of public administration? In E. Ongaro & S. Van Thiel (Eds.), *The Palgrave Handbook of Public Administration and Management in Europe* (pp. 991–1009). Palgrave Macmillan. https://doi.org/10.1057/978-1-137-55269-3_50.

Christensen, T., & Lægreid, P. (2007a). The whole-of-government approach to public sector reform. *Public Administration Review*, 67(6), 1059–1066. https://doi.org/10.1111/j.1540-6210.2007.00797.x.

Christensen, T., & Lægreid, P. (2007b). *Transcending New Public Management: The Transformation of Public Sector Reforms* (1st ed.). Routledge. https://doi.org/10.4324/9781315235790.

De Bruijn, H., & Dicke, W. (2006). Strategies for safeguarding public values in liberalized utility sectors. *Public Administration*, 84(3), 717–735. https://doi.org/10.1111/j.1467-9299.2006.00609.x.

De Vries, M., & Nemec, J. (2013). Public sector reform: An overview of recent literature and research on NPM and alternative paths. *International Journal of Public Sector Management*, 26(1), 4–16. https://doi.org/10.1108/09513551311293408.

De Swaan, A. (1988). *In Care of the State: Health Care, Education and Welfare in Europe and the USA in the Modern Era*. Oxford University Press.

Eriksen, E. O. (2023). Three modes of administrative behaviour: differentiated policy implementation and the problem of legal certainty. *Journal of European Public Policy*, 30(12), 2623–2642. https://doi.org/10.1080/13501763.2022.2125047.

Esping-Andersen, G. (1990). *The Three Worlds of Welfare Capitalism*. Polity Press. https://pagotto.wordpress.com/wp-content/uploads/2018/05/the-three-worlds-of-welfare-capitalism-1990.pdf.

Flinders, M., & Skelcher, C. (2012). Shrinking the quango state: five challenges in reforming quangos. *Public Money & Management*, 32(5), 327–334. https://doi.org/10.1080/09540962.2012.703410.

Hansen, M. B., Thomassen, A. O., & Toriesen, D. O. (2023). Guest editorial: Historical trends and emerging issues in public management education. *International Journal of Public Sector Management*, 36, 289–299. https://doi.org/10.1108/IJPSM-07-2023-352.

Hospital Healthcare Europe (HHE) (2007). *Ireland's health chiefs accused over cancer scandal*. Hospital Healthcare Europe. https://hospitalhealthcare.com/news/irelands-health-chiefs-accused-over-cancer-scandal/.

Hibbing, J. R., & Theiss-Morse, E. (2002). *Stealth Democracy: Americans' Beliefs About How Government Should Work*. Cambridge University Press. https://doi.org/10.1017/CBO9780511613722.

Hood, C. (1991). A public management for all seasons? *Public Administration*, 6(3), 3–19. https://doi.org/10.1111/j.1467-9299.1991.tb00779.x.

Hood, C. (2011). *The Blame Game. Spin, Bureaucracy, and Self-Preservation in Government*. Princeton University Press.

Hvidman, U., & Andersen, S. C. (2015). Perceptions of public and private performance: Evidence from a survey experiment. *Public Administration Review, 76*(1), 111–120. https://doi.org/10.1111/puar.12441.

Jakobsen, M., James, O., Moynihan, D., & Nabatchi, T. (2019). JPART virtual issue on citizen-state interactions in public administration research. *Journal of Public Administration Research and Theory, 29*(4), e8–e15. https://doi.org/10.1093/jopart/muw031.

Klijn, E.-H., Koppenjan, J., Spekkink W., & Warsen R. (2015). *Governance Networks in the Public Sector* (1st ed.). Routledge. https://doi.org/10.4324/9781315887098.

Lægreid, P., & Verhoest, K. (Eds.) (2010). *Governance of Public Sector Organizations: Proliferation, Autonomy and Performance* (1st ed.). Palgrave Macmillan. https://doi.org/10.1057/9780230290600.

Lee, D., & Van Ryzin, G. G. (2020). Bureaucratic reputation in the eyes of citizens: An analysis of US federal agencies. *International Review of Administrative Sciences, 86*(1), 183–200. https://doi.org/10.1177/0020852318769127.

Majone, G. (2001). Two logics of delegation: Agency and fiduciary relations in EU governance. *European Union Politics, 2*(1), 103–122. https://doi.org/10.1177/1465116501002001005.

Marvel, J. D. (2015). Public opinion and public sector performance: Are individuals' beliefs about performance evidence-based or the product of anti-public sector bias? *International Public Management Journal, 18*(2), 209–227. https://doi.org/10.1080/10967494.2014.996627.

Meynhardt, T. (2009). Public value inside: What is public value creation? *International Journal of Public Administration, 32*(3–4), 192–219. https://doi.org/10.1080/01900690902732632.

Mintzberg, H. (1980). Structure in 5's: A synthesis of the research on organization design. *Management Science, 26*(3), 322–341. https://doi.org/10.1287/mnsc.26.3.322.

Moore, M. H. (1997). *Creating Public Value: Strategic Management in Government*. Harvard University Press.

Morgan, G. (2006). *Images of organization* (3rd ed.). Sage Publications.

Osborne, S. P. (Ed.) (2010). *The New Public Governance? Emerging Perspectives on the Theory and Practice of Public Governance*. Routledge.

Osborne, S. (2021). *Public Service Logic: Creating Value for Public Service Users, Citizens, and Society Through Public Service Delivery* (1st ed.). Routledge. https://doi.org/10.4324/9781003009153.

Overman, S., & Van Thiel, S. (2016). Agencification and public sector performance: A systematic comparison in 20 countries. *Public Management Review, 18*(4), 611–635. https://doi.org/10.1080/14719037.2015.1028973.

Pestoff, V. (2018). *Co-Production and Public Service Management: Citizenship, Governance and Public Services Management* (1st ed.). Routledge. https://doi.org/10.4324/9781351059671.

Parliamentary Inquiry Committee of the Dutch Senate (POC) (2012). Lost connections?: Summary of main findings of the parliamentary enquiry by the Dutch Senate into privatization and agencification of central government services. https://www.eerstekamer.nl/behandeling/20121030/lost_connections_summary_of_main.

Polidano, C. (1999). *The new public management in developing countries*. Institute for Development Policy and Management.

Pollitt, C. (2005). Ministries and agencies: Steering, meddling, neglect and dependency. In M. Painter & J. Pierre (Eds.), *Challenges to state capacity: Global trends and comparative perspectives* (1st ed., pp. 112–136). Palgrave Macmillan. https://doi.org/10.1057/9780230524194_7.

Pollitt, C., & Bouckaert, G. (2011). *Public Management Reform: A Comparative Analysis* (3rd ed.). Oxford University Press.

Pollitt, C., & Dan, S. (2013). Searching for impacts in performance-oriented management reform: A review of the European literature. *Public Performance & Management Review, 37*(1), 7–32. https://doi.org/10.2753/PMR1530-9576370101.

Pollitt, C., Talbot, C. Caulfield, J., & Smullen, A. (2005). *Agencies: How Governments Do Things Through Semi-Autonomous Organizations* (1st ed.). Palgrave Macmillan. https://doi.org/10.1057/9780230504868.

Randma-Liiv, T., & Drechsler, W. (2017). Three decades, four phases: Public administration development in Central and Eastern Europe, 1989–2017. *International Journal of Public Sector Management, 30*(6–7), 595–605. https://doi.org/10.1108/IJPSM-06-2017-0175.

Schillemans, T., Overman, S., Fawcett, P., Flinders, M., Fredriksson, M., Lægreid, P., Maggetti, M., Papadopoulos, Y., Rubecksen, K., Rykkja, L. H., Salomonsen, H. H., Smullen, A., Verhoest, K., & Wood, M. (2021). Conflictual accountability: Behavioral responses to conflictual accountability of agencies. *Administration & Society, 53*(8), 1232–1262. https://doi.org/10.1177/00953997211004606.

Thomas, J. C. (2012). *Citizen, Customer, Partner: Engaging the Public in Public Management* (2nd ed.). Routledge. https://doi.org/10.4324/9781315707013.

Tompkins, J. R. (2005). *Organization Theory and Public Management* (1st ed.). Wadsworth Publishing.

Torfing, J., Andersen, L. B., Greve, C., & Klausen, K. K. (2020). *Public Governance Paradigms: Competing and Co-Existing.* Edward Elgar Publishing. https://doi.org/10.4337/9781788971225.

Tyler, T. R., & Fagan, J. (2008). Legitimacy and cooperation: Why do people help the police fight crime in their communities. *Ohio State Journal of Criminal Law, 6*(1), 231–276. http://hdl.handle.net/1811/73064.

Van de Walle, S. (2016). When public services fail: A research agenda on public service failure. *Journal of Service Management, 27*(8), 831–846. https://doi.org/10.1108/JOSM-04-2016-0092.

Van der Meer, J., Vermeeren, B., Van Thiel, S., & Steijn, B. (2023). The bureaucrat, the entrepreneur, and the networker: Developing and validating a measurement scale for civil servants' role perceptions. *Public Administration Review, 84*(3), 500–518. https://doi.org/10.1111/puar.13702.

Van der Wal, Z., De Graaf, G., & Lasthuizen, K. (2008). What's valued most? Similarities and differences between the organizational values of the public and private sector. *Public Administration, 86*(2), 465–482. https://doi.org/10.1111/j.1467-9299.2008.00719.x.

Van Slyke, D. M., & Roch, C. H. (2004). What do they know, and whom do they hold accountable? Citizens in the government–nonprofit contracting relationship. *Journal of Public Administration Research and Theory, 14*(2), 191–209. https://doi.org/10.1093/jopart/muh013.

Van Thiel, S. (2004). Trends in the public sector: Why politicians prefer quasi-autonomous organizations. *Journal of Theoretical Politics, 16*(2), 175–201. https://doi.org/10.1177/0951629804041120

Van Thiel, S., & Migchelbrink, K. (2023). Blame or karma? The attribution of blame in the childcare benefits affair. *Recht Der Werkelijkheid/Journal of Empirical Research on Law in Action, 44*(2), 13–34. https://doi.org/10.5553/RdW/138064242023044002002.

Verhoest, K., Van Thiel, S., Bouckaert, G., & Lægreid, P. (Eds.) (2012). *Government Agencies: Practices and Lessons from 30 Countries* (1st ed.). Palgrave Macmillan. https://doi.org/10.1057/9780230359512.

Vibert, F. (2007). *The Rise of the Unelected: Democracy and the New Separation of Powers*. Cambridge University Press. https://doi.org/10.1017/CBO9780511491160.

Williamson, O. E. (1981). The economics of organization: The transaction cost approach. *American Journal of Sociology, 87*(3), 548–577. https://doi.org/10.1086/227496.

Wynen, J., Kleizen, B., Verhoest, K., Lægreid, P., & Rolland, V. (2020). Just keep silent…: Defensive silence as a reaction to successive structural reforms. *Public Management Review, 22*(4), 498–526. https://doi.org/10.1080/14719037.2019.1588358.

Ecosystems: the word that would be king?

by Adina Dudau

1. Introduction

As we navigate increasingly complex and interconnected societal and public administration challenges, the ecosystem approach is emerging as a pivotal framework for understanding and enhancing public service delivery, as well as the public administration configurations surrounding it. Public administration and public management research appears to be a late adopter of the paradigm, although it embraces previous paradigms promoting the interconnectivity of different interacting actors involved in public service design and delivery. Ecosystems have most recently emerged as a more actionable framing, particularly as examples of public service ecosystems seem to be ever more visible. For example, public transport ecosystems such as TransMilenio in Bogotá, Colombia, or Transport for London, UK, comprise public transit authorities, private transportation companies, urban planners, government agencies, technology providers, and users. Another example is that of urban planning ecosystems, which can include city planning departments, developers, non-profits, community organisations, environmental agencies, and residents. The Sustainable Sydney 2030 initiative in Australia is a good illustration of such ecosystems. It aims to create a sustainable urban environment through green building practices, public transport improvements, and community engagement for inclusive development.

Critical public service ecosystems are our national health systems. For example, the UK's National Health System (NHS) is a self-proclaimed comprehensive public service ecosystem of primary, secondary, tertiary and community healthcare providers (both public and private), policymakers, and patients, as well as interconnected suppliers, all underpinned by integrated care systems (including IT systems), as health data is shared across the system to improve patient outcomes and service efficiency. The integrative nature of this ecosystem was both an asset and a liability during the COVID-19 pandemic, and it became strikingly evident again in June 2024, when a cyber-attack on one private sector supplier's (a pathology laboratory) IT systems caused significant disruption across London health providers, decisively affecting patients' trust as their medical records got published on the dark web. It also affected health providers' ability to provide a wide range of treatments and inflicted what appears to be a long-lasting queue for future tests and treatments, thousands of patient appointments and hundreds of operations having been postponed because of the attack. In another chapter in this book, Greta Nasi explains the value of cybersecurity through the essential service ecosystem, analysing the value at risk at different ecosystem levels.

2. The trend: ecosystems theory in Public Administration and management

The term 'ecosystem' comes from the fields of biology and ecology, having been first coined by Arthur Tansley in 1935. It describes a system comprising both living entities (such as plants, animals, and microorganisms) and surrounding non-living elements (like air, water, and soil minerals) functioning and growing together. These living (biotic) and non-living (abiotic) parts are interconnected through the cycling of nutrients and the flow of energy. Ecosystems play a crucial role in providing vital services beneficial to humans, including purifying air and water, pollinating crops, regulating the climate, and maintaining nutrient cycles.

Our understanding of ecosystems has evolved since Tansley's 1935 conception (Pickett and Grove, 2009). The interconnectivity within the system and the dependency on the system (hence difficulty to transfer) have remained the key tenets of the theory, but organisational ecosystems are not required to be as long-lasting as natural ecosystems are. Governance concepts, including the openness or closed nature of ecosystems and the role of ecosystem managers or architects, are also evolving in management and organisational studies (Jacobides et al., 2018; Gulati et al., 2012).

In organisational contexts, ecosystems refer to a network or a complex, interdependent system that involves various entities – such as organisations, people, information, resources, and technologies – interacting with and adapting to each other (e.g. Granstrand and Holgersson, 2020; Iansiti and Levien, 2004; Teece, 2014; Adner, 2016; Jacobides et al., 2018). The concept includes not just the organisations directly involved in creating and distributing a product or service, but also the broader network of stakeholders such as suppliers, customers, regulators, competitors, and other entities that influence and are influenced by the value creation and delivery processes. Organisational ecosystems are dynamic and evolve over time, often requiring coordination and collaboration among diverse participants.

Ecosystems theory entered Public Administration via public service management, which has been influenced, in turn, by service marketing theories such as service-dominant logic (S-DL). S-DL proponents Lusch and Vargo define an ecosystem as a "relatively self-contained, self-adjusting system of resource-integrating actors connected by shared institutional arrangements and mutual value creation through service exchange" (Lusch and Vargo, 2014, p. 24). Considering the long-term benefit horizon of public services, shared institutional arrangements, protocols, and remits are certainly required in talking the public sector's 'wicked issues' (see Head's chapter in this book, which may explain the lure of ecosystems theory for our field. The disenchantment with the New Public Management and its overly insular focus on organisational economy, efficiency, and effectiveness (e.g. Osborne, 2018) may also have something to do with it. Public service ecosystems (Petrescu, 2019), as conceptualised through S-DL lenses, represent a broad and integrative framework for understanding how public services are created, exchanged, and maintained within interconnected networks of entities. Within them, value co-creation happens at macro (societal), meso (inter-organisational and community), micro (organisational), and sub-micro (individual) levels of analysis (Osborne et al., 2022).

In the past five years, ecosystems have received increasing attention from public service scholars (Liljeroos-Cork and Luhtala, 2024; Dudau et al., 2023a, b; Leite and Hodgkinson, 2023; Osborne et al., 2022). While the largest contingent of papers utilising the ecosystems framing has been published in *Public Management Review*, the home for public service management research, other top journals in our field have also hosted research utilising the theory, further substantiating the claim of a 'trend'. An analysis of the top five-ranked Public Administration journals in CABS Academic Journal Guide[1] illustrates this point:

Table 1. Ecosystems theory in top Public Administration journals

Journal	Number of articles with 'ecosystem*' in their abstract	Publication year	Central themes
PAR	6	2011	Natural ecosystems
		2019	Organisational (performance) ecosystems
		2019	Information ecosystem
		2022	Innovation ecosystem
		2022	Public service ecosystems
		2023	Public service ecosystems
Governance	1	2023	Public governance ecosystems
JPART	3	2002	Natural ecosystems restauration
		2011	Natural ecosystems restauration
		2014	Natural ecosystems restauration
PA	2	2012	Integrated nature design (Natura project)
		2022	Public service ecosystems
PMR	15	2019	Public service ecosystems
		2020	Organisational ecosystems
		2021	Organisational (social enterprise) ecosystems
		2022	Public service ecosystems
		2023	Organisational (NGO) ecosystems
			Public service ecosystems
			Public service ecosystems
			Public governance ecosystems
			Public service ecosystems
			Public service ecosystems
			Public service ecosystems
			Public service ecosystems
			Public service ecosystems
			Data ecosystems
			Organisational (performance) ecosystem

It looks like, before 2019, the concept of 'ecosystems' used in Public Administration and public management research only applied to natural systems. In 2019, PAR published two papers drawing on ecosystems and referring to organisational ecosystems on performance management (Munteanu and Newcomer, 2019) and information-related ecosystems (Robinson et al., 2019), whereas PMR published the call to arms on public service ecosystems (Petrescu, 2019), an extension of Osborne's (2018) public service logic. The dual focus (context specificity and interrelationality) of ecosystems is represented in these early works. Since 2019, there has been a burgeoning research interest in ecosystems, the most popular knowledge area extended through its application being public service ecosystems. Other aspects of public administration discussed through the ecosystem lens include innovation ecosystems (Fan et al., 2022), data ecosystems (Ruijer et al., 2023) and governance ecosystems (Calcara, 2022).

3. Is it a legitimate trend? Ecosystems' distinctiveness and usefulness for public administration and public management

Distinctiveness

While the trend of ecosystems in public administration seems apparent (and was signalled earlier by others who noticed a better fit with public administration and public management data than previous theories – see for example Kinder et al., 2022), we are yet to establish its unique offering and its usefulness in Public Administration and management theory and practice. Indeed, one might note a resemblance with other theories with which we may be more familiar in Public Administration and public management: autopoiesis, context, stakeholder, and network theory. Yet over the years, we have also acknowledged ways in which these theories' explanatory power has been challenged.

Autopoiesis theories describe the self-maintaining chemistry of living cells and extend to systems thinking about the nature of living organisms and organisations. The term 'autopoiesis' was coined by Chilean biologists Humberto Maturana and Francisco Varela in the 1970s. The theory focuses on the micro-level processes within systems, examining how individual components contribute to the system's self-maintenance. Applied to Public Administration and management, particularly as it was in the 1990s (e.g. Kickert, 1993; Morçöl, 1997; Brans and Rossbach, 1997), the theory sheds light on how interconnected public services maintain their coherence and functionality through internal processes. For instance, a network of healthcare providers develops self-regulating mechanisms to ensure consistent quality of care and efficient resource allocation, adapting to internal feedback and external demands. However, the uptake of autopoiesis outside biology has been limited. In Public Administration, there are not enough examples of such self-maintaining systems, particularly when considering unavoidable power and authority dynamics in the sector.

At a more macro level of analysis than autopoiesis theories we find the so-called 'context theories', which advance the idea that public management and policy outcomes are heavily influenced by the specific contexts in which they are implemented. For example, two of its main proponents, Christopher Pollitt and Geert Bouckaert, argue that context matters significantly in understanding the effectiveness and dynamics of public management reforms and practices (Pollitt and Bouckaert, 2011). When applied to interconnected public services, context theories suggest that the design and implementation of services must be tailored to the specific socio-cultural, economic, and political environments of the communities they serve. For example, public health services in urban areas may need different strategies compared to rural areas due to varying demographic and socio-economic contexts. What context theories do well is explain the interdependencies between the elements within a system, but they insufficiently account for practices across contexts.

At a meso level of analysis we find the stakeholder theory, which stipulates that the association between entities and their stakeholders is swayed by the preferences of the most significant stakeholders. This significance is determined by stakeholders' power, legitimacy, and urgency (Freeman, 1984; Mitchell et al., 1997). The idea of stakeholder prominence is contested in the context of intricate organisational and inter-organisational structures designed to address complex challenges such as poverty or climate change (Dentoni et al., 2018; Cottafava and Corazza, 2021). In these situations, valuable insights and solutions might arise from partners traditionally deemed less obvious. Additionally, stakeholder theory and stakeholder management lack the dynamism required of a nuanced analysis of an organisational context, partners, and strategic directions. As suggested by Lebec and Dudau (2023), ecosystems theory might provide solutions to these obstacles, offering insightful perspectives for understanding and illustrating stakeholders' contributions to organisations, especially those operating within networks addressing vague and inherently complicated social issues.

Finally, perhaps the most widespread theory that comes close to the principles and axioms of ecosystems is the 'network theory', which offers a useful mapping of structured relationships in public services. Network theory is primarily structured around the idea of nodes (actors) and links (relationships), focusing on the direct interactions and connections between individual entities. While this is indeed useful in the analysis of these relationships, it oversimplifies complex public service environments. Public services often involve multiple stakeholders with varying degrees of influence and power, and the linear and binary nature of network theory does not adequately capture the nuances of these interactions. It overlooks the indirect, multidimensional, and dynamic interactions that are typical in public services, as well as the influence of socio-political factors and cultural norms. It also fails to account for the adaptability and evolution of public service systems. In a public service context, the environment is constantly changing due to policy shifts, economic changes, and social dynamics, which network theory, with its static representation of relationships, struggles to model effectively. It does not fully encompass the feedback loops, emergent properties, and adaptive mechanisms that are intrinsic to public service systems. This limitation hinders its ability to predict how changes in one part of the system might impact the whole, making it less effective for strategic planning and policymaking.

Kinder et al. (2021, 2022) have also pointed out that network theory, with its emphasis on centrally controlled networks, often limits trust and learning due to its rigid structure of pre-defined roles and relationships. In such a framework, interactions and collaborations are often dictated by top-down governance (Klijn et al. 2015). This top-down approach can lead to uniform outcomes, as it lacks flexibility and responsiveness to the diverse and evolving needs of users. In the context of public services, this rigidity impedes the ability to adapt to local contexts and individual user needs, leading to a one-size-fits-all service delivery that may not be optimal. In contrast, ecosystems theory, as exemplified by Kinder et al.'s (2021, 2022) Finnish data, can offer a more adaptive approach. In the absence of central direction, ecosystems allow for the emergence of bottom-up governances, which are more responsive to the logic of practice that suits both users and street-level professionals. This approach facilitates learning from practice and fosters trust, as it is more aligned with the actual needs and preferences of users. The varied user needs give way to diverse emergent governance options, each legitimate in its context. These governances are not imposed top-down, but are 'pulled' by users' needs, leading to service delivery that is more quality-oriented and personalised, as opposed to being solely cost-driven. This shift towards user-centricity in public services, where outcomes are influenced by user-defined preferences, represents a fundamental change from traditional, top-down governance models.

The Finnish case highlighted by Kinder et al. (2022) also highlights the significance of local context and culture in shaping public service delivery. The Nordic context, with its preference for pragmatic theory and practice iteration, favours informality and practicality over strict adherence to prescribed roles and relationships. Public service actors in this environment are not seen as merely rational agents; instead, they engage in listening and learning from users, focusing on personalised care plans, and figuring out practical delivery methods. This approach highlights the importance of context and culture in determining the most effective governance and management style for public services. It also suggests the power of ecosystems theory as a bridge between context and network theories.

Usefulness

The theory certainly shows promise for our field. For example, Kinder et al. (2021, 2022) show the potential of the ecosystems paradigm to confer a practice logic on public service quality resulting in active citizenship as an additional way of contributing to, and legitimising, quality in public services. Here, legitimacy encompasses the right and acceptance of an authority, usually a governing law (e.g. Laclau, 1990), which is, however debatably, predicated on its capacity to reflect the will and interests of the public. Earlier citizen participation work would support this perspective, claiming that participation facilitates the redistribution of power that enables the have-not citizens, presently excluded from the political and economic processes, to be deliberately included in the future (Arnstein, 1969).

While not everyone agrees on the link between public engagement (of either people or institutions) and public legitimacy (Nabatchi and Amsler, 2014; Braun and Busuioc, 2019), the argument that ecosystem approaches to governance can enhance public service legitimacy by reducing the distance between decision-makers and the public is certainly powerful (Kinder et al., 2022). Not only is it persuasive, it also seems useful, as participatory models of governance that embody a wide range of stakeholder perspectives tend to yield more innovative and effective solutions to public issues, contributing to stronger, more responsive, and more accountable governance structures (Fung, 2006, 2015).

If the usefulness of the theory is predicated on opportunities for more inclusive and legitimate governing forms, then expanding the breadth of participation further solidifies this legitimacy. The principle of inclusiveness asserts that the wider the range of stakeholders involved in the governance process, the more reflective and representative the decisions will be of the general populace. This approach strengthens public institutions by ensuring they are not only accountable but also transparent and responsive to the needs of a diverse society. The result, as argued by Gaventa and Barrett (2012), is the improvement of public services: more accountable and more representative and more responsive to the needs of the public. It follows, then, that public institutions that engage a broad spectrum of citizens, including marginalised and underrepresented groups, tend to develop policies and services that are more equitable and effective. This comprehensive approach to governance, which prioritises broad participation, is certainly suitable for analyses and prescriptions undertaken through ecosystem-theory lenses.

4. Responding to ecosystems: impact and future research directions

In Public Administration and management, we have responded to ecosystems with a considerable degree of enthusiasm in different aspects of public sector organising, from people management (e.g. corruption in civil service – in Dudau et al., 2023c), to performance measurement (Munteanu and Newcomer, 2019), value co-creation (Osborne et al., 2023), and service resilience (Leite and Hodgkinson, 2021). Indeed, it appears that ecosystems theory offers a promising direction in Public Administration research and practice, reflecting a shift towards more holistic, interconnected, and dynamic approaches to understanding and managing public administration processes and public services.

The research agenda must be further expanded to encompass not only the exploration of engagement's impact on institutional legitimacy, stability, and capacity, and the conditions under which the engagement of ecosystems participants is most likely to lead to positive legitimation outcomes, but also to investigate the distinct epistemic foundations of network and ecosystem analyses in public management. This involves a thorough examination of the differing theoretical underpinnings and methodological approaches inherent in these two perspectives.

Additionally, there is a pressing need to scrutinise how active agency (e.g. of street-level bureaucrats, of individual members of the public, of groups, etc.) is conceptualised within both network and ecosystem frameworks. Kinder et al. (2021, 2022) opened this avenue for us, but there is a further need to understand the role of individual and collective actors, and how their actions and interactions, underpinned by trust-building and learning, are perceived and incorporated within these analytical approaches. A connected issue is that of innovation and learning in ecosystems. Ecosystems theory can facilitate innovation in public administration by promoting learning and experimentation within and across organisations. By understanding the ecosystem as a dynamic learning environment, public administration can evolve more effectively through continuous feedback and adaptation.

Next, it may be beneficial to focus more on co-creation (or destruction – see Cui and Osborne, 2022) of value within ecosystems. Empirical research on this area has already started and is developing rapidly, but there are methodological challenges worth noting and identifying solutions to. Indeed, by shifting the focus from top-down service delivery to bottom-up and dialogical co-creation of value, ecosystems theory poses some methodological challenges to empirical investigation to do with boundary conditions, difficulty to generalise, localism, and difficulty to delineate the phenomena under study and the level of analysis. This also raises a spill-over problem: how do we extrapolate from implementation ecosystems, possibly most accessible for empirical investigation, to cross-sectoral policy integration? Indeed, the interconnected nature of ecosystems encourages a more integrated approach to policymaking. This is particularly relevant for addressing 'wicked problems' that span across different policy domains, requiring coordinated efforts across various sectors and levels of government.

Finally, as outlined in Leite and Hodgkinson (2020) and Dudau et al. (2023b), ecosystems theory raises the opportunity to investigate adaptability and resilience in the face of changing environments. In public administration, this perspective can help governments and agencies to be more responsive and flexible, adapting policies and services to evolving societal needs and challenges. There is substantial scope for development in this area, alongside a sustainability focus: ecosystems theory inherently promotes sustainability, as it considers the long-term impacts and interdependencies of policies and actions. This aligns with the growing emphasis on sustainable development in public governance.

Incorporating ecosystems theory into public administration research and practice encourages a more nuanced, flexible, and collaborative approach to governance, which is increasingly necessary in our complex and interconnected world, particularly in the face of unprecedented policy and public service access challenges post-COVID-19.

Notes

1. Chosen over alternatives such as the Scopus journal ranking on the basis of: (a) its relative stability over time; (b) the combination on metrics and expert qualitative evaluation of the journals; and (c) widespread, global use.

References

Adner, R. (2016). Ecosystem as structure: An actionable construct for strategy. *Journal of Management*, 43(1), 39–58. https://doi.org/10.1177/0149206316678451.

Arnstein, S. R. (1969). A ladder of citizen participation. *Journal of the American Institute of Planners*, 35(4), 216–224. https://doi.org/10.1080/01944366908977225.

Brans, M., & Rossbach, S. (1997). The autopoiesis of administrative systems: Niklas Luhmann on public administration and public policy. *Public Administration*, 75(3), 417–439. https://doi.org/10.1111/1467-9299.00068.

Braun, C., & Busuioc, M. (2020). Stakeholder engagement as a conduit for regulatory legitimacy? *Journal of European Public*, 27(11), 1599–1611. https://doi.org/10.1080/13501763.2020.1817133.

Cottafava, D., & Corazza, L. (2021). Co-design of a stakeholders' ecosystem: An assessment methodology by linking social network analysis, stakeholder theory and participatory mapping. *Kybernetes*, 50(3), 836–858. https://doi.org/10.1108/K-12-2019-0861.

Cui, T., & Osborne, S. P. (2022). Unpacking value destruction at the intersection between public and private value. *Public Administration*, 101(4), 1207–1226. https://doi.org/10.1111/padm.12850.

Dentoni, D., Bitzer, V., & Schouten, G. (2018). Harnessing wicked problems in multi-stakeholder partnerships. *Journal of Business Ethics*, 150(2), 333–356. https://doi.org/10.1007/s10551-018-3858-6.

Dudau, A., Stirbu, D., Petrescu, M., & Bocioaga, A. (2023a). Enabling PSL and value co-creation through public engagement: a study of municipal service regeneration. *Public Management Review*, 1–28. https://doi.org/10.1080/14719037.2023.2203148.

Dudau, A., Masou, R., Murdock, A., & Hunter, P. (2023b). Public service resilience post-Covid: Introduction to the special issue. *Public Management Review*, 25(4), 681–689. https://doi.org/10.1080/14719037.2023.2219690.

Dudau, A., Zyglidopoulos, S. C., Yang, W., & Li, Y. (2023c). Residual corruption in the Chinese civil service: Towards an ecosystem theory. *Academy of Management Proceedings*, 2023(1). https://doi.org/10.5465/AMPROC.2023.17710abstract.

Fan, D., Su, Y., & Huang, X. (2022). Nursery city innovation: A CELL framework. *Public Administration Review*, 82(4), 764–770. https://doi.org/10.1111/puar.13490.

Freeman, R. E. (1984). *Strategic Management: A Stakeholder Approach*. Pitman Publishing. https://doi.org/10.1017/CBO9781139192675.

Fung, A. (2006). Varieties of participation in complex governance. *Public Administration Review*, 66(s1), 66–75. https://doi.org/10.1111/j.1540-6210.2006.00667.x.

Fung, A. (2015). Putting the public back into governance: The challenges of citizen participation and its future. *Public Administration Review*, 75(4), 513–522. https://doi.org/10.1111/puar.12361.

Gaventa, J., & Barrett, G. (2012). Mapping the outcomes of citizen engagement. *World Development*, 40(12), 2399–2410. https://doi.org/10.1016/j.worlddev.2012.05.014.

Granstrand, O., & Holgersson, M. (2020). Innovation ecosystems: A conceptual review and a new definition. *Technovation*, 90–91, 1–12. https://doi.org/10.1016/j.technovation.2019.102098.

Gulati, R., Puranam, P., Tushman, M. (2012). Meta-organization design: Rethinking design in interorganizational and community contexts. *Strategic management journal*, *33*(6), 571–586. https://doi.org/10.1002/smj.1975.

Iansiti, M., & Levien, R. (2004). Strategy as ecology. *Harvard Business Review*, *82*(3), 68–78.

Jacobides, M. G., Cennamo, C., & Gawer, A. (2018). Towards a theory of ecosystems. *Strategic Management Journal*, *39*(8), 2255–2276. https://doi.org/10.1002/smj.2904.

Kickert, W. J. (1993). Autopoiesis and the science of (public) administration: Essence, sense and Nonsense. *Organization Studies*, *14*(2), 261–278. https://doi.org/10.1177/017084069301400205.

Kinder, T., Stenvall, J., Six, F., & Memon, A. (2021). Relational leadership in collaborative governance ecosystems. *Public Management Review*, *23*(11), 1612–1639. https://doi.org/10.1080/14719037.2021.1879913.

Kinder, T., Six, F., Stenvall, J., & Memon, A. (2022). Governance-as-legitimacy: Are ecosystems replacing networks? *Public Management Review*, *24*(1), 8–33. https://doi.org/10.1080/14719037.2020.1786149.

Klijn, E. H., & Koppenjan, J. F. M. (2012). Governance network theory: Past, present and future. *Policy and Politics*, *40*(4), 187–206. https://doi.org/10.1332/030557312X655431.

Laclau, E. (1990). *New Reflections on the Revolution of Our Time*. Verso.

Lebec, L., & Dudau, A. (2023). From the inside looking out: Towards an ecosystem paradigm of third sector organizational performance measurement. *Public Management Review*, *26*(7), 1988–2013. https://doi.org/10.1080/14719037.2023.2238724.

Leite, H., & Hodgkinson, R. (2023). Examining resilience across a service ecosystem under crisis. *Public Management Review*, *25*(4), 690–709. https://doi.org/10.1080/14719037.2021.2012375.

Liljeroos-Cork, J., & Luhtala, M. (2024). Value co-destruction through misintegration of resources within a public service ecosystem. *Public Management Review*, 1–24. https://doi.org/10.1080/14719037.2024.2366986.

Lusch, R. R., 2014. *Service-Dominant Logic: Premises, Perspectives, Possibilities*. Cambridge University Press. https://doi.org/10.1017/CBO9781139043120.

Maturana, H. R., & Varela, F. J. (1980). *Autopoiesis and Cognition: The Realization of the Living* (1st ed.). D. Reidel Publishing Company. https://doi.org/10.1007/978-94-009-8947-4.

Mitchell, R. K., Agle, B. R., & Wood, D. J. (1997). Toward a theory of stakeholder identification and salience: Defining the principle of who and what really counts. *Academy of Management Review*, *22*(4), 853–886. https://doi.org/10.2307/259247.

Morçöl, G. (1995). A Meno paradox for public administration: Have we acquired a radically new knowledge from the "new sciences". *Administrative Theory & Praxis*, *19*(3), 305–317. https://www.jstor.org/stable/25611228.

Munteanu, I., & Newcomer, K. (2020). Leading and learning through dynamic performance management in government. *Public Administration Review*, *80*(2), 316–325. https://doi.org/10.1111/puar.13126.

Nabatchi, T., & Amsler, L. B. (2014). Direct public engagement in local government. *The American Review of Public Administration*, *44*(4), 63S–88S. https://doi.org/10.1177/0275074013519702.

Osborne, S. P. (2018). From public service-dominant logic to public service logic: Are public service organizations capable of co-production and value co-creation. *Public Management Review*, *20*(2), 225–231. https://doi.org/10.1080/14719037.2017.1350461.

Osborne, S. P., Powell, M., Cui, T., & Strokosch, K. (2022). Value Creation in the Public Service Ecosystem: An Integrative Framework. *Public Administration Review, 82*(4), 634–645. https://doi.org/10.1111/puar.13474.

Petrescu, M. (2019). From marketing to public value: Towards a theory of public service ecosystems. *Public Management Review, 21*(11), 1733–1752. https://doi.org/10.1080/14719037.2019.1619811.

Pickett, S. T. A., & Grove, J. M. (2009). Urban ecosystems: What would Tansley do? *Urban Ecosystems, 12*(1), 1–8. https://doi.org/10.1007/s11252-008-0079-2.

Pollitt, C. (Ed.) (2013). *Context in Public Policy and Management: The Missing Link?* Edward Elgar Publishing.

Pollitt, C., & Bouckaert, G. (2011). *Public Management Reform: A Comparative Analysis of NPM, the Neo-Weberian State, and New Public Governance* (3rd ed.). Oxford University Press.

Ruijer, E., Dingelstad, J., & Meijer, A. (2023). Studying complex systems through design interventions probing open government data ecosystems in the Netherlands. *Public Management Review, 25*(1), 129–149. https://doi.org/10.1080/14719037.2021.1942533.

Tansley, A. G. (1935). The use and abuse of vegetational concepts and terms. *Ecology, 16*(3), 284–307. https://doi.org/10.2307/1930070.

Teece, D. J. (2014). A dynamic capabilities-based entrepreneurial theory of the multinational enterprise. *Journal of International Business Studies, 45*(1), 8–37. https://doi.org/10.1057/jibs.2013.54.

PART 5
FUTURES OF MANAGING THE CIVIL SERVICE

Shifting dynamics of advice: Non-state experts and private sector consultancies in public policy

by Rosie Collington

1. Introduction: policy challenges in the modern state

The policy challenges facing modern states look very different to those of half a century ago, when Public Administration scholarship in Europe first consolidated into a distinct research community. Since then, governments have become responsible for a growing number of social, economic, and – increasingly – environmental functions that politicians and public servants of the 1970s would scarcely have recognised. During the COVID-19 pandemic, for example, it was to governments that citizens and businesses turned to steer populations out of a health catastrophe and households and firms out of financial ruin. Following the enactment of the Paris Agreement in 2015, it is national governments that have become responsible for developing and coordinating domestic climate mitigation and adaptation strategies, marking a shift away from earlier market-led forms of climate governance (Falkner, 2016; Meckling and Allan, 2020). From demographic aging to natural disaster response and mounting homelessness, the diversity and scale of 'wicked' policy problems that governments are today understood as the responsible actor for navigating is unprecedented (Mazzucato and Kattel, 2018; Head, 2022; Head and Alford, 2015).

In part reflecting this expanded mandate, most OECD governments are also spending more than they ever have before, and government production costs as a percentage of GDP remain higher than they were before the 2008 financial crisis – despite a widespread commitment to reduce public sector budgets through austerity programmes over the following decade (Hood and Dixon, 2015; OECD, 2024). Many governments are nonetheless struggling to meet policy objectives that have long formed part of their mandate, from the provision of basic healthcare to tax administration and the regulation of emerging sectors, leading to arguments that the lines between what counts as a 'wicked' and 'normal' policy challenge are increasingly blurred (Peters, 2017). Over the past five decades, bureaucracies and their coordination have undergone radical transformations, shifting from more hierarchical to more market-based and networked forms in the wake of public sector reform agendas including New Public Management (NPM) and Joined-Up Governance (JUG) (Bouckaert et al., 2010; Pollitt and Bouckaert, 2017; Verhoest et al., 2007). At different junctures, across diverse policy domains, public sector organisations have been privatised, decentralised, outsourced, agencified, re-centralised, and insourced, and each wave of reform has left an indelible stamp on the bureaucracies that exist today.

The transformations of government bureaucracies and the evolution of policy challenges they encounter have been accompanied by the growing involvement of non-state actors as sources of expertise, advice, and capacity, from management consultants to legal and accounting professionals, academics, independent advisors, and, particularly in low- and middle-income countries, the contractors of international organisations (IOs) and public investment banks (PIBs). Notwithstanding some important contributions from within the field, however, the roles of these actors and the tasks for which governments have contracted them have remained only a marginal object of study in Public Administration and governance. Evidence from across the social sciences suggests that the complexity and uncertainty of policy challenges today, constrained capacity within public sector organisations, and growing struggles to secure legitimacy for action have created new opportunities for non-state actors to shape not only policy decisions but also bureaucratic processes. In this context, it is imperative to better understand the implications of this development, and how governments can meaningfully use external expertise and advice in ways that enable them to meet both current and future policy challenges. This chapter argues that the growing involvement of particularly management consultants, but also other actors, in policymaking and implementation processes around the world demands attention from the researchers who best understand the internal processes and politics of public sectors, and that this is critical for making sense of how governments succeed (or fail) in meeting the ever-evolving needs of the citizens they are responsible for serving.

2. The growing involvement of private sector actors in government bureaucracies

The involvement of non-state actors as sources of expertise and knowledge in government bureaucracies and policymaking is not a recent phenomenon, dating back to the emergence of early modern states, where it enabled them "to become more powerful and sophisticated and to construct empires and economies that were global in reach" (Ash, 2010). Nonetheless, the scale and scope of their activities in public sectors have grown dramatically over the past century, particularly in more recent decades. From the 1930s, external expertise increasingly came from actors organised in private sector firms, notably management consultancies (McKenna, 2010). This section briefly describes how the involvement of these actors evolved throughout this period, and related to broader trends in public administration reform and theory.

Given that what follows offers only a broad overview of general historical trends, it is worth noting at the outset that the scale and scope of non-state actors' involvement in public sectors, and the types of organisations involved in the provision of expertise and knowledge, has always diverged significantly across countries, broadly reflecting differences in administrative traditions and 'varieties of capitalism' (Saint-Martin, 2017; Seabrooke and Sending, 2022). Kipping (2021) has suggested that among the reasons why the United States became the birthplace of modern management consulting and the largest market for its services since its inception was the historically low extent of professionalisation and bureaucratisation of the government, itself related to a cultural suspicion of government (p. 37). The involvement of private sector consulting firms in the United States government increased substantially during the 1940s, as firms that had consolidated throughout the previous decade through the provision of advice to ailing companies in the aftermath of the Great Depression were invited to join the World War II effort and the post-war reconstruction (David, 2012; Kipping, 2021, 2019; McKenna, 2010). Individuals from firms including Booz Allen were directly employed to senior positions in the military (David, 2012), for example, and consultancies were subsequently commissioned to undertake critical analytical tasks for strategically important initiatives at the national level, such as the 1947 Hoover Commission (McKenna, 2010).

In subsequent decades, management consultancies also became increasingly involved in policymaking processes within Western European governments, tracking not only the establishment of consulting divisions in those countries (Saint-Martin, 2017), but also the more general proliferation of organisations established to provide advice to and influence government decisions, such as foreign policy and economic think tanks based within academic institutions (McGann, 2016). In particular, the growth of management consultants within the governments of Western Europe during the 1960s and 1970s has been linked to the expansion and changes in the role of computing within public administrations. In the UK, for example, the contracting of Arthur Andersen in this period was driven by the perception of a growing skills gap between public sector employees and consultants (Weiss, 2019).

The advent of neoliberal reforms in the 1980s catalysed the growth of management consultancies and think tanks within public administrations. The liberalisation of financial markets, the ensuing waves of mergers and acquisitions, and the reconfiguration of corporate governance norms towards shareholder-value maximisation facilitated the creation of new consulting services for private sector firms seeking to bolster productivity and generate support for management decisions among company boards (Mazzucato and Collington, 2023; McKenna, 2010). In the public sector, management consultancies in particular were contracted to provide advice on transferring companies into private hands, competitive tendering, and administrative reforms to increase efficiency and productivity of public sector employees (Hodge, 2006). In these roles, they acted as 'diffusers' and promoters of New Public Management, leading Hood and Jackson (1991) to coin the term 'consultocracy' to describe the influence of consultancies on public policy and decision-making (Hodge, 2006; Saint-Martin, 1998; Ylönen and Kuusela, 2019). In the United Kingdom, spending on management consulting services increased from £6 million in 1979 to £246 million in 1990 (Saint-Martin, 2017, p. 220), and similar patterns could be found elsewhere, notably in other liberal market economies, but also in countries such as France (Saint-Martin, 1998, p. 333). Saint-Martin (1998) describes the concerted strategies of multinational firms during this period to consolidate this influence through building "networks of expertise within the state" (p. 319), attesting to the challenges of clearly demarcating where demand ends and supply begins as drivers of growth in the consulting industry more generally (Mazzucato and Collington, 2023).

Governments beyond North America and Western Europe similarly experienced increased involvement of external actors in policy processes that went hand-in-hand with public sector and economic reforms that were frequently imposed through 'structural adjustment programmes' as conditions of loans from international financial institutions (IFIs). Management consultants have been described as the 'foot soldiers' of these organisations (Hodge, 2006), and were often contracted by them to oversee the privatisation of state-owned enterprises and public banks (Mazzucato and Collington, 2023, pp. 55–58). IFIs also increasingly deployed 'consultants' who were individually contracted by them to assist with the implementation of reforms through 'technical assistance', 'capacity building' and local training initiatives, which helped to create support for the reforms within public administrations (Broome and Seabrooke, 2015; Chwieroth, 2007).

Although the involvement of non-state actors in the policy activities of public administrations had steadily increased throughout the earlier decades of the 20th century, the period of neoliberalisation ushered in a rapid growth that benefited not only from the market-based nature of public sector and economic reforms, but also from the concomitant emergence of public choice ideas and the loss of trust in public sector employees and organisations vis-à-vis the private sector (Bouckaert, 2012; Van de Walle, 2011). Indeed, it is particularly in countries that most fervently adopted neoliberal reforms and where trust in the public sector and public services has remained low since the 1980s (cf. Van de Walle et al., 2008) that the scale and scope of involvement of non-state actors in public administrations has increased most dramatically ever since. With the emergence of Third Way ideas and 'networked' forms of governance in the 1990s, governments including the United Kingdom, the United States and Australia began to see growing involvement of actors including established management consultancies, non-governmental organisation (NGO) representatives and academics in policy decision-making processes, including through expert advisory bodies and councils (Craft and Halligan, 2017; Crowley and Head, 2017). Increasingly, outsourcing firms and NGOs were also contracted to directly deliver public services and manage strategic contracting arrangements (Bowman et al., 2015; Morphet, 2021; Pollitt and Bouckaert, 2017). In these new governance paradigms, governments and their public sectors were understood as critical actors in convening collective processes of policy objective-setting, but ideas about the relative efficiency and effectiveness of private sector actors in their implementation and the delivery of public services largely persisted (Mazzucato and Collington, 2023).

Indeed, even following the 2008 financial crisis and the adoption of public sector austerity programmes by OECD governments around the world, the structure of government production has continued to tilt further towards the growing involvement of external actors in public administration and services delivery, as shown in Figure 1 below. There is also evidence to suggest that in countries where the scale of central government spending on consulting contracts initially decreased in the early years of the 2010s, multinational consultancies in particular maintained widespread involvement in public administrations by offering to provide services at far below normal market rates. In the UK, for example, where the Coalition government elected in 2010 had committed to reducing spending on consultancies, it was reported that KPMG had "bid just £1 for some contracts worth millions" (Curtis, 2011). By 2019–2020, central government bodies were spending an estimated £1.2 billion on management consultancies (O'Dwyer, 2021) – up from £789 million in 2009–2010 (National Audit Office, 2010, p. 11).

Figure 1. Costs of goods and services used and financed by government as a percentage of total government production costs, OECD country average, 2007–2021

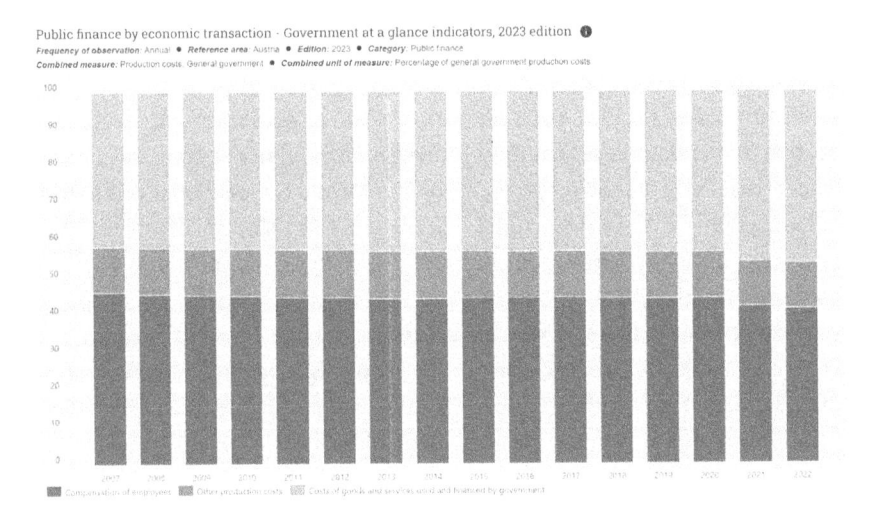

Source: OECD Stat (2023).

In summary, the nature of advice provided by external actors to governments since the post-war decades has largely reflected broader trends in public administration and ideas about the role of government in society. Management consultancies in particular have also been critical in the construction and promotion of these ideas. As the new policy challenges facing public sectors in the 2020s have become increasingly characterised by their complexity and uncertainty, it is worth exploring how the age of 'wicked' policy problems is shaping and being shaped by the influence of external experts, advisors, and consultants.

3. Experts, advisors, and consultants in responses to wicked policy problems

Originally coined in the 1970s (Rittel and Webber, 1973), the concept of 'wicked' policy challenges has gained popularity within public administration and governance research over the past decade to refer to policy demands that are complex, do not have immediate solutions, and require cross-sectoral and often experimental responses. They "typically cut across policy sectors and established levels of government [and] simultaneously affect all levels of society, diverse policy areas and sectors" (Alford and Head, 2017). In some cases, what is novel about policy areas described as 'wicked' is not that they are new societal challenges, but rather that governments have become responsible for navigating a collective response to them. The need to reduce carbon dioxide emissions has long been understood as a societal challenge, for example, but it is only in the past decade that governments have come to be recognised as the critical nodes "mediating emergent polycentric governance" (Dubash, 2021). While there is growing evidence that governments are increasingly involving non-state experts, advisors, and consultants in the development and implementation of responses to wicked policy challenges, this development and its implications have received only limited attention from public administration and governance researchers. Drawing on recent experiences with COVID-19 pandemic response and reflecting on emergent research from beyond the Public Administration field, what follows explores key drivers of increased involvement of non-state actors in wicked policy governance. The chapter concludes with reflections on the potential implications of this, and outstanding research questions for public administration and governance scholars.

The COVID-19 pandemic has widely been hailed as the epitome of a wicked policy challenge, with some researchers also describing it as a 'super wicked problem', a term previously used in reference to climate change, insofar as it has the characteristics of "time is running out, no central authority, those causing the problem also want to solve it, and policies irrationally discount the future" (Auld et al., 2021). Among other themes, public administration and policy researchers have explored what lessons can be gleaned from governments' responses to the pandemic for policy learning (Lee et al., 2020; Powell and King-Hill, 2020), bureaucratic agility (Kattel et al., 2022; Moon, 2020), public sector capacity (Kattel and Mazzucato, 2020; Weiss and Thurbon, 2021), and the interrelations between these for multilevel governance for future crises (Dunlop et al., 2020). The COVID-19 pandemic brought renewed attention among policymakers, practitioners, and citizens to the role of private sector actors in public policy processes and governance. In the first year of the pandemic, the involvement of management consultancies in particular reached an unprecedented scale and scope. While governments' uses of consultancies varied widely, patterns of growth could be seen across OECD countries (Mazzucato and Collington, 2023, pp. 11–17). The French Health Ministry, for example, had contracted consultancies for tasks related to the COVID-19 pandemic at an estimated value of €11 million between March 2020 and February 2021 (Braun and De Villepin, 2021). In the United Kingdom, where, as noted, spending on consultancies had been on the ascent throughout the previous decade, the value of contracts between central government bodies and consultancies reached £2.5bn in 2020–2021, with spending estimated to be double that of the previous year, driven in large part by contracts for pandemic-related tasks (O'Dwyer, 2021). Across the global economy, demand for consulting services across industries soared during the first years of the pandemic, with the UK consulting body, the Management Consultancies Association, suggesting that the sector grew by 16% between 2020 and 2021 (Consultancy.uk, 2022).

Notwithstanding some important contributions (cf. Vogelpohl et al., 2022), at the time of writing, research exploring why governments turned to management consultancies for support to deliver pandemic responses has been limited. Broader research on the involvement of consultancies and external expertise in wicked policy governance may nonetheless hold valuable insights.

The complexity and uncertainty that characterises wicked policy problems has been described as an important factor in governments' contracting of management consultancies in responses to them. Faced with new challenges and a perceived or real absence of internal expertise for responding to them, public sector managers employ consultancies to help make sense of emergent risks and their impacts, including through the use of algorithmic and digital tools, and develop policy options (Christensen and Collington, 2024). In her study of climate adaptation governance in the Australian government, for example, Keele (2021) shows how consultants "translate unfamiliar problems like climate change adaptation into familiar (techno-managerial) concepts that can be operationalized as tools then circulated, commercialized, and ultimately used by governments and businesses to tame the existential threats posed by dangerous climate change" (p. 69). Growing demand from public sector actors for consulting services in wicked policy governance thus reflects a broader tendency wherein evidence-informed advisory systems have been undermined as public sector managers come under pressure to make rapid decisions under conditions of unpredictability (Head, 2023).

As Head (2023) also notes, this context is exacerbated by the growing 'contestability' of expertise itself, which adds to the perceptions of uncertainty by policymakers about appropriate policy options. We might consider how this contestability interacts with issues of trust in government and public sector employees in policymakers' decisions to contract out critical tasks to private sector actors. The contracting of consultancies to serve as potential scapegoats, or, conversely, add legitimacy to decisions made by managers of private sector firms is well documented (Aschauer et al., 2022; Sturdy, 2011; Sturdy et al., 2010). In contexts of close media scrutiny and dissipating trust among political constituencies and publics, and particularly where these risks are compounded by the real or perceived wickedness of a policy problem, it is feasible that this is more often a key factor in public sector consultancy contracting decisions than is currently recognised. Interviews with employees working in governments at the outset of the COVID-19 pandemic attested to the role that a 'fog of war' mentality plays in such decisions (Mazzucato and Collington, 2023, p. 16).

Related to both these factors is the role of public sector capacity and its erosion in decisions to contract consultancies in governments. The loss of critical capabilities – or 'hollowing out' of the state – following decades of reforms that have shifted responsibility for public administration tasks and services to private sector actors, and from central government bodies to supra- and sub-state bodies, has been analysed extensively (Crouch, 2015; Dunleavy and Carrera, 2013; Head, 2023; Holliday, 2000; Pollitt and Bouckaert, 2017; Rhodes, 1994). Quantitative studies have established that NPM reforms did not result in reduced government production costs or increased 'efficiency' in the public sector (Alonso et al., 2015; Hood and Dixon, 2015), and the retrenchment of capabilities resulting from the contracting out of key functions has also been documented through case studies, including on public sector digital infrastructure (Collington, 2022). There is further evidence to suggest that public sector use of consultancies is associated with 'demand inflation', wherein demand for consulting services grows with greater use of consultancies, with general negative implications for organisational efficiency (Sturdy et al., 2022).

In wicked policy problems, particularly where they emerge quickly, the absence of capacity for delivering objectives can contribute to decisions to contract out tasks to management consultancies and other non-state actors, and indeed must also be recognised as contributing to the wickedness of a policy problem. The inherent complexity and uncertainty of policy challenges are compounded when public sector organisations lack the tools and skills for understanding and navigating stakeholder environments and assessing potential implications of risks and policy options. The erosion of public sector capacity is also related to the loss of trust in public sectors, where a decline in public sector effectiveness and public services quality undermines citizen support, suggesting that each of the factors discussed here – inherent policy wickedness, contestability of expertise, loss of trust, and the erosion of public sector capacity – interact to shape the involvement of non-state actors in wicked policy governance.

One final, important factor that is worth discussing here are the approaches and strategies of non-state actors in positioning themselves as valuable sources of knowledge and expertise in responses to wicked policy problems. In the years following the Paris Agreement, for example, large multinational consultancies invested heavily in establishing new sustainability divisions and expanding service lines that purported to fulfil the tasks governments were encountering, including through acquisitions of smaller, specialised sustainability consultancies (Christensen and Collington, 2024). Firms in sectors including engineering and construction also developed climate adaptation consulting services, joining the ranks of established consultancies among the "earliest 'winners' from the rapidly emerging and hugely contested domain of climate policy" (Keele, 2021, p. 56). Similarly, during the pandemic, large multinational consultancies were quick to establish new divisions and service lines purporting to offer solutions to the emergent challenges facing both governments and firms (Mazzucato and Collington, 2023). In the context that many public sectors find themselves in when confronting wicked policy problems in the 2020s, these efforts by non-state actors to be perceived as effective sources of supply should also be understood as an important dimension in the growing use of them by policymakers, pointing to the need for public administration and governance scholars to look beyond the formal boundaries of the state, perhaps drawing on perspectives from other social science disciplines, to understand contemporary developments and future challenges for the public sector.

4. Outstanding questions for public administration and governance research

Equipped with rigorous methodological approaches and a deep understanding of the inner workings of public sectors, public administration and governance scholars remain in prime position to confront emerging questions related to changing governance forms and the involvement of non-state actors in them. The developments explored in this chapter point to a number of research gaps and outstanding questions that researchers in these fields would be well poised to address, and which relate to other emerging research domains.

For one, it is pertinent to better understand what new forms of advice and expertise are being introduced into the public sector, and which actors are providing them. Government budget data can only tell us so much; as this chapter has described, the scale of management consultancy involvement in public sectors does not always correlate with government spending. Contracting information is inconsistent across governments, although in some countries recent transparency initiatives have created opportunities for better access to accurate data. These challenges should not preclude researchers from attempting to answer descriptive questions of 'who' and 'how much', but rather point to the need for rigorous qualitative approaches that public administration communities have advanced.

Further research is also needed to establish why public sector actors contract non-state actors in particular policy contexts, and how this relates to the broader challenges facing modern public administrations, from budgetary cuts to capacity erosion, declining or volatile citizen trust, and the complexity and uncertainty of policy areas. In particular, public administration researchers might explore how contracting decisions relate to formal bureaucratic structures within public sector organisations, and how external advice and expertise is mediated through changes in 'policy advisory systems' (Head, 2023, 2017).

The discussion in the preceding section of this chapter highlighted some implications of using management consultancies for public sector capacity, but some important gaps in knowledge endure about the consequences of non-state sources of knowledge and expertise in different contexts. Research on wicked policy governance has pointed to the importance of 'coordination capacity', for example (Christensen et al., 2019; Lægreid and Rykkja, 2015; Vitola and Senfelde, 2015). How might the involvement of non-state actors in wicked policy governance influence governments' ability to coordinate across actors within and beyond public administrations? Relatedly, how does the scale and scope of non-state actors' involvement affect public sector organisations' ability to learn and adapt as wicked policy problems evolve (Collington and Mazzucato, 2024; Mazzucato and Collington, 2023)? Both coordination capacity and public sector 'dynamic capabilities' require access to tacit or less-codifiable knowledge derived from routines and information about changes in the wider operating environment. We might consider how capacity becomes eroded through the loss of access to this knowledge across the interfaces of actors involved.

Perhaps most importantly for policy practitioners, further research is needed to better understand how public sector actors can effectively use external sources of advice and expertise. Modern governments do not work alone, and indeed citizens will continue to expect that they are able to harness knowledge and expertise from across societies to achieve policy objectives – whether from management consultancies, NGOs, think tanks, academics, firms, or other organisations. In particular, case studies exploring effective uses of non-state actors in the development and implementation of policies are needed to advance this understanding.

References

Alford, J., & Head, B. W. (2017). Wicked and less wicked problems: A typology and a contingency framework. *Policy and Society, 36*(3), 397–413. https://doi.org/10.1080/14494035.2017.1361634.

Alonso, J. M., Clifton, J., & Díaz-Fuentes, D. (2015). Did new public management matter? An empirical analysis of the outsourcing and decentralization effects on public sector size. *Public Management Review, 17*(5), 643–660. https://doi.org/10.1080/14719037.2013.822532.

Aschauer, F., Sohn, M., & Hirsch, B. (2022). How managers' risk perceptions affect their willingness to blame advisors as scapegoats. *European Management Journal, 40*(4), 606–617. https://doi.org/10.1016/j.emj.2021.09.004.

Ash, E. H. (2010). Introduction: Expertise and the early modern state. *Osiris, 25*(1), 1–24. https://doi.org/10.1086/657254.

Auld, G., Bernstein, S., Cashore, B., & Levin, K. (2021). Managing pandemics as super wicked problems: Lessons from, and for, COVID-19 and the climate crisis. *Policy Sciences, 54*, 707–728. https://doi.org/10.1007/s11077-021-09442-2.

Bouckaert, G. (2012). Trust and public administration. *Administration, 60*(1), 91–115. https://lirias.kuleuven.be/retrieve/216467.

Bouckaert, G., Peters, B. G., & Verhoest, K. (2010). *The Coordination of Public Sector Organizations: Shifting Patterns of Public Management* (1st ed.). Palgrave Macmillan. https://doi.org/10.1057/9780230275256.

Bowman, A., Erturk, I., Froud, J., Haslam, C., Johal, S., Leaver, A., Moran, M., & Williams, K. (2015). *What a Waste: Outsourcing and How it Goes Wrong*. Manchester University Press. https://doi.org/10.7228/manchester/9780719099526.001.0001.

Braun, E., & De Villepin, P. (2021, February 8). How consultants like McKinsey took over France. *Politico*. https://www.politico.eu/article/how-consultants-like-mckinsey-accenture-deloitte-took-over-france-bureaucracy-emmanuel-macron-coronavirus-vaccines/.

Broome, A., & Seabrooke, L. (2015). Shaping policy curves: Cognitive authority in transnational capacity building. *Public Administration, 93*(4), 956–972. https://doi.org/10.1111/padm.12179.

Christensen, R. C., & Collington, R. (2024). New development: climate consulting and the transformation of climate governance. *Public Money & Management*. 1–5. https://doi.org/10.1080/09540962.2024.2353672.

Christensen, T., Lægreid, O. M., & Lægreid, P. (2019). Administrative coordination capacity: Does the wickedness of policy areas matter? *Policy and Society, 38*(2), 237–254. https://doi.org/10.1080/14494035.2019.1584147.

Chwieroth, J. (2007). Neoliberal economists and capital account liberalization in emerging markets. *International Organization, 61*(2), 443–463. https://doi.org/10.1017/S0020818307070154.

Collington, R. (2022). Disrupting the welfare state? Digitalisation and the retrenchment of public sector capacity. *New Political Economy, 27*(2), 312–328. https://doi.org/10.1080/13563467.2021.1952559.

Collington, R. & Mazzucato, M. (2024). Beyond Outsourcing: Re-embedding the state in public value production. *Organization, 31*(7), 1136–1156. https://journals.sagepub.com/doi/10.1177/13505084231163931.

Consultancy.uk (2022, January 19). *UK consulting industry revenues hit £14 billion after double-digit growth*. Consultancy.uk. Retrieved March 3, 2022, from https://www.consultancy.uk/news/30179/uk-consulting-industry-revenues-hit-14-billion-after-double-digit-growth.

Craft, J., & Halligan, J. (2017). Assessing 30 years of Westminster policy advisory system experience. *Policy Sciences, 50*, 47–62. https://doi.org/10.1007/s11077-016-9256-y.

Crouch, C. (2015). The paradoxes of privatisation and public service outsourcing. *The Political Quarterly, 86*(S1), 156–171. https://doi.org/10.1111/1467-923X.12238.

Crowley, K., & Head, B. W. (2017). Expert advisory bodies in the policy system. In M. Brans, I. Geva-May, & M. Howlett (Eds.), *Routledge Handbook of Comparative Policy Analysis* (1st ed.), 181–198. Routledge. https://doi.org/10.4324/9781315660561-12.

Curtis, P. (2011, January 2). Whitehall supplier offers year's worth of free contracts while times are tough. *The Guardian*. https://www.theguardian.com/politics/2011/jan/02/kpmg-government-supplier-contracts-consultancy?CMP=share_btn_url.

David, R. J. (2012). Institutional change and the growth of strategy consulting in the United States. In T. Clark & M. Kipping (Eds.), *The Oxford Handbook of Management Consulting* (pp. 71–92). Oxford University Press. https://doi.org/10.1093/oxfordhb/9780199235049.013.0004.

Dubash, N. K. (2021). Varieties of climate governance: the emergence and functioning of climate institutions. *Environmental Politics, 30*(sup1), 1–25. https://doi.org/10.1080/09644016.2021.1979775.

Dunleavy, P., Carrera, L. N., & (2013). *Growing the Productivity of Government Services*. Edward Elgar Publishing. https://doi.org/10.4337/9780857934994.

Dunlop, C. A., Ongaro, & E. Baker, K. (2020). Researching COVID-19: A research agenda for public policy and administration scholars. *Public Policy and Administration, 35*(4), 365–383. https://doi.org/10.1177/0952076720939631.

Falkner, R. (2016). The Paris Agreement and the new logic of international climate politics. *International Affairs, 92*(5), 1107–1125. https://doi.org/10.1111/1468-2346.12708.

Head, B. W. (2022). *Wicked Problems in Public Policy: Understanding and Responding to Complex Challenges* (1st ed.). Palgrave Macmillan. https://doi.org/10.1007/978-3-030-94580-0.

Head, B. W. (2023). Reconsidering expertise for public policymaking: The challenges of contestability. *Australian Journal of Public Administration, 83*(2), 156–172. https://doi.org/10.1111/1467-8500.12613.

Head, B. W., & Alford, J. (2015). Wicked problems: Implications for public policy and management. *Administration & Society, 47*(6), 711–739. https://doi.org/10.1177/0095399713481601.

Hodge, G. A. (2006). The "consultocracy": The business of reforming government. In G. A. Hodge (Ed.), *Privatization and Market Development*. Edward Elgar Publishing. https://doi.org/10.4337/9781847204288.00015.

Holliday, I. (2000). Is the British state hollowing out? *The Political Quarterly*, 71(2), 167–176. https://doi.org/10.1111/1467-923X.00291.

Hood, C., & Dixon, R. (2015). *A Government that Worked Better and Cost Less? Evaluating Three Decades of Reform and Change in UK Central Government*. Oxford University Press. https://doi.org/10.1093/acprof:oso/9780199687022.001.0001.

Hood, C., & Jackson, M. (1991). *Administrative Argument*. Dartmouth Publishing Company.

Kattel, R., & Mazzucato, M. (2018). Mission-oriented innovation policy and dynamic capabilities in the public sector. *Industrial and Corporate Change*, 27(5), 787–801. https://doi.org/10.1093/icc/dty032.

Kattel, R., Drechsler, W., & Karo, E. (2022). *How to Make an Entrepreneurial State: Why Innovation Needs Bureaucracy*. Yale University Press. https://yalebooks.yale.edu/book/9780300227277/how-to-make-an-entrepreneurial-state/.

Keele, S. (2021). Taming uncertainty: Climate policymaking and the spatial politics of privatized advice. In C. Hurl & A. Vogelpohl (Eds.), *Professional Service Firms and Politics in a Global Era: Public Policy* (pp. 53–75). Palgrave Macmillan. https://doi.org/10.1007/978-3-030-72128-2_3.

Kipping, M. (2021). America first: How consultants got into the public sector. In C. Hurl & A. Vogelpohl (Eds.), *Professional Service Firms and Politics in a Global Era: Public Policy, Private Expertise* (pp. 29–52). Palgrave Macmillan. https://doi.org/10.1007/978-3-030-72128-2_2.

Kipping, M. (2019). Consultants and internationalization. In T. Da Silva Lopes, C. Lubinski, & H. J. S. Tworek (Eds.), *The Routledge Companion to the Makers of Global Business* (pp. 138–155). Routledge. https://doi.org/10.4324/9781315277813-11.

Lægreid, P., & Rykkja, L. (2015). Organizing for "wicked problems" – analyzing coordination arrangements in two policy areas: Internal security and the welfare administration. *International Journal of Public Sector Management*, 28(6), 475–493. https://doi.org/10.1108/IJPSM-01-2015-0009.

Lee, S., Yeo, J., & Na, C. (2020). Learning before and during the COVID-19 outbreak: A comparative analysis of crisis learning in South Korea and the US. *International Review of Public Administration*, 25(4), 243–260. https://doi.org/10.1080/12294659.2020.1852715.

Mazzucato, M., & Collington, R. (2023). *The Big Con: How the Consulting Industry Weakens our Businesses, Infantilizes our Governments and Warps our Economies*. Penguin Press.

Mazzucato, M., & Kattel, R., & (2020). COVID-19 and public-sector capacity. *Oxford Review of Economic Policy*, 36(Supplement 1), S256–S269. https://doi.org/10.1093/oxrep/graa031.

McGann, J. G. (2016). *The Fifth Estate: Think Tanks, Public Policy, and Governance* (1st ed.). Brookings Institution Press.

McKenna, C. D. (2010). *The World's Newest Profession: Management Consulting in the Twentieth Century* (Illustrated). Cambridge University Press. https://doi.org/10.1017/CBO9780511511622.

Meckling, J., & Allan, B. B. (2020). The evolution of ideas in global climate policy. *Nature Climate Change*, 10, 434–438. https://doi.org/10.1038/s41558-020-0739-7.

Moon, M. J. (2020). Fighting COVID-19 with agility, transparency, and participation: Wicked policy problems and new governance challenges. *Public Administration Review*, 80(4), 651–656. https://doi.org/10.1111/puar.13214.

Morphet, J. (2021). *Outsourcing in the UK: Policies, Practices and Outcomes* (1st ed.). Bristol University Press. https://doi.org/10.2307/j.ctv1ks0b6g.

National Audit Office (2010). *Central government's use of consultants and interims.* UK Government. https://www.nao.org.uk/wp-content/uploads/2010/10/1011488.pdf.

O'Dwyer, M. (2021, October 24). UK Public Sector Spending on Consultants More Than Doubles. *Financial Times.* https://www.ft.com/content/efdcaccf-a535-4ae8-afd0-8d0d70b1ed4b.

OECD (2024). *Government production costs.* oecd.org. https://doi.org/10.1787/44ec61e6-en.

Peters, B. G. (2017). What is so wicked about wicked problems? A conceptual analysis and a research program. *Policy and Society, 36*(3), 385–396. https://doi.org/10.1080/14494035.2017.1361633.

Pollitt, C., & Bouckaert, G. (2017). *Public Management Reform: A Comparative Analysis – Into the Age of Austerity* (4th ed.). Oxford University Press.

Powell, M., & King-Hill, S. (2020). Intra-crisis learning and prospective policy transfer in the COVID-19 pandemic. *International Journal of Sociology and Social Policy, 40*(9/10), 877–892. https://doi.org/10.1108/IJSSP-07-2020-0339.

Rhodes, R. A. W. (1994). The hollowing out of the state: The changing nature of the public service in Britain. *The Political Quarterly, 65*(2), 138–151. https://doi.org/10.1111/j.1467-923X.1994.tb00441.x.

Rittel, H. W. J., & Webber, M. M. (1973). Dilemmas in a general theory of planning. *Policy Sciences, 4,* 155–169. https://doi.org/10.1007/BF01405730.

Saint-Martin, D. (1998). The new managerialism and the policy influence of consultants in government: An historical–institutionalist analysis of Britain, Canada and France. *Governance, 11*(3), 319–365. https://doi.org/10.1111/0952-1895.00074.

Saint-Martin, D. (2017). Management consultancy and the varieties of capitalism. In M. Brans, I. Geva-May, & M. Howlett (Eds.), *Routledge Handbook of Comparative Policy Analysis* (1st ed.), 213–228. Routledge. https://www.taylorfrancis.com/chapters/edit/10.4324/9781315660561-14/management-consultancy-varieties-capitalism-denis-saint-martin.

Seabrooke, L., & Sending, O. J. (2022). Consultancies in public administration. *Public Administration, 100*(3), 457–471. https://doi.org/10.1111/padm.12844.

Sturdy, A. (2011). Consultancy's consequences? A critical assessment of management consultancy's impact on management. *British Journal of Management, 22*(3), 517–530. https://doi.org/10.1111/j.1467-8551.2011.00750.x.

Sturdy, A., Handley, K., Clark, T., & Fincham, R. (2009). *Management Consultancy: Boundaries and Knowledge in Action.* Oxford University Press. https://doi.org/10.1093/acprof:oso/9780199212644.001.0001.

Sturdy, A. J., Kirkpatrick, I., Reguera, N., Blanco-Oliver, A., & Veronesi, G. (2022). The management consultancy effect: Demand inflation and its consequences in the sourcing of external knowledge. *Public Administration, 100*(3), 488–506. https://doi.org/10.1111/padm.12712.

Van de Walle, S. (2011). NPM: Restoring the public trust through creating distrust? In T. Christensen & P. Lægreid (Eds.), *The Ashgate Research Companion to New Public Management* (1st ed.). Routledge. https://www.taylorfrancis.com/chapters/edit/10.4324/9781315613321-26/npm-restoring-public-trust-creating-distrust-steven-van-de-walle.

Van de Walle, S., Van Roosbroek, S., & Bouckaert, G. (2008). Trust in the public sector: is there any evidence for a long-term decline? *International Review of Administrative Sciences, 74*(1), 47–64. https://doi.org/10.1177/0020852307085733.

Verhoest, K., Bouckaert, G., & Peters, B. G. (2007). Janus-faced reorganization: Specialization and coordination in four OECD countries in the period 1980–2005. *International Review of Administrative Sciences*, 73(3), 325–348. https://doi.org/10.1177/0020852307081144.

Vitola, A., & Senfelde, M. (2015). An Evaluation of the cross-sectoral policy coordination in Latvia. *Public Policy and Administration*, 14(2), 236–249. https://doi.org/10.13165/VPA-15-14-2-06.

Vogelpohl, A., Hurl, C., Howard, M., Marciano, R., Purandare, U., & Sturdy A. (2022). Pandemic consulting: How private consultants leverage public crisis management. *Critical Policy Studies*, 16(3), 371–381. https://doi.org/10.1080/19460171.2022.2089706.

Weiss, A. E. (2019). *Management Consultancy and the British State: A Historical Analysis Since 1960.* (1st ed.). Palgrave Macmillan. https://doi.org/10.1007/978-3-319-99876-3.

Weiss, L., & Thurbon, E. (2021). Explaining divergent national responses to Covid-19: An enhanced state capacity framework. *New Political Economy*, 27(4), 1–16. https://doi.org/10.1080/13563467.2021.1994545.

Ylönen, M., & Kuusela, H. (2019). Consultocracy and its discontents: A critical typology and a call for a research agenda. *Governance*, 32(2), 241–258. https://doi.org/10.1111/gove.12369.

Flexibilisation of work and the future of public sector employment

by Adrian Ritz, Guillem Ripoll, and Lorenza Micacchi

1. Flexibilisation of work as an ongoing trend

The context of public servants' work is constantly changing. In recent times, three major disruptions have led to strategic responses of public organisations which are related to the future of the public sector workforce. Firstly, from a technological perspective, the use of new digital technologies such as artificial intelligence or sensor technologies change the service logic, work processes, and work environments of public organisations to an extraordinary degree (Margetts and Dorobantu, 2019). Secondly, value changes are emerging in modern societies, according to which labour is becoming less relevant for the identity formation of employees (Farrugia, 2019; Ainsworth and Ghin, 2021). A balanced approach to life is increasingly preferred to a lifelong commitment to an employer (Acheampong, 2021; Moltz, 2019). Thirdly, demographic change is in full swing and is triggering a labour shortage that will not spare the public sector (Ritz et al., 2023).

We argue that these disruptions in the work environment of public organisations are the cause of a major trend for the future public sector workforce, including future public human resources management: the flexibilisation of work. Flexibilisation of work is often subsumed under the title of 'New Work' (Bergmann, 2019) as a major shift in the working environment and employment conditions. However, flexibilisation of work in the public sector relates to two sides of the same coin: on the one hand, the need for a change in government to better face current and future challenges (e.g. the need for mobility within and beyond public employment) and, on the other hand, readiness for a change in the system and the potential implications of such flexibilisation in the sense of implementation measures (e.g. changes in employment regulation).

In recent times, the need for a change in government has been primarily due to disruptive challenges, giving little time to adapt to their implications.

The COVID-19 pandemic has been such a catalyst, forcing civil servants to adapt to the new environment by providing services in extreme circumstances, while updating their working habits like adopting new technologies, working remotely, and increasing collaboration across organisations and state levels. These changes then may lead to strategic responses related to more flexible working conditions for the public workforce and public personnel policies, showing the readiness for a change in the public personnel system.

By reflecting on the trend of flexibilisation of work and its implications for public organisations, with this chapter we aim to contribute to the following gaps in research. First, we set out the need for change as a result of the flexibilisation of public sector work at three levels: macro, meso and micro. Second, we identify potential drawbacks of flexibilisation, above all at the macro level. Lastly, we develop a framework which helps to better understand the reactions of public organisations to the trend of flexibilisation, which might result in different levels of implementation of flexibilisation of work.

2. Macro level: opportunities and drawbacks of flexibilisation for public personnel systems

The general trend of flexibilisation affects public personnel systems and shows the adaptation of these systems to contextual changes. However, public personnel systems are very stable institutional frameworks for public service (see also Nistotskaya in this volume). They function as the rule-of-law framework for the employment of private individuals by the government and define mutual rights and obligations between the state and the individual. In this way, public personnel systems are part of a wider institutional frame in which personnel policies, employment rules, and HR practices warrant the implementation of fundamental public values, such as rule of law, due process, objectivity, neutrality, expertise, independency, stability, inclusion, and division of power. These values are enshrined in the professional ethos of the civil service and influence citizens' trust in public institutions and their perceived legitimacy to a considerable degree (Ritz, 2019). In addition, civil service and its employment rules ensure competence and relevant skills for bureaucracy and thus contribute to the delivery, regulatory, control, coordination, or analytical capacities of the public sector (Lodge and Wegrich, 2014). Thus, public personnel systems represent a source of stability for public organisations guaranteed by the legal framework and its inherent values. However, this innate stability characterising the system might collide in a trade-off with the need for flexibility resulting from the above-mentioned disruptive changes.

Despite its notable stability, the public service in many countries has undergone significant changes in the last few decades, mainly related to the ongoing flexibilisation as an expression of markets as the dominant paradigm (Pollitt and Bouckaert, 2017; Bouckaert, 2023). For instance, the advent of New Public Management changed the focus more towards a performance orientation, instead of welfare-oriented working conditions and job security, and towards increased pay for performance elements (Boruvka and Perry, 2020), or fiscal austerity and the financial crisis led to job cuts and a reduction of career bureaucrats in public employment (Bach, 2016). This in turn increased the reliance on consultants and political advisors, which may undermine the stability of public service in a disruptive political and societal context (see also the contribution by Collington in this volume). However, these changes have not dramatically altered the 'face' of public personnel systems, which is still overall characterised by low turnover, limited job mobility, and lower pro-innovation attitudes (Lapuente and Suzuki, 2020; Suzuki and Hur, 2023). Thus, the combination of rather rigid system characteristics and a decline in the societal acceptance of public personnel systems may increase the pressure for flexibilisation from within and outside of the public sector.

Table 1 exemplifies the assumed changes caused by this pressure and the differences resulting from a more traditional and an increasingly transformed type of public personnel system, along the dimensions of employer interests, the employer–employee relationship, and core values (Ritz and Thom, 2019). Although public personnel reform is heavily context dependent and personnel systems differ in detail, the transformed system shows an overall tendency towards more openness, less uniformity, and greater flexibility.

First, there will be a further weakening of the high levels of job security and the unilateral, often legally guaranteed obligations of the state towards its employees. The public employer is to increase measures of flexibility using contract-based employment schemes, and its employer role follows organisational rather than individual interests, also giving opportunities for faster and more strategic restructuring of public organisations in a fast-changing environment. In a flexible and collaborative environment, the public employer is increasingly looking for the employee type of a 'system agent', able to co-create public value in networks, in contrast to the rule- and procedures-bound 'state agent'.

Second, the employer–employee relationship is moving away from a paternalistic and hierarchical relationship towards a more dynamic employment relationship with a wide variety of individualised conditions. For instance, mutual contract termination options will be used by both parties more often as the psychological contract changes from loyalty to employability. In addition, an increasing mobility of the workforce across sectoral and organisational boundaries (Frederiksen and Hansen, 2017) will help to transfer knowledge to the public sector and also allows public organisations to attract newcomers searching for sense-giving jobs.

Third, the debate about core values for which public personnel systems stand is increasingly stressing principles such as openness, flexibility, and agility due to the required digital skills and responsiveness (Mergel et al., 2021). However, as shown by Knies et al. (2022), time-honoured public sector values are less susceptible to change and new values need to be adapted to the existing ones (e.g. agility needs to respect due process). For example, in comparison to the private sector, public organisations are more likely to use equal opportunity programmes, but they are less susceptible to values like performance orientation, which might have as a consequence the more limited adoption of 'hard' human resources management practices such as pay for performance. Thus, although Table 1 exemplifies two different types of public personnel systems, in reality changes may happen on a continuum and be slower than assumed, and there may also be a layering of characteristics.

Table 1. Changing characteristics of public personnel systems

Dimension	Traditional personnel system	Transformed personnel system
Employer role and interests	– Unilateral dominance of the state – Obligations regarding employee interests and well-being – State agents with job security, autonomy, duty to serve and comply	– Bilateral contract-based employment – Focus on organisational interests and performance – System agents for co-creating public value in inter-organisational and inter-sectoral networks
Employer–employee relationship	– Safety-oriented long-term relationship – Recruitment and promotion based on examination, loyalty, tenured career, and seniority – Paternalistic and hierarchical relationship, low mobility – Stable participation along hierarchy	– Dynamic, developmental time-bound relationship – Value-, position-, and merit-based recruitment, promotion, and retention – Increasing mobility, mutual contract termination – Dynamic participation across hierarchy levels and teams
Core values	– Neutrality, accuracy and diligence – Expertise and qualification	– Openness, innovation and agility – Experience and collaboration – Inclusion and representation

As mentioned in section 1, the changing characteristics of public personnel systems relate to the need to better deal with contextual change. However, from a macro perspective the institutional conditions for flexibilisation and its potential drawbacks need to be considered. Flexibilisation of the core values of public personnel systems, the employer–employee relationship, and changing employer interests goes to the foundations of public service as an inherent element of meritocratic systems. Merit bureaucracy stands for high competence, ethical and behavioural norms supporting efficiency, professionalism, and the public interest, sustainable solutions, predictability, and resistance to the undue interference of politics in administration (see Nistotskaya in this volume). The latter aspect relates to the main concern about greater flexibilisation in today's Western world: the capture of public personnel systems by illiberal political actors and parties, which might retaliate and replace disloyal civil servants (see e.g. the contributions by Moynihan and Bach in this volume). For instance, taking advantage of increased mobility across sectors, an openly discriminatory government towards migrants might attract people with ethnocentric and xenophobic attitudes to the public service (see e.g. the Swedish case discussed by Nistotskaya in this volume). Thus, politicisation is a key characteristic for analysing public personnel systems. The intensity of this threat, however, differs across countries.

According to Dählstrom and Lapuente (2018), an important aspect of public personnel systems to analyse is their degree of politicisation, or, in other words, minister–mandarin relations and the separation between politicians and bureaucrats' careers (Pollitt and Bouckaert, 2017). In less politicised bureaucracies, civil servants' recruitment and career paths depend on merit-based criteria assessed through peer evaluations, establishing a deeply rooted loyalty to the profession, but not to the ruler. In contrast, more politicised bureaucracies have a significant number of political appointments, and to jump from the administrative arena to the political one is a common practice that signals the prominence of political-based promotion. In reality, politico-administrative systems are neither merit-based nor patronage oriented, but rather hybrid, including functional politicisation as relevant element of meritocratic bureaucracies (see Bach in this volume). Applying the logic of appropriateness (March and Olsen, 1989), institutions socialise individuals, describing the appropriate norms and values to be followed.

Thus, flexibilisation of institutions such as public personnel systems in terms of the separation between politics and administration and the system's openness and closedness, or its traditional versus transformed characteristics, may affect bureaucrats' socialisation and identity. These macro-level characteristics of public personnel systems provide different context-based signals to public employees, thus ultimately shaping their identity and behaviours. Therefore, from a liberal-democratic viewpoint, it is important that changes in public personnel systems through flexibilisation avoid political capture, be based on support for public values, and set the proper incentives to undermine greed, opportunism, and other integrity violations at the individual, micro level of public service (Dahlström and Lapuente, 2017).

In the next section we focus on HR practices as major link between the macro and micro level when it comes to the implementation of flexibilisation due to contextual change.

3. Meso level: flexibilisation of HR practices

At the organisational level, human resources management and its practices are responsible for the implementation of macro level public personnel systems and its policies. The trend of flexibilisation at this level is mainly driven by managerial strategies influencing personnel policies and practices. Since the COVID-19 crisis at the latest, most public organisations develop strategies related to the change of values, skills, and needs of future employees in times of labour shortages. Before discussing changing needs at the individual level in the last section of our chapter, we present in what follows changes in HR practices which exemplify the managerial implications of the flexibilisation trend at the meso level.

While the traditional bureaucracy rarely regards good quality human capital as a scarce resource, *HR recruiting* is challenged in a labour market where labour supply decreases due to demographic change (Berman et al., 2021). Flexibilisation will increase openness towards a more heterogeneous workforce and strengthen a 'developmental employability perspective' on public employees, characterised by a more dynamic view of the employer–employee relationship, qualifying employees and increasing their employability on the job market in exchange for engagement and performance, instead of a 'loyalty perspective' guaranteeing job security in exchange for loyalty and subordination. Recruiting in the public sector, above all in *Rechtsstaat*-oriented bureaucracies, is often characterised by uniform employment regulations (Lavigna and Hays, 2004). However, employing the future workforce means allowing differences in employment conditions without playing at secrecy. In addition, active sourcing as a recruitment strategy pays more attention to candidates' self-actualisation needs and asks for much more involvement of all employees, including senior civil servants, and not only of the recruiting department. Flexibilisation means more visibility of the traditionally 'hesitant, neutral' public employer on the labour market by selling its attractiveness through social media and other means (Thunnissen and Boselie, 2024).

HR retention is crucial for employee motivation. Public organisations, with their pro-social missions, stimulate public service motivation (Perry and Wise, 1990). With growing flexibility and changing psychological contracts, modern jobs increasingly reflect individual needs and identity, with employees desiring pride in their roles (Bouckaert, 2001). However, this does not mean that tangible rewards lose relevance, but instead that standardised compensation frameworks are limited due to evolving needs. Aligning the organisation's mission with incentives and individual needs is key to retaining employees (Ritz et al., 2023; Ripoll et al., 2023). Fairness and transparency in pay are important, but criticisms of opaque supervisor judgements exist. New pay approaches are directed towards democratic structures and employee participation, enhancing autonomy and commitment (Brück et al., 2021). The uniform base salary is supplemented by individual components, including time instead of money, based on individual needs and the organisation's financial situation. Thus, today's equality and standardisation-driven retention frameworks will face challenges from needs for individual participation and flexibility.

HR appraisal is often linked to compensation. In many countries, employee appraisal comes with incentivises (Hajnal and Staronova, 2021) and since the New Public Management reform at the latest, public organisations have been first class when it comes to the spread of systematic employee appraisal. In combination with new pay approaches, the appraisal function is changing. Developmental-oriented appraisal is increasing and seeks to enable an open, trustful, and in-depth dialogue, in contrast to rather coercive command-and-control-oriented appraisal (Jacobsen et al., 2013). Effective future public service is increasingly related to dynamic, iterative, and collaborative processes of experimentation (Torfing, 2019; Villa Alvarez et al., 2022). Command and control, as well as specific output goals, interferes with a learning- and collaboration-oriented approach to working (Lowe et al., 2020). In collaborative settings, appraisal also becomes more a result of a collaborative team perspective than a judgement by a single supervisor. In addition, decentralised appraisal structures without central control better allow transparent and direct feedback. The gaming situation of performance pay may further lose its role in motivating employees and more effective appraisal based on psychological insights is necessary, aiming at increasing interactional and procedural performance appraisal justice (Vidè et al., 2022).

Lastly, the trend of flexibilisation also impacts *HR development*. Although career orientation is an inherent characteristic of traditional public personnel systems, public organisations have a rather low reputation for career advancement (Bozeman and Ponomariov, 2009), with career perspectives more strongly associated with private sector employment (Kjeldsen and Jacobsen, 2013). However, the public sector could improve by establishing individualised career patterns beyond organisational boundaries. Protean and boundaryless career approaches can foster flexibility skills and self-actualisation (Grimland et al., 2012; De Caluwé et al., 2014). Facilitating across- and within-sector mobility, or offering vertical and horizontal career perspectives are coherent reactions to the flexibilisation trend and take into account the needs of future employees, such as younger workers' tendency for job-switching (Gallup, 2016). In addition, classical HR development measures, such as upskilling and reskilling or formal training agreements, help to address the implications of labour shortages. Due to the environmental change of digital transformation, recent foci of HR development activities are, for instance, related to business analytical skills (Paul and Tan, 2015), data literacy and data analytical skills (Dingelstad et al., 2022), and innovation skills (Vivona et al., 2019).

4. Micro level: changing needs of the future public workforce

The above-described changes in HR practices at the meso level need to be in alignment with the needs for future public servants as the trend of flexibilisation of work relates to changing needs in society. In the job market, public organisations are attractive employers if their offer fits the needs of job seekers (Ritz et al., 2023). Thus, to properly adapt HR practices and to both attract and retain a skilled workforce, public employers must know the needs and values of the future workforce. Generational literature is often used as argument for changing needs. It examines how personal and national or global events shape the attitudes and values of different age cohorts (Schuman and Scott, 1989). The Volcker Alliance (2023) reports that to attract young candidates, public service job ads should highlight real-world impact, promotion opportunities, job security, good salary, skill fit, and remote work options. Gallup's (2016) report also indicates that the so-called 'millennials' want to work for an organisation with a mission, a purpose, and opportunities for career development.

Despite a rather stereotypical view of generational differences of needs being common, the empirical evidence is mixed. Some studies show differences in job satisfaction, work values, or learning orientation (Wey Smola and Sutton, 2002; Davis et al., 2006; D'Amato and Herzfeldt, 2008). Others report no strong variations in these outcomes (Kowske et al., 2010; Roberts et al., 2010; Viechnicki, 2015; Gallup, 2016). For instance, the meta-analysis of Costanza et al. (2012) found no substantial generational differences in work-related outcomes. Research by Beier et al. (2022) suggests that age is a proxy for personal, environmental, historical, and random events that impact work attitudes and behaviours, which occur at different ages for different people within and between generations. Thus, within-generation differences might exceed between-generation differences, contributing to measurement errors in generational analysis.

Nevertheless, research evidence seems to agree on two major findings with regard to the overall trend across generations and over time in developed countries. First, the desire to have career success has decreased over the past few decades. Work is one of the basic units articulating our position in society, and to succeed at work also means to properly progress in life. Whereas this is more relevant to younger workers compared to older people (Offermann and Gowing, 1990; van der Heijden et al., 2009; van der Heijden et al., 2022), the value of career success in general is decreasing over time. Future employees no longer live for their career or for the public employer. The career has to fit into their overall life plan, and other factors, such as work–life balance, are gaining importance.

Second, self-enhancement and self-realisation have increased over time and are of high importance for employees. The satisfaction of material needs is high and the cultivation of the self becomes more relevant. Self-enhancement refers to the pursuit of self-directed goals, including new opportunities, challenges, and qualification options, which do not have to be related to work and career goals (Cassar, 2007). Although public sector organisations have their limitations in adapting to certain needs due to the institutional frame they are operating in, they may profit from this development due to their public service-oriented mission and resulting public service motivation (Ritz et al., 2016; Perry and Wise, 1990). Being socially accepted, signals related to high public value contribution might nurture the desire to see oneself in a positive light by associating with such positive values. Seeking association with public organisations as an employer helps individuals to maintain their positive self-evaluation, strengthens their own value-based identity, and elevates their status in society (Ritz et al., 2023).

Although not exhaustive, these two simple ideas reinforce the importance of reflecting upon the extent of transforming public personnel systems and changing HR practices in light of the changing needs of future public employees. This makes it possible to decide on the reaction strategies and implementation measures to be prepared for the trend of flexibilisation. In the following concluding section, we offer a framework for such reflections.

5. Conclusion and future research

Our contribution started with the argument that a major trend of flexibilisation of work is affecting public personnel systems at the macro level, HR practices at the meso level, and needs at the individual level. Whereas flexibilisation clearly leads to opportunities and drawbacks at the macro level, flexibilisation at the meso level is mainly driven by a managerial perspective generating opportunities for the public organisation in a changing environment in order to respond to the changing needs of individuals at the micro level.

We conclude our reflection by asking how flexibilisation unfolds in public organisations on the basis of two conditions. First, we argue that the type of public personnel system is relevant because, as shown in our discussion, these systems are heavily affected by this trend. We differentiate between traditional and transformed public personnel systems as described above. Second, we argue that the characteristics of the external environment represents a key variable affecting the unfolding of flexibilisation. Environmental cues result in higher or lower levels of environmental threats for public organisations like, for instance, undue politicisation as a result of illiberalism or external shocks such as the COVID-19 crisis. Figure 1 exemplifies our assumptions about four different reactions of public organisations to the trend of flexibilisation, which result in different levels of implementation of flexibilisation of work.

Figure 1. Public organisations' reaction to the trend of flexibilisation

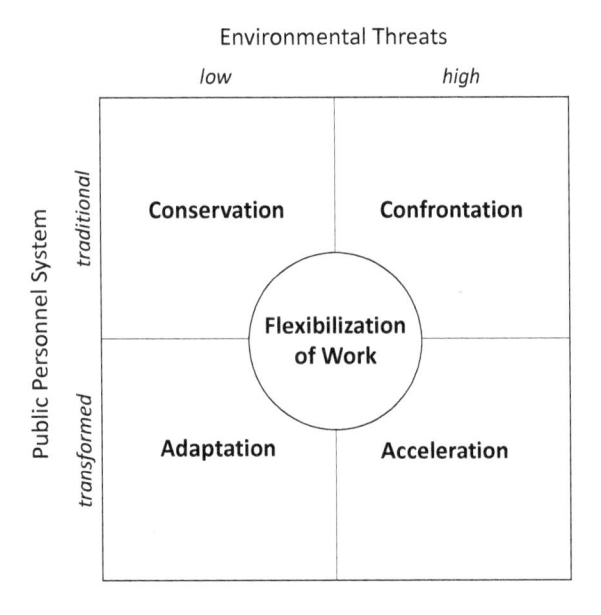

	Environmental Threats low	Environmental Threats high
Public Personnel System — *traditional*	Conservation	Confrontation
Public Personnel System — *transformed*	Adaptation	Acceleration

(Flexibilization of Work — center)

First, *conservation* of the institutional characteristics is the reaction to flexibilisation of work of a public organisation with a traditional personnel system in a stable environment with no major threats to the organisation. In such a situation, the organisation and its actors are not feeling a need for change and thus the implications of flexibilisation of work will rather be low for the bureaucracy, its personnel system, HR practices, and the individual employees.

Second, flexibilisation of work in a traditional system but a highly unstable environment with severe threats is assumed to lead to *confrontation*, because the administration will defend the system characteristics against the threats. For instance, flexibilisation in the sense of reduction of due process in employment rules is a great challenge for a public organisation facing undue political interference, as it may bring instability and unexpected HR release. Thus, HR is assumed to be reluctant to change its practices and individual bureaucrats will defend the system by opposition, opportunistic behaviour, union support, etc.

The third reaction mode of *adaptation* allows changes induced by the flexibilisation trend. Mobility of employees across and within organisational boundaries or less socialisation and infusion by traditional rules and values – as part of an open personnel system – nurtures positive attitudes towards reform, above all in a stable, non-threatening environment.

Fourth, flexibilisation of work is assumed to unfold in *acceleration* when the personnel system is transformed and environmental threats are high. Acceleration means dynamic reactions, which can lead to positive or negative shifts in the public organisation. For instance, the environmental threat of labour shortages may allow a transformed personnel system to embrace changing HR practices, such as open recruitment, with positive implications in terms of selection of less-qualified job seekers. However, this could also be at risk of lowering professionalism and losing integrity or highly public service-motivated job holders.

The above-mentioned reactions of public organisations to the trend of flexibilisation and its implications for macro-, meso- and micro-level variables depend on contextual settings and situational constraints, as exemplified in our matrix. Depending on the fit of these reactions to its context, the implementation of the flexibilisation trend might be more or less effective and, in some situations, an 'implementation gap' might occur. This means that this broader flexibilisation trend (which is induced by the evolution of the environment) might not become a full reality for an organisation and its HR practices.

We see four avenues for future research. Firstly, more knowledge is needed with regard to the trend of flexibilisation of work in the public sector itself.

How relevant are, for instance, temporal (e.g. part-time work), spatial (e.g. mobile office), structural (e.g. self-organisation), and contractual (e.g. self-determined salary) dimensions of flexibilisation for public organisations? Secondly, at the macro level, future studies could test the applicability of the proposed framework in different contexts and further explore potential mechanisms that might play a role in the various types of proposed reactions of public organisations. For instance, it would be of great interest to explore how traditional career-based versus transformed position-based systems adapt differently to flexibilisation as assumed in our matrix. In addition, we propose a qualitative, case-study-based research approach to test the applicability and validity of the model, and to explore its relationship with relevant outcome measures, such as public service performance, legitimisation, and trust in public service. Thirdly, at the meso level, future research should investigate how flexibilisation affects the change of HR practices. For this, we encourage carrying out comparative research and investigating the variance between distinct public organisations, for instance core administration and public corporations, or between different sectors, because the reaction to the trend of flexibilisation might differ due to the institutional context. Last but not least, it is of interest to gain more insights into the generalisability of the generational literature's claims about the changing needs of future public servants. More knowledge about within- and between-generation variation, as well as major and minor changes of needs, would certainly be of value for public sector HR practitioners in their task of implementing reactions to the trend of flexibilisation.

References

Acheampong, N. A. A. (2021). Reward preferences of the youngest generation: Attracting, recruiting, and retaining Generation Z into public sector organizations. *Compensation & Benefits Review*, 53(2), 75–97. https://doi.org/10.1177/0886368720954803.

Ainsworth, S., & Ghin, P. (2021). Public servants in reflection. In H. Sullivan, H. Dickinson, & H. Henderson (Eds.), *The Palgrave Handbook of the Public Servant* (1st ed., pp. 411–423). Palgrave Macmillan. https://doi.org/10.1007/978-3-030-29980-4_88.

Bach, S. (2016). Deprivileging the public sector workforce: Austerity, fragmentation and service withdrawal in Britain. *The Economic and Labour Relations Review*, 27(1), 11–28. https://doi.org/10.1177/1035304615627950.

Beier, M. E., Kanfer, R., Kooij, D. T. A. M., & Truxillo, D. M. (2022). What's age got to do with it? A primer and review of the workplace aging literature. *Personnel Psychology*, 75(4), 779–804. https://doi.org/10.1111/peps.12544.

Bergmann, F. (2019). *New Work New Culture: Work We Want and a Culture that Strenghtens Us.* John Hunt Publishing.

Berman, E. M., Bowman, J. S., Van Wart, M., & West, J. P. (2021). *Human Resource Management in Public Service: Paradoxes, Processes, and Problems* (7th ed.). CQ Press.

Boruvka, E., & Perry, J. L. (2020). Understanding evolving public motivational practices: An institutional analysis. *Governance*, 33(3), 565–584. https://doi.org/10.1111/gove.12460.

Bouckaert, G. (2001). Pride and performance in public service: Some patterns of analysis. *International Review of Administrative Sciences*, 67(1), 15–27. https://doi.org/10.1177/0020852301671002.

Bouckaert, G. (2023). The neo-Weberian state: From ideal type model to reality? *Max Weber Studies*, 23(1), 13–59. https://doi.org/10.1353/max.2023.0002.

Bozeman, B., & Ponomariov, B. (2009). Sector switching from a business to a government job: Fast-track career or fast track to nowhere? *Public Administration Review*, 69(1), 77–91. https://doi.org/10.1111/j.1540-6210.2008.01942.x.

Brück, C., Knauer, T., Meier, H., & Schwering, A. (2021). Self-set salaries and creativity. *Journal of Business Economics*, 91(1), 91–121. https://doi.org/10.1007/s11573-020-00985-z.

Cassar, G. (2007). Money, money, money? A longitudinal investigation of entrepreneur career reasons, growth preferences and achieved growth. *Entrepreneurship and Regional Development*, 19(1), 89–107. https://doi.org/10.1080/08985620601002246.

Costanza, D. P., Badger, J. M., Fraser, R. L., Severt, J. B., & Gade, P. A. (2012). Generational differences in work-related attitudes: A meta-analysis. *Journal of Business & Psychology*, 27(4), 375–394. https://doi.org/10.1007/s10869-012-9259-4.

Dahlström, C., & Lapuente, V. (2017). *Organizing Leviathan: Politicians, Bureaucrats, and the Making of Good Government*. Cambridge University Press. https://doi.org/10.1017/9781316822869.

Dahlström, C., Lapuente, V., & Teorell, J. (2010). *Dimensions of Bureaucracy. A Cross-National Dataset on the Structure and Behavior of Public Administration*. Quality of Government Institute, QoG Working Paper Series, 2010:13. https://www.gu.se/sites/default/files/2020-05/2010_13_Dahlstrom_Lapuente_Teorell.pdf.

D'Amato, A., & Herzfeldt, R. (2008). Learning orientation, organizational commitment and talent retention across generations: A study of European managers. *Journal of Managerial Psychology*, 23(8), 929–953. https://doi.org/10.1108/02683940810904402.

Davis, J. B., Pawlowski, S. D., & Houston, A. (2006). Work commitments of Baby Boomers and Gen-Xers in the IT profession: Generational differences or myth? *Journal of Computer Information Systems*, 46(3), 43–49. https://doi.org/10.1080/08874417.2006.11645897.

De Caluwé, C., Van Dooren, W., Delafortry, A., & Janvier, R. (2014). Sets of boundaryless careers in the public sector: The vanguard of a more mobile workforce?. *Public Personnel Management*, 43(4), 490–519. https://doi.org/10.1177/0091026014528479.

Dingelstad, J., Borst, R. T. & Meijer, A. (2022). 'Hybrid data competencies for municipal civil servants: An empirical analysis of the required competencies for data-driven decision-making'. *Public Personnel Management*, 51(4): 458–90. https://doi.org/10.1177/00910260221111744.

Farrugia, D. (2019). The formation of young workers: The cultivation of the self as a subject of value to the contemporary labour force. *Current Sociology*, 67(1), 47–63. https://doi.org/10.1177/0011392118793681.

Frederiksen, A., & Hansen, J. R. (2017). Increased importance of sector switching: A study of trends over a 27-year period. *Administration & Society, 49*(7), 1015–1042. https://doi.org/10.1177/0095399714555750.

Gallup (2016). *How Millennials Want to Work and Live.* Gallup. https://enviableworkplace.com/wp-content/uploads/Gallup-How-Millennials-Want-To-Work.pdf.

Grimland, S., Vigoda-Gadot, E., & Baruch, Y. (2012). Career attitudes and success of managers: The impact of chance event, protean, and traditional careers. *The International Journal of Human Resource Management, 23*(6), 1074–1094. https://doi.org/10.1080/09585192.2011.560884.

Hajnal, G., & Staronova, K. (2021). Changing patterns of individual performance appraisal systems for civil service in European Union countries: Toward a developmental or an incentivizing model. *International Journal of Public Sector Management, 34*(7), 748–764. https://doi.org/10.1108/IJPSM-02-2021-0051.

Jacobsen, C. B., Hvitved, J., Jacobsen, C. B., & Andersen, L. B. (2013). Command and motivation: How the perception of external interventions relates to intrinsic motivation and public service motivation. *Public Administration, 92*(4), 790–806. https://doi.org/10.1111/padm.12024.

Kjeldsen, A. M., & Jacobsen, C. B. (2013). Public service motivation and employment sector: Attraction or socialization? *Journal of Public Administration Research and Theory, 23*(4), 899–926. https://doi.org/10.1093/jopart/mus039.

Knies, E., Borst, R. T., Leisink, P., Farndale, E. (2022). The distinctiveness of public sector HRM: A four-wave trend analysis. *Human Resource Management Journal, 32*(4), 799–825. https://doi.org/10.1111/1748-8583.12440.

Kowske, B. J., Rasch, R., & Wiley, J. (2010). Millennials' (lack of) attitude problem: An empirical examination of generational effects on work attitudes. *Journal of Business and Psychology, 25*(2), 265–279. https://doi.org/10.1007/s10869-010-9171-8.

Lapuente, V., & Suzuki, K. (2020). Politicization, bureaucratic legalism, and innovative attitudes in the public sector. *Public Administration Review, 80*(3), 454–467. https://doi.org/10.1111/puar.13175.

Lavigna, R. J., & Hays, S. W. (2004). Recruitment and selection of public workers: An international compendium of modern trends and practices. *Public Personnel Management, 33*(3), 237–253. https://doi.org/10.1177/009102600403300301.

Lodge, M., & Wegrich, K. (2014). Introduction: Governance innovation, administrative capacities, and policy instruments. In M. Lodge & K. Wegrich (Eds.), *The Problem-solving Capacity of the Modern State: Governance Challenges and Administrative Capacities* (pp. 1–22). Oxford University Press. https://doi.org/10.1093/acprof:oso/9780198716365.003.0001.

Lowe, T., French, M., & Hawkins, M. (2020). Navigating complexity: The future of public service. In H. Sullivan, H. Dickinson, & H. Henderson, & (Eds.), *The Palgrave Handbook of the Public Servant* (1st ed., pp. 901–919). Palgrave Macmillan. https://doi.org/10.1007/978-3-030-29980-4_16.

March, J. G., & Olsen, J. P. (1989). *Rediscovering Institutions: The organizational Basis of Politics.* Free Press.

Margetts, H., & Dorobantu, C., & (2019). Rethink government with AI. *Nature, 568,* 163–165. https://doi.org/10.1038/d41586-019-01099-5.

Mergel, I., Ganapati, S., & Whitford, A. B. (2021). Agile: A new way of governing. *Public Administration Review, 81*(1), 161–165. https://doi.org/10.1111/puar.13202.

Moltz, M. C. (2019). Work-life balance and national context in attraction to public employment. *International Journal of Public Administration*, 42(4), 334–344. https://doi.org/10.1080/01900692.2018.1463247.

Offermann, L. R., & Gowing, M. K. (1990). Organizations of the future: Changes and challenges. *American Psychologist*, 45(2), 95–108. https://doi.org/10.1037/0003-066X.45.2.95.

Perry, J. L., & Wise, L. R. (1990). The motivational bases of public service. *Public Administration Review*, 50(3), 367–373. https://sangyubr.wordpress.com/wp-content/uploads/2012/02/the-motivational-bases-of-public-service.pdf.

Pollitt, C., & Bouckaert, G. (2017). *Public Management Reform. A Comparative Analysis* (4th ed.). Oxford University Press.

Ripoll, G., Ballart, X., Hernández, E., & Vandenabeele, W. (2023). "It's a match!": A discrete choice experiment on job attractiveness for public service jobs. *Public Management Review*, 1–35. https://doi.org/10.1080/14719037.2023.2239256.

Ritz, A. (2019). Öffentliche Personalsysteme im Wandel – weitere Reformschritte sind notwendig. *Dms – Der Moderne Staat – Zeitschrift für Public Policy, Recht und Management*, 12(1), 176–189. https://doi.org/10.3224/dms.v12i1.11.

Ritz, A., & Thom, N. (2019). *Public Management. Erfolgreiche Steuerung öffentlicher Organisationen* (6th ed.). Springer Gabler Wiesbaden. https://doi.org/10.1007/978-3-658-25875-7.

Ritz, A., Brewer, G. A., & Newmann, O. (2016). Public service motivation: A systematic literature review and outlook. *Public Administration Review*, 76(3), 414–426. https://doi.org/10.1111/puar.12505.

Ritz, A., Weißmüller, K. S., & Meynhardt, T. (2023). Public value at cross points: A comparative study on employer attractiveness of public, private, and nonprofit organizations. *Review of Public Personnel Administration*, 43(3), 528–556. https://doi.org/10.1177/0734371X221098153.

Roberts, B. W., Edmonds, G., & Grijalva, E. (2007). It is developmental me, not Generation Me: Developmental changes are more important than generational changes in narcissism—Commentary on Trzesniewski & Donnellan. *Perspectives on Psychological Science*, 5(1), 97–102. https://doi.org/10.1177/1745691609357019.

Schuman, H., & Scott, J. (1989). Generations and collective memories. *American Sociological Review*, 54(3), 359–381. https://doi.org/10.2307/2095611.

Suzuki, K., & Hur, H. (2023). Politicization, bureaucratic closedness in personnel policy, and turnover intention. *Governance*, 37(3), 993–1014. https://doi.org/10.1111/gove.12821.

Thunnissen, M., & Boselie, P. (2024). *Talent Management in Higher Education* (1st ed.). Emerald Publishing Limited. https://doi.org/10.1108/9781802626858.

Torfing, J. (2019). Collaborative innovation in the public sector: The argument. *Public Management Review*, 21(1), 1–11. https://doi.org/10.1080/14719037.2018.1430248.

Van der Heijden, B. I. J. M., De Lange, A. H., Demerouti, E., & Van der Heijde, C. M. (2009). Age effects on the employability–career success relationship. *Journal of Vocational Behavior*, 74(2), 156–164. https://doi.org/10.1016/j.jvb.2008.12.009.

Van der Heijden, B. I. J. M., Veld, M., & Heres, L. (2021). Does age matter? Examining career commitment as a moderator in the relationship between age-related HR/D practices and subjective career success for younger versus older academic staff. *Human Resource Development Quarterly*, 33(4), 405–425. https://doi.org/10.1002/hrdq.21463.

Vidè, F., Micacchi, L., Barbieri, M., & Valotti, G. (2021). The Renaissance of Performance Appraisal: Engaging Public Employees Through Perceived Developmental Purpose and Justice. *Review of Public Personnel Administration*, 43(4), 623–651. https://doi.org/10.1177/0734371X221116584.

Viechnicki, P. (2015). *Understanding Millennials in government: Debunking myths about our youngest public servants*. Deloitte University Press. https://www2.deloitte.com/content/dam/insights/us/articles/millennials-in-government-federal-workforce/DUP-1450_Millennials-in-govt_vFINAL_12.2.15.pdf.

Villa Alvarez, D. P., Auricchio, V., & Mortati, M. (2022). Mapping design activities and methods of public sector innovation units through the policy cycle model. *Policy Sciences*, 55(1), 89–136. https://doi.org/10.1007/s11077-022-09448-4.

Vivona, R., Demircioglu, M. A., Raghavan, A. (2019): Innovation and innovativeness for the public servant of the future: What, why, how, where, and when. In H. Sullivan & H. Dickinson (Eds.): *The Palgrave Handbook of the Public Servant*, 1–22. Palgrave Macmillan. https://doi.org/10.1007/978-3-030-29980-4_34.

Volcker Alliance (2023). *From Gen Z or Gen Z. Marketing Insights for Government Employers*. https://www.bi.team/wp-content/uploads/2023/12/LevelUp-Gov-From-Gen-Z-for-Gen-Z.pdf.

Wey Smola, K., & Sutton, C. D. (2002). Generational differences: Revisiting generational work values for the new millennium. *Journal of Organizational Behavior*, 23(4), 363–382. https://doi.org/10.1002/job.147.

The future of bureaucratic merit

by Marina Nistotskaya

1. Introduction

Bureaucratic merit, a system of human resource management in public bureaucracies that selects individuals based on qualifications, skills, and performance rather than connections, and protects them from politically motivated dismissals, is under pressure.

Some critics, particularly on the right-wing side of the political spectrum, argue that career protection makes bureaucrats less effective in their jobs and they should be more easily fired for poor performance (Sherk, 2021). Others, especially political winners of illiberal, populist, and autocratic persuasions, claim that meritocratic bureaucracy is part of a 'deep state' that aims to undermine their policies and, therefore, the will of people (for review of such claims, see Clark, n.d.; Wagner, 2023). Meritocratic bureaucracy has also been under pressure from the left. A new wave of critique highlights meritocracy as a system that preserves the power and influence of existing elites (Sandel, 2020). In addition, there are also those who point out that meritocratic bureaucracies may be inadequate for ensuring that bureaucrats represent the populations they serve (Riccucci and Van Ryzin, 2017), and merit-imbued impartiality may be a necessary, but not sufficient, condition for the welfare of present-day societies with heterogeneous populations (Suzuki and Demircioglu, 2021).

This chapter discusses these critiques and evaluates their merit against the accumulated knowledge base. It argues that while the subject is frequently and hotly debated, the public discourse is often superficial. Within scholarly debate on bureaucratic merit, many key topics, such as its relationship with efficiency or accountability to politicians and citizens, are either understudied or produce mixed results, or both. This makes it impossible to answer with certainty whether a merit bureaucracy remains the right model for organising Leviathan in democracies and offering realistic and efficacious reform prescription. This is a clarion call to the scholarship of Public Administration for conceptual and empirical clarity regarding the role we want public bureaucracy to play in modern governance.

2. Critique of bureaucratic inefficiency

Merit-based and tenure protection versus at-will systems

The inefficiency critique is not new. Bureaucratic slack became a subject of academic critique in the late 1960s with Niskanen's (1971) model of the budget-maximising bureaucrat. The 1978 Civil Service Reform Act in the US was motivated by President Jimmy Carter by the need to be able to "demote or fire incompetent workers without facing years of appeals" and to reward bureaucratic "performance rather than longevity" (cited in Clark, 2018). A perceived low level of public sector productivity was the main motivation for the New Public Management (NPM) reforms of the 1980s. This reasoning is also strikingly similar to the arguments sounded by the Trump administration already in 2018 (Clark, 2018), and continued by organisations like the Heritage Foundation (Dans et al., 2024) and the America First Policy Institute (AFPI) (Sherk, 2021), who see the return of political appointments and removal of tenure protection as the answer to the problem of bureaucratic inefficiency.

The argument in favour of political appointments tied to a particular government's time in office is both partisan and scholarly. The principal–agent theory holds that a closer alignment of the incentives between principal and agent would improve efficiency. As a result, partisan appointees would work on tasks that matter for politicians (and hence the electorate), and with greater zeal, and be more accountable to politicians (and therefore the electorate). When it comes to tenure protection, the argument that dismissal threats play an important role in eliciting high productivity of employees has a long tradition within economic analysis (Shapiro and Stiglitz, 1984). In the public sector, the absence of tenure protection makes dismissal threats credible, thereby motivating bureaucrats to work harder. Thus, hiring and firing 'at will' provides bureaucratic agents with "high-powered incentives" (Frant, 1996) to be both sensitive to the preferences of their political principals and work hard to satisfy those preferences.

Have these arguments found support in empirical data from the public sector? Unfortunately, despite many Western countries having experienced "a retreat from the institutionalized merit system that has (or had) been the standard way of organizing employment in the public sector" (Peters and

Pierre, 2004, p. 1), there is no systematic scholarship evaluating the effects of this first wave of politicisation. In other words, the core assumptions of the ineffectiveness critique had remained empirically untested (but see Battaglio, 2010; Bowman & West, 2006).

However, in the early 2000s, as the pendulum swung back and the virtues of merit bureaucracy were rediscovered (Miller, 2000; Olsen, 2006), a significant body of empirical work examining the effects of merit bureaucracy emerged. Since the pioneering study by Rauch (1995), numerous empirical studies have demonstrated that merit bureaucracy is associated with a myriad of positive government outputs (Boräng et al., 2018; Carpenter, 2002; Charron et al., 2017; Dahlström et al., 2012, 2021; Krause et al., 2006; Lewis, 2007) and broader societal outcomes, such as economic development, poverty, public health, corruption, democratisation, and democratic stability (Andersen and Krishnarajan, 2019; Charron et al., 2017; Cingolani et al., 2015; Colonnelli et al., 2020; Cornell et al., 2020; Dahlström et al., 2012; Evans and Rauch, 1999; Henderson et al., 2007; Miller, 2000; Nistotskaya and Cingolani, 2016; Rauch, 1995; Rauch and Evans, 2000). Furthermore, a recent systematic review identified 96 empirical publications related to merit bureaucracy and government performance, broadly defined and measured, published in 56 journals between 2014 and 2022 (Oliveira et al., 2024). It found that meritocratic appointments, tenure protection, and impartiality are robustly associated with higher government performance and lower corruption (Oliveira et al., 2024).

This research represents a formidable body of evidence against the latest iteration of the inefficiency critique. However, this evidence has not entered the current public discourse on the future of civil service reform on either side of the debate (Moynihan, 2023; Sherk, 2021). For instance, a policy paper by the AFPI (Sherk, 2021) that rationalised Donald Trump's plan to remove tenure protection for the majority of policy positions in the US federal government draws on none of the 96 articles featured in Oliveira et al.'s (2024) systematic review, despite the overwhelming majority of them being published before 2020.

Furthermore, despite empirical evidence overwhelmingly refuting the inefficiency claim, a small recent body of literature has shown that, under certain conditions, a politicised bureaucracy may improve outcomes within its area of responsibility (Rivera, 2020; Toral, 2024), or that certain types of politically misaligned bureaucratic agents (e.g. procurement officers) may underperform (Spenkuch et al., 2023). This evidence, which could be significant for the inefficiency camp, has not made significant inroads into the current public debate either.

This lack of integration of research evidence into current public discussions is a key reason why the ongoing debate on this subject in many countries remains superficial (Thomas, 2023). Consequently, "the blueprints [for the reform of the merit system] offered by both left and right are problematic" (McConnell et al., 2024), as they represent two radically opposed positions: preserving the status quo versus embracing radical deconstruction of the administrative state. Neither option reflects decades of research on the matter or suggests thoughtful, nuanced solutions to the legitimate question of how to improve the efficiency of the bureaucratic machine.

Implications for the research agenda

Various academic disciplines studying bureaucratic merit (see Asmus Olsen's chapter) can do more to advance public discourse and assist policy work on modernising the merit system. Beyond the obvious need for increased participation by scholars in public debate, there should be more empirical work isolating the mechanisms through which merit-based bureaucracies achieve efficiency. Several potential mechanisms have been suggested, such as higher competence, improved internal cohesion, codification of behavioural norms consistent either with the efficiency metrics or professional standards and ethos, longer-term horizons, and predictability (Boräng et al., 2018; Carpenter, 2014; Colonnelli et al., 2020; Cornell et al., 2020; Dahlström and Lapuente, 2017; Evans and Rauch, 1999; Miller, 2000; Miller and Whitford, 2016; Nistotskaya and Cingolani, 2016; Rauch, 1995). However, research on these mechanisms is still in its infancy (but see Nistotskaya and Cingolani, 2016). While social science research has moved beyond a mere affirmation of the association between X and Y and a greater demand has been placed on illuminating causal pathways, the bureaucratic merit scholarship has been out of step with these developments and needs improvement in this regard.

Secondly, since many proponents of a politicised bureaucracy recognise the efficiency benefits of merit-based recruitment for ensuring competence but not of tenure protection (Cummings, 2023; Sherk, 2021), the relationship between the two and their impact on efficiency needs to be empirically examined. Thus far, the empirical literature on the matter is sparse and inconclusive. While some studies have found that both merit-based recruitment and tenure protection improve bureaucratic performance (Nistotskaya and Cingolani, 2016; Ornaghi, 2016), Oliveros and Schuster (2018) suggest that the efficiency dividend is solely attributable to merit recruitment. Consequently, further research is necessary to isolate the individual impacts of tenure protection and meritocratic recruitment on bureaucratic efficiency, as well as to determine their relative strengths. It is also likely that the magnitude of these impacts is context-specific, which could generate more nuanced theoretical claims about the conditions under which the benefits of bureaucratic merit are fully developed or suppressed.

The picture of the determinants of bureaucratic efficiency is not complete without considering the links between methods not only of recruitment and dismissal, but also of promotions and assignment to different tasks and locations. Several studies that examined attributes other than recruitment and dismissals have provided rich insights into the matter. For example, Banik (2001) demonstrated that in India's sub-national governments it is not recruitment, but the power of transfer that is the most powerful "tool for politicians to extract obedience and compliance" from bureaucrats, and that arbitrary transfers undermine bureaucratic motivation to work for the benefit of the area. Understanding the broader range of factors (beyond recruitment and dismissals) that affect bureaucratic efficiency and their relative strength will potentially lead to realistic and efficacious reform choices.

Equally important is to understand how different 'mixes' of merit and non-merit personnel and their interactions affect bureaucratic performance. While partisan claims of bureaucratic inefficiency present bureaucracy as either fully meritocratic or fully politicised, extant literature has showed that in many countries around the world – ranging from the USA, Spain, Brazil, and the Dominican Republic to Balkan, African, and Asian democracies – merit and non-merit public managers often work side by side, even within the same organisations (Brierley, 2021; Colonnelli et al., 2020; Gjoksi, 2018; Oliveros and Schuster, 2018; Poocharoen and Brillantes, 2013). However, the literature on this matter is particularly scant. Krause et al.'s (2006) study on the optimal balance of merit and politicised personnel for maximising bureaucratic efficiency remains, to the best of the author's knowledge, the sole example of such research.

The discussion above has outlined the basic contours of a research agenda for scholars wishing to contribute to the important and recently heightened public debate on bureaucratic efficiency and ways of modernising merit systems. This agenda aims to bridge the gap between research, public discourse, and policy, ensuring that future reforms are grounded in robust evidence and nuanced understanding.

Diversity management and bureaucratic merit

The critique of bureaucratic inefficiency transcends the traditional merit versus politicisation debate. Advocates of diversity management argue that greater diversity is likely to enhance organisational performance (for a review, see Ding and Riccucci, 2023), implying that merit-based recruitment, geared to attract expertise and skills, may dampen diversity and, therefore, efficiency.

Having originated from research on the private sector workforce, this critique is not tailored exclusively to the public sector workforce. Consequently, "public administration research on diversity has not been theory driven" and predictions regarding the negative effect of diversity even on the basic functioning of public organisations are common (Ding and Riccucci, 2023, p. 1367). These observations clearly point to the direction that future research should take. The empirical literature on the effects of diversity in the public sector workforce is limited and yields mixed results. For example, while Shibeshi (2012) found that ethnic diversity among employees of US federal agencies was negatively related to organisation performance, Rasul and Rogger (2015) documented a large positive effect of ethnic diversity on completion rates of public sector projects in Nigeria. A recent meta-analysis of 37 quantitative studies concluded that the role of contextual factors is central in shaping the direction and magnitude of the diversity's impacts (Ding et al., 2021). However, the relationship between diversity and merit was examined only once.

Within the empirical milieu of US federal agencies, Park and Liang (2020) examined the relationship between agencies' adoption of merit-based human resource management practices, workforce gender and racial diversity, managerial commitment to diversity management, and organisational performance using survey and administrative data. The study found no direct association between workforce diversity and performance, but instead between merit and performance. More importantly, the positive effect of merit-based practices on organisational performance was amplified in agencies with a more diverse workforce in terms of gender (but not race) or greater diversity management efforts.

While the authors effectively identified the moderating effect of merit and diversity management on diversity's impact on performance, the next, arguably more demanding step, is to ascertain the mediation between these factors. This would shed light on the causal mechanisms at play. Causal evidence on the impact of merit versus other plausible pathways would provide a foundation for sound prescriptions for reforming the merit system. However, studies applying quasi-experimental methods are very limited within the bureaucratic merit scholarship, presenting a clear path for future research.

3. Critique of bureaucratic accountability

Accountability to politicians, sabotage and 'deep state'

The 'deep state' critique is also not new. In its current form, it is similar in kind to the age-old critique of bureaucratic accountability (or the lack thereof) to politicians, albeit not in degree. The academic literature has long ascertained that meritocratic bureaucrats have distinct preferences, which at times conflict with politicians' incentives (Finer, 1941; Friedrich, 1940; Miller, 2000; Wood, 1988). Max Weber problematised the issue as a matter of logical inconsistency between expertise and authority, writing "[t]he 'political master' finds himself in a position of the 'dilletante' who stands opposite the 'expert', facing the trained official who stands within the management of the administration" (Weber, 1946, p. 232). In contrast, the 'deep state' critique maintains that unelected, powerful bureaucrats simply hinder agenda of elected representative by "slow-walking, withholding information, leaking [...], and enlisting internal and external allies" (Sherk, 2022, p. 27), and instead secretly pursue their own goals.

For scholars acknowledging the distinct incentives of meritocratic bureaucrats, the central questions have revolved around whether this is a good or bad thing, and for what ends. Most concerns have centred on with the 'sabotage' of elected officials' policy goals by unelected bureaucrats either on the normative grounds related to democratic accountability or by positing that such 'sabotage' will generate negative consequences for society as a whole (Balla and Gormley Jr, 2017; Grindle, 2012; Skowronek, 1982; Wood, 1988). However, some scholars recognise the misalignment in preferences between principals and meritocratic agents as a feature that serves as an auxiliary constitutional and ethical safeguard on politicians, who often do not seek the public good but rather aim to satisfy short-sighted, pork barrel, or outright rent-seeking incentives (Brierley, 2020; Dahlström and Lapuente, 2017; Miller, 2000; Miller and Whitford, 2016; Nistotskaya and Cingolani, 2016). Ultimately, this misalignment is seen as a welfare-enhancing property of bureaucratic merit.

Leaving aside the normative elements of the critique, which revolve around values, ethics, and what ought to be rather than what is, and therefore cannot be resolved with empirical evidence, the problem with this literature, and by extension, with our struggle to effectively counter the populist rhetoric of the 'deep state', is that neither the claim of a sabotaging bureaucracy undermining the public good nor that of an above-politics, welfare-enhancing bureaucracy has accumulated sufficient empirical evidence to be thoroughly substantiated or refuted. This knowledge gap is hugely consequential. It allows the 'deep state' camp to perpetuate their rhetoric unopposed, further entrenching their narratives, and breeding citizen low confidence in merit-based administration (Simon and Moltz, 2022), which often leads to dissatisfaction with democracy, polarisation, and democratic backsliding (Bauer et al., 2021; Dahlberg and Holmberg, 2014). This unsubstantiated rhetoric has also fuelled populists' projects of bureaucracy re-politicisation, dismantling, and capture with questionable outcomes for both human well-being and democracy (Bauer et al., 2021; Peters and Pierre, 2004). Ultimately, without robust empirical evidence to clarify these claims, the debate remains mired in speculation and ideological conflict, making it impossible to answer with certainty whether a merit bureaucracy remains the right model for organising Leviathan and if it is necessary and sufficient for addressing the multiple challenges faced by societies.

Implications for the research agenda

The discussion above highlights the need for empirical studies that examine the social welfare effects of bureaucratic incentive structures both directly and under various levels and forms of political and societal oversight. This is no easy task, with the immediate hurdle being the lack of empirical data to facilitate such examination.

Presently incentive structures faced by bureaucrats are most often measured at the system level: through, for example, the extent of merit-based recruitment or tenure protection in a country. While the bureaucratic merit scholarship benefits from several such cross-country time-series datasets such as the expert survey of the Quality of Government Institute (Nistotskaya et al., 2021) or the Varieties of Democracy Institute at the University of Gothenburg or the commercially produced data on country risks (PRS Group, 2014), there remains a significant gap in cross-country data regarding the levels and forms of legislative, executive, judicial, media, or citizen oversight. This gap is critical because, as highlighted in a recent review article, "[o]nce bureaucrats are selected and deployed, these dynamics of bureaucratic oversight are a key determinant of public sector performance" (Brierley et al., 2023).

Furthermore, proxying individual incentives through organisational structures is not the most accurate way of measuring incentives, but extant empirical literature is dominated by this approach, with countries being a typical unit of analysis. As fruitful as this approach has been, bureaucratic incentives cannot be fully understood on the basis of organisational structures. This necessitates studies with individual-level data, which thus far has not been the strongest suit of the bureaucratic merit scholarship. The broader availability of individual-level data would also facilitate the deployment of quasi-experimental methods, as it simplifies the identification of a counterfactual group to estimate the impact of incentives.

Ideally, to be able to accurately discern potential effects of incentives, the data needs to combine both the organisational- and individual-level variables and to be over time. Acquiring comparative data of this kind is likely to surpass the efforts of individual researchers and necessitate collaboration with governments. Several initiatives, such as the Global Survey of Public Servants (GSPS) that seeks to provide "harmonized but granular data on public administration around the world" (Schuster et al., 2023), mark steps in the right direction.

Qualitative studies can also be a valuable method for testing the welfare effects of bureaucratic incentives. However, they have proven to be less popular among scholars of bureaucratic merit. One major obstacle is gaining access to bureaucratic sites for observations and other qualitative materials. In light of this challenge, comparative-historical studies seem to offer a promising alternative. For example, Andersen (2021) examined the variation in bureaucratic responsiveness to the political agenda of the day at constant levels of meritocracy in 19th-century Prussia and Imperial and Weimar Germany and found it is only a combination of high merit and high responsiveness that makes bureaucracy welfare-enhancing.

It is also important that empirical work is able to isolate specific mechanisms through which merit-based bureaucracies achieve outcomes that improve the welfare of all members of society (or, more precisely, improve outcomes for at least some without worsening them for others), such as increasing healthy years of life or ensuring access to safe drinking water. We need to ascertain with precision that specific incentives induced by merit-based recruitment or, alternatively, tenure protection removal are causally responsible for these improvements. However, the availability of large-N data suitable for such examination remains a significant challenge. In this context, qualitative research may provide valuable insights, as evidenced by developments in the adjacent field of state capacity (Brieba, 2018). Numerous completed and ongoing re-politicisation projects (Bauer and Becker, 2020; Bauer et al., 2021) can also be methodologically exploited within the natural experiment paradigm.

Accountability to citizens: representative bureaucracy and bureaucratic merit

The critique of accountability extends beyond just politicians; it also encompasses accountability to citizens. The reputed lack of bureaucratic accountability to the people they serve has sparked criticism of meritocratic bureaucracies among advocates of representative bureaucracy. This critique is increasingly relevant due to the growing diversity of populations in many countries worldwide. For example, in Sweden today 20% of the current residents are foreign born, including 14% of those born outside EU (Statistics Sweden, 2022). This demographic shift has prompted a demand for the nation's public sector workforce to reflect the diversity of its population.

The central question of this critique, from the standpoint of this chapter, is whether a representative bureaucracy or one with a diverse (though not necessarily representative) workforce outperforms a classic meritocratic bureaucracy in terms of both first-order outcomes, such as bureaucratic effectiveness, and second-order outcomes, like social welfare. The theoretical discussion, which has largely remained within the academic circles, has reached an impasse (Lim, 2006), and empirical research has yet to provide a resolution. A recent meta-analysis documented that the effects of representative bureaucracy on public organisational performance are highly contextualised (Ding et al., 2021). However, the level of institutionalisation of the merit system was not one of the contextual factors examined in the 80 quantitative studies included in the meta-analysis. Surprisingly, the empirical literature on representative bureaucracy does not engage with the bureaucratic merit scholarship, despite both aiming to explain bureaucratic performance and efficiency. Establishing such a dialogue is not merely an avenue for future research but a highway, essential for advancing our understanding of how different bureaucratic models impact government outputs and societal welfare.

An indication that the level of bureaucratic merit might be an important contextual factor moderating the effects of representative bureaucracy emerged from a recent study that found that where the levels of bureaucratic merit are relatively high, the quality of public services tends to be lower for citizens with lower education levels and lower incomes (Suzuki and Demircioglu, 2021). In other words, where the merit systems are older and relatively strongly institutionalised, bureaucratic merit maybe be a necessary but not sufficient condition for improved social welfare. This aligns with the conclusions drawn by Andersen (2021) regarding the impact of political responsiveness on bureaucratic quality within merit systems of the same level. Such research designs offer fresh insights and warrant broader application in future studies.

4. Meritocracy myth, equality, diversity, and inclusion (EDI), and bureaucratic merit

The 'meritocracy myth' critique of bureaucratic merit is equally not new. Qualifications and competence are two out of three core features of the merit system (Ingraham, 2006, p. 487), with the third one being the absence of political favouritism. The meritocracy myth critique revolves around the questions whether or not recruitment through a check of formal qualifications and competences enables equality, diversity, and inclusion, and whether preferential treatment of members of marginalised groups negatively affects bureaucratic quality?

Some have argued that meritocratic recruitment better enables members from all groups and classes to join public bureaucracy than patronage's opaque and personalistic criteria (Van Riper, 1958). However, there is also a deeply rooted belief that when it comes to formal qualifications and competence privileged groups will always have the upper hand over marginalised groups, as educational achievements are to a great extent just a reflection of existing socio-economic inequalities (Sandel, 2020). This 'myth of meritocracy' promoted a policy response in the form of various types of affirmative action policies, each differing in their intensity and scope. These policies are designed to address systemic inequalities and ensure that underrepresented groups have equitable opportunities in education and employment. While the consequences of such policies thus far have most strongly been felt in the US context, where EDI has been a longstanding agreed-upon goal, the increasing heterogeneity of populations and structural inequality in many countries worldwide will inevitably expand the relevance of these issues.

Despite their relevance, the literature on the relationship between merit, EDI, and bureaucratic performance in the context of the public sector workforce remains severely understudied and inconclusive. When evaluating the impact of affirmative action policies on bureaucratic quality, two studies are particularly noteworthy. While Lewis (2013) finds that in the US federal government, hiring based on veteran status lowers both the epistemic quality of the bureaucracy and its overall performance compared to merit hires, Sunam et al. (2022) documents that affirmative action in the Nepalese bureaucracy improves its competence, albeit only when compared to a patronage baseline.

Regarding the effect of merit-based recruitment on EDI, the empirical research is also limited and contradictory, with only two significant studies on the matter, each of which were set in the context of US civil service reform of the late 19th century. Kuipers and Sahn (2023) show that after the reform a salient underprivileged minority of the time – foreign-born whites – experienced substantial employment gains in public bureaucracy. In contrast, Moreira and Pérez (2022) show that the 1883 Pendleton Act reduced the share of individuals from lower socio-economic statuses.

The current literature fails to provide a satisfactory answer to the crucial and presently hotly publicly debated question of the relationship between merit, EDI, and bureaucratic efficiency. Consequently, it is not surprising that the quality of public discourse on this issue is overly simplistic and panders to established stereotypes, further exacerbating societal polarisation. This is evidenced, for example, by the recent debate over Claudine Gay's appointment and subsequent resignation as Harvard University President. Addressing this gap constitutes a large and important research agenda for scholars of bureaucratic merit.

5. Conclusion

Critics from various ideological perspectives challenge the meritocratic model on multiple fronts. From the right, the critique focuses on perceived inefficiencies and the need for greater political control over bureaucrats. This argument posits that career protections for bureaucrats can lead to complacency and hinder responsiveness to elected officials, who represent the electorate's will. From the left, critiques emphasise that meritocratic systems may perpetuate existing social inequalities by favouring those from privileged backgrounds who have better access to education and other resources. This advantage enables them to successfully navigate civil service exams and similar forms of meritocratic entry into bureaucracy. Furthermore, some argue that merit-based recruitment may not adequately reflect the diversity of the populations served by public bureaucracies, potentially leading to a lack of sensitivity to diverse societal needs. From both right and (sometimes) left, meritocratic bureaucracies are framed as part of a 'deep state' that obstructs politicians' agendas and portrays them as inherently antagonistic to democratic governance.

This chapter has evaluated the merits of these critiques against the accumulated knowledge base. It found that the ineffectiveness critique is largely unsupported by empirical evidence. Nearly 100 studies have demonstrated that merit-based recruitment, tenure protection, and impartiality are associated with higher government performance and societal benefits. However, the current public discourse often overlooks this robust body of evidence, leading to superficial and ideologically driven debates. On the other hand, the accountability and the myth of meritocracy critiques persist, largely due to the lack of a comparable body of evidence in bureaucratic merit scholarship to address these issues.

This situation is uncomfortable as it does not equip us to answer with precision the question – implicitly raised by these critiques – whether bureaucratic merit is a necessary and sufficient condition for addressing the evolving challenges faced by modern societies. It calls for conceptual clarity in Public Administration scholarship and allied disciplines regarding the role that public bureaucracy should play in the modern organisation of society, along with empirical responses to these critiques.

The implications for the research agenda are vast. Future efforts should, above all, illuminate the mechanisms through which merit-based systems achieve purported benefits. Integrating insights from representative bureaucracy and diversity management into the meritocracy debate is also crucial to understanding how diversity and representation can coexist with or enhance the meritocratic model.

Although the task in hand may seem daunting, a relevant example suggests otherwise. Through the 1970s, in both popular debate and scholarship the neglect of congressional oversight of the US federal bureaucracy became "a stylized fact", which was "widely and dutifully reported [...] often bemoaned, but almost never seriously questioned" (McCubbins and Schwartz, 1984, p. 165). However, this narrative was overturned by just three studies that posed relevant and precise research questions and employed innovative methodologies (McCubbins et al., 1987; McCubbins and Schwartz, 1984; McCubbins et al., 1989). Consequently, already in 1991 Wood and Waterman (1991) argued that there was a new paradigm of political-bureaucratic relations, which ascertained that the US democratic institutions "shape nonelective public bureaucracies" (Wood and Waterman, 1991, p. 801), and led to significant bureaucratic oversight reforms like the establishment of the Office of Personnel Management (OPM).

Rigorous and innovative research has the potential to challenge entrenched narratives and drive pragmatic reforms of bureaucracy. Among the measures that can expedite progress in bureaucratic merit scholarship, embracing its interdisciplinary nature and fostering collaboration are essential. Leveraging the digitalisation of data production, including open government data, can also significantly enhance research capabilities, as well as forming partnerships with governments. Moreover, scholars of bureaucratic merit should prioritise communicating their research to the public effectively in order to counter partisan criticism and ensure informed discourse on the merit system's role in democratic governance.

In sum, while the meritocratic model of bureaucracy has its challenges and critics, it remains a foundational element of societies with high levels of human well-being. However, continued research and nuanced public discussion are crucial for refining this model to meet the evolving needs of diverse societies.

References

Andersen, D. D. E. (2021). The limits of meritocracy in stabilizing democracy and the twin importance of bureaucratic impartiality and effectiveness. *Social Science History, 45*(3), 535–559. https://doi.org/10.1017/ssh.2021.15.

Andersen, D. D. E., & Krishnarajan, S. (2019). Economic crisis, bureaucratic quality and democratic breakdown. *Government and Opposition, 54*(4), 715–744. https://doi.org/10.1017/gov.2017.37.

Balla, S., & Gormley W. T. (2017). *Bureaucracy and Democracy: Accountability and Performance*. CQ Press. https://doi.org/10.4135/9781071801376.

Banik, D. (2001). The transfer raj: Indian civil servants on the move. *The European Journal of Development Research, 13*(1), 106–134. https://doi.org/10.1080/09578810108426783.

Battaglio, R. P. (2010). Public service reform and motivation: Evidence from an employment at-will environment. *Review of Public Personnel Administration, 30*(2), 341–363. https://doi.org/10.1177/0734371X10368224.

Bauer, M. W., & Becker, S. (2020). Democratic backsliding, populism, and public administration. *Perspectives on Public Management and Governance, 3*(1), 19–31. https://doi.org/10.1093/ppmgov/gvz026.

Bauer, M. W., Peters, B. G., Pierre, J., Yesilkagit, K., & Becker, S. (2021). *Democratic Backsliding and Public Administration: How Populists in Government Transform State Bureaucracies*. Cambridge University Press. https://doi.org/10.1017/9781009023504.

Boräng, F., Cornell, A., Grimes, M., & Schuster, C. (2018). Cooking the books: Bureaucratic politicization and policy knowledge. *Governance, 31*(1), 7–26. https://doi.org/10.1111/gove.12283.

Bowman, J. S, & West, J. P. (2006). Ending civil service protections in Florida government: Experiences in state agencies. *Review of Public Personnel Administration, 26*(2), 139–157. https://doi.org/10.1177/0734371X06286978.

Brieba, D. (2018). State capacity and health outcomes: Comparing Argentina's and Chile's reduction of infant and maternal mortality, 1960–2013. *World Development, 101*, 37–53. https://doi.org/10.1016/j.worlddev.2017.08.011.

Brierley, S. (2020). Unprincipled principals: Co-opted bureaucrats and corruption in Ghana. *American Journal of Political Science, 64*(2), 209–222. https://doi.org/10.1111/ajps.12495.

Brierley, S. (2021). Combining patronage and merit in public sector recruitment. *The Journal of Politics, 83*(1), 182–197. https://doi.org/10.1086/708240.

Brierley, S., Lowande, K., Potter, R. A., & Toral, G. (2023). Bureaucratic politics: Blind spots and opportunities in political science. *Annual Review of Political Science, 26*, 271–290. https://doi.org/10.1146/annurev-polisci-061621-084933.

Carpenter, D. (2002). *The Forging of Bureaucratic Autonomy: Reputations, Networks, and Policy Innovation in Executive Agencies, 1862–1928*. Princeton University Press. https://doi.org/10.2307/j.ctv10crfk2.

Carpenter, D. (2014). *Reputation and Power: Organizational Image and Pharmaceutical Regulation at the FDA*. Princeton University Press. https://www.jstor.org/stable/j.ctt7t5st.

Charron, N., Dahlström, C., Fazekas, M., & Lapuente, V. (2017). Careers, connections, and corruption risks: Investigating the impact of bureaucratic meritocracy on public procurement processes. *The Journal of Politics*, 79(1), 89–104. https://doi.org/10.1086/687209.

Cingolani, L., Thomsson, K., & de Crombrugghe, D. (2015). Minding Weber more than ever? The impacts of state capacity and bureaucratic autonomy on development goals. *World Development*, 72, 191–207. https://doi.org/10.1016/j.worlddev.2015.02.016.

Clark, C. S. (2018, July 3). After 40 years, a Look Back at the Unlikely Passage of Civil Service Reform. *Government Executive*. https://www.govexec.com/management/2018/07/after-40-years-look-back-unlikely-passage-civil-service-reform/149458/ .

Clark, C. S. (n.d.). Deconstructing the Deep State: Donald Trump isn't the first president to be deeply skeptical of the institutions and people he now leads. *Government Executive*. https://www.govexec.com/feature/gov-exec-deconstructing-deep-state/.

Colonnelli, E., Prem, M., & Teso, E. (2020). Patronage and selection in public sector organizations. *American Economic Review*, 110(10), 3071–3099. https://doi.org/10.1257/aer.20181491.

Cornell, A., Knutsen, C. H., & Teorell, J. (2020). Bureaucracy and growth. *Comparative Political Studies*, 53(14), 2246–2282. https://doi.org/10.1177/0010414020912262.

Cummings, D. (2023). Vote Leave, Brexit, COVID, and No. 10 with Boris. *Manifold*, 28. https://www.manifold1.com/episodes/dominic-cummings-vote-leave-brexit-covid-and-no-10-with-boris-28/transcript.

Dahlberg, S., & Holmberg, S. (2014). Democracy and bureaucracy: How their quality matters for popular satisfaction. *West European Politics*, 37(3), 515–537. https://doi.org/10.1080/01402382.2013.830468.

Dahlström, C., & Lapuente, V. (2017). *Organizing Leviathan: Politicians, Bureaucrats, and the Making of Good Government*. Cambridge University Press. https://doi.org/10.1017/9781316822869.

Dahlström, C., Fazekas, M., & Lewis, D. E. (2021). Partisan procurement: Contracting with the United States federal government, 2003–2015. *American Journal of Political Science*, 65(3), 652–669. https://doi.org/10.1111/ajps.12574.

Dahlström, C., Lapuente, V., & Teorell, J. (2012). The merit of meritocratization: Politics, bureaucracy, and the institutional deterrents of corruption. *Political Research Quarterly*, 65(3), 656–668. https://doi.org/10.1177/1065912911408109.

Dans, P., Chretien, S., & Hemenway, T. (2024). *Building for a conservative victory through policy, personnel, and training: Get the facts*. Presidential Transition Project. https://www.project2025.org/.

Ding, F., & Riccucci, N. M. (2023). How does diversity affect public organizational performance? A meta-analysis. *Public Administration*, 101(4), 1367–1393. https://doi.org/10.1111/padm.12885.

Ding, F., Lu, J., & Riccucci, N. M. (2021). How bureaucratic representation affects public organizational performance: A meta-analysis. *Public Administration Review*, 81(6), 1003–1018. https://doi.org/10.1111/puar.13361.

Evans, P., & Rauch, J. E. (1999). Bureaucracy and growth: A cross-national analysis of the effects of "Weberian" state structures on economic growth. *American Sociological Review, 64*(5), 748–765. https://doi.org/10.1177/000312249906400508

Finer, H. (1941). Administrative responsibility in democratic government. *Public Administration Review, 1*(4), 335–350. https://doi.org/10.2307/972907.

Frant, H. (1996). High-powered and low-powered incentives in the public sector. *Journal of Public Administration Research and Theory, 6*(3), 365–381. https://doi.org/10.1093/oxfordjournals.jpart.a024317.

Friedrich, C. (1940) [2000]. Public policy and the nature of administrative responsibility. In Tadao Miyakawa (Ed.), *The Science of Public Policy: Essential Reading in Policy Sciences II. Volume VII, Policy Process Part III*, 114–132. Routledge.

Gjoksi, N. (2018). *Weber in the Balkans: contested party–state relations in reforming the civil service in Albania and FYR Macedonia, 2000–13*. PhD thesis European University Institute. https://doi.org/10.2870/518742.

Grindle, M. S. (2012). *Jobs for the Boys*. Harvard University Press. https://www.jstor.org/stable/j.ctt24hk8t.

Henderson, J., Hulme, D., Jalilian, H., & Phillips, R. (2007). Bureaucratic effects: "Weberian" state agencies and poverty reduction. *Sociology, 41*(3), 515–532. https://doi.org/10.1177/0038038507076620.

Ingraham, P. W. (2006). Building bridges over troubled waters: Merit as a guide. *Public Administration Review, 66*(4), 486–495. https://doi.org/10.1111/j.1540-6210.2006.00608.x.

Krause, G. A., Lewis, D. E., & Douglas, J. W. (2006). Political appointments, civil service systems, and bureaucratic competence: Organizational balancing and executive branch revenue forecasts in the American states. *American Journal of Political Science, 50*(3), 770–787. https://doi.org/10.1111/j.1540-5907.2006.00215.x.

Kuipers, N., & Sahn, A. (2023). The representational consequences of municipal civil service reform. *American Political Science Review, 117*(1), 200–216. https://doi.org/10.1017/S0003055422000521.

Lewis, D. E. (2007). Testing Pendleton's premise: Do political appointees make worse bureaucrats? *The Journal of Politics, 69*(4), 1073–1088. https://doi.org/10.1111/j.1468-2508.2007.00608.x.

Lewis, G. B. (2013). The impact of veterans' preference on the composition and quality of the federal civil service. *Journal of Public Administration Research and Theory, 23*(2), 247–265. https://doi.org/10.1093/jopart/mus029.

Lim, H.-H. (2006). Representative bureaucracy: Rethinking substantive effects and active representation. *Public Administration Review, 66*(2), 193–204. https://doi.org/10.1111/j.1540-6210.2006.00572.x.

McConnell, M., Negroponte, J., O'Keefe, S., Hayden, M., & Loy, J. (2024, June 18). Opinion: We have run federal agencies. Here's what the civil service needs. *The Washington Post*. https://www.washingtonpost.com/opinions/2024/06/18/fix-civil-service-experience-partisanship/.

McCubbins, M. D., & Schwartz, T. (1984). Congressional oversight overlooked: Police patrols versus fire alarms. *American Journal of Political Science, 28*(1), 165–179. https://doi.org/10.2307/2110792.

McCubbins, M. D., Noll, R. G., & Weingast, B. R. (1987). Administrative procedures as instruments of political control. *The Journal of Law, Economics, and Organization, 3*(2), 243–277. https://doi.org/10.1093/oxfordjournals.jleo.a036930.

McCubbins, M. D., Noll, R. G., & Weingast, B. R. (1989). Structure and process, politics and policy: Administrative arrangements and the political control of agencies. *Virginia Law Review, 75*, 431–482. https://doi.org/10.2307/1073179.

Miller, G. (2000). Above politics: Credible commitment and efficiency in the design of public agencies. *Journal of Public Administration Research and Theory, 10*(2), 289–328. https://doi.org/10.1093/oxfordjournals.jpart.a024271.

Miller, G. J., & Whitford, A. B. (2016). *Above politics: Bureaucratic Discretion and Credible Commitment.* Cambridge University Press. https://doi.org/10.1017/CBO9781139017688.

Moreira, D., & Pérez, S. (2022). *Who Benefits from Meritocracy?* Technical report, National Bureau of Economic Research. https://www.nber.org/system/files/working_papers/w30113/w30113.pdf.

Moynihan, D. (2023, November 27). Trump Has a Master Plan for Destroying the "Deep State". *The New York Times.* https://www.nytimes.com/2023/11/27/opinion/trump-deep-state-schedule-f.html.

Niskanen, W. A. (1971). *Bureaucracy and representative government.* Routledge. https://doi.org/10.4324/9781315081878.

Nistotskaya, M., & Cingolani, L. (2016). Bureaucratic structure, regulatory quality, and entrepreneurship in a comparative perspective: Cross-sectional and panel data evidence. *Journal of Public Administration Research and Theory, 26*(3), 519–534. https://doi.org/10.1093/jopart/muv026.

Nistotskaya, M., Dahlberg, S., Dahlström, C., Sundström, A., Axelsson, S., Mert Dalli, C., & Alvarado Pachon, N. (2021). *The Quality of Government Expert Survey 2020 (Wave III): Report.* Quality of Government Institute, QoG Working Paper Series 2021:2. https://www.gu.se/sites/default/files/2021-03/2021_2_Nistotskaya_Dahlberg_Dahlstrom_Sundstrom_Axelsson_Dalli_Alvarado%20Pachon.pdf.

Oliveira, E., Abner, G., Lee, S., Suzuki, K., Hur, H., & Perry, J. L. (2024). What does the evidence tell us about merit principles and government performance? *Public Administration, 102*(2), 668–690. https://doi.org/10.1111/padm.12945.

Oliveros, V., & Schuster, C. (2018). Merit, tenure, and bureaucratic behavior: Evidence from a conjoint experiment in the Dominican Republic. *Comparative Political Studies, 51*(6), 759–792. https://doi.org/10.1177/0010414017710268.

Olsen, J. P. (2006). Maybe it is time to rediscover bureaucracy. *Journal of Public Administration Research and Theory, 16*(1), 1–24. https://doi.org/10.1093/jopart/mui027.

Ornaghi, A. (2016). *Civil Service Reforms: Evidence from U.S. Police Departments.* Technical report, MIT. https://www.eief.it/files/2017/01/02-jmp_ornaghi.pdf.

Park, S., & Liang, J. (2020). Merit, diversity, and performance: Does diversity management moderate the effect of merit principles on governmental performance? *Public Personnel Management, 49*(1), 83–110. https://doi.org/10.1177/0091026019848459.

Peters, G., & Pierre, J. (Eds.) (2004). *Politicization of the Civil Service in Comparative Perspective: The Quest for Control.* Routledge. https://doi.org/10.4324/9780203799857.

Poocharoen, O.-o., & Brillantes, A. (2013). Meritocracy in Asia Pacific: Status, issues, and challenges. *Review of Public Personnel Administration*, 33(2), 140–163. https://doi.org/10.1177/0734371X13484829.

PRS Group (2014). *International Country Risk Guide Methodology*. PRS Group. https://www.prsgroup.com/wp-content/uploads/2012/11/icrgmethodology.pdf.

Rasul, I., & Rogger, D. (2015). The impact of ethnic diversity in bureaucracies: Evidence from the Nigerian civil service. *American Economic Review*, 105(5), 457–461. https://doi.org/10.1257/aer.p20151003.

Rauch, J. E. (1995). Bureaucracy, infrastructure, and economic growth: Evidence from US cities during the progressive era. *The American Economic Review*, 85(4), 968–979. https://www.nber.org/system/files/working_papers/w4973/w4973.pdf.

Rauch, J. E., & Evans, P. B. (2000). Bureaucratic structure and bureaucratic performance in less developed countries. *Journal of Public Economics*, 75(1), 49–71. https://doi.org/10.1016/s0047-2727(99)00044-4.

Riccucci, N., & Van Ryzin, G. (2017). Representative bureaucracy: A lever to enhance social equity, coproduction, and democracy. *Public Administration Review*, 77(1), 21–30. https://doi.org/10.1111/puar.12649.

Rivera, C. V. (2020). Loyalty or incentives? How party alignment affects bureaucratic performance. *The Journal of Politics*, 82(4), 1287–1304. https://doi.org/10.1086/708337.

Sandel, M. J. (2020). *The Tyranny of Merit: What's Become of the Common Good?* Penguin UK.

Schuster, C., Mikkelsen, K. S., Rogger, D., Fukuyama, F., Hasnain, Z., Mistree, D., Meyer-Sahling, J., Bersch, K., & Kay, K. (2023). The global survey of public servants: Evidence from 1,300,000 public servants in 1,300 government institutions in 23 countries. *Public Administration Review*, 83(4), 982–993. https://doi.org/10.1111/puar.13611.

Shapiro, C., & Stiglitz, J. E. (1984). Equilibrium unemployment as a worker discipline device. *The American Economic Review*, 74(3), 433–444. https://www.jstor.org/stable/1804018.

Sherk, J. (2021, May 26). Increasing Accountability in the Civil Service. *America First Policy Institute*. https://americafirstpolicy.com/issues/increasing-accountability-in-the-civil-service.

Sherk, J. (2022, February 1). Tales From the Swamp: How Federal Bureaucrats Resisted President Trump. *America First Policy Institute*. https://americafirstpolicy.com/issues/20222702-federal-bureaucrats-resisted-president-trump.

Shibeshi, S. (2012). *Relationship between ethnic diversity and organizational performance of U.S. federal agencies (Order No. 3548772)*. PhD thesis, Walden University.

Simon, C. A., & Moltz, M. C. (2022). Confidence in merit-based public administration in the context of right-wing authoritarian populism. *Administration & Society*, 54(6), 995–1018. https://doi.org/10.1177/00953997211045609.

Skowronek, S. (1982). *Building a New American State: The Expansion of National Administrative Capacities, 1877–1920*. Cambridge University Press. https://doi.org/10.1017/CBO9780511665080.

Spenkuch, J. L., Teso, E., & Xu, G. (2023). Ideology and performance in public organizations. *Econometrica*, 91(4), 1171–1203. https://doi.org/10.3982/ECTA20355.

Statistics Sweden (2022). Population in Sweden by country/region of birth, citizenship and Swedish/foreign background, 31 December 2022. https://www.statista.com/statistics/525675/

sweden-number-of-inhabitants-by-region-of-birth/#:~:text=Of%20Sweden's%20total%20 population%20of,from%20Asia%2C%20with%20856%2C000%20people.

Sunam, R., Pariyar, B., & Shrestha, K. K. (2022). Does affirmative action undermine meritocracy? "Meritocratic inclusion" of the marginalized in Nepal's bureaucracy. *Development Policy Review*, *40*(1). https://doi.org/10.1111/dpr.12554.

Suzuki, K., & Demircioglu, M. A. (2021). Is impartiality enough? Government impartiality and citizens' perceptions of public service quality. *Governance*, *34*(3), 727–764. https://doi.org/10.1111/gove.12527.

Thomas, A. (2023, May 24). Appointed on Merit: the Value of an Impartial Civil Service. *Institute for Government*. https://www.instituteforgovernment.org.uk/publication/civil-service-impartiality.

Toral, G. (2024). How patronage delivers: Political appointments, bureaucratic accountability, and service delivery in Brazil. *American Journal of Political Science*, *68*(2), 797–815. https://doi.org/10.1111/ajps.12758.

Van Riper, P. P. (1958). *History of the United States Civil Service*. Row, Peterson.

Wagner, E. (2023, March, 21). Trump Vows to "Shatter the Deep State," Revive Schedule F and Move More Agencies Out of DC. *Government Executive*. https://www.govexec.com/workforce/2023/03/trump-vows-shatter-deep-state-revive-schedule-f-and-move-more-agencies-out-dc/384266/.

Weber, M. (1946). *The Theory of Social and Economic Organization*. Talcott Parsons (Ed.). Oxford University Press.

Wood, B. D. (1988). Principals, bureaucrats, and responsiveness in clean air enforcements. *American Political Science Review*, *82*(1), 213–234. https://doi.org/10.2307/1958066.

Wood, B. D., & Waterman, R. W. (1991). The dynamics of political control of the bureaucracy. *American Political Science Review*, *85*(3), 801–828. https://doi.org/10.2307/1963851.

The functional politicisation of the merit civil service: From responsive to subservient bureaucracy?

by Tobias Bach

1. Introduction

The relationship and boundaries between politics and administration are fundamental topics in the study of Public Administration, and several observers have identified the politicisation of the bureaucracy as a key trend in recent decades (Peters and Pierre, 2004). Many scholars in the field are interested in documenting the scope of patronage appointments, how they have changed over time, and the often-problematic consequences they bring. This focus implies a tendency to empirically examine 'positive' cases with considerable levels of politicisation, with the United States being an important example with a vast body of scholarship on political appointees (Lewis, 2008).

This study takes a different direction and provides insights on the relationship and interactions between politics and administration in countries with a merit-based civil service (see also the chapter by Nistotskaya in this volume). These countries exhibit low levels of patronage, yet the roles and interactions of senior civil servants with executive politicians are characterised by political considerations and embedded norms of political responsiveness among bureaucrats. This is what I call the paradox of meritocracy: whereas political considerations are largely irrelevant when it comes to recruitment and promotion of civil servants, their day-to-day work is characterised by high levels of functional politicisation, which means they must consider the political aspects of policy development and implementation (Hustedt and Salomonsen, 2014). The first part of this chapter provides evidence for the persistence of merit-based recruitment in selected countries and illustrates institutional variation among merit-based systems.

In contexts where patronage appointments are common, politicians can ensure the bureaucracy's responsiveness to their policy preferences by strategically placing ideological allies in key positions in the bureaucracy. In merit-based bureaucracies, political responsiveness is ensured through the above-mentioned norms of responsiveness to the government of the day. Put differently, incoming ministers must be confident that the bureaucracy serves them equally well as their predecessors from a different party. However, civil servants must balance the norm of responsiveness against competing norms such as legality or truthfulness (Christensen and Opstrup, 2018). An important insight is that merit-based bureaucracies display a high awareness of the distinct role and duties of bureaucrats and politicians operating in a political context. Yet despite these strong norms, politicians may still disregard civil service advice, and bureaucrats may refrain from speaking truth to power to protect their own career (Bischoff, 2023). There are signals that the demand for political responsiveness is increasingly overriding other legitimate concerns in interactions between politicians and bureaucrats in merit-based bureaucracies. This study provides some indications that responsiveness is increasingly turning into subservience in merit-based bureaucracies. Most empirical insights come from Norway, a small and wealthy country in Northern Europe, while occasional examples from countries such as Denmark or the Netherlands are also included.

2. The persistence of merit-based bureaucracy

This chapter takes its starting point in the widespread claim that bureaucracies in developed economies have become more politicised over time. A widely used definition describes politicisation as "the substitution of political criteria for merit-based criteria in the selection, retention, promotion, rewards, and disciplining of members of the public service" (Peters and Pierre, 2004, p. 2). Thus understood, the concept of politicisation overlaps with the notion of patronage appointments or "the power of political actors to appoint individuals by discretion to nonelective positions in the public sector" (Panizza et al., 2019, p. 148). This section focuses on politicisation understood as patronage, regardless of whether such patronage is perfectly legal (formal politicisation, see Hustedt and Salomonsen, 2014) or whether political criteria are applied for positions legally defined as merit-based. Well-known examples of formal politicisation are political appointees in the US (Lewis, 2008) and "political civil servants" in Germany (Bach and Veit, 2018), but scholars have also studied how politicians seek to influence the careers of regular civil servants (Doherty et al., 2019).

In their comparative book on public management reforms, Pollitt and Bouckaert (2017) include mandarin–minister relations as a key characteristic of politico-administrative regimes. They highlight several aspects of those relations, including whether career paths of senior civil servants and politicians are separated or overlapping, whether senior civil servants have known party-political sympathies, and how secure their positions are when they do not meet performance expectations or when there is a change in the political leadership. These are essential aspects of mandarin–minister relations which can be used to distinguish politicised from merit-based policy bureaucracies. Policy bureaucracies include organisations such as ministries or departments whose main tasks are "developing and maintaining public policy" (Bach and Wegrich, 2020, p. 525).

There are no clear indications that countries with strongly merit-based policy bureaucracies in Northern Europe have shifted towards a more patronage-based model. However, it is important to note that measuring trends over time requires longitudinal data, which is often not readily available. As a starting point, looking at cross-sectional data can provide some useful indications of the position of these countries relative to more patronage-based systems. For instance, the expert survey conducted by the Quality of Government Institute (QoG) can offer valuable insights into this comparison.

The latest QoG expert survey included questions specifically on recruitment to positions in central government (Nistotskaya et al., 2021). Their indicator of merit-based recruitment is based on the following question: "To what extent are appointments to bureaucratic positions in the central government based on individuals' merits – such as knowledge, skills and job-related experience?" Focusing on Europe, countries such as Norway (#1), the Netherlands (#3), Sweden (#5), the United Kingdom (#9) and Denmark (#11) have some of the world's most merit-based central government bureaucracies. Another question addresses patronage as a separate dimension: "To what extent are appointments to bureaucratic positions in central government based on the political and/or personal connections of the applicant?" When reversing the order from high to low patronage, we find Norway (#1), Denmark (#6), the Netherlands (#9) and the United Kingdom (#10) among the world's least patronage-based central governments. For this indicator, Sweden does not rank among the least patronage-based countries, confirming the picture of a somewhat stronger political influence on appointments demonstrated in the literature (Christiansen et al., 2016).

Another source of comparative information is the Coordinating for Cohesion in the Public Sector of the Future COCOPS survey of senior civil servants (Hammerschmid et al., 2016), which provides an insider perspective rather than expert assessments. The survey asked about the actual use of politicians' appointment powers through the following question, which respondents could answer on a seven-point scale from strongly disagree (1) to strongly agree (7): "Politicians regularly influence senior-level appointments in my organization". Analysing COCOPS data from 18 countries, Bach et al. (2020) found that Scandinavian (Iceland, Denmark, Finland, Norway) and Anglo-Saxon (Ireland, United Kingdom) countries had the lowest average scores of political influence on appointments. Among continental European countries, the Netherlands is ranked the lowest, scoring only slightly higher than Denmark. In contrast to the QoG expert survey, Denmark ranks among the least politicised countries in the COCOPS survey, whereas Norway and Sweden were close to countries like Germany and Hungary which are typically considered to be fairly politicised. One possible explanation for the differences observed is that Norway and, to a lesser extent, Sweden have experienced a continuous increase in the number of political appointees since the 1970s. In contrast, Denmark has only seen a very modest increase in political appointees, with each minister having only one or two advisers (Kolltveit, 2016).

The above-mentioned studies are cross-sectional and cannot say anything about trends unfolding over time, yet several recent studies analyse careers and tenure of senior civil servants in longitudinal designs. A comparison of the tenure of permanent secretaries in Denmark and Norway (1970–2020) shows that the careers of permanent secretaries in Denmark are 'immune' to minister or wholesale government changes, whereas wholesale government changes in Norway come with a slightly higher risk of turnover among permanent secretaries (Askim et al., 2024). The article suggests that these differences result from institutional differences between a "pure merit civil service" where ministers are assisted by advisers without executive authority (examples include Denmark and the Netherlands) and a "hybrid merit civil service" where politically appointed state secretaries are wedged between the minister and the permanent secretary (examples include Norway, Sweden, and Germany) (Askim et al., 2024). In Denmark, ministers are highly dependent on permanent secretaries "to control the portfolio as they have nobody else to resort to for the mixture of professional-political advice they demand" (Askim et al., 2024, p. 347). That study provides evidence of the effects of different mixes of personnel hired on meritocratic and political grounds, respectively, which according to Nistotskaya (this volume) is an important area of research on meritocratic bureaucracy.

A number of other studies using career data highlight the persistence of merit-based recruitment, although some of them also provide indications for politicisation. A recent study on political elites in Denmark finds that political and administrative careers in central government are clearly separated

(Binderkrantz et al., 2023). In a study of top civil servants in the Netherlands, Van Dorp (2023) shows that party politics does play a significant role for making it to the top of the administrative hierarchy. However, the pool of candidates for those positions consists of highly ranked and experienced civil servants, which means that political criteria may play a role but come in addition rather than instead of merit-based criteria (a similar finding was made in Germany, see Bach and Veit, 2018).

Finally, Trangbæk (2022) studied career trajectories of Danish top civil servants since 1925 and explicitly focuses on changes over time. Amongst other things, her analysis shows how careers have become more diverse, with more top civil servants coming from outside the ministry they are leading. In addition, her analysis indicates a growing importance of positions conferring 'political craft', such as being a secretary to a minister or having experience from coordinating ministries such as the Prime Minister's Office or the Ministry of Finance. This finding resonates with the study by Van Dorp (2023), who finds that "experience in the PMO served as a stepping stone for future appointments" (p.191). All in all, although there are some indications of politicisation in what traditionally have been considered merit-based bureaucracies, the overall pattern is one of persistent patterns of merit-based recruitment.

3. The paradox of meritocracy and its problems: from responsive to subservient bureaucracy?

From a bird's eye comparative perspective, the meritocratic model may be misunderstood as one with a highly autonomous bureaucracy where politicians have limited possibilities to exercise control over bureaucracy. However, this impression is misleading, as a lack of patronage (as one important instrument of political control over bureaucracy) does not mean that bureaucracies are out of control. Bersch and Fukuyama (2023) distinguish several mechanisms of bureaucratic autonomy, where powers of appointment, promotion, and removal must be seen in conjunction with mechanisms such as procedural limitations on discretionary decision-making. A potential challenge of this type of analytical approach is the problem of observational equivalence (Pollack, 2002): the absence of observable control behaviour by politicians may either imply that bureaucrats are guilty of "the crime of runaway bureaucracy" (McCubbins et al., 1987, p. 247), or they may be perfectly compliant which would equally well explain the absence of control behaviour.

Therefore, low levels of political patronage should not be misunderstood as the absence of political responsiveness among policy bureaucrats. This is because merit-based bureaucracies uphold strong norms of loyalty towards their political principals in combination with norms of party-political neutrality. An important implication is that merit-based bureaucracies display high levels of "functional politicization" (Hustedt and Salomonsen, 2014) or "political craft" (Bach and Veit, 2018). In a functionally politicised bureaucracy, providing political-tactical advice to executive politicians is an integral part of the work of policy bureaucrats (Christensen and Opstrup, 2018; Hustedt and Salomonsen, 2018). Arguably, the ability of policy bureaucrats to provide political-tactical advice is a pre-condition for the continuous existence of a merit-based civil service. Assuming that there is a demand for political types of support for executive politicians in any system of government, then this support must be provided by someone (Bach and Hustedt, 2023). In a context with an almost exclusively meritocratic civil service, political-tactical advice must necessarily be provided by the civil service (unless politicians can rely on outside actors such as party apparatuses). If politicians do not receive political-tactical advice from the civil service, they are likely to look for alternative sources of advice.

There is some empirical evidence that low levels of patronage go together with high levels of functional politicisation. Christiansen et al. (2016) conducted a survey among civil servants in Denmark and Sweden. Overall, respondents in both countries report that they provide relatively more policy advice than political-tactical advice. However, Danish civil servants provide significantly more political-tactical advice and significantly less policy advice than Swedish civil servants. Moreover, Danish civil servants "express a much better understanding of what is going on within the political leadership in their department" (Christiansen et al., 2016, p. 1243). These authors describe their results as "a crowding out effect of functional politicisation" (p.1245), whereby policy advice becomes less relevant in a context characterised by high functional politicisation. This is what I call "the paradox of meritocracy": meritocratic policy bureaucracies may look apolitical from the outside, but they cannot function without a significant degree of functional politicisation.

A functionally politicised merit-based bureaucracy must carefully balance potentially conflicting values (Opstrup et al., 2024). In a seminal piece, Jacobsen (1960) highlighted how policy bureaucrats must pay attention to loyalty to the political leadership, political neutrality (which means they must be ready to serve any government), and professional autonomy. In particular, balancing loyalty and professional autonomy may prove challenging. The value of loyalty towards the minister still stands very strong in Norway. A key mantra is that bureaucrats should never put their minister in a difficult situation ("*å stille statsråden i forlegenhet*"). A former permanent secretary wrote that "it is hard to imagine how absolute this loyalty to the minister feels" (own translation, Hildrum, 2017, p. 33). This loyalty also applies to "difficult ministers", which will simply increase the pressure on permanent secretaries to protect the permanent ministerial staff. Yet there is also a potential danger that loyalty trumps professionalism (or truthfulness) when bureaucrats' loyalty turns into subservience, anticipating their minister's policy preferences, and refraining from providing advice they know ministers do not like (Hildrum, 2017).

The challenges of balancing fundamental but potentially conflicting values in a merit bureaucracy are illustrated by Bischoff (2023). She analyses how and why civil servants in Denmark responded to vignettes in which a civil servant is asked to assist the minister, yet complying with this would be clearly illegal. In other words, she investigates how civil servants balance political responsiveness and the obligation to act in accordance with the law. Her analysis shows that one quarter of survey respondents did "choose political responsiveness over legal obligations" (p. 1483) in their answers to the vignettes. Important reasons for compliance (and hence going against the obligation of legality) include expectations of negative career consequences and the notion that responsibility is with those giving an order, not those receiving the order (but the results obviously also show that a majority would not comply and stick to the legality principle). Interestingly, those further down the hierarchy are more likely to comply (which dovetails with the 'pushing up responsibility' explanation). An important lesson is the following: "This shows that, even in a strongly meritocratic system, the bureaucracy does not necessarily constitute a strong bulwark against legal violations" (Bischoff, 2023, p. 1493). This is a particular relevant insight for current debates about democratic backsliding (Lotta et al., 2023; Moynihan, 2022) and whether and how the bureaucracy should resist undue political interference (Schuster et al., 2022; Yesilkagit, 2021; Yesilkagit et al., 2024). If bureaucrats must fear negative career consequences, such as not being considered for promotion, they may refrain from reminding ministers of legal or other concerns that normally should constrain executive power (see also Opstrup et al., 2024).

Although patronage remains at comparatively low levels in merit-based bureaucracies, there are indications of an increase in functional politicisation in merit bureaucracies, which may result in tensions between executive politicians and policy bureaucrats (Bach and Wegrich, 2020). One indicator of increasing tensions is anecdotal evidence (often in the form of scandals of different sorts) in which politicians' demands are at odds with key administrative values or in which bureaucrats are considered as being too responsive to politicians (Hustedt and Salomonsen, 2018). In Denmark, there have been recurrent discussions about the norms and values guiding the work of policy bureaucrats and how they should handle dilemmas (Askim et al., 2024). Those discussions resulted in an explicit code of conduct (published in 2015), which delineates seven duties of civil servants, although similar norms had been defined in various parliamentary decisions earlier (Christensen and Opstrup, 2018).[1] A very similar code of conduct was adopted by the Norwegian government a few years later, explicitly following the Danish example.[2] Amongst others, those codes of conduct outline norms of political responsiveness, legality, truthfulness, professionalism, and party-political neutrality. Importantly, they are guidelines for how to deal with potential dilemmas, in which there normally are no easy answers, especially when it comes to defining the line between what is (un)acceptable behaviour of politicians and bureaucrats. As noted by Hustedt and Salomonsen (2018, p. 85), "defining 'the line' appears to be a recurrent and latent issue for merit-based bureaucracies in contemporary societies".

While related to appointments rather than interactions, the following example illustrates how established boundaries between politics and administration are being pushed in a meritocratic context. In 2020 a centre-right government in Norway appointed Frank Bakke Jensen (who was minister of defence at that time) to the administrative position of head of the Fisheries Agency. There were several problems: the minister only applied to the position several weeks after the deadline and he had a job interview before sending his application. Moreover, he never appeared on the public list of applicants (which is mandatory according to freedom of information legislation). Although the government argued he was the most qualified applicant for the position, there were clear doubts about his professional competence for the position. The appointment decision resulted in heavy criticism from the parliamentary opposition, including an open hearing in parliament, because the appointment of incumbent ministers to non-elected offices was largely considered inappropriate and had not been practised for more than a century. However, this is an informal rule, and after apologising, the government got away with the appointment.

This episode provides an example of the strong reliance on informal norms governing democracies, which at the same time makes them vulnerable to the exploitation of legal prerogatives following the letter rather than the spirit of the law (Levitsky and Ziblatt, 2019). While this example gained considerable public attention, the majority of day-to-day decision-making processes in policy bureaucracies, where bureaucrats face dilemmas and adhere to a very strong norm of political responsiveness, often remain unknown to the public. This is a key challenge for merit-based bureaucracies where there is an inherent risk that bureaucrats are crossing 'the line' and doing party-political work. In Norway, the presence of a small number of political appointees may have played a role in preventing career bureaucrats from encountering such dilemmas (Kolltveit, 2016). The next section sketches some lessons for how to address growing levels of functional politicisation and potential challenges.

4. How to avoid loyalty turning into subservience in merit-based bureaucracies?

The main argument of this chapter is that low levels of politicisation as patronage go hand in hand with high levels of functional politicisation (related arguments are made by Askim et al., 2024; Christensen and Opstrup, 2018; Hustedt and Salomonsen, 2018). In the following I briefly sketch some implications of a trend towards increasing levels of functional politicisation and the inherent risks of responsiveness turning into subservience in merit-based bureaucracies.

The sustainability of the merit-based model relies on a high degree of political responsiveness of the bureaucracy. If politicians find that the permanent bureaucracy does not serve them adequately, they are likely to look for other sources of advice, or they may seek to strengthen their grip on appointments to career civil service positions. However, especially unexperienced politicians or politicians with a populist ideology which is critical towards 'the elite' may question the loyalty of the bureaucracy. Therefore, it is crucial that politicians are aware about the strong loyalty of the policy bureaucracy and its ability to serve different political masters equally well (and this is something that bureaucrats frequently underline as a highly important aspect of their professional role). At the same time, the bureaucracy itself must also cultivate an awareness of fundamental norms and values. After all, it is bureaucrats themselves who will be 'teaching' norms and values about political-administrative relations to politicians, especially in merit-based systems.

The nature of those fundamental norms and values, which often are informal (cf. the controversial appointment case mentioned above), formulated as guidelines (cf. Denmark and Norway), and which provide guidance rather than definitive answers in dilemma situations, implies that they are vulnerable to "unprincipled principals" (Schuster et al., 2022). As the analysis of Bischoff (2023) shows, a significant share of bureaucrats in one of the most meritocratic civil services of the world would obey a political order rather than defend the principle of legality. A related analysis demonstrates that the norms of truthfulness and professionalism are more easily pushed aside compared to legality (Christensen and Opstrup, 2018). Anecdotal evidence suggests that bureaucrats engage in self-restraint in proposing policy alternatives or providing information when they anticipate a negative reaction by political leaders (Hildrum, 2017). In other words, even though the countries covered in this chapter are clearly not among those facing immediate threats of democratic backsliding, the challenges in the relation between politics and administration are not unlike those related to bureaucracies' roles as potential defenders of liberal democracy in the context of democratic backsliding (Yesilkagit et al., 2024).

In an essay on the role of bureaucracy in standing up against populist leaders, Yesilkagit (2021) highlights that bureaucrats must be conscious of their role as guardians of constitutional values which stretch beyond the priorities of the government of the day. The experiences in merit-based bureaucracies may provide a partial answer to the question of how to strengthen the bureaucracy's constitutional role. A corollary of (increases in) functional politicisation in merit-based contexts are explicit debates about the norms and values guiding interactions between politicians and bureaucrats. Those debates serve the function of making both the duties of the civil service and the boundaries of political authority explicit and providing justifications for standing up to excess demands for loyalty from executive politicians and speaking truth to power. As we have seen above, explicit guidelines and informal norms may not prevent politicians from taking problematic action behind closed doors, but they are likely to raise the political costs of such actions.

Moreover, entrusting bureaucrats with the role of defending liberal democracy creates another challenge, namely that "bureaucratic perceptions may simply reflect value conflicts between bureaucrats and political principals and diverging views of what the 'public interest' constitutes given the multitude of public values" (Schuster et al., 2022, p. 419). If bureaucrats actively seek to prevent elected politicians from pursuing their political agendas, bureaucrats themselves will contribute to undermining democratic values (Schuster et al., 2022). Therefore, an important issue to address is how policy bureaucrats can (and do) distinguish between a decision or policy that is legitimate (although it may be less optimal to address a given policy problem) and one that potentially undermines the foundations of liberal democracy.

Hence, an important lesson is that hiring on merit seems to be a necessary, but not a sufficient condition for ensuring that civil servants dare speak truth to power. My analysis concurs with the observations of Nistotskaya in this volume that research on meritocratic bureaucracy should address the mechanisms underlying the superior performance of meritocratic bureaucracies and that it should move beyond meritocratic recruitment as the main indicator of meritocracy. There is a clear need to better understand the norms and practices guiding the decisions of bureaucrats in meritocratic contexts and their interactions with politicians.

5. How to study the paradox of politicisation: longitudinal and comparative studies of merit-based bureaucracies

The concluding section briefly highlights some directions for how the fields of Public Administration and Political Science may address some of the issues raised in this chapter. First, a more general point is that researchers need longitudinal data to study any kind of trend, which also applies to the study of political-administrative relations. Many important research questions in Public Administration are about temporal dynamics, but scholars often lack an appropriate empirical foundation for rigorous longitudinal research designs (Murdoch et al., 2023). A growing body of research is studying career trajectories of civil servants (Askim et al., 2024; Trangbæk, 2022; Van Dorp, 2023) or combines career data with survey data (Doherty et al., 2019), providing relevant insights into the dynamics of politicisation as patronage.

In contrast, it is much more challenging to collect longitudinal data on the dynamics of functional politicisation. The study of such interactions will often require interview-based or ethnographic analyses (Trangbæk, 2021; van Dorp and 't Hart, 2019) that generate rich and contextual data which are more difficult to compare over time. A promising direction is to establish research infrastructures that enable the systematic and repeated collection of data. In Norway, a consortium of institutions has established the Panel of Public Administrators, which runs regular surveys among central government bureaucrats. Although most items are allocated through a time-sharing model, the consortium is now developing a set of standard questions which serves to create time series.[3]

Second, the field of Public Administration must engage in systematic comparative research. However, we must move away from the typical approach of collecting loosely related country chapters in edited volumes towards the collection of comparable data. This requires a truly collective effort that cannot be achieved by a single researcher or research group. The recently established research network Comparative Research on the Executive Triangle in Europe (CoREx), which is funded under the COST Action scheme, takes an important step into this direction.[4] CoREx will systematically collect data and analyse the institutional set-up of the executive triangle, which comprises ministers, ministerial advisers, and senior civil servants; these actors' career trajectories; their roles and interactions in policymaking; and questions related to accountability and transparency about the executive triangle. This network will study both merit-based and patronage-based bureaucracies. Although studying cases where patronage persists ('positive cases') may be considered more interesting and relevant for various reasons, it is equally important to study countries with strong meritocratic norms ('negative cases'). As the above discussion has shown, the fundamental questions about the dividing line between what is (not) acceptable are very similar across political systems. From a policy perspective, it will be especially relevant to get a better understanding of the mechanisms which sustain merit-based systems despite increasing pressures towards more political responsiveness.

Notes

1. https://medst.dk/media/9674/kodex_vii_english_version.pdf.
2. https://www.regjeringen.no/en/dokumenter/om-forholdet-mellom-politisk-ledelse-og-embetsverk/id2626841/.
3. https://www.uib.no/en/nfp.
4. https://www.cost-corex.com/ and https://www.cost.eu/actions/CA22150/.

References

Askim, J., Bach, T., & Christensen, J. G. (2024). Political change and administrative turnover in meritocratic systems. *West European Politics*, 47(2), 329–355. https://doi.org/10.1080/01402382.2022.2148195.

Bach, T., Hammerschmid, G., & Löffler, L. (2020). More delegation, more political control? Politicization of senior level appointments in 18 European countries. *Public Policy and Administration*, 35(1), 3–23. https://doi.org/10.1177/0952076718776356.

Bach, T., & Hustedt, T. (2023). Policy-making in the executive triangle – A comparative perspective on ministers, advisers and civil servants. In R. Shaw (Ed.), *Handbook on Ministerial and Political Advisers* (pp. 338–351). Edward Elgar Publishing. https://doi.org/10.4337/9781800886582.00034.

Bach, T., & Veit, S. (2018). The Determinants of promotion to high public office in Germany: partisan loyalty, political craft, or managerial competencies? *Journal of Public Administration Research and Theory*, 28(2), 254–269. https://doi.org/10.1093/jopart/mux041.

Bach, T., & Wegrich, K. (2020). Politicians and bureaucrats in executive government. In R. B. Andeweg, R. Elgie, L. Helms, J. Kaarbo, & F. Müller-Rommel (Eds.), *The Oxford Handbook of Political Executives* (pp. 525–546). Oxford University Press. https://doi.org/10.1093/oxfordhb/9780198809296.013.21.

Bersch, K., & Fukuyama, F. (2023). Defining bureaucratic autonomy. *Annual Review of Political Science*, *26*(1), 213–232. https://doi.org/10.1146/annurev-polisci-051921-102914.

Binderkrantz, A. S., Christensen, J. G., Christiansen, P. M., Nielsen, M. K., & Pedersen, H. H. (2023). Closed shutters or revolving doors? Elite career track similarity and elite sector transfers in Denmark. *European Journal of Political Research*, *63*(3), 1022–1041. https://doi.org/10.1111/1475-6765.12627.

Bischoff, C. S. (2023). Between a rock and a hard place: Balancing the duties of political responsiveness and legality in the civil service. *Public Administration*, *101*(4), 1481–1502. https://doi.org/10.1111/padm.12898.

Christensen, J. G., & Opstrup, N. (2018). Bureaucratic dilemmas: Civil servants between political responsiveness and normative constraints. *Governance*, *31*(3), 481–498. https://doi.org/10.1111/gove.12312.

Christiansen, P. M., Niklasson, B., & Öhberg, P. (2016). Does politics crowd out professional competence? The organisation of ministerial advice in Denmark and Sweden. *West European Politics*, *39*(6), 1230–1250. https://doi.org/10.1080/01402382.2016.1176368.

Doherty, K. M., Lewis, D. E., & Limbocker, S. (2019). Executive control and turnover in the senior executive service. *Journal of Public Administration Research and Theory*, *29*(2), 159–174. https://doi.org/10.1093/jopart/muy069.

Hammerschmid, G., Van de Walle, S., Andrews, R., & Bezes, P. (2016). *Public Administration Reforms in Europe: The View From the Top*. Edward Elgar Publishing.

Hildrum, E. (2017). Mellom lojalitet og servilitet. *Stat & Styring*, *27*(3), 32–35. https://doi.org/10.18261/ISSN0809-750X-2017-03-10.

Hustedt, T., & Salomonsen, H. H. (2014). Ensuring political responsiveness: Politicization mechanisms in ministerial bureaucracies. *International Review of Administrative Sciences*, *80*(4), 746–765. https://doi.org/10.1177/0020852314533449.

Hustedt, T., & Salomonsen, H. H. (2018). From neutral competence to competent neutrality? Revisiting neutral competence as the core normative foundation of western bureaucracy. In H. Byrkjeflot & F. Engelstad (Eds.), *Bureaucracy and Society in Transition: Comparative Perspectives* (pp. 69–88). Emerald Publishing Limited. https://doi.org/10.1108/S0195-631020180000033008.

Jacobsen, K. D. (1960). Lojalitet, nøytralitet og faglig uavhengighet i sentraladminstrasjonen. *Tidsskrift for samfunnsforskning*, *1*(4), 231–248.

Kolltveit, K. (2016). Spenninger i det politisk-administrative systemet: Erfaringer fra Norge. *Politica*, *48*(4), 481–496. https://doi.org/10.7146/politica.v48i4.131285.

Levitsky, S., & Ziblatt, D. (2019). *How Democracies Die*. Crown.

Lewis, D. E. (2008). *The Politics of Presidential Appointments: Political Control and Bureaucratic Performance*. Princeton University Press.

Lotta, G., Tavares, G. M., & Story, J. (2023). Political attacks and the undermining of the bureaucracy: The impact on civil servants' well-being. *Governance*, *37*(2), 619–641. https://doi.org/10.1111/gove.12792.

McCubbins, M. D., Noll, R. G., & Weingast, B. R. (1987). Administrative procedures as instruments of political control. *Journal of Law, Economics, & Organization*, *3*(2), 243–277. https://doi.org/10.1093/oxfordjournals.jleo.a036930.

Moynihan, D. P. (2022). Delegitimization, deconstruction and control: Undermining the administrative state. *The Annals of the American Academy of Political and Social Science, 699*(1), 36–49. https://doi.org/10.1177/00027162211069723.

Murdoch, Z., MacCarthaigh, M., & Geys, B. (2023). It's about time! Temporal dynamics and longitudinal research designs in public administration. *Public Administration Review, 83*(6), 1727–1736. https://doi.org/10.1111/puar.13758.

Nistotskaya, M., Dahlberg, S., Dahlström, C., Sundström, A., Axelsson, S., Dalli, C. M., & Pachon, N. A. (2021). *The Quality of Government Expert Survey 2020 (Wave III): Report*. The Quality of Government Institute, QoG Working Paper Series 2021:2. https://www.gu.se/sites/default/files/2021-03/2021_2_Nistotskaya_Dahlberg_Dahlstrom_Sundstrom_Axelsson_Dalli_Alvarado%20Pachon.pdf.

Opstrup, N., Christensen, J. G., Salomonsen, H. H., & Trangbæk, A. (2024). *Kodex VII: Et autoværn eller blot afstribning af kørebanen? Magtutredningen 2.0*. https://ps.au.dk/fileadmin/Statskundskab/Billeder/Forskning/Forskningsprojekter/Magtudredning/Essays/Tema3/Essay_af_Niels_Opstrup__Joergen_Groennegaard_Christensen__Heidi_Houlberg_Salomonsen___Amalie_Trangbaek.pdf

Panizza, F., Peters, B. G., & Ramos Larraburu, C. R. (2019). Roles, trust and skills: A typology of patronage appointments. *Public Administration, 97*(1), 147–161. https://doi.org/10.1111/padm.12560.

Peters, B. G., & Pierre, J. (2004). Politicization of the civil service: Concepts, causes, consequences. In B. G. Peters & J. Pierre (Eds.), *Politicization of the Civil Service in Comparative Perspective* (pp. 1–13). Routledge. https://doi.org/10.4324/9780203799857.

Pollack, M. A. (2002). Learning from the Americanists (again): Theory and method in the study of delegation. *West European Politics, 25*, 200–219. https://doi.org/10.1080/713869589.

Pollitt, C., & Bouckaert, G. (2017). *Public Management Reform: A Comparative Analysis – Into the Age of Austerity*. Oxford University Press.

Schuster, C., Mikkelsen, K. S., Correa, I., & Meyer-Sahling, J.-H. (2022). Exit, voice, and sabotage: Public service motivation and guerrilla bureaucracy in times of unprincipled political principals. *Journal of Public Administration Research and Theory, 32*(2), 416–435. https://doi.org/10.1093/jopart/muab028.

Trangbæk, A. (2021). *Life at the Top: Understanding Top Bureaucrats' Roles as the Link Between Politics and Administration*. Forlaget Politica.

Trangbæk, A. (2022). Does the cradle of power exist? Sequence analysis of top bureaucrats' career trajectories. *Governance, 36*(2), 609–627. https://doi.org/10.1111/gove.12688.

Van Dorp, E.-J. (2023). The practice and politics of secretary general appointments. *The American Review of Public Administration, 53*(5–6), 182–194. https://doi.org/10.1177/02750740231155408.

Van Dorp, E.-J., & 't Hart, P. (2019). Navigating the dichotomy: The top public servant's craft. *Public Administration, 97*(4), 877–891. https://doi.org/10.1111/padm.12600.

Yesilkagit, K. (2021). Can bureaucracy save liberal democracy? How public administration can react to populism. *Turkish Policy Quarterly, 20*(3), 31–38. http://turkishpolicy.com/article/1075/can-bureaucracy-save-liberal-democracy-how-public-administration-can-react-to-populism.

Yesilkagit, K., Bauer, M., Peters, B. G., & Pierre, J. (2024). The Guardian State: Strengthening the public service against democratic backsliding. *Public Administration Review, 84*(3), 414–425. https://doi.org/10.1111/puar.13808.

The disappearance of lower-grade bureaucrats

by Steven Van de Walle

1. Steering, not rowing: what has happened to the lower grades?

Becoming a civil servant has always been a path to social promotion, especially for citizens coming from less privileged backgrounds who could benefit either from merit-based recruitment or from political favours to obtain a position. Especially for less-educated citizens, a position as civil servant or public sector worker used to mean job security, a good pension, and a reasonable degree of social standing. Becoming a government clerk, mailman, railway worker, typist, driver, archival employee, cleaner, or coffee lady meant a step up from other low-skilled labour and created a mass of people with direct experience of, and representing, 'the state'.

There have been two 'golden ages' of mass public employment. One golden age was in the late 19th and early 20th century, when many modern public services developed: post offices, railways and railway stations, schools, the first social services. Public employment had a good reputation and was part of social promotion. Public services were 'agencies of change' and through public employment contributed to the state- and nation-building project (Weber, 1976; Van de Walle and Scott, 2011). Public services embody the nation-state and are a source of great pride. The other golden age happened in the 1970s. The 1970s saw the expansion of welfare state bureaucracies, as well as mass recruitment as an instrument to keep unemployment down in the wake of the oil crisis, with the government acting as an employer of last resort (Wilson, 1996). Public employment offered security and a good pension, even while not being entirely respected.

Public employment in the lower grades has been disappearing. The public sector increasingly relies on higher-skilled workers, often in policy functions (Page and Jenkins, 2005) rather than in operational ones. A government that steers but does not row no longer need rowers. These rowers increasingly work for external service providers, or their positions have become redundant through automation. Developments towards a normalisation of public employment, automation, upskilling, and privatisation have created a situation where permanent public employment is increasingly becoming a privilege for those with a higher level of education. Lower civil service grades have disappeared as a result of automation, and many manual jobs have been outsourced to private companies. Public sector organisations now mainly hire highly skilled civil servants, generally with a university degree. Tasks that were previously performed by an army of government workers are now merely planned and programmed by civil servants, and then implemented by hired hands or by computer programs.

The obvious efficiency gains aside, this trend has changed the meaning of public employment and may have created a disconnection between bureaucratic elites and the working class – them versus us. Current day populism has thrived on the story of disconnected bureaucratic elites and a self-serving state that works against the interest of the hard-working ordinary citizen. The disappearance of the working class from public employment means that a crucial connection between 'the state' and 'the people' has been broken.

Statistics for the UK Civil Service show that employment in the junior grades (AA/AO) declined from 47% to 38% between 2010 and 2016, whereas the share of all other grades has increased (Freeguard, 2016). A study on public employment in Dutch local government found that employment in the lowest personnel categories shrank from 11% to 2% in just two years (Vrooland and Davits, 2015). The Government Accountability Office found that increases in the US federal workforce mainly occur in "categories that require higher skill and educational levels" (GAO, 2014).

2. Why is this happening?

Good comparable data on public sector employment is scarce, which also makes explanations for evolutions in the data very tentative. We put forward four potential explanations.

A policy of having fewer, but better-educated civil servants

One of the objectives of major public sector reforms in the 1990s was to have fewer, but better (and better-paid) civil servants. This was to be achieved not only through different recruitment approaches, training, and early retirement, but also through changing the nature of work within public organisations.

This means that the disappearance of the working class has been at least partly the result of deliberate policy.

A desire to cut public employment numbers may have resulted in selective redundancies, whereby certain categories of public employees have been offered early retirement, whereas others have not, or whereby certain categories were more likely to take up early retirement offers. It remains to be seen though whether such government downsizing has actually taken place, or whether it was just rhetoric. Downsizing through focusing on older employees mainly affects those who have been employed in the 1970s – which was an era of major government expansion because of the use of government employment as a countercyclical economic policy, and because of the expansion of the welfare state. The recent recession also impacted on public employment and some groups may have been hit harder by selective dismissal, but evidence remains scarce.

Fewer, but better-educated civil servants can mean that certain tasks are done better, but may also signal over-education of civil servants for their jobs (Garibaldi et al., 2021). Higher-educated civil servants then replace less-educated ones, but they still largely do the same task. This phenomenon of displacement can relate to entire jobs, whereby, for example, a university-trained person takes over an administrative position from a clerk, or it can relate to parts of jobs, whereby, for instance, the coffee lady and the secretary are fired, and highly educated civil servants spend time making copies or preparing meeting rooms.

An alternative explanation could be that government tasks have become more complex, requiring higher-skilled officials. Indications that this could be the case can be found in expanding regulation and in the growth of collaborative networks. The emergence of a separate class of policy officials (Page and Jenkins, 2005) is also indicative of this trend.

Bits replace hands: automation and e-government

Automation is having a profound impact on the world of work (Brynjolfsson and McAfee, 2014). It is our second major potential explanation for the decline of working-class employment in the public sector. Repetitive simple tasks that were previously done by real people have been replaced by computers. Examples are simple acts such as registering unemployment days or opening and sorting tax returns. A smaller number of programmers and IT systems engineers have taken over. However, we also observe that public organisations delay automatisation because they still have a large stock of less-educated employees that are not near retirement age.

Changing ways of contacting government have also had an impact on government employment. Whereas traditionally government services were contacted in person or by mail, we have seen major growth in government contact centres. Increasingly, manning such call centres requires advanced skills, because employees have to deal with difficult cases that cannot easily be handled automatically. If this automation hypothesis is correct, one would expect a link between countries' advances in e-government and the share of less-educated public sector workers.

Still in the public sector, just no longer working for government: privatisation and outsourcing

The third explanation may be that the major transformation is not that the tasks of the less-educated people have disappeared, but that these tasks are simply no longer performed by government employees. Many manual tasks have been outsourced or privatised. Private security firms have taken over the work of police officers on guard duty, or the work of receptionists. Private catering companies have taken over the job of the government canteen cook and coffee lady. Many utility companies and public transport companies are now in private hands. The result is that positions that used to fall under a civil service statute are now 'normal' private jobs. The people doing these jobs still indirectly work in the public sector, but they no longer work for government.

The changing political opportunity structure of public employment

The fourth explanation is a very different one. Public employment takes an important place in systems of patronage (Grindle, 2012), and often is an important spoil for election winners. A promise to create new jobs in government, and especially giving jobs to one's electorate, can attract voters. Such political strategies have in the past resulted in excessive numbers of public personnel. This political opportunity structure has largely disappeared in developed countries. Handing out public jobs for political reasons is largely seen as unacceptable, in an environment where meritocracy has become the dominant and accepted discourse when talking about public sector recruitment. Calls for shrinking a bloated government apparatus also makes it difficult for politicians to run on a platform that promises public jobs as spoils. This changing political opportunity structure is related to another major transformation in society: the decline of the mass political party and the individualisation of politics (Van Biezen et al., 2012). Having smaller and professional parties has reduced the need to reward large numbers of loyal party members with government jobs after a successful election.

3. Effects: declining government legitimacy and rise of the new public service multinationals

The implications of the disappearance of the working class from the public sector go beyond human resources management in government. We outline two important implications that will require a response from both government and the Public Administration research community. One is the potential decline of government legitimacy among parts of the population because they are absent from public employment. The other is the rise of public service trans- or multinationals, whereby employment for public service provision is shifting to (large) private sector companies.

Government is not us: the delegitimation of bureaucracies

Michael Young's satirical *The rise of the meritocracy* (1958) starts with a chapter on the civil service model, guided by competitive entry and merit. It paints a dystopian picture of a society where merit is defined by education. A disconnection between government (administrators) and citizens has also been a recurring theme in the Public Administration literature (King et al., 1998). When large segments of the population no longer work for government, or know anyone in their direct environment who does, government risks becoming a foreign body. People as a result rely on (social) media for their information on government, and they no longer see opportunities for social advancement though government employment.

Public employment is a way of connecting citizens to government (Groeneveld and Van de Walle, 2010; Riccucci et al., 2014). Using the terminology of representative bureaucracy, absence of passive representation may lead to a feeling of disenfranchisement (Krislov, 1974). The resulting absence of active representation may mean government is less able to take the view and concerns of less-educated citizens on board when making policies and designing public services. In addition, a low level of education is often also associated with other characteristics such as ethnic background or place of residence. The result is a loss of government legitimacy among substantial groups of the population and changing attractiveness of the government as an employer.

Negative stereotypes of bureaucrats are abundant (Willems, 2020), and are stronger among people working outside of government (Bertram et al.,

2022). Bureaucratic bashing thrives when such stereotypes exist, and this has a negative impact on policy implementation, morale, and recruitment (Garrett et al., 2006). The delegitimation of public administration is further fuelled by populist politics. Populism makes a distinction between the real, pure people and an elite that does not work for the general interest of the people (Mudde, 2004). Bureaucrats often feature prominently in populist discourse as a group that is out of touch, unaccountable, and disconnected from the people.

The rise of the new public service multinationals

The second major implication of the disappearing working class from public employment is that a new economic sector has emerged: that of private companies delivering public services. These companies employ large numbers of relatively low-educated employees in jobs and sectors such as street cleaning, security, water provision, public transport, prison services, or health. Well-known examples of such companies are Serco, Veolia, and Falck. In 2013, Wilks already estimated that the public service industry in the UK employs 1.2 million people, accounting for 6% of GDP (Wilks, 2013). Increasingly, such companies are taking over traditional serial bureaucratic jobs as well. For instance, in Belgium Sodexo has been in charge of handling training subsidy applications and payments for small companies on behalf of the Flemish government. These companies increasingly operate multinationally. Clifton and Díaz-Fuentes (2008) have called them "public service transnationals". This has potential implications not only for the type and quality of work (see e.g. Flecker and Hermann, 2011) but also potentially for how their employees identify with (national) government or with public service, and the public service ethos (Koumenta, 2016). In addition, governments' dependence on such providers may result in a loss of knowledge about these service sectors and thus, eventually, undermine governments' capacity to steer and procure such services. The size of some of the private public service providers also raises concerns about the limited competition in these markets. Labour sociologists have expressed concerns about the precarious nature of much of the employment in this sector (Standing, 2011).

4. What should the public sector do?

The public sector is an important actor on the labour market. Yet using government employment as a policy tool (to reduce precariousness or to create legitimacy) is contested, to say the least. It risks putting the efficiency and effectiveness of public administration in second place by sidelining the

HR requirements of operational services. It also creates a risk that public employment will (again) be used for party-political or patronage purposes. Still, the public sector needs to carefully reflect on its outsourcing policies and its future role as a model employer or standard-setter on the labour market.

There have been some initiatives whereby governments have deliberately reverted to hiring lower-skilled workers into government employment. Examples are insourcing of previously outsourced tasks (e.g. the insourcing of cleaning staff by the Dutch government, or processes of remunicipalisation (Wollmann et al., 2010)), the recruitment of poverty experts to support policymakers in understanding their target groups, or the creation of targeted traineeship programmes.

This means public sectors need to reflect on their ambition to remain, or again become, a model employer, and use their leverage as the most important employer to steer or set standards in the labour market (Groeneveld and Steijn, 2016). With the disappearance of the working class from public sector employment, the public sector's ability to be a model employer has changed. It now needs to act through its procurement of services, rather than through directly acting as an employer. The traditional role of public sector unions is also likely to further change (Bach and Kessler, 2012). More particularly, their activities may again become more sector-based, rather than following a public–private divide.

5. What does this mean for Public Administration research?

For Public Administration research, two parallel trends are important to monitor. One is the changing composition of the traditional public sector workforce; the other is the growing workforce in public service provision outside of the traditional public sector.

First, there is a need for more and better description of the trends we set out in this chapter. How fast are lower grades disappearing from our public sectors? Is this phenomenon happening at the same pace in all countries and policy sectors? What explains the pace of change? And if the process is indeed happening, what is the main driver behind it? This requires a systematic and cross-national mapping that requires even more fine-grained data than what has so far been collected as part of other large-scale research initiatives (see e.g. Gotschall et al., 2015). It also means moving beyond the discipline's focus on studying differences *between* permanent and contractual employment (see e.g. Demmke, 2016, but also the chapter by Ritz et al. in this volume) in the public sector and instead focusing on trends *within* these types of employment.

Second, our discipline needs to understand the implications of this trend. If lower grades are indeed disappearing, what does this mean for the legitimacy of the public sector and bureaucrats? And how will changes in the public sector workforce influence the legitimacy of governments and democratic systems? This means the old topic of representative bureaucracy becomes more important than ever. More elaborate empirical work is needed on active and symbolic representation, with a specific focus on social class. This also opens avenues for closer collaboration with political scientists studying populism (see also the chapter by Bauer in this volume).

Public Administration research has traditionally focused on civil servants or policymakers working within classic bureaucracies. However, a massive and increasing number of employees work for various for-profit public service providers, many of which are organised cross-nationally. Traditional research topics from our discipline such as those related to public service motivation, discretion, or public value are also relevant to address in relation to these groups of workers. Employees of private public service providers are predominantly studied by labour sociologists, who tend to focus on different types of research questions, such as those related to precarious work. Managers of these private public service providers are predominantly studied from an operational management perspective. Public Administration research needs to step into this gap.

References

Bach, S., & Kessler, I. (2012). *The Modernisation of the Public Services and Employee Relations: Targeted Change*. Palgrave Macmillan.

Bertram, I., Bouwman, R., & Tummers, L. (2022). Socioeconomic status and public sector worker stereotypes: Results from a representative survey. *Public Administration Review*, 82(2), 237–255. https://doi.org/10.1111/puar.13461.

Brynjolfsson, E., & McAfee, A. (2014). *The Second Machine Age: Work, Progress, and Prosperity in a Time of Brilliant Technologies*. WW Norton & Company.

Clifton, J., & Díaz-Fuentes, D. (2008). The new public service transnationals: Consequences for labour. *Work Organisation, Labour and Globalisation*, 2(2), 23–39. https://doi.org/10.13169/workorgalaboglob.2.2.0023.

Demmke, C. (2016). *Doing Better with Less? The Future of the Government Workforce: Politics of Public HRM Reforms in 32 Countries*. Peter Lang. https://doi.org/10.3726/978-3-653-07180-1.

Flecker, J., & Hermann, C. (2011). The liberalization of public services: Company reactions and consequences for employment and working conditions. *Economic and Industrial Democracy*, 32(3), 523–544. https://doi.org/10.1177/0143831X10389201.

Freeguard, G. (2016, October 6). *The Civil Service in 2016 – smaller, older, better gender balance*. Whitehall Monitor blog. Institute for Government. http://www.instituteforgovernment.org.uk/blog/14701/the-civil-service-in-2016-in-eight-charts/.

Garibaldi, P., Gomes, P., & Sopraseuth, T. (2021). Public employment redux. *Journal of Government and Economics*, 1, 1–32. https://doi.org/10.1016/j.jge.2021.100003.

Garrett, R. S., Thurber, J. A., Fritschler, A. L., & Rosenbloom, D. H. (2006). Assessing the impact of bureaucracy bashing by electoral campaigns. *Public Administration Review*, 66(2), 228–240. https://doi.org/10.1111/j.1540-6210.2006.00575.x.

Gottschall, K., Kittel, B., Briken, K., Heuer, J.-O., Hils, S., Streb, S., & Tepe, M. (2015). *Public Sector Employment Regimes: Transformations of the State as an Employer* (1st ed.). Palgrave Macmillan. https://doi.org/10.1057/9781137313119.

Government Accountability Office (GAO) (2014). *Federal Workforce: Recent trends in federal civilian employment and compensation*. GAO-14-215. http://www.gao.gov/products/GAO-14-215.

Grindle, M. S. (2012). *Jobs for the Boys: Patronage and the State in Comparative Perspective*. Harvard University Press. https://doi.org/10.4159/harvard.9780674065185.

Groeneveld, S., & Steijn, B. (2016). Management of human resources: Trends and variation. In S. Van de Walle & S. Groeneveld (Eds.), *Theory and Practice of Public Sector Reform* (pp. 178–193). Routledge.

Groeneveld, S., & Van de Walle, S. (2010). A contingency approach to representative bureaucracy: power, equal opportunities and diversity. *International Review of Administrative Sciences*, 76(2), 239–258. https://doi.org/10.1177/0020852309365670.

King, C. S., Stivers, C., & Box, R. C. (1998). *Government is Us: Strategies for an Anti-Government Era*. Sage Publications.

Koumenta, M. (2011). Modernization, privatization, and the public service ethos in the United Kingdom. In D. Marsden (Ed.), *Employment in the Lean Years: Policy and Prospects for the Next Decade* (pp. 199–212). Oxford University Press. https://doi.org/10.1093/acprof:osobl/9780199605439.003.0014.

Krislov, S. (1974). *Representative Bureaucracy*. Prentice Hall.

Mudde, C. (2004). The populist Zeitgeist. *Government and Opposition*, 39(4), 541–563. https://doi.org/10.1111/j.1477-7053.2004.00135.x.

Page, E. C., & Jenkins, B. (2005). *Policy Bureaucracy: Government with a Cast of Thousands*. Oxford University Press. https://doi.org/10.1093/acprof:oso/9780199280414.001.0001

Riccucci, N. M., Van Ryzin, G. G., & Lavena, C. F. (2014). Representative bureaucracy in policing: Does it increase perceived legitimacy? *Journal of Public Administration Research and Theory*, 24(3), 537–551. https://doi.org/10.1093/jopart/muu006.

Standing, G. (2011). *The Precariat: The New Dangerous Class*. Bloomsbury Academic.

Van Biezen, I., Mair, P., & Poguntke, T. (2012). Going, going, ... gone? The decline of party membership in contemporary Europe. *European Journal of Political Research*, 51(1), 24–56. https://doi.org/10.1111/j.1475-6765.2011.01995.x.

Van de Walle, S., & Scott, Z. (2011). The political role of service delivery in state-building: Exploring the relevance of European history for developing countries. *Development Policy Review*, 29(1), 5–21. https://doi.org/10.1111/j.1467-7679.2011.00511.x.

Vrooland, V., & Davits, R. (2015). *Verrassende wendingen gemeentelijk verzuim*. Gemeente.nu. https://www.gemeente.nu/loopbaan/ontwikkeling/verrassende-wendingen-gemeentelijk-verzuim/.

Weber, E. (1976). *Peasants into Frenchmen: The Modernization of Rural France, 1870–1914*. Stanford University Press. https://doi.org/10.1515/9780804766036.

Wilks, S. (2013). *The Political Power of the Business Corporation*. Edward Elgar Publishing.

Willems, J. (2020). Public servant stereotypes: It is not (at) all about being lazy, greedy and corrupt. *Public Administration, 98*(4), 807–823. https://doi.org/10.1111/padm.12686.

Wilson, W. J. (1996). When work disappears. *Political Science Quarterly, 111*(4), 567–595. https://doi.org/10.2307/2152085.

Wollmann, H., Baldersheim. H., Citroni, G., McEldowney, J., & Marcou, G. (2010). From public service to commodity: The demunicipalization (or remunicipalization?) of energy provision in Germany, Italy, France, the UK and Norway. In H. Wollmann & G. Marcou (Eds.), *The Provision of Public Services in Europe: Between State, Local Government and Market* (pp. 168–190). Edward Elgar Publishing. https://doi.org/10.4337/9781849807227.00015.

Young, M. D. (1958). *The Rise of the Meritocracy*. Transaction Publishers.

PART 6
FUTURES OF STUDYING PUBLIC ADMINISTRATION

Using Public Administration research to strengthen 'futures thinking' in the public sector

by Jeroen Maesschalck

1. Introduction

While anticipating the future has always been important for public sector organisations, it becomes all the more crucial in the "turbulent" (Ansell et al., 2024) and "dangerous" (Roberts, 2020) times we are said to live in. Geert Bouckaert, whose retirement is the occasion for this volume, has made this point emphatically. Indeed, 'Public Administration and Futures' was one of the three themes in the 'European Perspectives for Public Administration Project' that he championed with Werner Jann (Bouckaert and Jann, 2020a). Specifically, Bouckaert and Jann argued for the use of utopias and dystopias as a way to inspire thinking about the future and to turn Public Administration (PA) into a 'trendsetter' that shapes future agendas instead of a discipline that trails behind agendas set by others (Bouckaert and Jann, 2020b, p. 33). In addition to this utopia approach, PA has seen various attempts to draw from the growing field of 'futures studies' to "work with the future" (Poli, 2022). These attempts often occurred in the context of strategic management (e.g. Joyce, 2020; Roberge, 2013) and typically used scenario development as their most important technique (e.g. Kitsing, 2020; Vesnic-Alujevic et al., 2019). Most of these 'futures thinking' exercises emphasise the creative collection of new ideas and perspectives, often relying on consultations of a broad scope of stakeholders and experts. This chapter critically reflects on that focus on collecting new information for futures thinking. Specifically, it argues that futures thinking exercises could also benefit from available knowledge that is drawn from existing PA research. While it might not seem obvious to use empirical research (which by definition focuses on current or past events) for futures thinking, this chapter will argue that this is not only possible, but also very useful.

The chapter starts with a brief introduction to the field of 'futures studies' or 'futures thinking' and then presents a simplified three-step version of a typical futures thinking exercise. It then proposes two ways in which insights from PA research can contribute to such an exercise: (a) by providing concepts and empirical knowledge that help to develop 'prototypes'; and (b) by providing background knowledge to test (or to 'wind tunnel') these prototypes against various scenarios. Having thus illustrated how PA research can strengthen futures thinking exercises, the chapter concludes with some reflections on how, vice versa, futures thinking techniques can also strengthen PA research.

2. Futures thinking: an introduction

This section briefly introduces the field referred to as "futures studies" (Sardar, 2010) or "futures thinking" (Inayatullah, 2008), with "futures" deliberately in the plural to emphasise the open and pluralistic nature of the discipline. This field is characterised by continuous debates over definitions and approaches (e.g. Kristóf and Nováky, 2023). Inayatullah (1990, 2013), for example, distinguishes between four approaches to futures thinking: predictive-empirical (aimed at predicting, typically relying on linear forecasting), cultural-interpretative (aimed at understanding competing images of the future), critical (aimed at disturbing existing power relations by questioning categories and evoking other scenarios), and participatory (emphasising consultation among stakeholders). Another illustrative classification is Miller et al.'s (2018, pp. 59–60) distinction between three ways of "using the future". First, 'optimisation of the future' is a closed approach to the future: it imposes patterns from the past on the future, thus privileging causal-predictive methods. Typical tools of this approach are trend extrapolation and predictive scenario building. Second, the 'contingent futures' approach prepares for surprises that we already recognise and anticipate. It uses tools such as the Delphi method and simulations. Third, the 'novel futures' approach moves beyond the previous two and aims at identifying unknown unknowns (as opposed to the known unknowns), by emphasising imagination and openness.

While the emphasis in futures thinking was originally more on what Inayatullah (1990) described as the predictive-empirical approach and Miller et al. (2018, pp. 59–60) as the optimisation approach, the field of futures studies now increasingly emphasises the other, non-predictive approaches (Dator, 1998; Miller, 2007). Thus, instead of aiming to predict the future, in its current state the field of futures studies rather aims to open up alternative futures (Inayatullah, 2013, p. 41) or to anticipate the future (Miller et al., 2018).

Anticipation then is "the form the future takes in the present" (Miller, 2018a, p. 2). It allows us to "use the future" in the present and the capacity to do so has been called "futures literacy" (Miller, 2018b). From this perspective, "the future is not a territory to map and conquer, but a source of new opportunities for the present" (Poli, 2022, p. 113). The aim of exercises in futures thinking then is to allow "people, organizations and communities to make explicit choices between different possible futures" (Poli, 2022, p. 139). This broader perspective on futures studies, aimed at opening up alternative futures, will be the perspective in the remainder of this chapter.

3. Futures thinking in three consecutive steps

The futures studies field has used a wide array of tools and techniques, such as literature reviews, expert panels, trend extrapolation, brainstorming, interviews, the Delphi method, environmental scanning, SWOT analysis, modelling, morphological analysis, futures wheel, citizen panels, gaming, visualisation, design labs, weak signals analysis, and polygon futures (e.g. Bishop et al., 2007; Glenn and Gordon, 2009; Popper, 2008; Tõnurist and Hanson, 2020, pp. 45–72). As this array of techniques is overwhelming, many authors or (educational) institutions have offered comprehensive models that assemble some of these techniques into a stepwise process to produce foresights. For example, Hines and Bishop's (2013) "framework foresight" approach offers a manual consisting of six consecutive steps, while Burrows and Gnad's (2018) "anticipatory governance" model contains four steps, as does Bezold's (2020) "aspirational futures" approach and Poli's (2022) model to "work with the future". A look at these and other (e.g. Slaughter and Hines, 2020) stepwise manuals suggests that there are essentially three consecutive basic steps that can be found in all of them. The remainder of this section briefly presents these three steps, reflecting on their possible application in a public sector context.

The analysis usually starts with a delineation and description of the domain or topic to be explored (e.g. an organisation, a policy issue, or a policy field (Hines and Bishop, 2013, p. 33)) and a description of the driving forces shaping that domain or topic. This is often a very broad map of political, economic, social, technical, environmental, legal (PESTL) and other (e.g. military/security (Burrows and Gnad, 2018, p. 14)) factors. In some models (e.g. Burrows and Gnad, 2018), this first step also includes the analysis of weak signals (or emerging issues) aimed at "identifying future problems/possibilities at their earliest possible emergence rather than waiting until they are fully formed and powerful trends" (Dator, 1998, p. 306). When addressing driving forces, it is important to understand that they are interdependent, certainly in the context of public administration and public policy. For example, catastrophes, as Braithwaite (2024) points out, can cascade into each other, as when, for instance, a natural disaster cascades into a financial crisis, which in turn increases pressure for political violence.

Following the delineation and description of the driving forces, most manuals move on to the development of 'alternative futures' of the organisation's context as shaped by those driving forces. These alternative futures are often presented as scenarios. Given the emphasis within the futures studies field on opening up multiple futures, scenarios are not only the best-known but probably also the most "archetypical" (Bishop et al., 2007, p. 5) product of futures studies. There is an impressive array of techniques for scenario development (Bishop et al., 2007; Börjeson et al., 2006; Cordova-Pozo and Rouwette, 2023). Probably the best known is the Royal Dutch Shell/Global Business Network matrix approach (Schwartz, 1996). It generates four plausible scenarios, defined by two dimensions in a two by two matrix. Those two dimensions represent the two main uncertainties facing the domain within which the futures thinking exercise will occur. Other approaches use generic categories of scenarios that are to be specified for the topic or field that is the object of the futures thinking exercise. For example, the well-known 'framework foresight' approach distinguishes between four archetypical scenarios: continuation (or baseline), collapse, new equilibrium, and transformation (Dator, 1998, p. 305; Hines, 2020, pp. 206–207). Another fourfold classification takes a more normative view: business as usual, best case, worst case, and outlier (Inayatullah, 2008, p. 17; Schwartz, 1996). Other approaches are much more open in the types and number of scenarios to be developed. Instead of specifying generic types of scenarios, they propose techniques to develop scenarios (e.g. visualisation, role playing, probability trees, modelling, etc. (Bishop et al., 2007)). What all these approaches to scenario development share is the aim, typical for futures thinking, to take a very broad and creative view so as to move beyond the obvious. When applied in a context of PA, this implies that such exercises should go far beyond the areas and issues with which PA researchers are most comfortable. Hence, the scenarios should not only address issues like decreasing trust in institutions, democratic backsliding, or geopolitical dynamics, but also issues like global warming or migration that usually receive much less attention in PA (Pollitt, 2017).

In the final step (or steps), the manuals typically move from scenarios about the environment to actual strategic options that the organisation or network of organisations can take internally in response to those scenarios.

Thus, step 3 is the stage when futures thinking gradually moves into (strategic) planning (Hines, 2020, pp. 209-210). It is useful to note that this distinction between scenarios in the environment of the public sector organisation (step 2) and strategies within the public sector organisation (step 3) is not always clearly made in futures thinking exercises in the context of PA. For example, Kitsing's typology of five 'governance scenarios' (Kitsing, 2020) and the EU's Joint Research Center's four scenarios of the future of government (Vesnic-Alujevic et al., 2019) amalgamate these two steps. While there might be good reasons to do so, the discussion below will show that a clear distinction between step 2 and step 3 is crucial for the futures thinking exercise that is proposed here. The strategic options that are to be generated in step 3 can take various forms. They can be framed as 'strategic scenarios' (Börjeson et al., 2006; Miller, 2007), developed with the aim to describe the possible consequences of various decisions, showing how they can vary depending on the various external scenarios that were developed in step 2 (Börjeson et al., 2006, p. 728). The strategic options can also be framed as 'prototypes' that can then be tested by 'wind tunnelling' them against the various scenarios developed in step 2, in the same way as a prototype of an aeroplane is tested in a wind tunnel (Bouwman et al., 2012; van der Merwe, 2008, pp. 232-233). Thus, wind tunnelling or "policy stress testing" is "a strategic foresight tool that compares a stakeholder's current strategic choices against the scenarios produced" (Kelemen and Fergnani, 2020). In a fortunate match of metaphors, such wind tunnelling exercises can be seen as an increasingly important way of dealing with the 'turbulent' context (Ansell et al., 2024) in which we live.

The following two sections will now argue that PA research can particularly contribute to this third step, by helping (a) with the development of the prototypes and (b) with the wind tunnelling of those prototypes.

4. Using Public Administration research to develop prototypes

The first way in which PA research can contribute to step 3 is by providing the conceptual framework to develop prototypes. Such prototypes can be developed at various levels of analysis: for a particular organisational subunit or organisation, for a network of organisations, for a policy field, for a regulatory regime, etc. A prototype is "an experiential learning tool used for testing a desired product or service" (Greyson, 2020, p. 88). It could be a physical tool, an artefact representing a particular future, or indeed a particular organisational design. The field of futures studies offers many, often participatory, techniques to develop and test such prototypes. However, this chapter argues that such techniques might usefully be complemented with insights from existing PA research. Specifically, PA's extensive literature on models and paradigms provides the language as well as insights to develop such prototypes. It offers useful classifications of 'basic building blocks' and recommendations on how these can be assembled in prototypes. Four examples can illustrate this.

First, probably the best-known typology of basic building blocks is the triad 'hierarchy, market, network'. PA research has produced an extensive literature on the benefits and risks of these three basic types and on the many ways in which they can be combined (e.g. Meuleman, 2008). As Bouckaert (2023) points out, these three concepts can refer to the locus of activities (state, private for-profit business, not-for-profit), but they can also refer to three drivers or mechanisms that can be used within various sectors, organisations, or organisational units. These building blocks are usually assembled in models or paradigms, often used as ideal types ("methodological tool to interpret reality" (Bouckaert, 2023, p. 14)) and sometimes also as normative ideals or 'omegas' (Pollitt and Bouckaert, 2017) of reform trajectories. Bouckaert (2023), for example, shows how the relative importance of the three basic components differs in three well-known PA paradigms: New Public Management (emphasis on market), New Public Governance (emphasis on network), and the Neo-Weberian State (emphasis on hierarchy). He also shows how, even within a particular paradigm, the relative importance of the building blocks can evolve, depending on the overall context. Such reflections about the advantages and disadvantages of particular combinations of the basic building blocks can be a very useful source of inspiration for those who want to develop and test a prototype for a particular public sector organisation or public sector field.

A second example of a typology of basic building blocks is the fourfold typology of grid-group cultural theory: hierarchy, individualism, egalitarianism, and fatalism (Douglas, 1970; Hood, 1998). While the first three largely resemble hierarchy, market, and network, the fourth type, 'fatalism', adds a building block that is less common in normative ideals, but observable in the reality of the public sector. Prototype developers can draw from the small research tradition in PA that has presented paradigms as well as real-life organisations as combinations of these four basic building blocks (6, 2003; Lodge, 2009; Maesschalck, 2004a; Verweij and Thompson, 2006). A third example is offered by Torfing et al.'s (2020) classification of seven public governance paradigms. While their discussion does not systematically use basic building blocks, it does specify five dimensions on which the seven paradigms vary, some of which resemble the basic building blocks (Torfing et al., 2020, pp. 151–165). For example, 'centralised control' could be seen as an indicator of hierarchy, 'use of incentives' as an indicator of market, and 'societal involvement' as an indicator of network. Fourth, Pollitt and Bouckaert (2017, pp. 26–29) take a more pragmatic approach and opt not to work with basic building blocks but with 'public management tools', such as contracting out, executive agencies, or service user boards. In a culinary metaphor, they consider these tools as the "dishes/*plats*", while theoretical paradigms (as well as real-life reform programmes) can be seen as menus that combine various dishes. Again, this is a useful classification for those who want to design a specific prototype or '*plat*'.

Some of these authors also offer an important additional recommendation to those who would want to develop prototypes: the importance of 'requisite variety' and thus the need to combine the basic building blocks. According to this recommendation, variation within institutional design is not only an empirical phenomenon, but also a goal to be aimed at. For example, while Bouckaert's (2023) preference for the Neo-Weberian State paradigm implies an emphasis on 'hierarchy', he also recognises that a sufficient degree of market and network are necessary as well. The recommendation to combine the basic building blocks is particularly well developed in the tradition of grid-group cultural theory. A series of studies, in PA as well as related disciplines, has shown that combining cultural theory's four basic building blocks in a 'polyrational', 'clumsy', or 'hybrid' way can make an institution or a policy more viable (6, 2003; Ney and Verweij, 2015; Verweij and Thompson, 2006). This is also consistent with the recent literature on 'robust governance', which argues that combining basic approaches is particularly relevant in times of turbulence. By "maintaining multiple repertoires" (Ansell et al., 2023, p. 9) or "strategic polyvalence" (Ansell et al., 2021, p. 953), organisations are better prepared for a range of different futures (Ansell et al., 2024, p. 43). For the same reason, this literature on robustness recommends hybrids such as "coordinated autonomy" (Capano and Toth, 2023) or "bounded autonomy" (Ansell et al., 2021, p. 953) as approaches to prepare for crisis. Of course, this is not to say that all combinations of the basic building blocks are inherently good. Some can undermine viability (6, 2003), create unnecessary contradictions (Torfing et al., 2020, p. 181) or generate serious ethical problems (Maesschalck, 2004b). PA research's many empirical studies of administrative reform offer useful insights about the advantages and risks of various combinations of the basic building blocks in various environments. That knowledge can help with the development of a prototype that is appropriate for a particular context.

5. Using Public Administration research to wind tunnel the prototypes

PA research is useful not only for the development of a particular prototype, but also for the 'wind tunnelling' of that prototype. It is not sufficient to know that a prototype is adequate for a particular context, we also want to know whether it will remain viable in the future or, more precisely, in various futures. Hence, we need a thought experiment in which the prototype is tested against the various scenarios that were developed in step 2. The aim is to imagine how the prototype would fare in these various scenarios in order to assess its robustness. Suppose, by way of example, that we selected an organisation prototype for the police organisation in a particular country that focuses on digital governance and relies on the "intelligent center/devolved delivery" model (Dunleavy and Margetts, 2023). How would this fare in a scenario in which serious floodings combine with large power and internet outages? Or how would it fare in a scenario in which, as part of hybrid warfare, a cyber-attack on the police's network combines with widespread violent protests fuelled by AI-powered distribution of fake news? These are just two examples that particularly focus on crisis scenarios. Of course, the prototype will be wind tunnelled against the other scenarios developed in step 2 as well, some of which possibly more optimistic. This intense assessment of the prototype against various scenarios requires constant questioning of assumptions and thus offers many critical learning opportunities (van der Merwe, 2008, p. 233). It allows advisors as well as decision-makers to see which revisions are necessary to make the prototype more robust. There are at least two ways in which PA empirical research can contribute to this wind tunnelling exercise.

First, the most obvious way in which PA research can help with this thought experiment is by providing insights on how similar prototypes performed in similar circumstances in the past. Given that the very aim of the development of scenarios is to imagine the unimaginable, the amount of relevant research might be limited. It is nevertheless possible that particular scenarios have occurred somewhere at some point and that useful lessons can already be drawn from how governments responded to those. The growing body of research on how governments responded to COVID-19 (e.g. Ansell et al., 2021; Boin and Lodge, 2021), for example, is an obvious source to help wind tunnelling prototypes for other crisis scenarios. Another source could be research on how public administrations in fragile states have dealt with conditions of fragility as caused by, for example, a surge in political violence or organised crime's infiltration of the state apparatus. Bearing in mind Roberts' warning in his chapter for this volume that states in the Global North should prepare for fragility, this certainly is an exercise worth considering.

Second, the wind tunnelling thought experiment also creates opportunities to think about prototypes in a more dynamic way. Instead of looking at prototypes as entirely fixed set-ups, it could be useful to design them from the outset in a modular way. They would then be seen as a set of well-prepared instruments and approaches that can be applied progressively depending on how the environment evolves. PA scholars are certainly aware of the need for such dynamic approaches. Bouckaert (2023), for example, recognises the need to understand 'sequential' and 'simultaneous' dynamics between hierarchy, market, and network. Nevertheless, actual theoretical insights on how such building blocks could be selected and in which order this should be done remain very limited. One very promising concept to guide this dynamic approach to prototyping and wind tunnelling comes from a field adjacent to PA: regulation. Specifically, Braithwaite's notion of 'meta-strategy', i.e. a strategy for selecting and sequencing strategies (Braithwaite, 2021, p. 206; 2022, p. 439), can be helpful here. Applied for our purposes, a meta-strategy would not only help with selecting the appropriate mix of building blocks to design a prototype, but would also provide guidance on how this selection could be adapted over time to the evolution of various scenarios. Probably the best-known example of such a meta-strategy is "responsive regulation" (Ayres and Braithwaite, 1992). This strategy helps regulators to choose among various regulatory strategies (often represented as layers in a pyramid that escalate in degree of deterrence) depending on the reactions of those who are regulated. This could act as a source of inspiration for a similar theory for choosing and sequencing hierarchy, market, and network, particularly for prototypes of regulatory regimes. Another promising example of a meta-strategy is Braithwaite's (2024) concept of "iterative responsiveness to complexity". Having listed the many complex catastrophes that are threatening our society, Braithwaite questions the truism that complex problems by definition need complex solutions. He offers a list of examples of 'simple' solutions that have proved very helpful in dealing with complex catastrophes. Thus, the meta-strategy he proposes is to start with a simple solution by default, and gradually move to more complex solutions as the situation requires, relying on an iterative evaluation of how these solutions perform. This meta-strategy might also guide the wind tunnelling exercise that is proposed here. For example, while the prototype could start from a design based on the characteristics of, say, an ideal-type version of the Neo-Weberian State paradigm, wind tunnelling this design against various scenarios could inspire iterative adaptations that would make the design gradually more complex.

Using meta-strategies like the two just discussed in a wind tunnelling exercise offers a useful complement to the approach that more and more authors propose as an answer to growing complexity and turbulence: 'bricolage' (Carstensen et al., 2023; Van de Walle, 2014) or the creative (re)use of a heterogeneous repertoire of existing solutions in the same way as a bricoleur uses and reuses old materials. While bricolage has obvious advantages, its weakness is that, like the bricoleur, it only uses what is mentally and practically available. The added value, compared to bricolage, of futures thinking in general and of using meta-strategies in wind tunnelling exercises specifically, is that they help to expand the repertoire of solutions by making them mentally conceivable. This in turn also invites a reflection on what can be done now in preparation, so as to make sure that some of these solutions are available when needed in the future.

6. Conclusion

There has been no shortage of complaints that PA research is not useful for practice (e.g. Pollitt, 2017; Roberts, 2020). This chapter suggest that one way in which PA research can be practically useful is by contributing to futures thinking. Specifically, it proposed two ways in which PA research can do that. First, PA research can inspire the design of prototypes by offering basic building blocks as well as tested ways of combining those building blocks in models or paradigms. With its extensive literature on the pros and cons of the various models and paradigms, it can help to conceptualise prototypes in a systematic way. It can also help to unearth normative assumptions that might remain implicit in a traditional futures thinking exercise that ignores existing PA research because it focuses only on the creative development of new ideas. Second, with its extensive knowledge about the impact of models and its suggestions for meta-strategies, PA research can support the exercise of wind tunnelling the prototype against various possible futures as presented in various scenarios. In doing so, it contributes to the main advantage of wind tunnelling: helping to expand the repertoire of solutions by making them mentally conceivable and practically possible.

Of course, the approach proposed in this chapter offers only one way in which PA can contribute to futures thinking in the public sector. PA research also has useful insights to offer on how to strengthen the capacity of the public sector to anticipate various futures and thus to make public sector organisations more "futures literate" (Miller, 2018b). Tōnurist and Hanson (2020, pp. 115–116), for example, refer to various core government structures (e.g. HR, open forms of strategic planning, creation of competence centres, etc.) that can contribute to anticipatory innovation in the public sector. Noting that "the work on anticipatory innovation governance is just in its beginnings" (Tõnurist and Hanson, 2020, p. 112), they propose a series of topics that deserve further research. Likewise, the rapidly growing literature on 'robust governance' (Ansell et al., 2023; Ansell and Trondal, 2018) draws from other literatures to suggest topics and approaches that can be a source of inspiration for futures thinking in the public sector. Ansell et al. (2024, pp. 44–46), for example, list a series of strategies of 'vigilance' that can make public sector organisations more future-oriented. Another important line of relevant PA research are studies into the conditions under which the results of futures thinking exercises are actually used by policymakers (e.g. Fobé and Brans, 2013).

While this chapter focused on how PA research can contribute to practice-oriented exercises in futures thinking, it should be noted that, conversely, these thought experiments might actually also benefit academic PA research itself. This is possible in at least two ways. First and most obviously, researchers also reflect about the future of public administration. In fact the volume to which this chapter is a contribution is an example of such a reflection by PA academics. This chapter argues that such exercises can be enriched by techniques like scenario development, prototyping, and wind tunnelling. More generally, the field of future studies offers an impressive amount of other techniques and methodologies (e.g. Delphi, morphological analysis, futures wheel, visualisation, design labs, etc.) that can also inspire academic PA. With their emphasis on inclusiveness, creativity, and questioning assumptions, these techniques can help to surface 'uncomfortable knowledge' (Rayner, 2012; Saltelli and Giampietro, 2017) by turning the spotlight on blind spots within PA research. Second, the prototyping and wind tunnelling exercises proposed in this chapter offer a way to enrich the academic debates about models and paradigms. Instead of the search for the ultimate paradigm, this chapter proposes to develop specific prototypes as particular combinations of the basic building blocks. These prototypes are not seen as normative standards or 'omegas' of reform (Pollitt and Bouckaert, 2017), but simply as experimental designs that need to earn their worth during tests against a broad range of imaginative scenarios. Such a pragmatic approach might be a refreshing addition to the existing, sometimes sterile 'paradigm wars' in academic PA.

References

6, P. (2003). Institutional viability: A neo-Durkheimian theory. *Innovation: The European Journal of Social Science Research*, *16*(4), 395–416. https://doi.org/10.1080/1351161032000163593.

Ansell, C. K., Sørensen, E., & Torfing, J. (2021). The COVID-19 pandemic as a game changer for public administration and leadership? The need for robust governance responses to turbulent problems. *Public Management Review*, *23*(7), 949–960. https://doi.org/10.1080/14719037.2020.1820272.

Ansell, C. K., Sørensen, E., & Torfing, J. (2023). Public administration and politics meet turbulence: The search for robust governance responses. *Public Administration*, *101*(1), 3–22. https://doi.org/10.1111/padm.12874.

Ansell, C. K., & Trondal, J. (2018). Governing turbulence: An organizational-institutional agenda. *Perspectives on Public Management and Governance*, *1*(1), 43–57. https://doi.org/10.1093/ppmgov/gvx013.

Ansell, C. K., Sørensen, E., Torfing, J., & Trondal, J. (2024). *Robust Governance in Turbulent Times*. Cambridge University Press. https://doi.org/10.1017/9781009433006.

Ayres, I., & Braithwaite, J. (1992). *Responsive Regulation: Transcending the Deregulation Debate*. Oxford University Press.

Bezold, C. (2020). Aspirational futures. In R. Slaughter & A. Hines (Eds.), *The knowledge base of futures studies 2020* (pp. 143–156). Association of Professional Futurists and Foresight International.

Bishop, P., Hines, A., & Collins, T. (2007). The current state of scenario development: An overview of techniques. *Foresight*, *9*(1), 5–25. https://doi.org/10.1108/14636680710727516.

Boin, A., & Lodge, M. (2021). Responding to the COVID-19 crisis: A principled or pragmatist approach? *Journal of European Public Policy*, *28*(8), 1131–1152. https://doi.org/10.1080/13501763.2021.1942155.

Börjeson, L., Höjer, M., Dreborg, K.-H., Ekvall, T., & Finnveden, G. (2006). Scenario types and techniques: Towards a user's guide. *Futures*, *38*(7), 723–739. https://doi.org/10.1016/j.futures.2005.12.002.

Bouckaert, G. (2023). The neo-Weberian state: From ideal type model to reality? *Max Weber Studies*, *23*(1), 13–59. https://doi.org/10.1353/max.2023.0002.

Bouckaert, G., & Jann, W. (Eds.) (2020a). *European perspectives for public administration: The way forward*. Leuven University Press. https://doi.org/10.11116/9789461663078.

Bouckaert, G., & Jann, W. (2020b). The EPPA-project. In G. Bouckaert & W. Jann (Eds.), *European perspectives for public administration: The way forward* (pp. 21–42). Leuven University Press. https://doi.org/10.11116/9789461663078.

Bouwman, H., Haaker, T., & de Reuver, M. (2012). Some reflections on the high expectations as formulated in the Internet Bubble era. *Futures*, *44*(5), 420–430. https://doi.org/10.1016/j.futures.2012.03.004.

Braithwaite, J. (2021). Street-level meta-strategies: Evidence on restorative justice and responsive regulation. *Annual Review of Law and Social Science*, *17*, 205–225. https://doi.org/10.1146/annurev-lawsocsci-111720-013149.

Braithwaite, J. (2022). *Macrocriminology and Freedom*. ANU Press. https://doi.org/10.22459/MF.2021.

Braithwaite, J. (2024). *Simple Solutions to Complex Catastrophes: Dialectics of Peace, Climate, Finance, and Health.* Springer Nature Switzerland. https://doi.org/10.1007/978-3-031-48747-7.

Burrows, M. J., & Gnad, O. (2018). Between "muddling through" and "grand design": Regaining political initiative – The role of strategic foresight. *Futures, 97,* 6–17. https://doi.org/10.1016/j.futures.2017.06.002.

Capano, G., & Toth, F. (2023). Thinking outside the box, improvisation, and fast learning: Designing policy robustness to deal with what cannot be foreseen. *Public Administration, 101*(1), 90–105. https://doi.org/10.1111/padm.12861.

Carstensen, M. B., Sørensen, E., & Torfing, J. (2023). Why we need bricoleurs to foster robust governance solutions in turbulent times. *Public Administration, 101*(1), 36–52. https://doi.org/10.1111/padm.12857.

Cordova-Pozo, K., & Rouwette, E. A. J. A. (2023). Types of scenario planning and their effectiveness: A review of reviews. *Futures, 149,* 103153. https://doi.org/10.1016/j.futures.2023.103153.

Dator, J. (1998). Introduction: The future lies behind! Thirty years of teaching futures studies. *American Behavioral Scientist, 42*(3), 298–319. https://doi.org/10.1177/0002764298042003002.

Douglas, M. (1970). *Natural symbols: Explorations in Cosmology.* Random House. https://archive.org/details/naturalsymbolsex00doug/page/n3/mode/1up.

Dunleavy, P., & Margetts, H. (2023). Data science, artificial intelligence and the third wave of digital era governance. *Public Policy and Administration.* https://doi.org/10.1177/09520767231198737.

Fobé, E., & Brans, M. (2013). Policy-oriented foresight as evidence for policy making: Conditions of (mis)match. *Evidence & Policy, 9*(4), 473–492. https://doi.org/10.1332/174426413X662789.

Glenn, J. C., & Gordon, T. J. (2009). *Futures Research Methodology: Version 3.0.* Millennium Project, Washington, DC.

Greyson, M. (2020). Design for the abstract qualities of futures studies. In R. Slaughter & A. Hines (Eds.), *The Knowledge Base of Futures Studies 2020* (pp. 86–97). Association of Professional Futurists and Foresight International.

Hines, A. (2020). Framework foresight: Exploring futures the Houston way. In R. Slaughter & A. Hines (Eds.), *The Knowledge Base of Futures Studies 2020* (pp. 196–214). Association of Professional Futurists and Foresight International.

Hines, A., & Bishop, P. C. (2013). Framework foresight: Exploring futures the Houston way. *Futures, 51,* 31–49. https://doi.org/10.1016/j.futures.2013.05.002.

Hood, C. (1998). *The Art of the State. Culture, Rhetoric, and Public Management.* Clarendon Press. https://doi.org/10.1093/0198297653.001.0001.

Inayatullah, S. (1990). Deconstructing and reconstructing the future: Predictive, cultural and critical epistemologies. *Futures, 22*(2), 115–141. https://doi.org/10.1016/0016-3287(90)90077-U.

Inayatullah, S. (2008). Six pillars: Futures thinking for transforming. *Foresight, 10*(1), 4–21. https://doi.org/10.1108/14636680810855991.

Inayatullah, S. (2013). Futures studies: Theories and methods. In N. Al-Fodham (Ed.), *There's a Future: Visions for a Better World* (pp. 37–66). BBVA Group. http://www.metafuture.org/library1/FuturesStudies/Futures-Studies-theories-and-methods-published-version-2013-with-pics.pdf

Joyce, P. (2020). Governing for the future: Means, ends and disconnects. In G. Bouckaert & W. Jann (Eds.), *European Perspectives for Public Administration* (pp. 85–102). Leuven University Press. https://doi.org/10.2307/j.ctvv417th.9.

Kelemen, B., & Fergnani, A. (2020). The futures of terrorism against China in the Greater Middle East. *Futures, 124*, 102643. https://doi.org/10.1016/j.futures.2020.102643.

Kitsing, M. (2020). Scenarios as thought experiments for governance. In G. Bouckaert & W. Jann (Eds.), *European Perspectives for Public Administration* (pp. 103–126). Leuven University Press. https://doi.org/10.2307/j.ctvv417th.10.

Kristóf, T., & Nováky, E. (2023). The story of futures studies: An interdisciplinary field rooted in social sciences. *Social Sciences, 12*(3), 192. https://doi.org/10.3390/socsci12030192.

Lodge, M. (2009). The public management of risk: The case for deliberating among worldviews. *Review of Policy Research, 26*(4), 395–408. https://doi.org/10.1111/j.1541-1338.2009.00391.x.

Maesschalck, J. (2004a). Approaches to ethics management in the public sector: A proposed extension of the compliance-integrity continuum. *Public Integrity, 7*(1), 21–41. https://www.tandfonline.com/doi/abs/10.1080/10999922.2004.11051267.

Maesschalck, J. (2004b). The impact of new public management reforms on public servants' ethics: Towards a theory. *Public Administration, 82*(2), 465–489. https://doi.org/10.1111/j.0033-3298.2004.00403.x.

Meuleman, L. (2008). *Public Management and the Metagovernance of Hierarchies, Networks and Markets: The Feasibility of Designing and Managing Governance Style Combinations*. Springer Science & Business Media. https://doi.org/10.1007/978-3-7908-2054-6.

Miller, R. (2007). Futures literacy: A hybrid strategic scenario method. *Futures, 39*(4), 341–362. https://doi.org/10.1016/j.futures.2006.12.001.

Miller, R. (2018). Introduction: Futures literacy: Transforming the future. In R. Miller (Ed.), *Transforming the Future: Anticipation in the 21st century* (pp. 1–12). Taylor & Francis. https://www.taylorfrancis.com/chapters/oa-edit/10.4324/9781351048002-1/introduction-riel-miller.

Miller, R. (Ed.) (2018b). *Transforming the Future: Anticipation in the 21st Century*. Taylor & Francis. https://doi.org/10.4324/9781351048002.

Miller, R., Poli, R., & Rossel, P. (2018). The discipline of anticipation: Foundations for futures literacy. In R. Miller (Ed.), *Transforming the Future: Anticipation in the 21st Century* (pp. 51–65). Routledge. https://www.taylorfrancis.com/chapters/oa-edit/10.4324/9781351048002-3/discipline-anticipation-riel-miller-roberto-poli-pierre-rossel.

Ney, S., & Verweij, M. (2015). Messy institutions for wicked problems: How to generate clumsy solutions? *Environment and Planning C: Government and Policy, 33*(6), 1679–1696. https://doi.org/10.1177/0263774X15614450.

Poli, R. (2022). *Working with the Future: Ideas and Tools to Govern Uncertainty*. EGEA.

Pollitt, C. (2017). Public administration research since 1980: Slipping away from the real world? *International Journal of Public Sector Management, 30*(6-7), 555–565. https://doi.org/10.1108/IJPSM-04-2017-0113.

Pollitt, C., & Bouckaert, G. (2017). *Public Management Reform: A Comparative Analysis – Into the Age of Austerity* (4th ed.). Oxford University Press.

Popper, R. (2008). How are foresight methods selected? *Foresight, 10*(6), 62–89. https://doi.org/10.1108/14636680810918586.

Rayner, S. (2012). Uncomfortable knowledge: The social construction of ignorance in science and environmental policy discourses. *Economy and Society, 41*(1), 107–125. https://doi.org/10.1080/03085147.2011.637335.

Roberge, I. (2013). Futures construction in public management. *International Journal of Public Sector Management*, 26(7), 534–542. https://doi.org/10.1108/IJPSM-06-2012-0074.

Roberts, A. (2020). *Strategies for Governing: Reinventing Public Administration for a Dangerous Century*. Cornell University Press.

Saltelli, A., & Giampietro, M. (2017). What is wrong with evidence based policy, and how can it be improved? *Futures*, 91, 62–71. https://doi.org/10.1016/j.futures.2016.11.012.

Sardar, Z. (2010). The namesake: Futures; futures studies; futurology; futuristic; foresight – what's in a name? *Futures*, 42(3), 177–184. https://doi.org/10.1016/j.futures.2009.11.001.

Schwartz, P. (1996). *The art of the long view: Planning for the future in an uncertain world*. Crown.

Slaughter, R., & Hines, A. (Eds.) (2020). *The Knowledge Base of Futures Studies 2020*. Association of Professional Futurists and Foresight International.

Tõnurist, P., & Hanson, A. (2020). *Anticipatory Innovation Governance: Shaping the Future Through Proactive Policy Making*. OECD. https://doi.org/10.1787/cce14d80-en.

Torfing, J., Andersen, L. B., Greve, C., & Klausen, K. K. (2020). *Public Governance Paradigms: Competing and Co-Existing*. Edward Elgar Publishing. https://doi.org/10.4337/9781788971225.

Van de Walle, S. (2014). Building resilience in public organizations: The role of waste and bricolage. *The Innovation Journal*, 19(2).

van der Merwe, L. (2008). Scenario-based strategy in practice: A framework. *Advances in Developing Human Resources*, 10(2), 216–239. https://doi.org/10.1177/1523422307313321.

Verweij, M., & Thompson, M. (2006). *Clumsy Solutions for a Complex World: Governance, Politics and Plural Perceptions*. Palgrave Macmillan. https://doi.org/10.1057/9780230624887.

Vesnic-Alujevic, L., Stoermer, E., Rudkin, J.-E., Scapolo, F., & Kimbell, L. (2019). *The Future of Government 2030+: A Citizen Centric Perspective on New Government Models*. Publications Office of the European Union. https://doi.org/10.2760/145751.

The future of a scattered field: Challenges and opportunities

by Asmus Leth Olsen

When we attempt to characterise the state of the art in Public Administration, we tend to define the research frontier by a set of journals and maybe a few books. These journals typically carry the name of "American" or "International" journal of "Public Administration", "Public Management" or "Public Policy". We read and cite these journals and a couple of books when making our own contributions to the field. We also do meta-reviews or meta-studies to aggregate our knowledge across these journals on topics like public–private partnership (Wang et al., 2018), job satisfaction (Cantarelli et al., 2016), public service motivation (Ritz et al., 2016), the use of theories (Hattke and Vogel, 2023), or the usefulness of different methods (Hansen and Tummers, 2020; Bouwman and Grimmelikhuijsen, 2016). Reading, keeping up to date, and aggregating our knowledge along the research frontier is a difficult as well as important task. However, the knowledge accumulated by a set of journals is only relevant if it represents the full body of evidence on the issues at hand. Drawing on recent evidence and my own observations, I will argue in this piece that journals in Public Administration are not the primary frontier for research concerning many problems and puzzles related to the field of Public Administration.

We have spent a good deal of the past decade re-vitalising the discussion about the *relevance* of other fields and disciplines to the study of Public Administration (Wright, 2011; Hustedt et al., 2020). Most prominent has been the revival of Behavioural Public Administration (Olsen, 2015; Grimmelikhuijsen et al., 2017) which explicitly has called for the integration of psychological theories and Public Administration problems as first argued for by Simon (1996) more than 70 years ago. However, these discussions have side-stepped a more fundamental point: neighbouring fields and disciplines produce research that is not just *relevant* to Public Administration. The trend in these fields is that they now also produce large amounts of high-quality research which must be regarded as de facto Public Administration research by any meaningful definition. We need to accept Public Administration, as a field beyond the restrictions of a set of journals and some classic books.

I will argue that accepting the trend line of Public Administration as a field beyond journals confronts us with the serious challenge of defining the state of the art for any meaningful research question. I will also argue that the inclusion of research on Public Administration issues from other academic fields and disciplines offers us opportunities to resolve two major issues in 'our' field: (a) a much more diverse set of non-Western cases studied with (b) more rigorous methods for causal inference. In that sense, the extension of our field solves our two primary inferiority complexes. I end by outlining a five-point plan of how to escape a field-centric view of Public Administration and evolve into a 'true field' that embraces all research on our field of interest without discriminating against where and how it was published.

1. Trends at the research frontier: my favourite pieces of Public Administration research from recent years

Research is not formally a competition, but I often find myself thinking about what my favourite pieces of public administration research are. From the past couple of years, what follow are among my favourite pieces of research on public administration, reflecting four major clusters of research which I often myself aspire to add to.

First, a trend of focusing on representative bureaucracy and discrimination in citizen–state interaction has long been a major topic in Public Administration, with recent and renewed interest as most Western countries become increasingly diverse. Some examples are as follows: Goncalves and Mello (2021) aim to estimate if racial bias in policing is a product of a few bad apples or a more systemic problem. It turns out that racial bias in Florida police is largely systemic and not just a few flawed individuals running amok. Studying all-female police departments in India, Jassal (2020) finds that representation through gender separation has unintended consequences that do not benefit women victims of crimes or the public's view of women police officers. In a US setting, Peyton et al. (2022) find via clever experiments that citizens overestimate minority representation in the police force and increase their support for mild forms of affirmative action if corrected in these beliefs.

Second, there has been an explosion of research on administrative burdens in public administration since the publication of Herd and Moynihan (2019). A few examples are as follows: In the US, Fishbane et al. (2020) show that re-designing messages to appear in court can massively reduce failure to appear in court for low-level offences. This has huge benefits for the individual citizen summoned by the court and economically for society as a whole. Sabety et al. (2023) study a New York City intervention to reduce friction in accessing primary care for undocumented immigrants. The intervention increases self-reported access and leads to fewer emergency department visits. Using a natural experiment in the assignment of interview dates for the re-certification process for the Supplemental Nutrition Assistance Program in the US, Homonoff and Somerville (2021) clearly identify how late assignments induce an administrative burden which ultimately cuts rightful recipients off the programme. Third, topics surrounding motivation, crowding, recruitment, and retention in the public sector have long been central to the field (Ritz et al., 2016) and the trend continues with new novel methods. There is rich development in this area, but a few examples could be as follows. Ashraf et al. (2020) resolve the seemingly fundamental tension between pro-sociality and talent in a large-scale field experiment to fill healthcare positions in Zambia. For the marginal applicant, additional career benefits do not highlight a trade-off as candidates in the treatment group are both more talented and pro-social. Khan et al.(2019) exploit the fact that some tax bureaucrats in Pakistan can choose geographically attractive locations based on previous performance, which boosts tax collection for those bureaucrats particularly affected by the scheme. Via a field experiment in Rwanda, Leaver et al. (2021) clearly show that teachers assigned a pay-for-performance scheme increase pupil learning in primary school relative to teachers assigned to a fixed wage scheme.

Fourth, bureaucratic politics and the relationship between politics and administration are at the core of the Public Administration field (Dahlström and Lapuente, 2022) and have become fashionable again due to current tensions in world politics. The international trend is reflected in the following examples: Using the total population of public sector workers in Brazil, Colonnelli et al. (2020) find strong evidence that political considerations lead to the selection of less-qualified bureaucrats. In Ghana, Brierley (2020) shows that bureaucrats' perception of political discretion matters for their ability to withstand corrupt behaviour. If bureaucrats are under the impression that politicians have great discretion, then they are more likely to facilitate their corrupt behaviour. Finally, back in Brazil, Hjort et al. (2021) show in a field experiment that strong evidence-based policy can more easily diffuse and be adopted by municipalities.

In summary, public administration research is alive and well, handling topical issues using diverse global cases and strong causal methods.

2. The trend challenge: a field beyond journals

There is just one minor issue: none of the examples listed above are published in traditional Public Administration journals. They are all printed in general interest science journals (Fishbane et al., 2020; Peyton et al., 2022), journals in economics (Ashraf et al., 2020; Colonnelli et al., 2020; Hjort et al., 2021; Khan et al.2019; Leaver et al., 2021; Homonoff and Somerville, 2021) or political science journals (Sabety et al., 2023; Brierley, 2020). Can we accept them as Public Administration research? Not if we rely on a journal-centric definition of 'our' field.

However, it is research that at face value seems to be almost impossible to distinguish from the questions, topics, and puzzles which researchers in Public Administration (as defined by a set of journals) usually care about. The examples stated above also fit any scholarly definition of Public Administration that we provide our students with across textbooks. That is, research that deals with "the management of public programs" (Denhardt, Denhardt and Blanc, 2013, p. 1), "what government can properly and successfully do, and secondly, how it can do these proper things with the utmost possible efficiency and at the least possible cost both of money and of energy" (Dimock, 1937, p. 29) or "public leadership of public affairs directly responsible for executive action" (Appleby, 1947, p. 95).

While all different, these definitions point to a view of Public Administration as a field of study that can be captured by definitions that place the demarcation line of the field slightly differently (Hustedt et al., 2020; Pollitt, 2014). As Bouckaert and Jann (2020, p. 34) argue: "PA is not a (traditional) discipline and should not strive to become one. It's a research platform or research field, a community of interest combining and using different disciplines and methods." Echoing this sentiment, Pollitt (2010, p. 292) says: "What unifies public administration is its subject – the state, the public sector, and the public realm – not its aims, theories, or methods". Or as Raadschelders (2011, p. 147) puts it, "public administration is a field of study defined by its material object".

The field of Public Administration is not directly obliterated by my ability to identify a dozen strong pieces of public administration research published outside the field (as defined by its journals). How representative are the examples listed above? In Olsen et al., (2023), we provide a detailed analysis of public administration research published in top economics journals. Qualitatively these analyses also seem to cover research on public administration in general science journals and political science which were among the examples cited in the previous section. The overall conclusion is that Public Administration research in economics is of the same order of magnitude as the full field of (quantitative) Public Administration research. If we add Public Administration research published in the other social science disciplines then we easily end at the conclusion that the centre of gravity of research on public administration is outside the field of Public Administration.

All this would be fine if strong connections and citation patterns existed between the other disciplines and the field of Public Administration. This is, however, not the case. Wright (2011) shows that the Public Administration field has very weak co-citation networks with 'our' disciplines of law, management, and political science. Naturally, some of the work in these disciplines is only marginally relevant to Public Administration. However, if we focus on research outside disciplines that fit a mainstream definition of Public Administration then the pattern is the same. In Olsen et al. (2023), we show that in 138 pieces of research on Public Administration published in Economics, there are less than 10 references to any article published in a Public Administration journal. The pattern is not much better the other way around, as Public Administration journal articles have cited just about 20% of the 138 Economics.

It is fair to say that the journal-centric Public Administration field and the rest of public administration are two almost perfectly separated worlds looking at the same empirical reality. Naturally, a limit of the above is a focus on journals and not books. Public Administration has produced some classics in book format that are widely cited in other fields – just consider the works of Herbert Simon – and it could be worth exploring whether books produce more cross-field citations.

3. The trend opportunity: diversity and causality at the new research frontier

The lack of citations between Public Administration in our journals and public administration in other journals implies that we quite explicitly have been working with a very narrow definition of the field: *Public Administration is Public Administration if it is published in a Public Administration journal*. However, if we are true to the field view of Public Administration as defined by its "subject – the state, the public sector, and the public realm – not its aims, theories, or methods" (Pollitt, 2010, p. 292), then we should embrace the newfound treasure trove of public administration research published out of sight of the field's journals.

Importantly, this newfound research offers us opportunities to patch up serious flaws found only within the journal-centric Public Administration field. I will here focus on two: (a) the neglect of cases from the Global South; and (b) the call for stronger causal methods. Recently, there has been a focus on case studies in the journal-centric Public Administration field (Roberts, 2018; Bertelli et al., 2020; Hattke and Vogel, 2023; 2023). In a large-scale study of theories in Public Administration, Hattke and Vogel (2023) finds that of the countries mentioned in the articles, 56% are Anglo-Saxon and 29% are continental European. If we look more specifically at quantitatively oriented Public Administration and with hand-coding (but slightly different categories) of the actual cases studied then we find very similar numbers: about 50% are from the US and 40% other Western countries (Olsen et al., 2023).

Some of the most populous states in the world with large and important governance issues are virtually absent from the journal-centric Public Administration field. This includes India, Nigeria, Brazil, and Indonesia. Looking closer at the journal-centric Public Administration field, we can see that the European cases mostly centre on Benelux and Scandinavia. The second most studied case in quantitative research in the top journals of Public Administration is Denmark (Olsen et al., 2023).

This stands in sharp contrast to public administration research from outside the field. As we saw in the earlier examples, they were rich on cases from the Global South, with studies from Pakistan, Brazil, Zambia, Rwanda, and Ghana, along with multiple studies from the United States. This was not a coincidence: hand-coding of public administration research published in Economics journals (Olsen et al., 2023) shows that about half of the cases studied are non-WEIRD (i.e. countries that are not Western, educated, industrial, rich, and democratic) (Henrich et al., 2010). Thus while Denmark is the second most studied case in quantitative Public Administration in our journals, India is the second most studied case (after the US) in public administration research in Economics (Olsen et al., 2023).

This casts the under-representation of the Global South in Public Administration in a very different light. The under-representation is only found in the journal-centric Public Administration field. However, if we extend public administration research to outside fields and disciplines, we are offered a rich body of research on a diverse set of cases from the Global South. Thus, by extending our field beyond journals we also relieve concerns about the external validity and relevance of Public Administration research to countries outside the West. While the inclusion of 'foreign' public administration at first seems like a destabilising force, it actually patches the research frontier on what is perhaps the biggest threat to the relevance of the journal-centric Public Administration field.

A similar story can be told about the journal-centric Public Administration field's concern about the state of causal and experimental Public Administration. Our field has seen a surge of survey experimental work in the past decade (Bouwman and Grimmelikhuijsen, 2016). Key to the spread of experiments has been the Behavioural Public Administration movement (Grimmelikhuijsen et al., 2017), which has used psychology as a transport belt for one of psychology's favourite tools: the survey experiment. However, there have been concerns about our relatively late adoption of experimental research relative to other fields (James et al., 2017) and lack of attention to detail in experimental designs (Jilke et al., 2016). More recently the concern revolves around too strong of an emphasis on survey experiments, and too little work using field and quasi-experiment (Hansen and Tummers, 2020) with mostly stronger external validity and direct relevance for practitioners (James et al., 2017).

As the Behavioural Public Administration movement has paved the way for experimental methods, originally used in another disciplines (Grimmelikhuijsen et al., 2017), the implicit (or sometimes very explicit) ideal is that we now have to redo our research on all the important Public Administration topics from an experimental approach. The work is needed to reach a new equilibrium of research methods in a field dominated by regression analysis on observational data and case studies using various qualitative data sources.

This line of argument is fine. However, public administration research from outside the field offers an alternative: again, as for the diversity of our cases, our inferiority complex on causal methods stems from a journal-centric view of the field. The examples of research listed in the first section all use different field or quasi-experimental methods (sometimes in companion with survey experiments). More thorough investigation shows that this is quite representative of parts of public administration research outside the field, which overall relies much more on field and quasi-experimental methods (Olsen et al., 2023). They do so at the expense of fewer kitchen-sink regressions on observational data and survey experiments in student populations which partly characterise quantitative work in our field.

In summary, any inferiority that a journal-centric view of the field might induce in terms of the diversity of cases or causal credibility of our methods can largely be solved by extending the view of the field to Public Administration research published in other disciplinary journals.

4. The future: Public Administration in the next decade

If you remember one point from this text then let it be: we need to accept Public Administration as a field beyond a set of journals. The scattered nature of the field beyond the journals leaves us with important decisions about the future direction of the field as it plays out in our journals. In Olsen et al. (2023), I outlined an intentionally provocative path for the future of our field: we can have a meaningful couple of decades in front of us where we analyse, discuss, and dissect motivation, burdens, and discrimination in the cases of Scandinavia, Benelux, and the handful of New World Anglo-Saxon countries. These are important places with mature welfare states servicing hundreds of millions of citizens. If this is the path we choose, we should more explicitly recast ourselves as WEIRD Public Administration: the study of Public Administration in countries that are Western, educated, industrial, rich, and democratic (Henrich et al., 2010).

An alternative, and more constructive, path for the future could be a reformulation of Public Administration as an integrator of knowledge across fields and disciplines (Olsen et al., 2023). Here is a five-point plan we could start implementing tomorrow which would markedly shift the direction of our field over the coming decade:

1. Correct the scientific record: Conduct reviews and meta-studies on the major topics in Public Administration based on research across journals. This genre is already present in our field but too often journal-centric. We need reviews and meta-studies that aggregate Public Administration research from a journal-agnostic point of view.
2. Reform the educational curriculum: Rewrite our textbooks and restructure our education to reflect the full body of knowledge on Public Administration from all fields and disciplines. Again, some areas already do this to some extent (like work on motivation), but it needs to be our *modus operandi* in all matters of teaching material.
3. Change publishing incentives: Commit editors and reviewers at our journals to only accept papers that are fully agnostic about what journals they cite; for example, work in economics can be cited at any rate in a Public Administration journal. This is potentially the most difficult one and strong norms and incentives are stacked against it. It will require a collective effort where more senior people with good tenure positions could move the needle for the next generation.
4. Publish broadly: Aim to publish Public Administration work in general science journals and in journals of other fields and disciplines. The analysis above clearly shows an appetite for our research questions in these

journals, but the question is whether we have the right methodological skills and general ability to move our subject matter out of a sub-field state of mind and onto the big stages of science.
5. Be integrative in research communication: Communicate research on Public Administration from all fields and disciplines to the media and practitioners. The final point is the lowest-hanging fruit and merely requires us to read Public Administration broadly with a focus on non-PA journals.

Some of the above points of action will require several radical steps, which all stem from the fact that we need to abandon the idea that the journals of our field are a representative record of the research on public administration. Overall, these steps all follow a very basic logic: if we are a field that has committed ourselves to studying a relatively well-defined piece of the world, then we need to take every single piece of research regarding this piece of the world seriously if it aims to say something meaningful.

References

Appleby, P. H. (1947). Toward better public administration. *Public Administration Review, 7*(2), 93–99. https://doi.org/10.2307/972751.

Ashraf, N., Bandiera, O., Davenport, E., & Lee, S. S. (2020). Losing prosociality in the quest for Talent? Sorting, selection, and productivity in the delivery of public services. *American Economic Review, 110*, 1355–1394. https://doi.org/10.1257/aer.20180326.

Bertelli, A. M., Hassan, M., Honig, D., Rogger, D., & Williams, M. J. (2020). An agenda for the study of public administration in developing countries. *Governance, 33*(4), 735–748. https://doi.org/10.1111/gove.12520.

Bouckaert, G., & Jann, W. (2020). Lessons and next steps. In G. Bouckaert & W. Jann (Eds.), *European Perspectives for Public Administration* (pp. 455–465). Leuven University Press. https://doi.org/10.2307/j.ctvv417th.28.

Bouwman, R., & Grimmelikhuijsen, S. (2016). Experimental public administration from 1992 to 2014: A systematic literature review and ways forward. *International Journal of Public Sector Management, 29*(2), 110–131. https://doi.org/10.1108/IJPSM-07-2015-0129.

Brierley, S. (2020). Unprincipled principals: Co-opted bureaucrats and corruption in Ghana. *American Journal of Political Science, 64*(2), 209–222. https://doi.org/10.1111/ajps.12495.

Cantarelli, P., Belardinelli, P., & Belle, N. (2016). A meta-analysis of job satisfaction correlates in the public administration literature. *Review of Public Personnel Administration, 36*(2), 115–144. https://doi.org/10.1177/0734371X15578534.

Colonnelli, E., Prem, M., & Teso, E. (2020). Patronage and selection in public sector organizations. *American Economic Review, 110*(10), 3071–3099. https://hdl.handle.net/10419/262694.

Dahlström, C., & Lapuente, V. (2022). Comparative bureaucratic politics. *Annual Review of Political Science, 25*, 43–63. https://doi.org/10.1146/annurev-polisci-051120-102543.

Denhardt, R. B, Denhardt, J. V., & Blanc, T. A. (2013). *Public Administration: An Action Orientation*. Cengage Learning.

Dimock, M. E. (1937). The study of administration. *American Political Science Review, 31*(1), 28–40. https://doi.org/10.2307/1948041.

Fishbane, A., Ouss, A., & Shah, A. K. (2020). Behavioral nudges reduce failure to appear for court. *Science, 370*(6517). https://doi.org/10.1126/science.abb6591.

Goncalves, F., & Mello, S. (2021). A few bad apples? Racial bias in policing. *American Economic Review, 111*(5), 1406–1441. https://www.jstor.org/stable/27027861.

Grimmelikhuijsen, S., Jilke, S., Olsen, A. L., & Tummers, L. (2017). Behavioral public administration: Combining insights from public administration and psychology. *Public Administration Review, 77*(1), 45–56. https://doi.org/10.1111/puar.12609.

Hansen, J. A., & Tummers, L. (2020). A systematic review of field experiments in public administration. *Public Administration Review, 80*(6), 921–931. https://doi.org/10.1111/puar.13181.

Hattke, F., & Vogel, R. (2023). Theories and theorizing in public administration: A systematic review. *Public Administration Review, 83*(6), 1542–1563. https://doi.org/10.1111/puar.13730.

Henrich, J., Heine, S. J., & Norenzayan, A. (2010). The weirdest people in the world? *Behavioral and Brain Sciences, 33*(2–3), 61–83. https://doi.org/10.1017/s0140525x0999152x.

Herd, P., & Moynihan, D. P. (2019). *Administrative Burden: Policymaking by Other Means*. Russell Sage Foundation. https://doi.org/10.7758/9781610448789.

Hjort, J., Moreira, D., Rao, G., & Santini, J. F. (2021). How research affects policy: Experimental evidence from 2,150 Brazilian municipalities. *American Economic Review, 111*(5), 1442–1480. https://doi.org/10.1257/aer.20190830.

Homonoff, T., & Somerville, J. (2021). Program recertification costs: Evidence from SNAP. *American Economic Journal: Economic Policy, 13*(4), 271–298. https://doi.org/10.1257/pol.20190272.

Hustedt, T., Randma-Liiv, T., & Savi, R. (2020). Public administration and disciplines. In G. Bouckaert & W. Jann (Eds.), *European Perspectives for Public Administration* (pp. 129–465). https://www.jstor.org/stable/j.ctvv417th.11.

James, O., Jilke, S. R., & Van Ryzin, G. G. (2017). *Experiments In Public Management Research: Challenges and Contributions*. Cambridge University Press. https://doi.org/10.1017/9781316676912.

Jassal, N. (2020). Gender, Law Enforcement, and Access to Justice: Evidence from All-Women Police Stations in India. *American Political Science Review, 114*(4), 1035–1054. https://doi.org/10.1017/S0003055420000684.

Jilke, S., Van de Walle, S., & Kim, S. (2016). Generating usable knowledge through an experimental approach to public administration. *Public Administration Review, 76*(1), 69–72. https://www.jstor.org/stable/24757493.

Khan, A. Q., Khwaja, A. I., & Olken, B. A. (2019). Making moves matter: Experimental evidence on incentivizing bureaucrats through performance-based postings. *American Economic Review, 109*, 237–270. https://doi.org/10.1257/aer.20180277.

Leaver, C., Owen, O., Serneels, P., Zeitlin, A. (2021). recruitment, effort, and retention effects of performance contracts for civil servants: Experimental evidence from Rwandan primary schools. *American Economic Review, 111*(7), 2213–2246. https://doi.org/10.1257/aer.20191972.

Olsen, A. L. (2015). "Simon said," we didn't jump. *Public Administration Review, 75*(2), 325–326. https://doi.org/10.1111/puar.12330.

Olsen, A. L., Bendtsen, K.-E., & van Leeuwen, P. (2023). *The Identity Crisis of Public Administration. Public Administration Beyond Our Journals.* [Working Paper]. https://osf.io/23tqy.

Peyton, K., Weiss, C. M., & Vaughn, P. E. (2022). Beliefs about minority representation in policing and support for diversification. *Proceedings of the National Academy of Sciences, 119*(52). https://doi.org/10.1073/pnas.2213986119.

Pollitt, C. (2010). Envisioning public administration as a scholarly field in 2020. *Public Administration Review, 70*, S292–S294. https://doi.org/10.1111/j.1540-6210.2010.02289.x.

Pollitt, C. (2014). *The Changing Face of Academic Public Administration.* Address to SNSPA, Bucharest. https://snspa.ro/wp-content/uploads/2018/06/Lectio_Prima_Christopher_Pollit.pdf.

Raadschelders, J. C. N. (2011). The future of the study of public administration: Embedding research object and methodology in epistemology and ontology. *Public Administration Review, 71*(6), 916–924. https://doi.org/10.1111/j.1540-6210.2011.02433.x.

Ritz, A., Brewer, G. A., & Neumann, O. (2016). Public service motivation: A systematic literature review and outlook. *Public Administration Review, 76*(3), 414–426. https://doi.org/10.1111/puar.12505.

Roberts, A. (2018). The aims of public administration: Reviving the classical view. *Perspectives on Public Management and Governance, 1*(1), 73–85. https://doi.org/10.1093/ppmgov/gvx003.

Sabety, A., Gruber, J., Bae, J. Y., & Sood, R. (2023). Reducing Frictions in Health Care Access: The ActionHealthNYC Experiment for Undocumented Immigrants. *American Economic Review: Insights, 5*(3), 327–346. https://doi.org/10.1257/aeri.20220126.

Simon, H. A. (1996). *Models of My Life.* MIT Press.

Wang, H., Xiong, W., Wu, G., & Zhu, D. (2018). Public–private partnerships in Public Administration discipline: A literature review. *Public Management Review, 20*(2), 293–316. https://doi.org/10.1080/14719037.2017.1313445.

Wright, B. E. (2011). Public administration as an interdisciplinary field: Assessing its relationship with the fields of law, management, and political science. *Public Administration Review, 71*(1), 96–101. https://doi.org/10.1111/j.1540-6210.2010.02310.x.

The rise of open science and public access: Implications for Public Administration research

by Mary K. Feeney

1. Trend: the rise of open science

The open science movement is fully upon us, but many of the implications of this movement remain ahead of us. Open science refers to the effort to make the conduct of science (e.g. methods, procedures, and practice) and science outputs (e.g. publications, data, samples, software, code) publicly accessible. While the open science movement within the academy was popularised largely in response to demands for solutions to fraud and the replication crisis, outside the academy it is driven by a demand for equal public access to knowledge and science. The Universal Declaration of Human Rights states that we all have a right to "share in scientific advancement and its benefits" (UDHR, Article 27(1)). This implies a right to participate in the scientific process and share in its benefits.

The United Nations Educational, Scientific, and Cultural Organization (UNESCO) outlines pillars of open science with six principles: open methodology, open source, open data, open access, open peer review, and open educational resources (UNESCO, 2022). The open science movement is based on the premise that transparent and accessible science will advance knowledge sharing, enable the cumulation of science, and ensure the public can benefit more readily from science outcomes. Open science seeks to improve replication and verification of scientific results while combatting fraud and unequal access to knowledge. Transparency of scientific method, design, and analysis enables replication and reproducibility. Replication ensures confirmation of findings, advances trust in the science, and furthers scientific training. Reproducibility advances validity and transferability of findings. Open science advances education and communication of science, by sharing knowledge beyond narrow research communities of experts. The ethos and goals of open science directly align with many values we promote in the field of Public Administration – transparency, openness, public goods production, public engagement, and advancement of social outcomes through public access.

The open science movement is being embraced by many academic researchers, governments, and research funders and propelled by advances in information and communication technologies. The open science trend affects multiple components of public administration scholarship, from open access issues in peer-reviewed journal publications, availability of pre-prints on third-party websites, and requirements for open access to datasets and analytical code, to accessible sharing of educational materials. These changes in expectations related to the conduct, production, reporting, and publication of research results have direct implications for academic training, research costs and workload, collaboration and competition patterns, and equitable access to knowledge and research evidence for policy and practice. In this chapter, I outline where we are in the open science movement, the implications of open science for Public Administration, from publishing and academic journals to data-sharing and education, and how the community of Public Administration scholars could and should respond.

2. What is the evidence for this trend?

Publishing and open access

While the open science movement began within the academic community (Dominik et al., 2022), it is formally advanced by governments and funding institutions, especially in the case of publicly funded research. One of the most immediate outcomes of the open science movement, for scholars, has been the open access movement in our academic journals. Plan S is the foundation of the open access (OA) publishing movement. In September 2018, cOAlition S, an international consortium of European research organisations and funders filed a complaint to academic publishing. Supported by the European Commission and European Research Council, Plan S outlines nine principles that include call for open access to the results of publicly funded research, for transparency in publicly funded research, for all authors and institutions to retain copyright to their publications, ideally through Creative Commons Attribution licence, and critically for OA publication fees to be covered by funders or research institutions, not individual researchers (cAOlition S, 2023). Plan S set the stage for negotiations with publishing organisations, library subscription orders, and author agreements about copyright and licensing.

In Public Administration today, the results of the implementation of Plan S are most evident in our journals among Dutch, Danish, and German authors, with the Dutch leading the way. The Dutch Research Council (NWO) requires compliance with Plan S for all research published after 1 January 2021, and aims for 100% open access immediately upon publication. Much of the success of the implementation of Plan S can be attributed to Dutch universities developing successful transformative agreements with many academic publishers, including Elsevier, Springer, and Wiley, and the prevalence of public funding for Public Administration research, including open access publishing fees, in the Netherlands. A quick scan of JPART and PAR in the last three years shows the result of this effort – most open access articles in both journals are from authors based at European institutions. And among OA articles, the majority are attributed to authors based in the Netherlands, Denmark, and Germany.

While we can all agree that putting research articles in front of a paywall is good for increasing public access to research results, requiring researchers to pay for open access has the unintended result of creating other types of inequity in our research system (Dominik et al., 2022; Ross-Hellauer, 2022; Shu and Lariviere, 2024). According to Taylor & Francis, articles that are open access have 95% more citations and seven times as many downloads as those behind the paywall.[1] My own calculations while serving as editor at JPART was that within two years open access publications had, on average, 1.5 times the citations of those without OA. Thus, those authors who can afford OA get a boost to their research impact (Ross-Hellauer, 2022), while others, especially those from developing countries, face additional financial burdens (Shu and Lariviere, 2024). Research finds that authors of OA articles are more likely to be male, senior, federally funded and working at more prestigious universities (Olejniczak and Wilson, 2020) and there is more geographic diversity among non-OA articles (Smith, 2022). Flipping the paywall from readers paying to authors paying exacerbates inequality of research access and impact and goes against the ethos of the open science movement and the spirit of Plan S. Moreover, requiring authors to pay for OA fees has resulted in larger budget lines in research grants going to pay OA fees (e.g. profits for publishers), instead of supporting research (Shu and Lariviere, 2024).

While European governments have led the effort to make the results of publicly funded research publicly accessible through open access, the United Kingdom and United States are taking a different approach. Universities in the UK promote the 'green' open access route by posting research results to institutional repositories (rather than paying for open access) (Dominik et al., 2022). In 2022, the White House's Office of Science Technology Policy released a memorandum on public access to federally funded research, commonly referred to as the Nelson Memorandum. The Nelson Memo relies on the FAIR principles (Findable, Accessible, Interoperable, and Re-usable) in its definition of public access, requiring free, immediate, and equitable access to results from federally funded research (Wilkinson et al., 2016). Specifically, the Nelson Memorandum calls for broad and expeditious sharing of peer-reviewed publications and associated scientific data. The requirement does not come with funding, requirements for open access, or specifications of who should cover the cost of purchasing open access in academic journals or the costs of curating and sharing data.

The unfunded mandate in the US has had immediate impacts on the research community, institutions, and funders, who are scrambling to understand the requirements and their implications. Unlike Plan S, the US does not require researchers to publish using OA. It requires researchers to share the data underlying published articles immediately (without embargo) and post the research article to a publicly accessible repository. To avoid OA fees, authors can post the article to a repository provided by the funding agency (e.g. NIH's PubMed or NSF's Public Access Repository), a research institution (e.g. Princeton's Open Access Repository, Illinois Data Bank), or a third party (e.g. ResearchGate, SSRN, Dataverse, Qualitative Data Repository). By not requiring the payment of OA fees, the US policy does not drive additional profits to publishing houses or require researchers to set aside limited research funds for publication fees. Unlike the European approach, which provides funding support for OA and resulted in negotiated deals with for-profit publishers, the Nelson Memorandum places the onus on researchers and institutions to comply with public access requirements. In both cases, these policies have put the power of the state and public research funding behind the open science movement. These policies are also being furthered by private foundations. Starting in 2025, the Gates Foundation will require grantees to make research results publicly available through pre-prints and will no longer allow grant funds to be used for publisher OA fees. This policy aligns with an earlier 2017 policy by the Chan Zuckerberg Initiative (Brainard, 2024). Requiring public access to the results of publicly funded research not only advances the open science movement, but also aligns with Public Administration values of transparency, accessibility, and the advancement of public good. I think we can all agree that research resulting from taxpayer money should be freely available and accessible to the public – we might even go so far as to argue that all Public Administration research (if we intend it to be impactful) should be freely available and accessible to the public.

Open research practices

The principles and values underlying the open science movement parallel the values highlighted in Public Administration – transparency, public value creation, equal access, accountability, and public goods production through knowledge advancement. The practice of open science directly impacts the scholarly field as Public Administration researchers are under increasing demands to make their research publicly accessible. The field now has a few open access journals, including the *Journal of Behavioral Public Administration* (JBPA) and the *Journal of Public and Nonprofit Affairs* (JPNA). Top journals in the field facilitate open access through Open Select (hybrid open access). Additionally, leading journals (e.g. PAR) encourage and in some cases (e.g. JPART) require data underlying research published in the journal to be made publicly available, when ethically possible. When I served as editor at JPART (2019–2024), we required publishing authors to share materials that make their method and data collection transparent and replicable.[2] We required authors to include, for example, interview protocols, survey instruments, and data sources as part of their article or online appendices. We required authors to post their data (when ethically possible) to a publicly accessible repository, rather than making data available upon request – a process that results in bias and inconsistent data access based on author whims. In rare cases, we experienced push back from authors, but in most cases, after a conversation about the importance for open science, reproducibility, replication, and transparency, authors complied with the requirement. It was helpful to remind authors that by posting their data, syntax, and code to a repository, they were claiming ownership of that intellectual output and able to ensure their work and data would be replicable and citable, since datasets in repositories are assigned DOIs (digital object identifiers) and create a public record of the work.

Technology as an open science enabler

The open science movement has rapidly proceeded in part due to advancements in information and communication technologies. The movement away from print journals to online access enables faster and potentially more equitable access to academic peer-reviewed publications. Advancements in big data, digitisation in government, and cloud computing have made data and code access and sharing possible and more affordable.

Researchers have access to peer-reviewed articles via online academic libraries and Google Scholar, and the public now has more access via public libraries, Google Scholar, and pre-print sites such as ResearchGate, Social

Science Research Network (SSRN), National Bureau of Economic Research (NBER), university repositories, and direct request to researchers. These websites, search engines, and technological advances operating outside of traditional academic, for-profit publishing houses have increased access to research outputs for the public and academic scholars working in less wealthy institutions and nations. Open access in academic journals – from fully OA journals to for-profit journals with tiered OA options – has moved a portion of peer-reviewed academic research results in front of the paywall, making them available to anyone with an internet connection. These shifts in academic publishing practice are the direct result of pressures from the open science community and enabled by technology advancements.

The traditional publishing model is dying; for example, many journals no longer print hard-copy issues. In the next decade, we can expect the movement away from volumes and issues being released and instead published articles moving straight to websites with DOIs. Ideally, soon we will not be using citations with volumes, issue numbers, and page numbers, but instead citing DOIs, which serve the same purpose but are designed for the digital age. We might see the prestige of traditional publishing houses and journals wane as they fail to compete with more interactive, faster-producing systems like NBER and arXiv. We might also see academic collectives form through professional associations or on their own to pool their voluntary labour as authors, reviewers, and editors and cut out profit-seeking publishing houses altogether. Professional associations that rely heavily on the traditional publishing model for revenue will need to shift to more flexible, openly accessible models.

Government open data

The open science movement, in particular open methodology, open source, and open data principles, are greatly served by advancements in big data, computing, and digital storage capacities. Data repositories abound – making it easier and cheaper for researchers to share data and code and post research results. For Public Administration scholars, this movement also means more and better access to government data. As governments digitise their services, they are better able to develop and manage open data portals, enabling researchers and cities to access data. It is obvious that much of the top-notch Public Administration research coming out of Denmark in the last decade is the direct result of the Danish government's commitment to digitisation and collaboration with academic researchers. With all government activities digitised, researchers working with the government can track programme development and outcomes, test variations in policy and practice, and use that evidence to advance government practice and public outcomes.

Yet there remain examples of fully digitised governments (e.g. Estonia, Taiwan, China) where Public Administration scholarship is not in step. Estonia is one of the most digitised nations in the world, but we do not see Public Administration scholars in Estonia churning out research for international consumption. China is another example, where the state collects reams of administrative data, but researcher access to these data remains a challenge. Still, as more and more governments digitise and engage in the open data and open science movement, Public Administration scholars will see expanding opportunities to test research questions and use evidence to enhance government performance and public outcomes. Given this opportunity for Public Administration scholarship to advance in step with government open data movements, it would behove us – as a field – to collectively advocate for government open data.

3. Is this a desirable trend? What will be the positive/negative effects?

Hell yes! The open science movement absolutely is a desirable movement for Public Administration. It has real implications for improving our science, and more important the impact of our science on practice, policymaking, and public outcomes. Public access to information and data is better for science and for society. We are seeing the beginning of the positive outcomes of data-sharing for checking science. For example, Data Colada (https://datacolada.org/about) debunked multiple studies in economics, psychology, and management that were found to advance results based on flawed or fabricated data (Lewis-Kraus, 2023). Replicating findings helps to ensure more honest, trustworthy science (Korbmacher et al., 2023). Reproduction enables the advancement of theory, by re-testing hypotheses in new contexts. For the social sciences, especially an applied field like Public Administration, replicability strengthens the evidence we put into management and policy practice.

Additionally, with advancements in the government open data movement, we see more transparency in government, accountability, and opportunities for engagement with citizens and citizen science. Citizen science is a key component of the open science movement – engaging the public in science for the good of society. Public administration scholars should be at the forefront of these efforts. Researchers and citizens alike can access government data for research purposes and can advocate and lobby for improved governance in their communities. Partnerships between Public Administration scholars and government agencies looking to leverage their administrative data offer opportunities to improve government service provision and Public Administration scholarship. Of course, responsible use of data is critical, but increased access to reliable government data has the potential to transform our field.

4. What are potential negative outcomes?

The open science movement does not come without costs and threats to academic scholarship. Potential obstacles and barriers include opposition to change, increased workload and costs, growth in predatory journals and the demise of the traditional publication model, information overload, and exacerbating inequity. First, no one likes change – even those who say they do often end up resisting change. Altering our research and publishing practice takes time, effort, and resources. Making research documentation, instruments, protocols, and data available upon publication is good research practice. But ensuring data and code are confidential, stripped of identifiers, and sharable takes time and effort. Researchers need training and incentives to do this work – and support staff to ensure quality open science. Engaging in organised research practice can make these steps easier, but it still takes time and effort. Curating secure datasets for public access requires expertise, especially when navigating complex, confidential, or higher-risk data. Without reasonable training and compensation for these efforts, we are asking researchers to do more without reward. Additionally, producing publicly available data and research results could overwhelm the public domain. How do we ensure interested parties can find high-quality research results and evidence; how do we help users find the signal in the noise?

Inequality

Inevitably, the resources required to achieve public access can exacerbate inequalities in Public Administrative research across institutions, nations, research types, and researcher communities (Ross-Hellauer, 2022; Siriwardhana, 2015). Researchers at well-resourced institutions and in wealthier nations are more likely to have access to the training and technical support required to engage in open science (Siriwardhana, 2015). First, we already see patterns emerging across researchers who have access to financial resources to pay open access fees as compared to those without (Ross-Hellauer, 2022). Second, the architecture and structure of public access resources and platforms have been designed by researchers in resource-rich nations and institutions, thus potentially creating bias against those taking alternative approaches (Bezuidenhout and Chakauya, 2018; Okune et al., 2021). Third, there are inequities in the patterns of who is most susceptible to predatory journals (Shamseer et al., 2017). Additionally, some types of research are more easily made accessible. For example, the provision of meta-data for some types of data (e.g. detailed socio-cultural data, data with personal identifiers, tacit data, data from very small groups) requires more careful curation than large, de-identified administrative datasets. Differences across data type result in vast differences in how resource intensive it is for researchers to provide publicly accessible results and data. And often collaborative research efforts result in clashes between norms and expectations about data-sharing (e.g. many government agencies and researchers are not open to sharing their data).

Within our Public Administration research community, like all other scientific fields, some demographic groups are more widely represented in specific sub-fields or methods associated with various sub-fields (NCSES, 2023). The burden of complying with public access data requirements will create varying costs and differently affect communities of researchers in specific sub-fields or using particular methodologies. Furthermore, the current technological architecture is only beginning to address the needs of qualitative researchers, but still failing to create simple solutions for those working with non-codifiable data or data that are collectively owned (Carroll et al., 2019). These inequities are something we should be tracking and paying attention to as the open science movement continues.

5. What should we do to respond to open science trends?

As a field, we should not only respond to the open science movement, but we should also work to lead that movement. We should not wait for open science and the assorted changes to our work life happen, but instead embrace an open science ethos and work to implement it in our research, teaching, and practice. This begins with adopting open science practices in our research, working to advance open government data, and training the next generation to do research in a more collaborative, open way.

It is critical that we as a field recognise the value of open science and the need for our research training efforts to prepare scholars for this type of work. PhD programmes must train researchers to document their research processes in transparent, accessible ways. We need to train researchers early and often on data storage, protection, and sharing best practices and we need the institutional support and resources to engage in best practice. These additional training and resource requirements bring the inevitable threat of exacerbating current inequities and creating new ones. Meeting public access requirements from curating and storing datasets to ensuring public access to peer-reviewed publications requires training, expertise, and technical capacity, and rewards and recognition for that work.

Education and training

A key part of training Public Administration scholars for open science is ensuring we are well educated on the range of community-governed or government-funded repositories (e.g. Open Science Framework, Welcome Open Research, Zenodo) and commercial product suites that may or may not meet standards of public access (Andrews, 2020). It is critical that Public Administration researchers have the expertise necessary to make well-informed decisions about open science platforms and products (Matthews, 2023). Similarly, Public Administration researchers should leverage no-cost pre-print servers (e.g. arxiv.org) and publicly accessible institutional publication repositories. If the field shifts toward these venues in favour of costly open access options (e.g. Gold Open Access, hybrid access, diamond, bronze, etc.), we will be eliminating another form of inequitable knowledge access. Guiding researchers toward reputable open access peer-reviewed journals, pre-print servers, and repositories and away from predatory journals should be a key part of research training in all scientific fields. This is especially key for ensuring public access to high-quality research and ensuring scholars can distinguish between predatory and legitimate journals – a threat that disproportionately affects researchers working in lower-resourced nations and institutions (Shamseer et al., 2017). Education on issues of open science, predatory journals, and data access should be standard in any Public Administration programme and something promoted and facilitated by our professional societies. This educational effort should not be limited to PhD trainees, but also include training for experienced researchers unfamiliar with evolving open science expectations.

Support and rewards

It will be important to support and reward open science activities. Funding agencies should increase support for these extra costs for training and conducting research. Research institutions need to recognise and reward open science activities, including developing and archiving publicly available data, code, research, and educational materials. Evaluation, promotion, and tenure review activities should include reporting open science activities and the ways in which scholars have engaged in advancing public access to research activities and outputs. Advancing knowledge is key to evaluating academic science; the accessibility of that knowledge should be a core component of that evaluation.

Collaboration

The UNESCO recommendation on Open Science offers a framework for supporting global collaboration – recognising that truly open science means participation in and access to scientific benefits for all. Public administration scholars should think more globally in their collaborations with trainees, practitioners, and other researchers. Open scholarship means moving toward collaborative open science training, mentoring, and supervision that creates a more open, inclusive research culture (Azevedo et al., 2023). Public access to research data and government data should enable more and better collaboration in the Public Administration research community. Scientific knowledge is cumulative. Measurement improvement depends on multiple tests of measures in varying contexts. By making research protocols accessible, we enable others to test the validity and reliability of our measures. Accessible data enables multiple researchers to test data from multiple angles, address various questions, and ultimately reduce bias and error in data analysis. While some fear that sharing data and research protocols will result in theft of ideas, it is also the case that by placing our ideas, draft papers, data and analysis, and code on public access platforms we are marking that work as our own. Once assigned a DOI, the research is traceable and citable. By shifting our focus to advancement of knowledge in a collaborative community, rather than peer-reviewed publication alone, we can begin to acknowledge, value, and recognise advancements through research production, instrument design, and data curating. The open science movement is an opportunity for us to begin to account for all steps of the research process and move toward a culture of collaborative knowledge advancement.

Open education

An important principle in the open science movement that has yet to receive much attention in the field of Public Administration is open education. A key component to open science is ensuring research training and education orient science participants and users toward open science, but also that our science be delivered through accessible educational outputs. With the growth in online education and teaching, many in Public Administration are facing questions of who owns course materials, lecture notes, presentations, and so on. Online courses typically require the course to be packaged in advance and the institution delivering the course generally owns the materials developed by the instructor in their employment. While many of us have faced questions of when and how to share course syllabi, materials, lecture notes, or assignments, few to none of our professional associations or research institutions have led the charge to advance open education or integrate open science in our educational training. Azevedo et al. (2022) offer a Framework for Open and Reproducible Research Training (FORRT; https://forrt.org) that seeks to advance open scholarship in higher education and advance open science goals of transparency, reproducibility, and integrity. They argue that bringing open science culture to pedagogical communities can improve research and practice. Teaching is a product of our science and therefore a science outcome that should be publicly accessible. FORRT seeks to advance open science through open teaching and mentoring practice, open-source educational resources, and initiatives to co-create materials that lower barriers to entry and make science outputs more accessible.

As a field committed to the advancement of social and public goods and seeking to advance the practice of Public Administration, we are well positioned to take a lead in open education. How would the field advance if we began sharing our curriculum design in a more intentional manner – with one another, but also with the public? Do we have an obligation to make the textbooks that we write publicly accessible? These are discussions not currently happening in our field – among faculty, at academic conferences, among deans, in our professional associations, or with our accreditation bodies.

6. What are the impacts on the Public Administration research agenda?

As with any novel change in science, we need to be expert, knowledgeable users. We need to train students and seasoned researchers for this new era of open science. Open science will enable more participatory governance and collaboration with communities. Open education will provide more expert training and knowledge to those who cannot afford or access formal Public Administration education. Embracing open science through open government should make it easier for PA scholars to engage with and advise governments on policymaking and practice.

We need to shift our thinking to Public Administration science as cumulative and collaborative, not isolated and competitive. We need to reward public access and data-sharing. We need to prioritise using publicly funded, openly accessible platforms and create mechanisms to equitably get materials in front of paywalls (e.g. payments for OA exacerbate inequality). Open science is the responsibility of individual researchers, academic professional associations, accreditation bodies, research institutions, research funders, and governments.

We must change our mindset from one of competing to produce publications to collaborating to produce impactful knowledge. The focus on publications has used academic voluntary labour to enrich for-profit publishing houses, resulting in an academic currency that is only available to some and perpetuates an unsustainable growth model. We should be focused on creating knowledge, not competing for limited publication space in the pages of a journal. The digital age means page space is no longer limited. We do not need pages in a journal, we need good research producing strong evidence to drive effective policy and administrative practice. As an academic community we can best produce this evidence through collaboration, making the outputs of our research publicly accessible, and focusing on a knowledge and data commons.

Here are a few avenues for action:
- Adopt an ethos of open science:
  - Change our mindset from churning out publications to producing impactful knowledge. Less is more; we should be publishing high-quality research rather than more research.
  - Move toward collaboration and away from competition.
  - Engage in citizen science.

- Adopt better digital practices in our work:
  - Use DOIs for citations, rather than volume, issue, and page numbers.
  - Get an ORCID number: this is your knowledge and research output tracker.
  - Familiarise ourselves with best practices for open science and open data. Data Colada has an excellent guide including practical solutions for minor issues, for example how to make permanent links to referenced materials and our own scholarship.
  - Commit to public access for our research. Make our own research and data collection protocols, datasets, and publications publicly accessible.
  - Commit to open education by making educational materials publicly accessible.

- Reform our PhD curriculum to train researchers for open science in research production, data curation and sharing, and publication sharing (e.g. posting pre-prints).
- Advocate for government open data.

– Update our institutions:
- Reward scholars who are actively advancing open science. Step 1 is to act informally when writing letters of recommendation, reviewing articles, annual reviews, or tenure reviews. Step 2 is formal change at your institution.
- Encourage and reward citizen science and engaged research with local governments.
- Reform our professional associations to be more future-oriented and lead on issues of open science.
  – Host workshops, seminars, and training at conferences on best practice and providing up-to-date information on public access platforms.
  – Work with our professional associations, especially those that own journals, to move toward fully open, public access peer-reviewed publication.
  – Create innovative, flexible publishing networks or servers to generate value, rather than relying on revenue from the old, closed science publishing model.
- Lobby your university and colleagues to make teaching materials (syllabi, slides, reviews) publicly accessible.
- Lobby public administration accreditation organisations and professional associations to push for open government data.
- Prepare for the demise of the traditional publishing industry. It is coming; what do we want the next generation of peer-reviewed research to look like?

Notes

1. These numbers are reported on the Taylor & Francis webpage and based on citations received by June 9, 2021, for articles published 2016–2020 in journals listed in Web of Science® as reported in the Digital Science's Dimensions platform. Download data based on usage in 2018–2020 for articles published 2016–2020. Retrieved on January 20, 2024, from https://www.tandfonline.com/openaccess/openselect.

2. Note that we made this requirement for papers that were conditionally accepted. Given the newness of these requirements, we did not want to add the additional burden to submitting authors (editors and reviewers) to provide data and code with all submissions. In some cases, reviewers or editors requested data or code and each time authors complied. As people become more used to open science norms, we should expect data and code submission to become a standard component of peer review.

References

Andrews, P. (2020). The platformization of open. In M. P. Eve & J. Gray (Eds.), *Reassembling Scholarly Communications: Histories, Infrastructures, and Global Politics of Open Access* (pp. 265–276). MIT Press. https://doi.org/10.7551/mitpress/11885.003.0027.

Azevedo, F., Liu, M., Pennington, C. R., Pownall, M., Evans, T. R., Parsons, S., Elsherif M. M., Micheli, L., Westwood, S. J., & FORRT (2022). Towards a culture of open scholarship: the role of pedagogical communities. *BMC Research Notes, 15*(75). https://doi.org/10.1186/s13104-022-05944-1.

Brainard, J. (2024). Gates foundation places bold bet on preprints. *Science, 384*(6691), 18. https://doi.org/10.1126/science.adp6029.

Carroll, S. R., Herczog, E., Hudson, M., Russell K., & Stall S. (2021). Operationalizing the CARE and FAIR principles for indigenous data futures. *Scientific Data, 8*(108). https://doi.org/10.1038/s41597-021-00892-0.

cOAlition S (2023). Plan S: Making full & immediate Open Access a reality. Retrieved on December 23, 2023 from https://www.coalition-s.org/addendum-to-the-coalition-s-guidance-on-the-implementation-of-plan-s/principles-and-implementation/.

Dominik, M., Nzweundji, J. G., Ahmed, N., Carnicelli, S., Jalaluddin, N. S. M., Rivas, D. F., Narita, V., Enany, S., & Rojas, C. R. (2022). Open SCIENCE – For whom? *Data Science Journal, 21*(1), 1–8. https://doi.org/10.5334/dsj-2022-001.

Dutch Research Council (NWO). Open access publishing. Retrieved on December 31, 2023 from https://www.nwo.nl/en/open-access-publishing.

Korbmacher, M., Azevedo, F., Pennington, et al. (2023). The replication crisis has led to positive structural, procedural, and community changes. *Communications Psychology, 1*(3). https://doi.org/10.1038/s44271-023-00003-2.

Lewis-Kraus, G. (2023, September 30). They Studied Dishonesty. Was Their Work a Lie? *The New Yorker*. https://www.newyorker.com/magazine/2023/10/09/they-studied-dishonesty-was-their-work-a-lie.

National Center for Science and Engineering Statistics (NCSES) (2023, January 30). NSF's NCSES releases report on Diversity Trends in STEM Workforce and Education. U.S. National Science Foundation. https://new.nsf.gov/news/diversity-and-stem-2023.

Office of Science and Technology Policy (2022, August 25). *Ensuring Free, Immediate, and Equitable Access to Federally Funded Research [Memorandum]*. Executive Office of the President. Retrieved on December 5, 2023 from https://www.whitehouse.gov/wp-content/uploads/2022/08/08-2022-OSTP-Public-access-Memo.pdf.

Olejniczak, A J., & Molly, J. W. (2020). Who's writing open access (OA) articles? Characteristics of OA authors at Ph.D.-granting institutions in the United States. *Quantitative Science Studies*, *1*(4), 1429–1450. https://doi.org/10.1162/qss_a_00091.

Parsons, S., Azevedo, F., Elsherif, M. M., Guay, S., Shahim, O. N., Govaart, G. H., Norris, E., O'Mahony, A., Parker, A. J., Todorovic, A., & Pennington, C. R. (2022). A community-sourced glossary of open scholarship terms. *Nature Human Behavior, 6,* 312–318. https://doi.org/10.1038/s41562-021-01269-4.

Ross-Hellauer T. (2022). Open science, done wrong, will compound inequities. *Nature, 603*(7901), 363. https://www.nature.com/articles/d41586-022-00724-0.

Ross-Hellauer, T., Reichmann, S., Cole, N., Fessi A., Klebel, T., & Pontika N. (2022). Dynamics of cumulative advantage and threats to equity in open science: A scoping review. *Royal Society Open Science, 9*(1), 1–22. https://doi.org/10.1098/rsos.211032.

Shamseer, L., Moher, D., Maduekwe, O., Turner, L., Barbour, R., Clark, J. Galipeau, J., Roberts, J., & Shea B.J. (2017). Potential predatory and legitimate biomedical journals: Can you tell the difference? A cross-sectional comparison. *BMC Medicine, 15*(1), 28. https://doi.org/10.1186/s12916-017-0785-9.

Shu, F., & Larivière, V. (2024). The oligopoly of open access publishing. *Scientometrics, 129*(1), 519–536. https://doi.org/10.1007/s11192-023-04876-2.

Siriwardhana, C. (2015). Promotion and reporting of research from resource-limited settings. *Infectious Diseases, 8,* 25–29. https://doi.org/10.4137/IDRT.S16195.

Smith, A. C., Merz, L., Borden, J. B., Gulick, C. K., Kshirsagar, A. R., & Bruna, E. M. (2022). Assessing the effect of article processing charges on the geographic diversity of authors using Elsevier's "Mirror Journal" system. *Quantitative Science Studies, 2*(4), 1123–1143. https://doi.org/10.1162/qss_a_00157.

UNESCO (2022). Understanding open science. Retrieved on December 31, 2023 from https://doi.org/10.54677/UTCD9302.

United Nations (n.d.). *A Universal Declaration of Human Rights. Resolution adopted by the General Assembly on 10 December 1948.* https://undocs.org/en/A/RES/217(III).

Wilkinson, M. D., Dumontier, M., Aalbersberg, Ij. J., et al. (2016). The FAIR Guiding Principles for scientific data management and stewardship. *Scientific Data, 3*(1), 9. https://doi.org/10.1038/sdata.2016.18.

CONCLUSION

Which futures for the public sector?

by Geert Bouckaert

1. Trends in democratic societies impacting the link between society and the (administrative) state

Since the published works of the philosophers Rousseau (1712–1778) on citizens and state sovereignty, and Montesquieu (1689–1755) on the three branches of the state, and since Tocqueville's (1805–1859) work on democracy in America, the concepts and the practices of democracies have evolved in cyclical terms with ups and with downs, especially in the 20th century.

In post-communist 1989 Europe, some politicians-philosophers, such as Vaclav Havel (1936–2011; Czechoslovakian president from 1989–1992, and Czech president from 1993–2003), and Tadeusz Mazowiecki (1927–2013; Polish Prime Minister from 1989–1991), were thinking and acting in terms of ideals of post-democratic systems. In his 1978 essay 'The Power of the Powerless', Havel pleads for an 'existential revolution' which needs to "go significantly beyond the framework of classical parliamentary democracy" (Havel in Vladislav, 1986, p. 119). In his August 1989 speech for the Polish Parliament, Mazowiecki argued in favour of a general civic democracy beyond existing realities (Babiuch-Luxmoore, 1992, p. 251). Even when they were not very concrete on what this could look like, they wanted to go beyond existing Western democracies.

The current pressure on our democratic systems from polarisation, populism, and illiberalism results in a debate on more or less, and on different models of democracy. The shifting roles of leadership, social media with influencers, and digital platforms with unidentified actors and algorithms result in accelerating dynamics and debates on the occasion of elections and their shifting outcomes for the legislative and executive branches of our states. Even within the European Union, there is no obvious and safe place that ultimately protects us from these realities.

The future way of administering or governing our democratic states seems to demonstrate the need for more and different forms of participation and interfaces. This is also based on fundamental philosophical debates on how to combine, on the one hand, increasingly complex systems which need to be governed in a collaborative way (Barandiarán et al., 2023), and on the other hand citizens expecting to be involved at different stages, in different degrees and ways, in realising priorities and sustainable goals for our policies in our societies.

This triggers the question of whether we need more and better direct or indirect (representative) involvement, participation, collaboration, deliberation, etc., or less, and how different this should be from current models. This leads to the issue of the nature and the interactions of political, administrative, and civic leadership and 'elites'. This interaction requires levels and types of trust between all those involved. OECD trust surveys (OECD, 2022) demonstrate that citizens want to be taken into account. Trust becomes a *'sine qua non'* for democratic governance (Bouckaert, 2009; OECD, 2023). This results in the question of how to bring in governance expertise and from whom. There is, on the one hand, the policy-related content of complex governance systems (energy, mobility, environment, economy, agriculture, justice, health, etc.), and on the other hand the transparent and fair procedures for design, decision-making, implementation, and evaluation. In combination, this should lead to mechanisms for responsible and accountable governance, but in practice this is often not sufficiently the case. The old debate about centralisation (size) versus decentralisation, with a 'trade-off' between 'efficiency' and 'democracy' (Dahl and Tufte, 1937) is enlarged to a systemic debate of efficient and democratic governance.

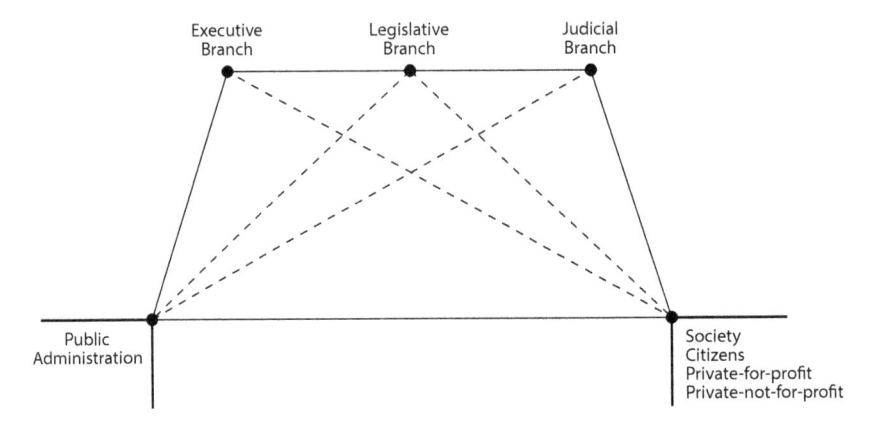

Figure 1. Governing democracy with democratic governance

The systemic question of how to govern democracy with which model(s) of democratic governance in a turbulent world resurfaces the old debates about how citizens relate to a sovereign state, how different functions of the state should be allocated to different branches, and how a layered bureaucracy and administration should relate to and support these branches in interaction with a society consisting of citizens, private-for-profit, and private-not-for-profit organisations (Fig. 1).

This always was a major topic for utopian designs. In the history of utopias, Thomas More's (1478–1535) famous Utopia (1516) addressed first all the dysfunctions of the state, and then offered the alternative of the Isle of Utopia. In the 20th century, the number of dystopias surpassed the number of utopias (Bouckaert, 2020; see also Achten et al., 2016).

Major political ideologies also have societal omegas as ultimate ideals of their political programmes. Since the end of the 1970s, economic liberalism has resulted in market-driven New Public Management for public sector reforms, as actively promoted by the OECD. Parallel economic policy prescriptions by the IMF and the World Bank pushed for globalism with trade liberalisation, privatisation, and fiscal, budgetary, and monetary policies which minimised fiscal pressure and public sectors. This became official in the Washington Consensus (1989).

Stretching liberalism into neoliberalism by stating that 'market' is always better than 'state', and by focusing almost purely on 'efficiency', in combination with a tax race to the bottom by cutting costs and budgets, resulted in a minimal state with a minimal administration with sub-critical capacity. In some countries, it resulted in 'deconstructing' the administrative state (Kettl, 2017; see also the contributions of Bauer, of Moynihan, and of Riccucci in this volume).

Following a pure logic of consequences (as efficient results), without asking which consequences for whom, resulted in parts of society being excluded from services and policies. In some cases, chasing results was possible when standardisation or algorithms neglected relevant information on citizens. This resulted in the increasing neglect of a logic of appropriateness (March and Olson, 2011), up to neglecting important rights of citizens. The childcare benefit and the Groningen natural gas scandals in the Netherlands under the leadership of right-wing conservative Prime Minister Rutte, and the Robodebt scheme in Australia under conservative governments (Podger, 2024) are evidence of how a pure focus on results wiped out appropriateness from the public sector. The US case (Moynihan, and Riccucci in this volume) becomes a supreme example of actively dismantling the administrative state.

Preaching and practising a mechanism which does not combine the two logics of consequences and appropriateness (Bouckaert, 2022a), but replaces a logic of appropriateness with a single logic of consequences, results in accepting exclusion and violation of the rights of (weak) citizens. This major feeling of exclusion has resulted not only in political consequences but also in 'voice' and 'exit' (as Hirschman once labelled it). In some countries, this has resulted in major parts of the population making the leap to anti-elitist politics, which in some places has been captured by illiberalism. This becomes a fine example of dialectics of first a liberal 'thesis', then a neoliberal 'anti-thesis', resulting in an illiberal 'synthesis' as a temporary and intermediate stage, which in itself becomes a thesis that could trigger its own anti-thesis for the future.

This dialectic political rollercoaster implies that solutions from the past will not work for the future. It also implies that the supporting public sector and administration is a car on this rollercoaster that needs to adjust to centrifugal and centripetal forces simultaneously. This means that, within the politico-administrative system, public administration is pressured to be smaller and bigger, internally and externally (with consultants) focused, autonomous and dependent, neutral-inclusive (as in defending the rule of law) and biased-exclusive.

Unfortunately, on this politico-administrative rollercoaster, there is no calm 'eye' in the centre of the hurricane. It means that public administration cannot and will not stay out of this vortex. Thinking in terms of balancing, or of trade-offs, or in the best case of paradoxes, will most probably not work in a sustainable way (Pollitt and Bouckaert, 2017). This leads to the sharp systemic debates demanding a new vision on Public Administration for the future.

The classical three branches of the state – legislative, executive, and judicial (Fig. 1) – have been developed within liberal democracies to be independent in order to balance power within the frame of the rule of law and the constitutions of our states.

There are variations and historical dynamics in designing systems that have resulted in degrees of imbalance, especially between the legislative and executive branches in the 20th century. There is a general impression that the executive branch has gained power and momentum vis-à-vis the legislative branch. However, there was always a reality of a reliable, predictable, and independent judicial branch. This seems to be changing, resulting in a judicial branch which is becoming politicised and therefore dependent, leading to unpredictable or changing positions which violate the legal 'acquis', fundamental rights, and even the rule of law itself. This is happening in

Hungary, and recently in Poland (see also Bauer in this volume). There is also evidence (see both Moynihan and Riccucci in this volume) of a shift in this direction in the US. The purpose of a balanced system, which separates the three powers so that they are autonomous and balanced, shifts to a system with a dominating branch, which results in dependent and imbalanced powers.

The dynamics of imbalanced branches of power could be driven by the legislative (populist), by the executive (authoritarian), or by the judicial (politicised) branch, impacting the other two branches in different ways. It also impacts the administrations of each of the three branches, not just the administration of the executive.

On the legislative side, in majoritarian systems, the combination of increased and polarised gaps between the two equally major parties, and the disproportion between the number of votes and the number of seats (also by actively gerrymandering districts), results in perceptions of elections as being not democratic and stolen by a 'majority'. However, in proportional election systems, where coalitions and 'compromises' are politically obvious, the shift to the extremes (left and right) with a fragmented and a shrinking centre creates an almost 'empty' political centre. In combination with the unwillingness to make a coalition and compromise with one of the extremes, this results in long periods of caretaker governments (for Belgium, see Bouckaert and Brans, 2012). In some countries this results in needing to have new elections to make centre coalitions more 'feasible'. This becomes a self-fulfilling mechanism when elections are no longer a crucial part of the solution to build a new coalition. Democratic elections then lose their legitimising capacity to be part of solving the problem of replacing the current government.

On the judicial side, replacing judges in a political way, or containing judicial autonomy, including by parliament, results in a weakening of the judiciary by reducing it to being subject to the executive or the legislative. Turning the courts into a tool for the executive prevents them from balancing the executive, and safeguarding the 'rule of law', not the 'rule by law'.

On the executive side, Western countries have three types of different politico-administrative systems (Bouckaert, 2022b). The US, a prototype for a spoil system, increases the size of its spoil to increase control over its administrative system, in combination with an active deconstruction of the administrative state (Kettl, 2017). In France, there is a typical osmosis of politics and top civil servants via their elite educational systems, which are in transformation. This is happening in combination with an increased outsourcing of strategic expertise to consultants (see Collington in this volume). In the UK, the top of the civil service is separate from the political executive, in a strict way. However, increasingly top executive politicians are surrounded by permanent advisors that replace the top civil servants. These combined trends within the three types of politico-administrative systems are exacerbated by a political class which in general distrusts administrations, and prefers direct communication. This leads to a centripetal and centrifugal momentum for the administrations, which suffer from reduced legitimacy at the political level. This, in turn, creates a dilemma for administrations between being neutral or being loyal.

2. Macro levels of disruption impacting the functioning of the administrative state

Adding to populist and authoritarian disruptions of the politico-administrative systems, crises (plural) become recurrent and chronical, and start shaking the system itself. These multiple crises and system quakes change the nature of administrating, managing, or governing our public sectors in society (Bouckaert and Galego, 2024). The classical sequence of 'normality'–'crisis'–'handling crisis'–'back to normal' is becoming 'old school' PA. We are moving to simultaneously ensuring standard operating procedures for delivery of services (health, security, mobility, education, etc.) with chronical crises governance.

Even when different authors use different concepts for system quakes, such as turbulence, or poly-crises (see Head in this volume), most research on crises is on the possible preparedness and first handling of the events (Jugl, 2023). Almost no research is conducted on questions of how to adjust our multilevel administrative systems for flexibility, resilience, and adaptabilty in a sustainable way (see Roberts in this volume), or on dynamic hybridity (see Randma-Liiv and Nõmmik in this volume).

This will also require a blend and hybridity of the academic PA community to ensure legal frames (law) and legitimacy (political sciences). To these classical academic PA communities, crises-specific academic expertise needs to be added (health, digital, hydrology, etc.). We will have to build and change our academic teams with such speed and flexibility that this matches the speed and complexity of the crises and the testing of 'solutions' to handle crises.

One of the consequences of these crises and shocks is enhanced societal conflicts, which may require more interventions for security and authority. It is remarkable how many key authors assume situations of 'stability' (see Roberts in this volume), and societal harmony which allows to get 'Public Value' (Moore, 1995; see also Van Thiel in this volume), based on "profiles of courage" for ethical public leadership (Moore, 1995, p. 294), even when Moore considers "doubtful assumptions and unwarranted cynicism" (ibid., p. 297). This tension between shared and enthusiastic 'mission'-driven programmes (Mazzucato, 2022) versus opposite strategies triggers a question of to what extent strategies are wishful thinking and embrace a (naïve) harmony via an imagined shared understanding of the 'common good'.

Of course, the 17 SDGs (2015–2030) have been developed and agreed upon by an almost global political leadership, and these followed the shared agreement on the Millennium Objectives (2000–2015) for developing countries. Indeed, this generates potential 'Public value' and 'mission-driven' programmes and organisations. However, the shifting political arenas, combined with the crises, result more in societal and political conflicts than in harmony, and more in disputes than in consensus. The implication for public sector administrations is that they are squeezed between polarised parties and opinions, and between major societal and political actors. This impacts decision-making processes for policies, investments, and organisational service delivery, which are not solved by only consultations, collaborations, and participations. It also impacts the contents of these policies by shifting to exclusion rather than inclusion, even when legally defined. It pushes administrations to the edge of existing constitutional and rule-of-law-based legal frameworks.

When stability becomes the exception rather than the standard position, a context of irreversible constitutional fragility of states, even in Western countries, could become reality (see Roberts in this volume). Hopefully, it first will not have to get worse, before it gets better. But 'hope' is not a strategy; therefore, Public Administration needs to be ahead of these realities.

3. Dilemmas leading to contradictions for the administrative state

Merit versus representative versus deconstructed administrations

Even when most research on the link between types of bureaucracies (merit-based, representative, tenured, or not) and their 'performance' (effectiveness, and social welfare) (see Bach, and Nistotskaya in this volume) is on (at least until now) stable liberal democracies, the initial assumption of having a functioning bureaucracy as part of a solid democracy is not (yet) questioned. However, the shift to illiberal systems, which intend to deconstruct administrations and operate in contexts of 'rule by law' rather than 'rule of law', creates a new context for administrations, whether they are based on merit or not, or whether they are representative or not.

Combined with an increasing conviction that traditional ('deep' state) administrations are incompatible with illiberal and populist governments, more evidence on how traditional administrations can be well performing will not necessarily convince those who are principally opposed to these 'elite' administrations.

Bach's 'paradox of meritocracy' (in this volume) clearly shows that a combined attention to loyalty to political leadership, political neutrality, and professional autonomy may result in a bureaucracy which becomes functionally politicised and which does not even resist legal violations. This could easily lead to democratic backsliding. This is the case even when there is sufficient evidence that effective bureaucracies are fundamental to democratic societies, their welfare, and well-being.

Fast changing blueprints of administrations

Since public administrations will not be in the quiet eye of the hurricane of changes, politico-administrative relations and administrations as such will be affected in a reactive or a pro-active way, in at least three dimensions.

First, simultaneously combining traditional service delivery with crises governance and system quakes will require variable capacity which can ensure fast-shifting volumes (people and budgets) and types of activities (legal competencies), including between levels of government. This kind of flexibility will be embedded in political turbulence. To the extent that the public personnel systems are not adjusted to realities, this could lead to reactive adaptation or even pro-active acceleration (see Ritz et al. in this volume). One of the components of flexibility is not only the reduction of numbers, but also the substitution and transformation of the qualifications. Lower-grade bureaucrats are disappearing (see Van de Walle in this volume), and various types of competencies are upgraded.

Second, replacing tenure with floating contracts and consultants (see Collington in this volume) could result in sub-critical capacity in the public sector. International consultancy companies have been very successful in organising demand, and matching supply by defining and delivering ideas, from an operational to a strategic level. This has correlated with the neoliberal agenda to reduce public sector capacity, in terms of FTE. It has also resulted in a shift from public sector capacity to contracting out services to these private service companies, without firm proof that this is economic, efficient, and sustainably effective for the public sector and its administration.

Third, these dynamics will be further amplified by a pressure to combine and replace human with artificial capacity (see Moon et al., and Meijer in this volume). There is a general agreement that AI will affect governance of the public sector, and the role of the public sector in society. It is not clear yet how AI will change the nature of the public sector in society as such. Whether it will (also) become a 'platform' of datasets, which will have to use hard and soft regulation to run the societal-government 'platform' and its 'actors', is not clear. The combination of hierarchy, markets, and networks will create hybridity, which requires a clear vision on how to organise responsibility and accountability. Special attention will need to be paid to 'algorithms' which combine datasets for 'decisions'. This will require a clear vision on how to regulate algorithms and how to audit these, since self-regulation will probably not work. Even when this has all the potential to become a positive transition, and even when there are concerns about how this will impact governments and administrations in society, there is evidence of new types of criminality and major disruptions by cyber-attacks, which will also require a new type of 'ecosystem' (see Nasi, and Dudau in this volume), which implies a new way of organising the public sector and its interactions as such.

'Neutral' responses versus 'engaged' communication to citizens

One of the direct links and communication channels of the public sector with society is via street-level bureaucrats (SLBs). Their role and position has been affected significantly. The emergence of AI and algorithms has put pressure on the relevance of SLBs in supporting and decision-making activities. There has been a movement to replace SLBs with digital tools. This is also related in some cases to the disappearance of lower-level bureaucrats, even when some SLBs are not necessarily lower-level bureaucrats (see Van de Walle in this volume). The embeddedness in political dynamics has impacted these SLBs (see Lotta in this volume) in such a way that responses vary from acceptance to resistance.

It is becoming increasingly relevant to use different clusters of citizens based on those who trust and believe in the government and its administrations, and those who do not. This impacts how to communicate with different citizen target groups. In an increasingly polarised and populist political environment, tailored and differentiated communication between 'public administration' and 'citizens' becomes crucial. Distinctions need to be made according to different levels of trust, satisfaction, perceptions, expectations, or participation. The difficulties are not just about the extremes, but even more about the in-between grey zones of sceptic and undecided citizens (see Canel in this volume). Most probably, absence or loss of communication or replacement of public communication by alternative truth-generating sources is contributing to the dismantling of state functions.

Regulating for 'public value': to be or not to be?

In the oscillating debate and practice on whether the state or the market should be in charge of delivering services, the in-between third way of markets 'regulated' by the state sounded like a win-win way of organising and sharing responsibilities for delivery. The history of 'regulation' has been dynamic and fluctuates between closer to the market, as self-regulation, or closer to the state. The realities of failing self-regulation or red-tape regulation burdens demonstrate the tensions, trade-offs, and contradictions for regulation as a policy tool. Lodge (in this volume) moves to a regulatory state 2.0 as one possible scenario for regulatory futures in a state, depending on the strength of the regulator's and the regulatee's capacity.

However, next to the state as a hierarchy (H), and the market (M), networks (N) are becoming relevant and crucial in society, such as digital and social networks. Within the governance space consisting of three dimensions (H, M, and N), three types of models have been developed (Pollitt and Bouckaert, 2017; Bouckaert, 2023). New Public Management (NPM) as a dominant model is based on market mechanisms, including within the public sector. It assumes that markets will not only regulate themselves, but also the networks, and even hierarchies. The pure and dominant model of New Public Governance (NPG) is based on network mechanisms. It also assumes that networks are self-regulated, and could regulate markets and hierarchies. Finally, the dominant model of the Neo-Weberian State (NWS) is hierarchy based, and founded in the rule-of-law and a constitutional democracy. It also regulates markets and networks. Obviously, reality consists of blends and hybrids of these three pure systems, and HMN need to be combined, depending on policy specific features. Nevertheless, there is a decision to be made for the dominant driver of the governance space: hierarchy, or market, or networks.

4. How will futures for the public sector impact futures for Public Administration, or vice versa: how could futures for Public Administration impact futures for the public sector?

The central question is how realities are affecting the academic research field of Public Administration. Do and will research agendas follow realities? This could and should be a starting point to make sure that ultimately academic research in the field of Public Administration gets ahead of realities and is able to inspire practices and reforms. This is the central question of the 'relevance' of research for current and future practice.

The scattered field of Public Administration is contingent on national contexts, and it is dominated by academics from stable countries, not fragile ones (see Roberts in this volume). It is also contingent on distributed academic disciplines (see Olson in this volume), and is dominated by academics from some dominant disciplines. If it is the case that research in Public Administration should or could save the (administrative) state, it will have to go for open and shared research (Feeney in this volume) and use future-oriented research strategies (Maesschalck in this volume).

Public Administration is a field within social sciences, and a platform for several classical and 'new' academic disciplines (data sciences, psychology, anthropology, etc.) which need to be integrated and consolidated in their focus on the state, its politico-administrative system, and within society at large. This kaleidoscopic view of the 'whole of government' within the 'whole of society' invites us to be more horizontal than vertical in academic university infrastructures.

Public Administration is also, as a social science, not only empirical but also normative in its focus and its purpose. The wording of, for example, 'good' for governance, or 'quality' for delivery, or 'efficient' and 'effective' for measurement covers and even hides normative positions which should be made explicit. Operationalising these concepts already demonstrates some of the hidden normative positions. However, this is not just an operational discussion of which public values should be taken into account. The fundamental and perhaps ultimate normative question to be raised within Public Administration is how governance can be organised with or without democracy, and with or without a rule-of-law-based constitutional framework. Public Administration is normative in its purpose when it makes explicit which omega is the ultimate purpose, as in a utopian way of stating an ideal. For Norbert Elias (1897–1990), 'utopia' should (again) become part of a social science research toolkit. 'Utopia' as a social science technique allows Public Administration to look at potentials for possible futures. Utopias put more emphasis on teleological rationalities, rather than on causal mechanisms. For Elias, this helps to re-evaluate the role of imagination in social sciences, as opposed to fatalism or mere pragmatism. Developing utopias becomes a scientific method to define directions to transform realities, rather than just abstract dreams (Elias, 2014).

5. 'Jumping' to conclusions for Public Administration: taking stock of possible futures

This book has discussed several challenges for our Western politico-administrative systems, with the purpose of looking for futures of our (administrative) states, and with the intention of impacting our field of Public Administration. This requires not only solid analyses of what is going on, but also imagination, normative views, and courage to be ahead of extrapolated realities.

The combinations of (authoritarian) populism and illiberalism, with turbulence caused by major crises and system quakes, and digital transformations, impact the current politico-administrative systems. This affects all interactions: between the three branches of the state (legislative, executive, judicial), between the civil service and the executive, and between society (citizens, NGOs, private for-profit companies) and government, parliament, the judiciary, and administrations. It also impacts dynamics within society, with changing attitudes vis-à-vis hierarchies, markets, and networks. Obviously, this has a bearing on the capacity and the functioning of the traditional civil service.

Our PA research focuses too much on stable countries and not enough on fragile countries. It focuses too much on lower levels of questions (policy cycles and management) and not enough on 'grand' questions, which include discussions on governance with or without democracy, on governance with or without government, on fragile and failed states, or on democratic backsliding.

As academics, we need to ask these three questions of 'what can we know?', 'what should we do?', and 'what can we hope for?'. From my perspective, this results in 10 tentative and hypothetical conclusions for 'futures for the public sector':

1. *Deliberative democracy* should complement and support representative democracy, and should also be complemented by *collaborative governance*.
2. *Trust* is the ultimate demonstration of the performance of a system. This should not only include trust of society in the public sector, but also trust of the public sector in society, and trust within the public sector and between its state branches. Assessing 'trust' should be systematic and recurrent; trust in governance requires adjusted communication strategies.
3. Stronger independence should be ensured, with responsibility and accountability for all three branches (legislative, executive, judicial), at all levels of government.

4. Relying on professional values and individual ethos of the civil service is necessary but not sufficient. There is also a need for a 'rule-of-law'-based foundation and framework to ensure an equilibrated and mutually reinforced *logic of consequences, with a logic of appropriateness.*
5. NWS, the *Neo-Weberian State*, is better equipped for a legitimate and sustainable governance space, much more so than NPM (markets) and NPG (networks), since it combines inclusive service delivery, effective crises governance, and sustainable innovation; PA should contribute to protecting and re-inventing state hierarchy based on a rule-of-law-driven constitutional democracy. This 'hierarchy' is open, also horizontal, and participatory in its leadership and accountability, and hybrid in its combination with markets and networks.
6. The public governance space should prepare and reform for a flexibility and variability which *combines simultaneously, not sequentially, day-to-day service delivery with chronical crises governance*, consolidated across levels of government.
7. The public sector should reform and prepare for a shift from connected core organisations with (related) databases, to connected core databases with (related) organisations. The core entities of the public sector will shift from public sector organisations to public databases. *Public sector/service governance will become public database governance, which includes AI as a driver of policy and service.*
8. Since the 17 Sustainable Development Goals will not be realised by 2030, our academic field of Public Administration has the intellectual duty to use 'our' three horizontal SDGs (SDG11: strong local communities; SDG16: strong institutions, peace, and justice; and SDG17: partnerships across government and society) to *focus on effective, accountable, and inclusive governance of the three Ps (People, Planet, Prosperity).*
9. Since academic communities are increasingly accessible beyond languages and cultures, there is a need for *more comparative research and fair academic dialogues*, taking different (non-Western) cultures into account, *also and especially from communities in fragile countries.*
10. Since 'futures' are permanent and dynamic, there is a need for our critical academic reflections and research on *futures within Public Administration to also be organised in a permanent, dynamic, and forward rolling way.* This should be explicit in all PA research strategies. A teleological (utopian) methodology should complement a causal thinking.

The ultimate purpose of this book is not just to take stock, or to extrapolate a bit, or to just react according to a normative framework. The focus is on being ahead of problems and tensions or even on curbing dystopian futures into desirable and possible futures, in a voluntaristic and positive way. This is what all participants in the seminar, and in this book, share. From a voluntaristic perspective, we have a strong belief that our research makes a difference and contributes to a public sector in society that will be better in our futures. I hope this book helps to inspire and motivate young researchers for the rest of this century.

References

Achten, V., Bouckaert, G., & Schokkaert, E. (Eds.) (2016). *A Truly Golden Handbook: The Scholarly Quest for Utopia*. Leuven University Press. https://doi.org/10.11116/9789461662347.

Babiuch-Luxmoore, J. (1992). Het personalisme en de oppositie in Polen. In L. Bouckaert & G. Bouckaert (1992). *Metafysiek en Engagement* (pp. 221–254). Acco.

Barandiarán, X., Canel, M. J., & Bouckaert, G. (Eds.) (2023). *Building Collaborative Governance in Times of Uncertainty: Pracademic Lessons from the Basque Gipuzkoa Province*. Leuven University Press. https://doi.org/10.11116/9789461665058.

Bertelli, A. M., & Schwartz, L. J. (2022). *Public Administration and Democracy: The Complementarity Principle*. Cambridge University Press. https://doi.org/10.1017/9781009217613.

Bertelli, A. M. (2021). *Democracy Administered: How Public Administration Shapes Representative Government*. Cambridge University Press. https://doi.org/10.1017/9781316755167.

Bouckaert, G. (2009). Trust and public administration. *Administration*, 60(1), 91–115. https://lirias.kuleuven.be/retrieve/216467.

Bouckaert, G. (2020). From Public Administration in Utopia to Utopia in Public Administration. In G. Bouckaert & W. Jann (Eds.), *European Perspectives for Public Administration: The Way Forward* (pp. 71–83). Leuven University Press. https://doi.org/10.2307/j.ctvv417th.8.

Bouckaert, G. (2022a). A "Government Positioning System" (GPS) for reform. In E. Colombo (Ed.), *Le istituzioni e le idee. Studi indisciplinati offerti a Fabio Rugge per il suo settantesimo compleanno*. Giuffrè Francis Lefebvre.

Bouckaert, G. (2022b). Public management and politics: Oxymoron or new political paradigm for the state sector? In A. Ladner & F. Sager (Eds.), *Handbook on the Politics of Public Administration* (pp. 138–148). Edward Elgar Publishing. https://doi.org/10.4337/9781839109447.00019.

Bouckaert, G. (2023). The Neo-Weberian State: From ideal type model to reality? *Max Weber Studies*, 23(1), 13–59. https://doi.org/10.1353/max.2023.0002.

Bouckaert, G., & Galego, D. (2024). System-quake Proof "Systemic Resilience Governance": Six Measures for Readiness. *Global Policy*, 15(S6), 97–105. https://doi.org/10.1111/1758-5899.13433.

Bouckaert G., & Brans, M. (2012). Governing without government: Lessons from Belgium's caretaker government. *Governance: An International Journal of Policy, Administration, and Institutions*, 25(2), 173–176. https://doi.org/10.1111/j.1468-0491.2012.01579.x.

Dahl, R. A., & Tufte, E. R. (1973). *Size and Democracy*. Stanford University Press.

Elias, N. (2014). *L'utopie*. La découverte.

Havel, V. (1978). The Power of the Powerless. In J. Vladislav (Ed.) (1986), *Vaclav Havel or Living in Truth* (pp. 36–122). Meulenhoff Amsterdam in association with Faber and Faber.

Jugl, M. (2023). Administrative characteristics and timing of governments' crisis responses: A global study of early reactions to COVID-19. *Public Administration*, 101(4), 1408–1426. https://doi.org/10.1111/padm.12889.

Kettl, D. F. (2017). The clumsy war against the "Administrative State". *Public Administration Review*, 77(5), 639–640. https://doi.org/10.1111/puar.12834.

Koliba, C. (2024). Liberal democratic accountability standards and public administration. *Public Administration Review*, 1–11. https://doi.org/10.1111/puar.13831.

March, J. G., & Olson, J. P. (2011). The logic of appropriateness. In R. E. Goodin, M. Moran, M. Rein (Eds.), *The Oxford Handbook of Political Science*. Oxford University Press. https://doi.org/10.1093/oxfordhb/9780199548453.003.0034.

Mazzucato, M. (2022). *Mission Economy: A Moonshot Guide to Changing Capitalism*. Penguin Press.

Moore, M. H. (1995). *Creating Public Value: Strategic Management in Government*. Harvard University Press.

OECD (2022). *Building Trust to Reinforce Democracy: Main Findings from the 2021 OECD Survey on Drivers of Trust in Public Institutions*. OECD Publishing. https://doi.org/10.1787/b407f99c-en.

OECD (2023). *Government at a Glance 2023*. OECD Publishing. https://doi.org/10.1787/3d5c5d31-en.

Podger, A. (2024). Public administration developments in Australia: Lessons an NPM leader might today draw from NWS. *Journal of Policy Studies*, 39(2), 63–79. https://doi.org/10.52372/jps39206.

Pollitt, C., & Bouckaert, G. (2017). *Public Management Reform: A Comparative Analysis – Into the Age of Austerity* (4th expanded ed.). Oxford University Press.

List of contributors

Bach, Tobias, Department of Political Science, University of Oslo, Norway
Bauer, Michael W., Florence School of Transnational Governance, European University Institute, Italy
Bouckaert, Geert, KU Leuven Public Governance Institute, Belgium
Canel, María José, Faculty of Media & Communication Sciences, Complutense University of Madrid, Spain
Collington, Rosie, Institute for Innovation and Public Purpose, University College London, UK, and Department of Organization, Copenhagen Business School, Denmark
Dudau, Adina, Adam Smith Business School, University of Glasgow, UK
Feeney, Mary K., Frank and June Sackton Chair and Professor, School of Public Affairs, Arizona State University, USA
Head, Brian W., School of Political Science, University of Queensland, Australia
Hondeghem Annie, KU Leuven Public Governance Institute, Belgium
Lee, Seulgi, Institute of Future Government, Yonsei University, South Korea
Lodge, Martin, Department of Government, The London School of Economics and Political Science, UK
Lotta, Gabriela, Getulio Vargas Foundation, Brazil
Maesschalck, Jeroen, Leuven Institute of Criminology, KU Leuven, Belgium
Meijer, Albert, Utrecht University School of Governance, the Netherlands
Micacchi, Lorenza, KPM Center for Public Management, University of Bern, Switzerland
Moon, Jae M., Institute of Future Government, Yonsei University, South-Korea
Moynihan, Donald, J. Ira and Nicki Harris Family Professor of Public Policy, Ford School of Public Policy, University of Michigan
Nasi, Greta, Department of Social and Political Sciences, Bocconi University, Italy
Nistotskaya, Marina, Quality of Government Institute, Department of Political Science, University of Gothenburg
Nõmmik, Steven, Tallinn University of Technology, Estonia
Olsen, Asmus Leth, Department of Political Science, University of Copenhagen, Denmark
Park, Ire, Institute of Future Government, Yonsei University, South Korea
Park, Seungkyu, Institute of Future Government, Yonsei University, South Korea
Randma-Liiv, Tiina, Tallinn University of Technology, Estonia
Riccucci, Norma M., Rutgers University, Newark, USA
Ripoll, Guillem, School of Economics and Business, University of Navarra, Spain
Ritz, Adrian, KPM Center for Public Management, University of Bern, Switzerland

Roberts, Alasdair, University of Massachusetts Amherst, USA
Steen Trui, KU Leuven Public Governance Institute, Belgium
Van de Walle, Steven, KU Leuven Public Governance Institute, Belgium
Van Thiel, Sandra, Erasmus School of Social and Behavioural Sciences, Erasmus University Rotterdam, the Netherlands